DEMOCRACIES IN AMERICA

DEMOCRACIES IN AMERICA

KEYWORDS FOR THE NINETEENTH CENTURY AND TODAY

Edited By

D. BERTON EMERSON

AND

GREGORY LASKI

OXFORD
UNIVERSITY PRESS

Great Clarendon Street, Oxford, OX2 6DP,
United Kingdom

Oxford University Press is a department of the University of Oxford.
It furthers the University's objective of excellence in research, scholarship,
and education by publishing worldwide. Oxford is a registered trade mark of
Oxford University Press in the UK and in certain other countries

© D. Berton Emerson and Gregory Laski 2023

The moral rights of the authors have been asserted

First Edition published in 2023

Impression: 1

Published in the United States of America by Oxford University Press
198 Madison Avenue, New York, NY 10016, United States of America

British Library Cataloguing in Publication Data

Data available

Library of Congress Control Number: 2022941168

ISBN 978–0–19–886569–8 (hbk.)
ISBN 978–0–19–287187–9 (pbk.)

DOI: 10.1093/oso/9780198865698.001.0001

Printed and bound by
CPI Group (UK) Ltd, Croydon, CR0 4YY

These abstract terms which abound in democratic languages, and which are used on every occasion without attaching them to any particular fact, enlarge and obscure the thoughts they are intended to convey; they render the mode of speech more succinct and the idea contained in it less clear. But with regard to language, democratic nations prefer obscurity to labor. I do not know, indeed, whether this loose style has not some secret charm for those who speak and write among these nations. As the men who live there are frequently left to the efforts of their individual powers of mind, they are almost always a prey to doubt; and as their situation in life is forever changing, they are never held fast to any of their opinions by the immobility of their fortunes. Men living in democratic countries, then, are apt to entertain unsettled ideas.

Alexis de Tocqueville, Democracy in America (1840)

Tell us how things are today, thus allowing the possibility that they might be different tomorrow. This articulation, this noticing and describing, does not necessarily constitute civic participation, but it does at the very least mean throwing one's hat in the ring; it means anteing into the game of our democracy.

Quiara Alegría Hudes, "A World of Cousins," in Education and Equality (2016)

Foreword

Educators are often told—increasingly through legislative mandate—to teach "just the facts." But in a country where various groups seem to hold to their own set of "facts," what are the shared facts to be taught about democracy? This is the question with which *Democracies in America* wrestles.

I was trained in the law, a discipline people seek in order to answer the question, "Is this legal?" Frighteningly unsatisfying as it may be, the best answer is most often, "It depends." After reading this book, a reader might also answer whether the United States is a democracy with "it depends."

I see in this volume a resource for those who don't want simple answers. Indeed, uncomfortable answers are this book's currency as it explores the vocabulary of democracy, using the period between 1789 and 1914 as an anchor to build this understanding.

The power of the essays in *Democracies in America* lies in the ways the contributors highlight the many tensions inherent in constitutional democracy, exposing the fragility of pillars we hold dear and take as firm. That is a lesson that would serve us well to heed.

Why ask a practitioner in the K-12 education space to write the Foreword for this book? I imagine the question the editors would want answered is how these "meditations about democracy" can hope to shape how young people should understand democracy.

Are we a republic or a democracy? We asked this specific question as part of the Educating for American Democracy (EAD) initiative, for which I served as Chair of the Steering Committee. EAD brought together more than 300 teachers, scholars, students, and leaders from the private and public sectors—representing viewpoint, professional, and demographic diversity—to produce *The Roadmap to Educating for American Democracy* for K-12 history and civics excellence. We ultimately chose the term "constitutional democracy" to resolve the tensions between a populist and an elitist representative form of governance. To educators, our choice of this particular phrase will matter less than the replicable process of inquiry and debate that led us to that choice.

EAD outlines a vision of the future of history and civic education in the United States. *The EAD Roadmap* is made up of seven themes, each supported by US history and civics questions. The questions parallel the process that *Democracies in America* employs—deep explorations of vocabulary and concepts, refusing to accept a surface-level understanding of who "We the People" are, for example. As I read the essays in *Democracies in America*, I kept in mind the challenge for educators embodied in EAD Design Challenge 1:

> How can we help students understand the full context for their roles as civic participants without creating paralysis or a sense of the insignificance of their own agency in relation to the magnitude of our society, the globe and shared challenges?

The energy and sense of possibility that animates young people is critical to democracy. We erode innocence and agency at our own peril. Cynicism is the enemy of learning. So, what then? Is this just an intellectual exercise? How should educators engage in democracy education?

To that complex question, I only offer that the answers to the questions in *The Roadmap* and those raised in *Democracies in America* reflect the values of the community in which they are taught. Whether considering matters of law or the vocabulary of democracy, the variances in meaning and evolution in understanding are shaped through our individual and collective lived experiences. Since teaching about democracy involves teaching a set of values, it is an inherently political act, whether or not educators share their personal values explicitly.

As educators consider their role in the formation of citizens, they should read *Democracies in America* from the perspective of the contributions of individuals and groups of people not as heroes but as shapers of ideas and institutions, as dissenters and movement leaders, who have shaped the world today and provided guidance about how to contribute to "a more perfect union." In knowing more about the historical and current vocabulary of democracy, readers will find inspiration to shape their own values and stimulate their actions in concert with others in continuing to shape democracies in America.

Louise Dubé

Acknowledgments

This book has been in development for a long time, and our contributors have stuck with us through it all, delivering excellent essays and sharing sage advice. Our first thanks go to them. For imparting their wisdom about making edited collections material, we thank Julia Stern, Kathleen Diffley, and Andreea Deciu Ritivoi. Danielle Zawodny Wetzel, Robert Cavalier, and Sarah Daly generously gave us ideas about keywords pedagogy and resources for teaching about democracy. Paul Erickson connected us with the Commission on the Practice of Democratic Citizenship at the American Academy of Arts and Sciences and the fantastic work they have done to advocate for a reinvention of American democracy. Engaged students and treasured colleagues at Carnegie Mellon University, the United States Air Force Academy, and Whitworth University helped us to focus our concept, as did the anonymous reviewers at Oxford University Press. Manifold thanks to Jacqueline Norton for believing in this project from the beginning and for seeing it through amid many disruptions and delays. Our gratitude goes as well to Hannah Doyle, Jamie Mortimer, and the production team, especially project manager Vaishnavi Ananthasubramanyam and copyeditor Sally Evans-Darby, at Oxford for bringing us across the finish line. We gratefully acknowledge Jessica Hinds-Bond for creating the index and proofreading the manuscript. Final thanks to our friends and families for the countless tangible and intangible ways in which they have made this volume both necessary and possible.

An earlier, small-scale incarnation of this project appeared in a special forum on democracy in *J19: The Journal of Nineteenth-Century Americanists* 5, no. 2 (2017): 361–403. Danielle Allen's piece first appeared there as "A Democracy, If You Can Keep It." Chapters in this book by James Sanders, Sandra M. Gustafson, and Jason Frank also expand on essays that were originally part of that forum. All material is reprinted with permission of the University of Pennsylvania Press.

Nancy Rosenblum's contribution is adapted from her 2016 book *Good Neighbors: The Democracy of Everyday Life in America*. We are grateful to Princeton University Press for permission to reprint.

We also acknowledge the following for allowing us to publish passages that serve as epigraphs to various sections of this book:

The University of Chicago Press for the extract from Quiara Alegría Hudes's essay in Danielle Allen, *Education and Equality*. Copyright © 2016 by the University of Chicago.

The Feminist Press for the extract from Frances Ellen Watkins Harper's speech as collected in Frances Smith Foster, ed., *A Brighter Coming Day: A Frances Ellen Watkins Harper Reader*. Copyright © 1990 by Frances Smith Foster.

W. W. Norton & Company, Inc. for the extract from Jill Lepore, *These Truths: A History of the United States*. Copyright © 2018 by Jill Lepore.

Metropolitan Books, an imprint of Henry Holt and Company, and Verso Books, reproduced with permission of The Licensor through PLSclear, for the extract from Astra Taylor's *Democracy May Not Exist, but We'll Miss It When It's Gone*. Copyright © 2019 by Astra Taylor. All rights reserved.

Contents

About the Editors and Contributors

Danielle Allen is James Bryant Conant University Professor at Harvard University and Director of Harvard's Edmond J. Safra Center for Ethics. She is the author of *Talking to Strangers: Anxieties of Citizenship since Brown vs. the Board of Education* (University of Chicago Press, 2004), *Our Declaration: A Reading of the Declaration of Independence in Defense of Equality* (Norton/Liveright, 2014), and *Education and Equality* (University of Chicago Press, 2016), among many other books. She is a principal investigator for Educating for American Democracy and a cochair of the American Academy of Arts and Science's Commission on the Practice of Democratic Citizenship.

Angélica María Bernal is Associate Professor of Political Science at the University of Massachusetts Amherst, where she specializes in founding and refounding processes, popular constitutionalism, and Indigenous rights and social movements in Latin America. Her first book, *Beyond Origins: Rethinking Founding in an Age of Constitutional Democracy* (Oxford University Press, 2017), was awarded the First Book Award, Honorable Mention, in the Foundations of Political Theory section of the American Political Science Association. She is a former and current Fulbright Fellow to Ecuador and is currently working on a book on Indigenous protest and resistance against natural resource extraction and emergent philosophies of anti-extractivism.

Jean Ferguson Carr is Associate Professor Emerita of English at the University of Pittsburgh, where she directed the Composition and Women's Studies programs and won university awards for graduate mentoring and leadership in diversity. She is a coauthor of *Archives of Instruction: Nineteenth-Century Rhetorics, Readers, and Composition Books in the United States* (Southern Illinois University Press, 2005), which won the 2006 Mina Shaughnessy Prize given by the Modern Language Association. She is a coeditor, with Dave Bartholomae, of the Pittsburgh Series in Composition, Literacy, and Culture and a textual editor of two volumes of *The Collected Works of Ralph Waldo Emerson* (Harvard University Press, 1979, 1983).

Christopher Castiglia is Distinguished Professor of English at the Pennsylvania State University. He is the author of several studies of nineteenth-century American literature, including *Bound and Determined: Captivity, Culture-Crossing, and White Womanhood from Mary Rowlandson to Patty Hearst* (University of Chicago Press, 1996), *Interior States: Institutional Consciousness and the Inner Life of Democracy in the Antebellum United States* (Duke University Press, 2008), and *The Practices of Hope: Literary Criticism in Disenchanted Times* (New York University Press, 2017). He was, with Dana D. Nelson, a founding editor of *J19: The Journal of Nineteenth-Century Americanists*.

Russ Castronovo is Tom Paine Professor of English and Director of the Center for the Humanities at the University of Wisconsin–Madison. He is the author of many books on literature and politics, including *Fathering the Nation: American Genealogies of Slavery and Freedom* (University of California Press, 1995), *Necro Citizenship: Death, Eroticism, and the Public Sphere in the Nineteenth-Century United States* (Duke University Press, 2001), *Beautiful Democracy: Aesthetics and Anarchy in a Global Era* (University of Chicago Press, 2007), and *Propaganda 1776: Secrets, Leaks, and Revolutionary Communications in Early America* (Oxford University Press, 2014). He is a coeditor, with Dana D. Nelson, of *Materializing Democracy: Toward a Revitalized Cultural Politics* (Duke University Press, 2002).

Tess Chakkalakal is Associate Professor of Africana Studies and English at Bowdoin College. She is the author of *Novel Bondage: Slavery, Marriage, and Freedom in Nineteenth-Century America* (University of Illinois Press, 2011), which earned the Robert K. Martin Prize for best book on American literature and was named "a must read" by *Choice*. She is a coeditor of *Jim Crow, Literature, and the Legacy of Sutton E. Griggs* (University of Georgia Press, 2013), a critical edition of Sutton E. Griggs's *Imperium in Imperio* (West Virginia University Press, 2022), and a new edition of Charles Chesnutt's journals and literary memoranda, forthcoming from Oxford University Press.

Elizabeth Maddock Dillon is Distinguished Professor of English at Northeastern University. Her *New World Drama: The Performative Commons in the Atlantic World, 1649–1849* (Duke University Press, 2014) won the Barnard Hewitt Award for Outstanding Research in Theatre History. She also authored *The Gender of Freedom: Fictions of Liberalism and the Literary Public Sphere* (Stanford University Press, 2004) and coedited *The Haitian Revolution and the Early United States: Histories, Geographies, Textualities* (University of Pennsylvania Press, 2016). She is a codirector of the Futures of American Studies Institute and has formerly served as Chair of the American Literature Section of the Modern Language Association.

Louise Dubé is Executive Director of iCivics. She chaired the steering committee for Educating for American Democracy. Funded by the National Endowment for the Humanities and the US Department of Education, as well as the William and Flora Hewlett Foundation and the Howard and Geraldine Polinger Family Foundation, the initiative offers a roadmap to reinvigorate twenty-first-century K-12 US history and civics education. Dubé began her career as an attorney in Montreal, Canada, and holds a law degree from McGill University, as well as an MBA from Yale.

William Duffy is Associate Professor and Director of Graduate Studies in the English department at the University of Memphis, where he specializes in rhetorical theory, communication ethics, and the teaching of writing. His articles have appeared in such journals as *Literacy in Composition Studies*, *Rhetoric Review*, and *College English*, and his recent book *Beyond Conversation: Collaboration and the Production of Writing* was published by Utah State University Press (2021).

D. Berton Emerson is Associate Professor in the Department of English at Whitworth University. He has written essays and reviews that have appeared in *American Literature, ESQ, Nineteenth-Century Literature*, and the *Los Angeles Review of Books*. With Gregory Laski, he edited an interdisciplinary forum on "democracy" in the long nineteenth century that appeared in *J19: The Journal of Nineteenth-Century Americanists*. He is currently completing a book manuscript titled "American Literary Misfits: Vernacular Aesthetics and Imagined Democracies, 1828–1861."

Jason Frank is John L. Senior Professor of Government at Cornell University, where he teaches political theory. He is the author of *Constituent Moments: Enacting the People in Postrevolutionary America* (Duke University Press, 2010), *Publius and Political Imagination* (Rowman & Littlefield, 2013), and *The Democratic Sublime: On Aesthetics and Popular Assembly* (Oxford University Press, 2021). He is also a coeditor of *Vocations of Political Theory* (University of Minnesota Press, 2001) and editor of *A Political Companion to Herman Melville* (University Press of Kentucky, 2013). His political commentary has appeared in *Boston Review* and the *New York Times*.

John Funchion is Associate Professor of English at the University of Miami. He is the author of *Novel Nostalgias: The Aesthetics of Antagonism in Nineteenth-Century US Literature* (Ohio State University Press, 2015) and a coeditor, with Keri Holt and Edward Watts, of *Mapping Region in Early American Writing* (University of Georgia Press, 2015). His essays have appeared in *ESQ: A Journal of Nineteenth-Century American Literature and Culture*, *Early American Literature*, *Modern Language Quarterly*, *Modernist Cultures*, and *The Henry James Review*. He also belongs to a research team whose project, "Multi-Disciplinary Analyses of the Nature and Spread of Unsubstantiated Information Online," secured funding from the National Science Foundation's Secure and Trustworthy Cyberspace program.

David Gold is Professor of English, Education, and Women's and Gender Studies at the University of Michigan, specializing in rhetoric and writing. His work includes *Rhetoric at the Margins: Revising the History of Writing Instruction in American Colleges, 1873–1947* (Southern Illinois University Press, 2008); the collection *Rhetoric, History, and Women's Oratorical Education: American Women Learn to Speak* (Routledge, 2013), coedited with Catherine Hobbs; *Educating the New Southern Woman: Speech, Writing, and Race at the Public Women's Colleges, 1884–1945* (Southern Illinois University Press, 2014), coauthored with Catherine Hobbs; and the collection *Women at Work: Rhetorics of Gender and Labor* (University of Pittsburgh Press, 2019), coedited with Jessica Enoch.

Sandra M. Gustafson is Professor of English and Concurrent Professor of American Studies at the University of Notre Dame. Her books include *Eloquence Is Power: Oratory and Performance in Early America* (University of North Carolina Press, 2000) and *Imagining Deliberative Democracy in the Early American Republic* (University of Chicago Press, 2011). Gustafson edited the journal *Early American Literature* for a decade and is currently a member of the editorial team of the *Norton Anthology of American Literature*. The National Endowment for the Humanities (NEH) has awarded her three grants: two for book projects and one for an NEH summer seminar on democracy.

Jack Jackson is Associate Professor of Politics at Whitman College, where he teaches political theory and US constitutional law. He is the author of *Law Without Future: Anti-Constitutional Politics and the American Right* (University of Pennsylvania Press, 2019). He is also a coeditor, with Martha Fineman and Adam Romero, of *Feminist and Queer Legal Theory: Intimate Encounters, Uncomfortable Conversations* (Routledge, 2009). Other writing by Jackson has appeared in *Theory & Event*, *History of the Present*, *Rethinking Marxism*, *Contemporary Political Theory*, and *n +1*. In 2016 he held the Fulbright Research Chair in Constitutional and Political Theory at McGill University.

Gregory Laski is the author of *Untimely Democracy: The Politics of Progress after Slavery* (Oxford University Press, 2017), which won the American Literature Association's 2019 Pauline E. Hopkins Society Scholarship Award. Formerly a visiting faculty member at Carnegie Mellon University, Laski is currently a civilian associate professor of English at the United States Air Force Academy, where he cofounded the American Studies program. His writing has appeared in *American Literature, Callaloo*, and *The Chronicle of Higher Education*. He was a Mellon Fellow at the Newberry Library in 2021–22 and is at work on an intellectual history of revenge in the Reconstruction era.

Vincent Lloyd is Associate Professor of Theology and Religious Studies at Villanova University, where he also directs the Center for Political Theology. Lloyd researches and teaches about the philosophy of religion, religion and politics, and race. Among his many books on these topics are *Black Dignity: A Philosophy* (Yale University Press, 2022), *In Defense of Charisma* (Columbia University Press, 2018), *Religion of the Field Negro: On Black Secularism and Black Theology* (Fordham University Press, 2017), and *Black Natural Law* (Oxford University Press, 2016). He coedits the journal *Political Theology*.

Dana D. Nelson is Gertrude Conaway Vanderbilt Professor of English and former Chair of the English Department at Vanderbilt University. Her most recent books are *Bad for Democracy: How the Presidency Undermines the Power of the People* (University of Minnesota Press, 2008) and *Commons Democracy: Reading the Politics of Participation in the Early United States* (Fordham University Press, 2015). Nelson is a coeditor, with Russ Castronovo, of *Materializing Democracy: Toward a Revitalized Cultural Politics* (Duke University Press, 2002) and, with Christopher Castiglia, was a founding coeditor of *J19: The Journal of Nineteenth-Century Americanists*.

John Pell is Professor of English and Dean of the College of Arts and Sciences at Whitworth University. He specializes in rhetorical theory and history as well as pragmatism and human rights. His recent publications have appeared in *Present Tense: A Journal of Rhetoric in Society, Literacy in Composition Studies*, and the edited collection *Working with Faculty Writers* (Utah State University Press, 2013).

Padraig Riley is Visiting Associate Professor of History and Humanities at Reed College. He is the author of *Slavery and the Democratic Conscience: Political Life in Jeffersonian America* (University of Pennsylvania Press, 2015) and "Rethinking White Supremacy: Black Resistance and the Problem of

Slaveholder Authority," in *Revolutions and Reconstructions: Black Politics in the Long Nineteenth Century*, ed. Van Gosse and David Waldstreicher (University of Pennsylvania Press, 2020). His essays have also appeared in *Reviews in American History* and *The Journal of the Early Republic*, among other venues.

Alaina E. Roberts is Assistant Professor of History at the University of Pittsburgh. Her first book, *I've Been Here All the While: Black Freedom on Native Land* (University of Pennsylvania Press, 2021), uses archival research and family history to upend the traditional story of Reconstruction, connecting debates about Black freedom and Native American citizenship to westward expansion onto Native land. Her writing has also appeared in the *Western Historical Quarterly*, the *Journal of the Civil War Era*, *Southern Cultures*, the *Journal of the Gilded Age and Progressive Era*, *TIME* magazine, *High Country News*, and the *Washington Post*.

Nancy Rosenblum is Senator Joseph Clark Professor of Ethics in Politics and Government Emerita at Harvard University, where she served as Chair of the Department of Government. Her most recent book with Russell Muirhead is *A Lot of People Are Saying: The New Conspiracism and the Assault on Democracy* (Princeton University Press, 2019). Among her other books is *Good Neighbors: The Democracy of Everyday Life in America* (Princeton University Press, 2016). She is the editor of *Thoreau: Political Writings* (Cambridge University Press, 1996) and a coeditor of the *Annual Review of Political Science*.

James E. Sanders is Professor of History at Utah State University, specializing in Latin American Studies. His first book was *Contentious Republicans: Popular Politics, Race, and Class in Nineteenth-Century Colombia* (Duke University Press, 2004). His most recent book is *The Vanguard of the Atlantic World: Creating Modernity, Nation, and Democracy in Nineteenth-Century Latin America* (Duke University Press, 2014). Sanders's current project rethinks notions of a shared history of the broader Americas to challenge notions of American exceptionalism.

Mark Schmeller is Associate Professor of History at the Maxwell School of Citizenship and Public Affairs at Syracuse University. He is the author of *Invisible Sovereign: Imagining Public Opinion from the Revolution to Reconstruction* (Johns Hopkins University Press, 2016). Schmeller has received fellowships from the Mellon Foundation, the Library Company of Philadelphia, and the Charles Warren Center for Studies in American History at Harvard University. He is currently at work on a history of the 1826 kidnapping and murder of William Morgan, a Freemason who had threatened to reveal the secrets of the fraternal order.

Ariel Elizabeth Seay-Howard is a doctoral candidate and Graduate Ambassador in the Communication Department at Wayne State University. She is a cultural rhetorician; her research focuses on materiality, racial violence, and public memory. She has taught courses on public speaking, race and communication, activism and social change, and Black political thought. In addition, she has presented work on imposter syndrome, diversity and inclusion, lynching in America, and Black women in education at national and international conferences. Her Master's thesis was entitled "The Unheard Voices: A Critical Look at Black Women, Voice, and Education."

Michelle Sizemore is Associate Professor of English at the University of Kentucky. She is the author of *American Enchantment: Rituals of the People in the Post-Revolutionary World* (Oxford University Press, 2018), which argues that "enchantment" became a vital mode of enacting the people after the demise of traditional monarchical forms and investigates this phenomenon throughout a wide range of social and political rituals and literary and cultural discourses. She has published articles and reviews in *American Literary History*, *Legacy*, *Studies in American Fiction*, and other venues.

Derrick R. Spires is Associate Professor of English at Cornell University. He specializes in early African American and American print culture, citizenship studies, and African American intellectual history. His book *The Practice of Citizenship: Black Politics and Print Culture in the Early United States* (University of Pennsylvania Press, 2019) traces the parallel development of early Black print culture and legal and cultural understandings of US citizenship. *Practice* won the 2020 Bibliographical Society/St. Louis Mercantile Library Prize, the 2019 Midwest Modern Language Association (MLA) Book Prize, and the 2019 MLA First Book Prize.

Kyle G. Volk is Associate Professor of History and Chair of the Department of History at the University of Montana. His research focuses on the history of democracy, the problem of dissent and difference in American public life, and capitalism, law, and the American state. His first book, *Moral Minorities and the Making of American Democracy* (Oxford University Press, 2014), received the Organization of American Historians' Merle Curti Prize for Best Book in American Intellectual History and honorable mention for the Frederick Jackson Turner Prize for the Best First Book in American History. His current research explores the problem and politics of personal liberty in US history.

Edlie Wong is Professor of English at the University of Maryland, College Park. She is the author of *Racial Reconstruction: Black Inclusion, Chinese*

Exclusion, and the Fictions of Citizenship (New York University Press, 2015) and *Neither Fugitive nor Free: Atlantic Slavery, Freedom Suits, and the Legal Culture of Travel* (New York University Press, 2009). She is also a coeditor of a scholarly edition of George Lippard's *The Killers* (University of Pennsylvania Press, 2014). Her work has appeared in *Social Text, American Literary History, American Literature*, and *African American Review*. She is the recipient of fellowships from the National Endowment for the Humanities and the Mellon Foundation.

Introduction

Democracies in America: A User's Guide

D. Berton Emerson and Gregory Laski

Ask your neighbor, classmate, or colleague their thoughts about democracy in America and you will undoubtedly get many different responses. Some may assume it our natural condition, a presence as constant as the air we breathe. The more skeptical might consider it a concept once established yet now under threat and increasingly beyond recovery. Others may read it more cynically, suspicious that democracy has always been and will continue to be compromised by the interests of an empowered few. Still others may refuse the word altogether, holding that *oligarchy* better describes the national political structure or identifying in different terms—*justice*, *freedom*—a more compelling vision. Finding that democracy induces anxiety, too many may even prefer to ignore it completely.[1] In a contemporary United States marked by constituencies across the political spectrum who comfortably accept that all is well or, more likely, believe that their voices have gone unheard and their interests unheeded, *democracy* gets wielded in so many divergent directions as to be rendered nearly incoherent. Perhaps a recent commentator put it best: at present, we are "bewildered" by democracy.[2]

A generation ago, after two world wars and an ideological battle between East and West, liberal democracy purportedly enjoyed a global triumph over totalitarian communism.[3] In the twenty-first century, by contrast, this political system occupies a decidedly more precarious position. Increasing polarization, technological innovation, demographic change, and economic inequality, all decades in the making, are testing the limits of the constitutional structures imagined and established in the eighteenth and nineteenth centuries. *Can Democracy Work?*, *How Democracy Ends*, *How Democracies Die*, *Nervous States: Democracy and the Decline of Reason*, and *The People vs. Democracy* are

D. Berton Emerson and Gregory Laski, *Introduction: Democracies in America: A User's Guide* In: *Democracies in America: Keywords for the Nineteenth Century and Today*. Edited by: D. Berton Emerson and Gregory Laski, Oxford University Press. © D. Berton Emerson and Gregory Laski 2023. DOI: 10.1093/oso/9780198865698.003.0001

just a few examples of recently published books bearing moribund meditations.[4] Recent surveys back up such arguments. One oft-cited and potentially alarming appraisal has revealed that in the United States the so-called millennial generation holds little faith in democracy; only about 30 percent of those born after 1980 deem it "essential" to "live in a country that is governed democratically."[5] Interpreting such a response is not easy, and understanding precisely what "governed democratically" might have meant to the respondents is not completely clear. The survey included as potential "characteristics" of democracy, which respondents could affirm or reject, "People choose their leaders in free elections" and "The state makes people's incomes equal." In other words, by asking just what political equality has to do with economic equality, the survey raised a dilemma that has dogged democratic devotees and detractors for millennia. Put differently, if the results are bewildering, so too are the values implicit in the questions.

Such a state of affairs is not entirely new. When the Frenchman Alexis de Tocqueville published the second volume of *Democracy in America* in 1840, roughly fifty years after the ratification of the US Constitution, he sought to define the characteristics of an emerging order even as he complained about the difficulties inherent in that endeavor. A "deplorable consequence of democracy," Tocqueville wrote, was its effect on "language itself." Just as democracy disrupts social hierarchies and deracinates ancestral origins in the name of individualism, this system also unsettles the very means people use to articulate their ideas and express their commitments. Terms travel across social classes, with "vulgar" words showing up in "refined" contexts. Meanings get twisted, redefined, and reappropriated. And "abstract terms" seem to become completely untethered to "any particular fact." In that last condition, however, Tocqueville saw both possibility and peril. "Democratic nations are passionately addicted to generic terms and abstract expressions," he explained, "because these modes of speech enlarge thought and assist the operations of the mind by enabling it to include many objects in a small compass." And yet, although it promotes vision and creation, this linguistic imprecision also "makes expressions quicker but conceptions less clear. . . . In matters of language democracies prefer obscurity to labor." As an example, Tocqueville mentions "equality," one of his (and this book's) keywords. But he might as well have included the very term in the title of his famous study. For no matter what else it is and means, democracy is one of those "unsettled ideas."[6]

Authors and activists, politicians and ordinary people—before and after Tocqueville—have mined this expansiveness to different ends. This volume does not promise to narrow the range of meanings. Indeed, in making plural Tocqueville's title, *Democracies in America* asserts that democracy as an "unsettled idea," full of contradictions and perhaps irresolvable dilemmas, is not a bad thing. To the contrary, that condition of unsettlement is precisely what facilitates debate and discussion, contestation and conflict, hopeful revision and powerful protest: in short, the very lifeblood of democratic philosophy and practice. But this book does maintain—in fact, it unambiguously affirms—that doing this "hard work" requires a deliberate meditation on what democracy means and might mean. As the political theorist and volume contributor Danielle Allen has argued, a "shared vocabulary . . . should bind us all as Americans."[7] What words do we need to talk about the problems and promise of shared life in America? And what is the grammar and syntax required to turn that vocabulary into a living, breathing language? In short, how can we talk about democracy as it exists today?

Holding that a shared conversation about democracy is not only possible but urgently necessary, this book tackles these questions head-on and seeks to provide resources for responding. Acknowledging that the language of democracy is always provisional—always in need of assessment, revision, and reinvigoration—this volume offers a series of short, provocative meditations on twenty-five terms that can enrich the lexicon we employ to understand democracy in theory and practice. Penned by a group of intellectuals from various fields of study and written for a wide audience, the entries explore terms both commonplace (CITIZENSHIP and REPRESENTATION) and surprising (DISGUST and SHAM). Historically, the essays focus on a common period, roughly the decades preceding and following the publication of Tocqueville's study, what we call the *long nineteenth century*. This is an era that spans the vitality of the Revolutionary epoch, the contentious lead-up to the Civil War, the progress and regress of postwar Reconstruction, and the early reforms of the Progressive period. In connecting this foundational past to our present, *Democracies in America* invites readers to reflect on the meaning of this and related keywords to create a usable language of democracy that remains relevant across time. We maintain that a language that addresses the enduring dilemmas of democracy is the place to turn to and return to as a starting point for thinking about the many challenges that confront democratic citizens today. Ultimately, this book aspires to cultivate, for students and teachers in classrooms, as well as readers in libraries and cafés, a language to discuss, define, and refine the possibilities and problems of democracy in America.

When Is the Long Nineteenth Century?
And Why Focus on That Period?

Democracy does not simply have a history, "democracy *is* a history," Pierre Rosanvallon has argued, and therefore the study of this term must be situated in a "permanent dialogue between past and present."[8] This volume has chosen a particular past for this dialogue: US history happening between 1789—when the founding generation translated an imagined political system into a structural reality—and 1914, the dawn of the Progressive Era and the First World War. Other periods might have served as a point of reference to orient our inquiry: the twentieth century, with its transformative fights for inclusion based on race and gender and international engagements with multiple wars supposedly fought to defend democracy; or the Revolutionary era, prior to the consolidation of the Constitution and its manifold compromises. But these epochs are comparatively well known and enshrined in national historical consciousness via curricula and culture. And both periods, whether in the glories of the founding or in the rise to the position of global superpower, are fraught with presumptions of unquestioned triumph and the false reassurances of continuity and fulfillment.

Less so with the long nineteenth century. Although celebrated in Tocqueville's famous study, democracy in nineteenth-century America witnessed endless visions and revisions, conflicts and calamities, and was marked by compromises, successful and failed, breeding complications that have enduring relevance for our current moment. A brief smattering of instances illustrates this point. For example, in slavery, the Civil War, and especially Reconstruction, we find the sources and stories to understand abiding challenges such as systemic racism, mass incarceration, and income inequality, as well as acute crises such as the January 6, 2021, insurrection at the US Capitol, which sought to overthrow the results of the 2020 election and usurp the electoral will of the multiracial American people. Similarly, if women's suffrage today seems an indisputable democratic value, the contentious path to the Nineteenth Amendment, which spanned the antebellum and postbellum eras, reveals a complicated truth that not all women identified the vote with democratic power, an historical curiosity that seems ironically relevant in the waves of the #MeToo movement. What's more, the long nineteenth century was the world of Walt Whitman and Frederick Douglass, who attempted, from their sometimes significantly divergent experiences, and both before and after internal war, to write into being a democratic polity through poetry and prose, much as artists and intellectuals do now, albeit via different yet no less cutting-edge media. This period likewise saw enlightening debates about material legal structures such as the fraught relationship between states and the federal government and the major revision to the meaning of race and citizenship enshrined in the Fourteenth Amendment, all of which, in symbolic and structural ways, still resonate today.

Indeed, the issues we confront in the twenty-first-century United States—reactionary populism, racial division and discrimination, gender bias, income inequality, and the contours and boundaries of citizenship, to name just a few—are prefigured in the long nineteenth century. At times, as with the fight over the franchise or the quest of formerly enslaved Black people to secure equal rights, the resonances between then and now are instructive. In other instances—the shift from the local to the national as a point of political identification and site of governance, for example—the differences inform us about potential ways to rework present institutional structures such as congressional apportionment and the electoral college. Foregrounding these continuities and ruptures, we adopt this era as a shared point of historical reference in order both to shed light on the understanding and practice of democracy formed in this critical period and to explain how this epoch can help us take up discussions of democracy in the present.

Why Keywords? And Why *These* Keywords?

Democracies in America seeks a language for this conversation by turning to the keyword as a unit of meaning. In this, we take our cue from the British cultural historian Raymond Williams, who in the middle of the twentieth century published *Keywords: A Vocabulary of Culture and Society*, now a classic work that has inspired a number of projects focused on unpacking, unlocking, accessing, or organizing knowledge (as the term *key*word suggests), including an expansion and update of his project entitled *Keywords for Today: A 21st Century Vocabulary.*[9]

Williams began his effort in the wake of the Second World War, when he returned to civilian life from military service, only to find himself in what seemed a different world where everything, including the language those around him spoke, had changed. This particular experience gave rise to a more general insight into a profound truth about culture and politics and the role of language therein. "When we come to say 'we just don't speak the same language' we mean...that we have different immediate values or different kinds of valuation....In such a case, each group is speaking its native language, but its uses are significantly different, and especially when strong feelings or important ideas are in question. No single group is 'wrong' by any linguistic criterion, though a temporarily dominant group may try to enforce its own uses as 'correct.'"[10]

Language is especially relevant to democracy. If you have ever heard, or spoken, the phrase "but America is a *republic*, not a *democracy*," you get the gist. Williams was not talking explicitly about democracy (although that was one of his terms). Still, his point about the words he sought to define applies for our endeavor: "the problems of its meanings seemed to me inextricably bound up with the problems it was being used to discuss."[11] The term itself is a case in point: woven into its linguistic DNA, *demos* (people) and *kratos* (rule), are the immediate questions: "Who are the people?" and "Rule how?" As the intellectual historian James Kloppenberg has pointed out, grappling with these terms is the launching point for any conversation about democracy, for they lead to the "contested principles" and "premises" of this political form.[12] This is the "hard work" that Tocqueville noted was required for democratic deliberation and that the Americans he surveyed at least were unwilling to take up.

Importantly, however, the solution does not result from defining "people" and "rule"—or any other associated word or phrase—in an effort to fix their meaning. As Williams said of his *Keywords*, we also say of *Democracies in America*: this book is not a *dictionary* but a *vocabulary*. Where the former seeks to fix "proper meaning," always a limited and contingent task, a vocabulary seeks to clarify what "we share with others, often imperfectly, when we wish to discuss many of the central processes of our common life."[13] In this, the tension in how one person understands a term such as *equality* is not something to correct or resolve. Rather, the conflict is something to explore, for it will likely reveal a host of other problems—differences in experiences and how they inform our identities, and differences in power and access, to name only two. As thinkers such as Bonnie Honig and Astra Taylor have persuasively argued, democracy is rife with these sorts of dilemmas.[14] Articulating and debating these dilemmas through keywords reminds us that *language* is a crucial, if often neglected, component of civics education.[15]

With the selected terms, therefore, our book seeks to transform this vocabulary into a usable *language*. Language is composed not only of words but also a grammar and syntax that connects words and enables the formations of sentences—and, ultimately, claims. Accordingly, *Democracies in America* groups its keywords within four Parts, each of which has its own brief introduction that outlines a central problem and set of questions. The book begins with Part I, Preamble, which focuses on preliminaries and four principles that are crucial for—and arguably haunt, in some way—any attempt to define democracy, including the quandary of reducing "America" to the "United States." Part II, Institutions and Arrangements, features terms that we normally associate with the democratic procedures: REPRESENTATION, CITIZENSHIP, CONSTITUTION, and THE TOWN HALL MEETING, among others. Part III, Feelings, Attitudes, and Interdependence, features terms that we identify with the more personal, nonprocedural dimensions of democracy, such as DISGUST, COMFORT, and BELIEF. Because the personal and the political can never finally be separated, the juxtaposition of Parts II and III enacts yet another central dilemma: the constant collision of the individuated experience and collective life, and the way democracy appears to promise individual freedom and agency but also necessarily checks and limits that agency for the common good. Finally, Part IV, Ambitions and Distortions, explores the tendency for democracy's dreams to quickly become nightmares and how we can respond when this happens.

How to Read This Book and What to Do with It

Just as you might start with the opening lines of the Declaration of Independence or the Constitution before moving on to the list of grievances or the Bill of Rights, you might begin by reading the four terms that compose Part I to *Democracies in America*. After that, you can read the Parts in order or skip around. (To support the latter path, cross-references to other terms treated in this volume appear in SMALL CAPS.) The short introduction to each Part provides a sense of the central dilemma each grouping of words is engaging, and each entry in our volume concludes with recommendations for further reading that point to possible next steps for thinking about the term. The volume itself also ends by offering a meditation on possible paths for the future study of democracy.

After perusing one entry or many, you might use these resources to reflect on what you have learned in this book—and to revise it. Our Part divisions should be understood as simply one way of organizing these terms, which themselves are far from exhaustive. We could not include every useful word for talking about democracy, but this truth represents a possibility rather than a limitation. As noted earlier, the language we use to talk about democracy is always evolving. Perhaps you will respond to the book by asking what would happen if you moved a word from one Part to another to gain a different conceptual angle—if, say, THE COMMONS appeared in Part I rather than the final Part. If you are reading or teaching this work in a classroom, you might consider the many intersections and divergences between terms and across Parts; extend an entry to the present day; or revise a chapter using a different set of primary sources or different disciplinary lens. Maybe you would compose an entry on *race* or *gender*, collating insights from the many terms in the book that take up those concepts, which pervaded culture and politics in the long nineteenth century. You could compile a second volume of keywords and essays that prove just as crucial, if not more, to the lexicon of democracy, especially as the conditions we face change. What would an entry detailing the nineteenth-century prehistory of Black Lives Matter or #MeToo look like? The final project of a course might be to revise a single essay or group of essays—or, even better, to rework the entire book in a class-composed collection. Such projects might even spill outside of the classroom and into the campus community (or beyond) via a conversation series that explores how to talk about American democracy and its shared values across various boundaries and borders.

In this regard, finally, we hope that this volume contributes in a small way to the important work of two recent initiatives to strengthen American democracy: the Commission on the Practice of Democratic Citizenship, sponsored by the American Academy of Arts and Sciences, and the Educating for American Democracy project, sponsored by the National Endowment for the Humanities, the US Department of Education, and other entities. Made up of academics, philanthropists, media representatives, and leaders of nonprofit and civic organizations, the Commission conducted research on a massive scale across a two-year period, combining quantitative and qualitative methods to assess a number of factors that play a part in the functionality of democracy in the United States; from this work came a set of bipartisan recommendations to reinvigorate our political culture and institutions, grouped under the overarching aim of cultivating a sense of common purpose among Americans. The Educating for American Democracy project offers a curricular roadmap for cultivating such purpose by reviving civics education in K-12 classrooms and recommitting to the study of American history and politics on college campuses. Significantly, though both efforts were primarily designed by political scientists and historians, throughout their respective publications they regularly reflect on language: the Commission's report starts with an early definition of democracy and concludes with an appendix of key terms, while Educating for American Democracy displays a similar interest in seeking unity in its terminology, including a summary of the debates—and compromises—among the authors in arriving at their chosen language. Via our book's focus on keywords, then, we share the conviction that to realize democracy in the United States, we must bring words to life, recognizing the civic significance of language and its complexities. We hope that this project supports the "intentional forms" of "work, reckoning... conversation, and gathering that allow everyday citizens" to cultivate the belief that democracy demands and to help break free from the vicious circle in which this political form can get stuck.[16]

So, go ahead and turn the page. Follow our order or create one of your own. No matter the path you pursue, consider reading and reflecting with others on what you find here. Talk about the terms with your roommate, friend, cousin, or coworker; debate them in an intellectual community, classroom, or book club. Most importantly, make sure that you speak with someone whose worldview and experiences differ in some way from your own—or at least you presume that they differ. You might find that your own sense of EQUALITY or REPRESENTATION or MODERATION—or even *democracy*—diverges from theirs in fascinating ways. You might also find yourself unsettled by other discoveries. Hardly deplorable, that is precisely the kind of engagement—and enlargement—that democracy demands.

Notes

1. See Frances E. Lee and Nolan McCarty, eds., *Can America Govern Itself?* (Cambridge: Cambridge University Press, 2019), 1.
2. Adam Tooze, "Democracy and its discontents," *New York Review of Books*, June 6, 2019, https://www.nybooks.com/articles/2019/06/06/democracy-and-its-discontents.

3. The standard source is Francis Fukuyama and his projection that the dissolution of the Soviet Union marked the "end of history as such: that is, the end point of mankind's ideological evolution and the universalization of Western liberal democracy as the final form of human government." "The End of History?" *The National Interest* 16 (1989): 4. Scholars have debated and reevaluated this for the last three decades, Fukuyama chief among them.

4. See James Miller, *Can Democracy Work? A Short History of a Radical Idea, from Ancient Athens to Our World* (New York: Farrar, Straus, and Giroux, 2018); David Runciman, *How Democracy Ends* (New York: Basic Books, 2018); Steven Levitsky and Daniel Ziblatt, *How Democracies Die* (New York: Broadway Books, 2018); William Davies, *Nervous States: Democracy and the Decline of Reason* (New York: Norton, 2018); Yascha Mounk, *The People vs. Democracy: Why Our Freedom Is in Danger and How to Save It* (Cambridge, MA: Harvard University Press, 2018).

5. Roberto Stefan Foa and Yascha Mounk, "The Democratic Disconnect," *The Journal of Democracy* 27, no. 3 (2016): 5–17. It is worth noting that Foa and Mounk go on to recognize that "people can have an abstract allegiance to 'democracy' while simultaneously rejecting many key norms and institutions that have traditionally been regarded as necessary ingredients of democratic governance" (8). A survey from 2018 has yielded more sanguine yet still disconcerting reports on confidence in US democracy. See The Democracy Project, co-sponsored by the Bush Presidential Library, the Penn Biden Center, and the Freedom Project, https://www.democracyprojectreport.org.

6. Alexis de Tocqueville, *Democracy in America*, volume II, rev. ed., trans. Henry Reeve (1840; repr., New York: Colonial Press, 1899). Reeve's was the translation nineteenth-century Americans would have had access to, and so we quote from this text, which is freely available at http://xroads.virginia.edu/~HYPER/detoc/ch1_16.htm, notwithstanding the more authoritative renderings now in print, such as George Lawrence's translation, which appears in the Harper Perennial Modern Classics edition of *Democracy in America*, ed. J. P. Lawrence, or Gerald Beven's translation, featured in the Penguin Classics edition, ed. Isaac Kramnick.

7. Danielle Allen, "The road from serfdom: How Americans can become citizens again," *The Atlantic* 324, no. 6 (December 2019): 101, https://www.theatlantic.com/magazine/archive/2019/12/danielle-allen-american-citizens-serfdom/600778.

8. Pierre Rosanvallon, *Democracy Past and Future*, ed. Samuel Moyn (New York: Columbia University Press, 2006), 38, 37.

9. For instance, the New York University Press Keywords series includes volumes on American cultural studies, media studies, and environmental studies, to name just a few. In the first of these volumes, editors Bruce Burgett and Glenn Hendler highlight the value of a key to unlock an ensemble of meanings in their introduction to *Keywords for American Cultural Studies*, 2nd ed. (New York: New York University Press, 2014). Williams's volume was updated as *Keywords for Today:*

A 21st Century Vocabulary, ed. Colin McCabe and Holly Yanacek (New York: Oxford University Press, 2018).

10. Raymond Williams, *Keywords: A Vocabulary of Culture and Society*, rev. ed. (Oxford: Oxford University Press, 1983), 11.

11. Ibid., 15.

12. James T. Kloppenberg, *Toward Democracy: The Struggle for Self-Rule in European and American Thought* (New York: Oxford University Press, 2016), 6.

13. Williams, *Keywords*, 17, 14.

14. See Astra Taylor, *Democracy May Not Exist, but We'll Miss It When It's Gone* (New York: Henry Holt, 2019) and Bonnie Honig, "Difference, Dilemmas, and the Politics of Home," in Seyla Benhabib, ed., *Democracy and Difference: Contesting the Boundaries of the Political* (Princeton, NJ: Princeton University Press, 1996), 257–277.

15. In *Education and Equality* (Chicago, IL: University of Chicago Press, 2016), Danielle Allen advocates "verbal empowerment" as a key feature of civics education. See also Allen, "Here's one more question parents should think about during back-to-school season," *Washington Post*, September 5, 2019, https://www.washingtonpost.com/opinions/we-need-civics-education-in-schools-to-build-effective-democratic-citizens/2019/09/05/3280dea4-cfe6-11e9-b29b-a528dc82154a_story.html. Brook Thomas, in *Civic Myths: A Law-and-Literature Approach to Citizenship* (Chapel Hill, NC: University of North Carolina Press, 2007), 22–26, notes the overemphasis on the social sciences in civics education and advocates for the critical role of literature and language study. Responding to the "decline of a civic ethic" in the early 1990s, Sandra Stotsky's edited collection on *Connecting Civic Education and Language Education: The Contemporary Challenge* (New York: Teachers College Press, 1991) approached this concern from the vantage point of the classroom.

16. *Our Common Purpose*: *Reinventing Democracy for the 21st Century*, Commission on the Practice of Democratic Citizenship, American Academy of Arts and Sciences, June 2020, https://www.amacad.org/sites/default/files/publication/downloads/2020-Democratic-Citizenship_Our-Common-Purpose_0.pdf; quoted passage on 60. Educating for American Democracy, 2021, *Educating for American Democracy: Excellence in History and Civics for All Learners*, iCivics, March 2, 2021, www.educatingforamericandemocracy.org.

PART

I

Preamble

> It has often been said, in the twenty-first century and in earlier centuries, too, that Americans lack a shared past and that, built on a cracked foundation, the Republic is crumbling. Part of this argument has to do with ancestry: Americans are descended from conquerors and from the conquered, from people held as slaves and from the people who held them, from the Union and from the Confederacy, from Protestants and from Jews, from Muslims and from Catholics, and from immigrants and from people who have fought to end immigration. Sometimes, in American history . . . one person's villain is another's hero. But part of this argument has to do with ideology: the United States is founded on a set of ideas, but Americans have become so divided that they no longer agree, if they ever did, about what those ideas are, or were.
>
> Jill Lepore, *These Truths: A History of the United States* (2018)[1]

In its derivation from the Greek, "democracy" means people (*demos*) rule (*kratos*). That definition may seem simple enough, but complications quickly follow. Everything depends on who the "people" are and what it means to "rule." Who exactly count as "the people" and how do these people exert influence and control?

Similar ambiguities attend attempts to define "democracy" by way of its twin foundational values: liberty and equality. With liberty, are we interested in being free to do whatever we like or being free from restraints? With equality, what kind do we mean: Political? Legal? Economic? Racial? Gender? And, depending on the answer, what does it take to make equality real? Does liberty or equality have to come first? Is one more important than the other? How do the values of liberty and equality complement one another in a functioning democracy? And is America one? For that matter, what is the difference between "America" and the "United States"?

Addressing these questions is a must in a nation that allegedly cherishes the rule of law, especially when that rule of law is written down and available for all to interpret, as in the Constitution. For some, the job of democracy consists in ensuring the ideas of the founding are upheld. For others, the power of an amendable constitution means that "we the people" are always subject to change, and our rule of law must change with them. In both cases—and in myriad others—language and interpretation are crucial, adding extra intrigue to the dilemmas that have always plagued advocates of democracy.

At the heart of these debates across decades and centuries have been the precise definitions of what the governmental political system of the United States purports to be and precisely where the lines of legislation, execution, and adjudication might be drawn. Returning to the writings and speeches of founding figures like Alexander Hamilton and James Madison can tell us precisely what "democracy" meant to them in their moment (yes, they used that very word), which undoubtedly bears weight in ours. Lessons from times past can also help those seeking a balance between ostensibly divergent investments in liberty and equality. Important reminders and new insights arise when, for instance, revisiting public debates over personal liberty in relation to social reform movements such as temperance or the state-mandated requirements of the Fugitive Slave Law of 1850. The long nineteenth century has something to teach us, too, in the judicial rulings that determined the breadth and scope of the equal protection clause of the Fourteenth Amendment as it pertained to Chinese immigrants in San Francisco. And what more might we learn when we broaden our horizon beyond the jurisdiction of the United States alone and seek out meanings of democracy across the Americas?

In the twenty-first century, polarized partisan politics have apparently reached a new pitch and fervor. Some blame social media platforms, a 24/7 news cycle, and the disappearance of local news sources. Others highlight the retreat of civil institutions as a marker of declining trust in the responsiveness of politicians and governments. But there have always been different solutions to these enduring dilemmas of democracy, and hotly contested ideas that have stirred up fears, as historian Jill Lepore notes, of the imminent demise of the American experiment in collective self-rule.

Accordingly, this book's first Part, Preamble, features four keywords that will help us navigate these core questions and issues: DEMOCRACY VERSUS REPUBLIC, PERSONAL LIBERTY, EQUALITY, and SCALE. No matter what else you think the term can or should mean, talking about *democracy* productively presupposes an understanding of these concepts and the values, tensions, and complexities that emerge from them. Although language will always resist strict definition, engaging these terms across the centuries proves crucial for our present and future. As you read, consider: What are the building blocks of American democracy that emerge from this past, and how can we build on them today?

Note

1. Jill Lepore, *These Truths: A History of the United States* (New York: Norton, 2018), xvi.

I

Democracy versus Republic

Danielle Allen

The question of whether the United States counts as a democracy has
become a theme that introduces PARTISAN bickering. Although the
United States is now called a "democracy" in common parlance, some insist
that the only proper label for its political form is that of "republic." Take as
an example the education system of the state of Utah. The 1895 Utah
Constitution guarantees free public education to all, and the state code
(amended as of 2003) requires the state's public education system to "offer
a world-class core curriculum that enables students to successfully compete
in a global society, and to succeed as *citizens of a constitutional republic*."[1]
Utah's US Government and Citizenship Core, voted into effect in August
2010 by the Utah State Board of Education,[2] establishes as the first objective
of the first standard that students will "[i]nvestigate the ideas and events that
significantly influenced the creation of the United States Constitution and
the United States' form of government, a compound constitutional republic."
The third standard sets the expectation that "[s]tudents will understand the
distribution of power among the national, state, and local governments in
the United States federal system, or compound constitutional republic."
And the sixth standard, which requires that students understand the links
between the US and international systems, tasks students with comparing
"different political systems with that of the United States; e.g., dictatorship,
democracy, theocracy, monarchy, totalitarianism."[3] Students in Utah are
bound to learn that the United States is not and was never intended to be a
democracy. Will they have learned the right lesson?

The question of whether the United States is best understood as a republic
or a democracy is, in my view, a non-question. In fact, it can seem a real
question only if the compromises that secured the early American polity are

Danielle Allen, *Democracy versus Republic* In: *Democracies in America: Keywords for the Nineteenth Century and Today.*
Edited by: D. Berton Emerson and Gregory Laski, Oxford University Press. © D. Berton Emerson and Gregory Laski 2023.
DOI: 10.1093/oso/9780198865698.003.0002

obscured. In 1776, many of the founders invoked the idea of democracy as their goal. Take Samuel Adams, as an example, in this letter written to Benjamin Kent, dated July 27, 1776:

> New Govts are now erecting in the several American States under the Authority of the people. Monarchy seems to be generally exploded—and it is not a little surprising to me, that the Aristocratick Spirit which appeared to have taken deep Root in some of them, now gives place to that of Democracy. You justly observe that "the Soul or Spirit of Democracy is Virtue." No State can long preserve its liberty "where Virtue is not supremely honored." I flatter my self you are mistaken in thinking ours is so very deficient, and I do assure you, I find relief in supposing your Colouring is too high.[4]

During the heady days leading up to the Revolution, both before and after the Declaration of Independence, political matters were debated not in terms of whether to pursue a democracy or a republic but with regard to the question of how "popular" new political institutions ought to be. The question, in other words, was the degree to which popular sovereignty, rather than an aristocratic principle, ought to be the basis for the newly forming polities. This was the controversy John Adams worried would taint reception of his April 1776 pamphlet, *Some Thoughts on Government*. "In New England, the 'Thoughts on Government' will be disdained," John Adams wrote on May 12, 1776, to James Warren, "because they are not popular enough. In the Southern Colonies, they will be despised and detested, because too popular."[5] New England's politics were dominated by the structure of the democratic TOWN HALL MEETING; the Southern plantation economy tended toward more aristocratic political forms.

   The first period of founding saw extensive experimentation with possible forms of political institutions. The Pennsylvania Constitution chose a maximally popular structure, establishing a single unicameral legislature based in the franchise of all the freemen of the Commonwealth. In other words, Pennsylvania eschewed a structure with an upper "aristocratic" house to counterbalance a lower house. Thomas Paine was among the ardent supporters of this CONSTITUTION. In contrast, the Articles of Confederation rested not on a principle of popular sovereignty but on the authority of thirteen sovereign states. The purpose of the confederation was to "put them into a firm league of friendship with each other," and their Congress was in effect a location for league meetings.[6]

   Neither the wholly popular Pennsylvania Constitution nor the state-based system of the Articles of Confederation was stable. Each gave way to a new form during 1787–90 when the new US Constitution was developed and ratified and a new Pennsylvania Constitution was also created. Like the US Constitution, the new Pennsylvania Constitution included an upper house, though in this case members of both houses were to be elected by the citizens at a general election. The new state constitution also included a unitary executive in the form of an elected governor with a three-year term and veto power. As the debate about federal institutions unfolded, members of the founding generation discussed what the best name might be for the new political structures they were inventing, but they never came to a stable agreement. The terms "republic" and "democracy" both had their adherents.

James Madison, of course, offered the most full-throated criticism of the concept of a democracy, and it is his comments in *The Federalist Papers* 10 and 14 that are most commonly cited when arguing that the United States is a republic, not a democracy. In *Federalist* 14, for instance, he writes:

> The error which limits republican government to a narrow district, has been unfolded and refuted in preceding papers. I remark here only, that it seems to owe its rise and prevalence chiefly to the confounding of a republic with a democracy: And applying to the former reasonings drawn from the nature of the latter. The true distinction between these forms was also adverted to on a former occasion. It is, that in a democracy, the people meet and exercise the government in person; in a republic they assemble and administer it by their representatives and agents. A democracy consequently must be confined to a small spot. A republic may be extended over a large region.[7]

Madison sought to drive a wedge between the ideas of democracy and republic and closely linked the former to direct democracy, specifically as represented by ancient Athens. In contrast, he linked republics to mixed regimes in which aristocrats have roles distinct from those of the ordinary people. Rome, of course, was the model for that. Yet neither Madison's stark terminological clarity nor his history went without challenge, even in *The Federalist Papers* themselves.

Federalist 63 corrects an element of Madison's argument in *Federalist* 10 and 14. The authorship of this paper is attributed to both Hamilton and Madison. Since this essay critiques previous ones, if it was not Hamilton who wrote it, then Madison must be ventriloquizing someone's critique of his own earlier arguments. In *Federalist* 10 and 14, Madison held up ancient "pure democracies" as examples of what is wrong with democracy and why a republic is to be preferred; he refers explicitly to Athens as a pure democracy in *Federalist* 14. But the author of *Federalist* 63 points out that this

description of Athens is inaccurate: "[T]he position concerning the igno-
rance of the antient government on the subject of representation is by no
means precisely true in the latitude commonly given to it." The author of
Federalist 63 goes on to argue that the Athenians did after all employ REPRE-
SENTATION through the election of elite leaders; for instance, their nine
Archons. The disadvantage of "the democracies of Greece," the author con-
tinues, was not their political form but their limited geographical extent.[8]
This essay, in contrast to *Federalist* 10 and 14, defends the idea of democracy.

   Hamilton similarly revived the concept of democracy when he advocated for the new US Constitution in the New York ratifying convention.
Devoting an entire speech to confusion that had arisen over the words
"republic" and "democracy," he argued that the new Constitution formed
"a representative democracy." Here is an extract from his notes for his speech
of July 12, 1788:

> A republic a word used in various senses.
>
> Has been applied to aristocracies and monarchies....
>
> Again great confusion about the words. Democracy, Aristocracy, Monarchy...
>
> Democracy in my sense, where the whole power of the government in
> the people
>
> Aristocracy where whole sovereignty is permanently in the hands of a few for
> life or hereditary
>
> Monarchy where the whole sovereignty is in the hands of one man for life or
> hereditary.
>
> Mixed government when these three principles unite.
>
> *Consequence*, the proposed government a *representative democracy*.[9]

In Hamilton's formulation, the concept of democracy requires modifica-
tion. There are direct democracies, such as in ancient Athens, which made
only limited use of representation, and there are representative democracies,
such as the one he and his compatriots were inventing. In his definition of
democracy as conveying an unlimited commitment to popular sovereignty,
Hamilton signals the importance of that term. The term "democracy" con-
veys the fact that the polity's legitimacy rests in a principle of popular sovereignty, while the term "representative democracy" captures both the
centrality of popular sovereignty and the decision that such sovereignty be
exercised not directly but through the institutional form of representation.

   Hamilton was not alone in choosing to describe the new polity erected
on the foundations of the Constitution as a democracy. James Wilson, who

signed both the Declaration and the Constitution, and who was one of the first Supreme Court Justices, did as well. In the Pennsylvania ratification debates about the new US Constitution, he had this to say:

> There are three simple species of government—monarchy, where the supreme power is in a single person—aristocracy, where the supreme power is in a select assembly, the members of which either fill up, by election, the vacancies in their own body, or succeed to their places in it by inheritance, property, or in respect of some personal right or qualification—a republick or democracy, where the people at large retain the supreme power, and act either collectively or by representation.
>
> Each of these species of government has its advantages and disadvantages.....
>
> The advantages of democracy are, liberty, equal, cautious, and salutary laws, publick spirit, frugality, peace, opportunities of exciting and producing abilities of the best citizens. Its disadvantages are, dissensions, the delay and disclosure of publick counsels, the imbecility of publick measures retarded by the necessity of a numerous consent.
>
> . . . .
>
> What is the nature and kind of that government, which has been proposed for the United States, by the late convention? In its principle, it is purely democratical: but that principle is applied in different forms, in order to obtain the advantages, and exclude the inconveniences of the simple modes of government.[10]

The politics of the early United States were characterized by an argument over whether more democratic or more aristocratic approaches to politics should prevail. What mattered was how fully the principle of popular sovereignty was embraced. To suggest that a single term—whether "democracy" or "republic"—came to define the new political entity obscures the enduring argument over the question about popular sovereignty, and the history of specific compromises made to enable those who disagreed powerfully with one another to participate nonetheless as equal shareholders of the new set of public political institutions. Let's remember, with the ratifying conventions in each state, just how many people had to cast a vote on the new Constitution for it to be adopted. Plenty of people probably voted for the Constitution because they thought it created a "republic," but plenty of others probably did because they thought it forged a "representative democracy." A close look at the founding reveals not the exclusion of particular terms or ideas from the debate but instead the formation of an overlapping consensus. Moreover, it is clear from discussions at the time, such as those by Hamilton and Wilson, that the founders did not limit their usage of the term "democracy" to those variants that counted as direct democracies. For Hamilton and Wilson, "democracy" could refer to political systems that are based on a wholly popular foundation but nonetheless rely on representation for their operations.

The debate over just how popular our political institutions should be continues to this day. In some ways, the new Constitution reduced the influence of the popular principle, and in the late eighteenth and early nineteenth centuries, in the wake of its adoption, more states restricted voting rights before eventually widening them to their present latitude.[11] Yet in establishing a presidential system, elected from the national population, even if through an electoral college, the Constitution also paved the way for political newcomers like Andrew Jackson, Barack Obama, and Donald Trump to marshal popular support to overcome dynastic influence on politics. The fact of the matter is that the American political system can be called a democratic republic, a republican democracy, or even a representative democracy. All of these labels reveal a core feature of the system: the American founding built in perpetual contestation between masses and elites.

Notes

1. 2006 Utah Code 53A-1a-104, emphasis added, http://le.utah.govxcode/ Title53A/Chapter1a/53A-la-S104.thml.
2. "Understanding the Utah Core," Utah State Board of Education, http://www. utahpublicschools.org.
3. Utah State Standards, "Core Standards for Social Studies," 2010, pp. 25–27, http:// www.uen.org/core/core.do?courseNum=6210.
4. Samuel Adams to Benjamin Kent, July 27, 1776, in *Letters of Delegates to Congress, 1774–1789*, ed. Paul H. Smith et al. (Washington, DC: Library of Congress, 1976–2000), 25 vols., vol. 4, May 16, 1776–August 15, 1776.
5. John Adams to James Warren, May 12, 1776, in *Letters of Delegates to Congress, 1774–1789*, vol. 3, January 1, 1776–May 15, 1776.
6. Articles of Confederation (Lancaster, PA: Francis Bailey, 1777), 4, The Gilder Lehrman Institute of American History, https://www.gilderlehrman.org/sites/ default/files/inline-pdfs/T-04759.pdf.
7. "*The Federalist* Number 14, [30 November] 1787," *Founders Online*, National Archives, last modified October 5, 2016, http://founders.archives.gov/documents/ Madison/01-10-02-0185. Original source: *The Papers of James Madison*, vol. 10, 27 May 1787–3 March 1788, ed. Robert A. Rutland, Charles F. Hobson,

William M. E. Rachal, and Frederika J. Teute (Chicago, IL: University of Chicago Press, 1977), 284–289.

8. "*The Federalist* Number 63, [1 March 1788]," *Founders Online*, National Archives, last modified October 5, 2016, http:founders.archives.gov/documents/Hamilton/01-04-02-0213. Original source: *The Papers of Alexander Hamilton*, vol. 4, January 1787–May 1788, ed. Harold C. Syrett (New York: Columbia University Press, 1962), 561–569.

9. "New York Ratifying Convention. Notes for Speech of July 12 [1788]," *Founders Online*, National Archives, last modified October 5, 2016, http://founders.archives.gov/documents/Hamilton/01-05-02-0012-0060. Original source: *The Papers of Alexander Hamilton*, vol. 5, June 1788–November 1789, ed. Harold C. Syrett (New York: Columbia University Press, 1962), 149–156.

10. James Wilson, Monday, November 26, 1787, Ratification Debates, *Collected Works of James Wilson*, ed. Kermit L. Hall and Mark David Hall, with an introduction by Kermit L. Hall, and a bibliographical essay by Mark David Hall, collected by Maynard Garrison (Indianapolis, IN: Liberty Fund, 2007), vol. 1, 193, http://oll.libertyfund.org/titles/2072#Wilson_4140_1160.

11. Steven Mintz, "Winning the Vote: A History of Voting Rights," *History Now: The Journal of the Gilder-Lehrman Institute*, https://www.gilderlehrman.org/history-by-era/government-and-civics/essays/winning-vote-history-voting-rights. Note, in particular, the restriction on women's right to vote in New Jersey, increased restrictions on African American rights to vote in the early nineteenth century, and changes in the use of requirements for tax-paying and property ownership.

Further Reading

James Madison, Alexander Hamilton, and John Jay, *The Federalist Papers* (New York: Penguin Classics, 1987) is a key starting point for a full understanding of the debates at the founding. On the Declaration of Independence as a democratic document, see Danielle Allen, *Our Declaration: A Reading of the Declaration of Independence in Defense of Equality* (New York: Norton/Liveright, 2014). For more on the concept of popular sovereignty, see Jason Frank, *Constituent Moments: Enacting the People in Postrevolutionary America* (Durham, NC: Duke University Press, 2010) and Michelle Sizemore, *American Enchantment: Rituals of the People in the Post-Revolutionary World* (New York: Oxford University Press, 2018). Van Gosse documents the contestation over popular sovereignty by focusing on the extensive instances of African American men participating in electoral politics in the early United States in *The First Reconstruction: Black Politics in America from the Revolution to the Civil War* (Chapel Hill, NC: University of North Carolina Press, 2021).

2

Personal Liberty

Kyle G. Volk

On the eve of the American Revolution, British statesman Edmund Burke identified the "love of freedom" as the "predominating feature" of the American character. "This fierce spirit of liberty," he thought, was "stronger in the English Colonies probably than in any other people of the earth."[1] Perhaps unsurprisingly, American revolutionaries enshrined liberty in their Declaration of Independence and constitutions. Liberty would be the cornerstone of the American experiment, and over the next century and beyond it remained omnipresent in public life. On the stump and in campaign slogans, liberty provided politicos with rhetorical flourish and occasional purpose. On the road to war, liberty justified violence against the United States' North American and European adversaries. For renowned orators and ordinary citizens alike, liberty was what made their expanding empire exceptional.

To many, of course, Americans' veneration of liberty was sheer hypocrisy. Nowhere was this more evident than with racial slavery. Especially to the enslaved themselves, Frederick Douglass protested in his 1852 Fourth of July oration, Americans' "boasted liberty" was "unholy license" and "hollow mockery."[2] Yet to others, the coexistence of liberty and slavery bred no paradox. By the mid-nineteenth century, white southerners saw defending their liberty to enslave Black men, women, and children to be a cause worth fighting and even dying for. As Abraham Lincoln summarized in the middle of the Civil War, "We all declare for Liberty, but in using the same *word* we do not all mean the same *thing*." "The world," he lamented, "has never had a good definition of the word liberty, and the American people, just now, are much in want of one."[3]

Kyle G. Volk, *Personal Liberty* In: *Democracies in America: Keywords for the Nineteenth Century and Today.*
Edited by: D. Berton Emerson and Gregory Laski, Oxford University Press. © D. Berton Emerson and Gregory Laski 2023.
DOI: 10.1093/oso/9780198865698.003.0003

A protracted struggle over liberty—its meaning, scope, and significance—animated American democracy during the long nineteenth century. Perhaps less well known today is a particular yet vital strain: what contemporaries referred to as "personal liberty." A specific set of legal protections inherited from England, personal liberty during the nineteenth century became a malleable, politicized concept that powerfully stirred and structured Americans' struggles over the democratic state. Diverse Americans turned to personal liberty to safeguard national independence; to defend the rights of citizens and noncitizens from threats foreign and domestic; to galvanize and oppose reform crusades; to understand the stakes of slave emancipation; and to protect businesses and ways of life from threats of change and eradication. Deployments of personal liberty, then, varied by situation and changed over time. Nonetheless, they together made the protection of personal liberty not merely a periodic, individualistic concern but instead an ongoing, hotly contested public problem. Because it crystallized the central puzzles of the personal and the collective, self-determination and a collectively constituted life, that are packed within the idea of "self-rule," personal liberty became a key language of American democracy in its most formative period.

Members of the nineteenth-century American bench and bar understood personal liberty as a series of legal protections English subjects had won over the course of centuries to guard themselves from the arbitrariness of kings. As students of Sir William Blackstone's *Commentaries on the Laws of England* (1765), they learned that "personal liberty"—alongside "personal security" and "private property"—was one of three "principal" rights of the English people. To the famed English jurist, personal liberty was fundamentally about mobility. It consisted of the "power of locomotion, of changing situation, or moving one's person to whatsoever place one's own inclination may direct, without imprisonment or restraint, unless by due course of law." Beginning with Magna Carta and reinforced by the Petition of Right and in English law, the privilege of the writ of habeas corpus had become the most essential guarantee of personal liberty by ensuring that "no subject of England can be long detained in prison."[4]

In learned treatises, judges detailed the ways in which American lawmakers had adapted English personal liberty to the republic. In his *Commentaries on American Law* (1827), for example, the influential New York jurist James Kent explained that the "right to personal liberty" in the United States was protected by the "constitutional principle...that no person shall be deprived of his liberty without due process of law" and especially the constitutionally and legally secured "privilege of *habeas corpus*." From Joseph Story to Thomas Cooley, other leading judges followed Kent. They elaborated on varied legal and constitutional protections for personal liberty and echoed Blackstone (often explicitly) in emphasizing the crucial importance of habeas corpus provisions that protected individuals.[5] As Massachusetts jurist Theophilus Parsons concluded in 1878, "The most efficacious and indispensable of all the provisions of the constitution in respect to personal liberty" was the writ of habeas corpus.[6]

Early on, personal liberty transcended juridical pronouncements and odes to habeas corpus, becoming a critical language used to question unfreedoms that crippled not just individuals but wide swaths of Americans. It began in the earliest days of the republic amid sustained controversy over the impressment of American sailors by the British Empire. The British Navy had long rounded up sailors in seaports and aboard commercial vessels and forced them into the service of the empire for indeterminate lengths of time. To defend this compulsory labor regime and rebuff claims that it violated the vaunted traditions of English liberty, British officials mustered arguments of public necessity and the duty of mariners to defend the empire. As victims of impressment, British colonists had periodically objected, but the practice persisted, eventually becoming a grievance that American revolutionaries enumerated against King George III in the Declaration of Independence. Yet even after the Treaty of Paris of 1783 had established American independence, British impressment continued. During its wars against revolutionary and Napoleonic France, the British Navy forced some 10,000 Americans into service, challenging US sovereignty in the process. As John Quincy Adams wrote in 1808, this recurrent assault on Americans' "personal liberty" was "a malignity not inferior to that of murder." Something had to be done. War became the answer.[7]

The War of 1812 is aptly dubbed a second war of independence and a war for "Free Trade and Sailors' Rights," but it was also, as Congressman John C. Calhoun put it, a war to "defend...the personal liberties of our citizens." Before and during the conflict, hawks powered the American war machine with pleas for personal liberty. On the floor of Congress in 1811, for example, Representative Felix Grundy of Tennessee blasted the British "practice of impressing our seamen from merchant vessels" as an "unjust and lawless invasion of personal liberty."[8] As war lingered on and internal opposition mounted, personal liberty became a reason to stay the course and chastise dissenters. Speaker of the House Henry Clay was among those who applauded the Madison administration's "sacred regard for personal liberty" and lambasted Federalists who opposed a war "for the liberty of our seamen against foreign oppression."[9] But when proposals surfaced for American military conscription, the nation's purported reverence for personal liberty substantiated charges of despotism and became a reason to seek peace. America's "good constitution," the *New York Examiner* protested, "intended to secure to every free American all his rights, and above all, the right of personal liberty." If the war required Americans to "sacrifice" their own personal liberty, the *Examiner* concluded, "let us have peace—and we are willing to say, ANY PEACE."[10]

Controversies over impressment revealed two long-lasting tendencies. The first was the repeated identification of personal liberty as a constitutional right of CITIZENSHIP duly protected by government. That could require affirmative state power. As Representative Grundy thundered, British impressment called "loudly for the interposition of this government."[11] Yet when American leaders considered conscripting their own citizens, personal liberty justified restricting state power. Second, observers associated the denial of personal liberty with slavery. The right to personal liberty was something free citizens had and the enslaved did not. Impressed sailors— "compelled by violence" to serve and denied free movement—had become "military slave[s]." They were little different, one opponent of conscription declared, than the "West Indian or American slave." "Is not," this peace advocate asked, "our country already sufficiently disgraced and endangered by the ... million and a half of human beings ... held as slaves?" No need for America's democracy "of liberty and equal rights" to add to that number— and its own hypocrisy—by destroying the personal liberty of free citizens with forced military service.[12]

Impressment helped catalyze a degree of national introspection, pushing some Americans to consider homegrown unfreedoms anew. The imprisonment for debt—the legal power of creditors to incarcerate debtors as criminals—was one such area. "Do we not bluster," one opponent of the practice noted, "at a terrible rate if any other government touches the personal liberty of a citizen?" If British violations of sailors' liberty had driven the nation to war, shouldn't domestic policies placing the "personal liberty of the debtor in the power of creditor" be eradicated? As many embraced reform, chattel slavery again became the counterpoint. "If the object" of imprisoning debtors "is coercion," the *Providence American & Gazette* ridiculed in 1827, "why not give the creditor power to sell his debtor for a slave, to cut him up piece meal or at least to make him work with a chain round his neck till he works out the debt." Laws giving one citizen such power over another—particularly the power of confinement—should be abolished. Over the course of several decades, they gradually were.[13]

It was slavery itself, however, that most broadened the reach of personal liberty in American life. Antislavery northerners and proslavery southerners actually found a rare point of agreement here: the enslaved had no personal liberty. Antislavery intellectual Francis Wayland, for example, proclaimed that slavery violated "the personal liberty of man as a physical, intellectual, and moral being." "*Domestic Slavery*," he determined, was the "most common violation of personal liberty." Below the Mason–Dixon Line, proslavery legal scholar Thomas R. R. Cobb asserted that "the slave"—necessarily "under the absolute and uncontrolled dominion of his master"—had no "right of personal liberty." In fact, he summarized, "The right of personal liberty in the slave is utterly inconsistent with the idea of slavery."[14]

Any agreement, however, ended as antislavery northerners weaponized personal liberty to combat the rendition of fugitive slaves. The fugitive slave clause of the US CONSTITUTION had established enslavers' right to retrieve their property outside of their own state. Congress's Fugitive Slave Law of 1793 structured the process and provided masters or their agents the aid of magistrates, whether federal, state, or local. Kidnapping and other abuses followed as slave catchers could steal almost any Black person into slavery by accusing them of being a fugitive. Abolitionists used writs of habeas corpus and other legal devices to obstruct these "monstrous outrages upon personal liberty," and in the 1820s and 1830s they successfully lobbied for state laws that protected Black citizens, especially with guaranteed jury trials. After the US Supreme Court in *Prigg v. Pennsylvania* (1842) opened the door, northern states passed additional laws that forbade state officials from participating in the recapture of fugitives. Collectively, these "personal liberty laws," which pitted northern state governments against federal power, frustrated slavers and fanned the flames of sectional discord.[15]

They also politicized personal liberty, charting a path for increasing numbers of northerners to condemn not just slavery but also the Slave Power and its reach into the North. If slaveholders could use the federal government to assail the basic liberties of free Black citizens, what was to stop them from violating the rights of white northerners? Antislavery northerners had raised these concerns for decades, but the passage of the Fugitive Slave Law of 1850 poignantly put them center-stage. This powerful federal law enhanced slaveholders' ability to retrieve their property, including by denying jury trials to accused fugitives and by compelling ordinary citizens—even those with antislavery sensibilities—to aid in the rendition of fugitives. This draconian measure and its high-profile implementation laid bare to increasing numbers of northerners that white southerners had taken control of the federal government and were intent on growing its power to make slavery a national phenomenon. In 1852, Senator Charles Sumner captured the sentiment that would fuel northern defiance. "The true principles of our Political System," he affirmed, "all teach that [the Fugitive Slave Law] is a usurpation by Congress of powers that do not belong to it, and an infraction of rights secured to the States...A weapon so terrible to Personal Liberty the Nation has no power to grasp." To obstruct slaveholders' incursive federal government, antislavery northerners pushed through a new round of state-level personal liberty laws in the late 1850s. They helped bring the sectional crisis to a boil and, for southerners, became further reasons to secede from the Union.[16]

Wartime emancipation and the Thirteenth Amendment quieted debates over fugitive slaves but raised even larger questions about what personal liberty would mean for freed people. For so long, Americans had framed personal liberty and slavery as antithetical, but many now asked if personal liberty was simply the absence of slavery. Radical Republican congressman William Darrah Kelley was one of many activists who understood the gravity of the moment. Speaking about the "safeguards of personal liberty" in 1865, he observed:

> I know that slavery, in name, is ended; but you may change the name without changing the thing. If you leave four millions of laboring people at the South without the right to testify in open court, without the right to make a contract as any other person may, without the right of free education, such as is enjoyed by the children of Northern laboring people, you, in fact, leave slavery there.

Ensuring personal liberty required positive government action. Laws granting basic civil rights, voting rights for Black men, and government construction and funding of public schools were just the beginning. If policymakers didn't properly establish personal liberty, Kelley warned, the "slavery question" that had long divided the nation would lead inexorably

to an equally divisive "negro question" that would haunt the nation for
years to come. He was right.[17]

As struggles to reconstruct the South raged, personal liberty became
contagious elsewhere. In their fight against the Fugitive Slave Law, antislavery northerners had turned to it to justify resistance to invasive government power. This general anxiety received a jolt during the Civil War,
especially with President Abraham Lincoln's suspension of habeas corpus.
The trend continued in the decades after Appomattox as an array of reformers looked to solve public problems with coercive laws and new, more
aggressive modes of governance and policing. Laws mandating compulsory
attendance at public schools; protective yet restrictive labor legislation;
obscenity, speech, and advertising restrictions; compulsory vaccination laws;
racial segregation and eugenic measures; new urban police forces—all were
vital arms of the emerging Progressive-Era state that spurred objections
laced with encomiums to personal liberty. As the Quaker *Friends' Intelligencer*
summarized in 1901, "There is manifest just now a strong tendency toward
regulating the actions and activities of life 'by law'...a drift toward the
limitation of personal liberties." Soon, the author bemoaned, "the state will
decide what is good for us, and therefore what, in each waking hour, we
shall be engaged upon." For many, this tendency offended longstanding
traditions of governance and reverence for personal liberty.[18]

No issue did more to spur organized opposition to state power and hasten
personal liberty into public consideration than attempts to restrict alcohol
consumption by law. From the end of the Civil War through the 1920s,
the Prohibition Party, the Woman's Christian Temperance Union (WCTU),
the Anti-Saloon League, and other temperance groups looked to dry out
America with high-license statutes, local option laws, Sunday-closing
provisions, statewide prohibition laws, and eventually national prohibition
measures. Bigger government, reformers insisted, would liberate Americans
from the "bondage of intemperance." To antiprohibitionists, restrictive laws
threatened enslavement to the state and violated citizens' cherished personal
liberty, and they put those apprehensions at the forefront of their defiance.
Liquor dealers and other businessmen had led the charge against the prohibitory Maine Laws of the 1850s, and the United States Brewers' Association
had formed in response to federal alcohol taxes during the Civil War. But
in the Gilded Age, wet entrepreneurs and their allies, especially German
immigrants, broadened the antiprohibitionist appeal with new grassroots

organizations. They went by many names, but the most common was "Personal Liberty League" (PLL), the first of which formed in Massachusetts in 1867. From Boston to San Francisco, in cities and small towns, these associations proliferated, uniting local dissenters and becoming tied to state and national umbrella organizations. By the 1880s, this "important national political movement" had spread, as one observer noted, "like wild-fire." "[T]hey are to be found everywhere," the Connecticut Temperance Union bewailed, "and wherever found they are active and aggressive."[19]

PLLs mimicked the single-issue pressure politics of their temperance adversaries. Members "desert[ed] their party affiliations" to lobby politicos of both parties and to vote only for those who opposed prohibitory measures. They also practiced civil disobedience and challenged restrictive measures in courts. Equally important, they initiated public-opinion crusades to trumpet antiprohibitionism and undercut the legitimacy of restrictive liquor laws. The heart of their personal liberty politics was mass mobilization, which they achieved through forming associations, holding meetings and rallies, mailing "tons of literature," and posting propaganda in public spaces, especially inside saloons. In advance of Illinois's 1908 local option election, for example, the Decatur Organization of the Personal Liberty League held nightly gatherings to mobilize opposition to local prohibition. The prominent attorney Clarence Darrow was among the featured speakers who discussed such questions as "Does Prohibition Endanger Personal Liberty and Property?" As they resoundingly answered in the affirmative, PLLs saturated public discourse with arguments about property rights, search and seizure, religious liberty, and, in sum, an understanding of personal liberty that demanded not the absence of government but adherence to constitutionally prescribed limits on state power.[20]

For prohibitionists, PLLs advanced dangerous ideas that confused liberty with license, undermined law and order, and were unfit for a socially interdependent, modern society. Frances Willard, national president of the WCTU, was one of many dry champions to counter PLLs' conception of personal liberty. While campaigning in Iowa for a state constitutional amendment prohibiting the sale of alcohol in 1882, Willard broadcast that "a citizen's liberty is relative, not absolute" and that "all law" necessarily circumscribed individual liberty. Civilization mandated "the relinquishment of some part of a savage personal liberty" and it gave citizens "a freedom vastly broader, higher and more fruitful." This, she and others contended, was prohibitionists' goal: liberating citizens from drink so they could lead better, more productive, and ultimately freer lives. Achieving that goal necessitated legal restrictions on saloonkeepers' "liberty to enslave the drinker," which, Willard argued, was akin to destroying slaveholders' "liberty to enslave another class." Citing building codes, business regulations, restrictions on "profane" speech, and laws requiring people to wear clothing, Willard insisted that prohibiting the sale of alcohol was similar and in keeping with American traditions of protecting liberty with interventionist government. Over the next four decades, prohibitionists would elaborate on these ideas to justify their policies, including the Eighteenth Amendment and Volstead Act, and to repudiate their opponents who continued to contest prohibition with the language of personal liberty.[21]

As the struggle between prohibitionists and antiprohibitionists reveals, by the dawn of the twentieth century, two rather opposite perspectives on personal liberty were vying for dominance in American life. Where some sought to guard personal liberty by vigilantly monitoring innovative and intrusive modes of governance, others were turning to the state to, in their view, improve the actual conditions of liberty. Notably, these competing views were not only articulated by intellectuals and political leaders but had also become intimately tied to grassroots reform and antireform organizations and aired widely. Personal liberty and its attendant debates over state power would continue to animate modern democracy during the twentieth century. Most readily, when businessmen organized in the 1930s to thwart the New Deal's activist central state, it was no accident that they christened their organization the American Liberty League. Key leaders, in fact, had previously led antiprohibitionist organizations that preached personal liberty to demand the repeal of prohibition. And as COVID-19-driven battles over vaccines, state-mandated business closures, and mask ordinances have illustrated, personal liberty remains a contentious concern in the twenty-first century.

Notes

1. Edmund Burke, "Mr. Burke's Speech on Moving His Resolutions for Conciliation with the Colonies," in *The Works of the Right Hon. Edmund Burke*, vol. 1 (London, 1837), 186.
2. Frederick Douglass, *Oration, Delivered in Corinthian Hall, Rochester* (Rochester, NY: Lee, Mann & Co., 1852), 20.

3. Abraham Lincoln, "Address at Sanitary Fair, Baltimore, Maryland, April 18, 1864," in *Collected Works of Abraham Lincoln*, vol. 7 (New Brunswick, NJ: Rutgers University Press, 1953), 302.

4. William Blackstone, *Commentaries on the Laws of England. Book the First* (Oxford: Clarendon Press, 1765), 125, 130–131.

5. James Kent, *Commentaries on American Law*, vol. 2 (New York, 1827), 1, 22; Joseph Story, *Commentaries on the Constitution of the United States*, vol. III (Boston, MA, 1833), 206; Thomas Cooley, *A Treatise on the Constitutional Limitations which Rest Upon the Legislative Power of the States of the American Union*, 5th ed. (Boston, MA: Little, Brown, and Co., 1883), 360–429.

6. Theophilus Parsons, *The Personal and Property Rights of a Citizen of the United States* (Hartford, CT: Scranton and Co., 1878), 172–173.

7. Denver Brunsman, *The Evil Necessity: British Naval Impressment in the Eighteenth-Century Atlantic World* (Charlottesville, VA: University of Virginia Press, 2013), 38, 226, 244–247; John Quincy Adams, "Letter To the Hon. Harrison Gray Otis, a Member of the Senate of Massachusetts, on the present state of our National Affairs," *Colvin's Weekly Register* (Washington, DC), April 30, 1808.

8. *The Works of John C. Calhoun*, vol. 2 (New York: D. Appleton and Co., 1960), 3; "Mr. Grundy's Speech," *Niles Weekly Register* (Baltimore, MD), December 28, 1811.

9. "Mr. H. Clay's Speech," *Niles Weekly Register* (Baltimore, MD), February 13, 1813.

10. "Sailors' Rights; or, Impressments to be introduced into the American Service," *New York Examiner*, December 3, 1814.

11. "Mr. Grundy's Speech."

12. "Sailors' Rights;" "Impressment," *The Military Monitor* (New York), April 26, 1813; "Impressment and Conscription," *The Friend of Peace* (Cambridge, MA), January 1, 1821.

13. "We shall occasionally...," *Debtors' Journal* (Boston, MA), September 23, 1820; "Imprisonment for Debt," *Hopkinsian Magazine* 2, 21 (September 1827), 505; George Philip Bauer, "The Movement Against Imprisonment for Debt in the United States" (Ph.D. Dissertation, Harvard University, 1935).

14. Francis Wayland, *The Elements of Moral Science* (Providence, RI: Belknap & Hamersley, 1835), 220; Thomas R. R. Cobb, *An Inquiry into the Law of Negro Slavery in the United States of America* (Savannah, GA: W. Thorne Williams, 1858), 110.

15. "Review," *The Philanthropist* (Cincinnati, OH), March 6, 1838.

16. C. Edwards Lester, *Life and Public Services of Charles Sumner* (New York: United States Publishing Company, 1874), 144.

17. Hon. Wm. D. Kelley, *The Safeguards of Personal Liberty: An Address* (Philadelphia, PA: Social, Civil and Statistical Association of Colored People of Pennsylvania, 1865), 2–3.

18. "Restrictions on Personal Liberty," *Friends' Intelligencer* (Philadelphia, PA), October 5, 1901.

19. "Constitutional Prohibition," *Christian Recorder* (Philadelphia, PA), January 4, 1883; *Constitution of Councils of P. L. L. of Massachusetts, adopted by the Grand*

Council of the State of Massachusetts (Boston, MA, 1867); "Die Freisenneger Buerger," *Chicago* (IL) *Daily Inter-Ocean*, October 17, 1874; "A State Personal Liberty League," *Milwaukee Semi-Weekly Wisconsin*, April 28, 1875; "Forcing an Issue," *Milwaukee* (WI) *Daily Republican Sentinel*, August 23, 1882; *Minutes of the Twentieth Annual Convention of the Connecticut Temperance Union* (Hartford, CT, 1886), 15; *The Sixteenth Annual Report of the Connecticut Temperance Union* (Hartford, CT, 1882), 15.

20. "Forcing an Issue," *Milwaukee* (WI) *Daily Republican Sentinel*, August 23, 1882; "Fight Is Keen Against Liquor," *San Antonio* (TX) *Gazette*, April 4, 1908; "Anti-Local Option Calendar," *The Decatur* (IL) *Review*, March 30, 1908.

21. Frances Willard, "Personal Liberty," in Carolyn De Swarte Gifford and Amy R. Slagell, eds., *Let Something Good Be Said: Speeches and Writings of Frances E. Willard* (Urbana, IL: University of Illinois Press, 2007), 71–73.

Further Reading

Personal liberty has yet to find its historian. Important starting points include Michael Kammen's *Sovereignty and Liberty* (Madison, WI: University of Wisconsin Press, 1986) and *Spheres of Liberty* (Madison, WI: University of Wisconsin Press, 1986). Thomas D. Morris's *Free Men All* (Baltimore, MD: Johns Hopkins University Press, 1974) remains the best treatment of the personal liberty laws. Andrew Delbanco's *The War Before the War* (New York: Penguin, 2018) provides a useful overview of the controversy over fugitive slaves. On the politics of temperance and prohibition, see Kyle G. Volk, *Moral Minorities* (New York: Oxford University Press, 2014) and Lisa McGirr, *The War on Alcohol* (New York: Norton, 2016). On the changing conditions and ideas of liberty in modernizing America, see Barbara Young Welke, *Recasting American Liberty* (New York: Cambridge University Press, 2001) and Michael Willrich, *Pox* (New York: Penguin, 2011).

3

Equality

Edlie Wong

Equality has long served as the guiding principle for the American experiment in democracy, yet it remains one of the most elusive and contentious political concepts. The selfsame framers who declared that "all men are created equal" sanctioned legal slavery and racial oppression. Despite the frequent appearance of the word "equal" in the US CONSTITU-TION, the Reconstruction Amendments, passed in the wake of Civil War, marked the first time that the idea of equality—indeed, racial justice—appeared in a meaningful sense in this foundational document. Proposed in 1866 and ratified in 1868, the Fourteenth Amendment played a key role in transforming the United States into a more egalitarian democracy. It sought to establish a principle of "equal justice to all men and equal protection under the shield of the law."[1] Not only did the Fourteenth Amendment establish the territory of one's birth or *jus soli* as the basis for political membership, but it also extended the Fifth Amendment mandate of equal protection (of life, liberty, and property) beyond the federal government to the states. It was designed to strengthen the constitutional protection of equality.

Equality has many dimensions, but *legal* equality is a dimension as important as it is elusive. Constitutions aim to set up objective frameworks for governance, yet the interpretation of law based on these frameworks remains largely subjective. As a democracy based on the rule of law, the United States has long struggled with this inherent dilemma. This disjuncture between constitutional mandate and the application and adjudication of laws comes into sharpest focus during the post-Reconstruction era. The unsettled meaning of the Constitution's protection of equality became a cause for concern among African American writers and activists who witnessed the resurgence of violent white supremacy and Jim Crow laws in

Edlie Wong, *Equality* In: *Democracies in America: Keywords for the Nineteenth Century and Today.* Edited by:
D. Berton Emerson and Gregory Laski, Oxford University Press. © D. Berton Emerson and Gregory Laski 2023.
DOI: 10.1093/oso/9780198865698.003.0004

former Confederate states. The Constitution, Charles W. Chesnutt wrote, "would seem both comprehensive and conclusive...But a moment of reflection will show that it was neither. What constitutes race? When are rights equal or unequal? What is a denial of the equal protection of the laws? What are civil rights?"[2] In the closing decades of the nineteenth century, the Fourteenth Amendment became the "single most important text in constitutional adjudication."[3]

During this tumultuous period, the US Supreme Court issued a landmark equal protection ruling that has, since the mid-1900s, expanded the meaning and scope of equality. Surprisingly, this precedent had little impact on early Black civil rights struggles and was often cited in nineteenth-century rulings that advanced racial inequality and injustice. In *Yick Wo v. Hopkins* (1886), the US Supreme Court held for the first time that all persons, including noncitizens, were within the scope of the Fourteenth Amendment. It also ruled that facially neutral laws (laws without explicit discriminatory language) administered in a discriminatory manner violated the equal protection mandate. One legal commentator from the era declared that this "principle of the fundamental law...has made 'America' the very symbol and embodiment of all that is just and righteous in government, not alone protecting the unfortunate of our own nation from local hate and prejudice, but offering as well an asylum for the oppressed of other lands."[4] Yet the expansive principle set in *Yick Wo* did not alter the outcomes of subsequent equal protection challenges, including the landmark *Plessy v. Ferguson* (1896), which upheld the constitutionality of racial segregation. In the decade following *Yick Wo*, the court perfected a concept of formal equality that adhered to the language but not the practice of fair and equal treatment. This contradiction between the substance and form of equality remains an enduring dilemma for US democracy.

Now a staple of constitutional law textbooks, *Yick Wo* numbers among the most significant cases to ever come before the Supreme Court. Banned from US CITIZENSHIP with the passage of the 1882 Chinese Exclusion Act, immigrants from China faced escalating restrictions, xenophobia, and nativist attacks. The *San Francisco Evening Bulletin* noted that equal protection was "fine in theory" but not applicable to the Chinese, whose "habits, acquirements, and tendencies" placed them beyond the pale of "modern races of man."[5] It defended the Exclusion Act as a necessary measure, claiming bitterly that, "We can do nothing to elevate or reform them [the Chinese], for that would be discrimination, contrary to the Fourteenth Amendment."[6] Unable to naturalize and vote as citizens, Chinese immigrants turned to the courts to seek protection against discrimination. From 1881 to 1896, the Supreme Court heard seventeen cases involving Chinese immigrants from the Pacific Coast states. These cases represent an important if often over- looked element of US constitutional history, and the unanimous ruling in *Yick Wo* was highly unusual for the era's conservative court. Through this form of political contestation, Chinese legal activists challenged the mean- ing of equal protection and in the process helped define the national ideal of equality.

More than two decades before the *Yick Wo* case, despite suffering racial and economic restrictions, Chinese immigrants in California had managed to secure a foothold in the laundry industry. In 1861, Lee Yick immigrated from China and began a laundry business in San Francisco, which remained in continuous operation for the next twenty-two years. Wo Lee, the co-litigant in the case, had likewise continuously operated his San Francisco laundry for twenty-five years. In 1885, Yick and Lee ran afoul of a new city ordinance regulating laundry operations that was enforced only against the Chinese. In response to anti-Chinese public protests, the city passed more than a dozen ordinances intended to drive these laundries out of business or beyond the city limits. Public health officials and politicians fixated on these Chinese- run businesses—nine-tenths of which operated beyond Chinatown—as dangerous encroachments into otherwise white neighborhoods.[7] The city board of supervisors rejected all licensing petitions from Chinese laundry- men and granted all but one of the non-Chinese applications.[8] Forced to operate without licenses, Yick and Lee numbered among the 150 Chinese laundrymen the police arrested, although these same officers overlooked 80 other unlicensed white-owned laundries in operation.[9] The Tung Hing Tong Association, the Chinese laundrymen's guild, spearheaded the legal campaign to fight this racial discrimination.

In *Yick Wo v. Hopkins*, the court had to determine whether "strangers and aliens" like Yick and Lee were protected under the Fourteenth Amendment or any other part of the Constitution. The ruling in favor of the Chinese claimants appeared to make a powerful statement about equal protection. In the unanimous opinion, Justice Thomas Stanley Matthews declared that the "Fourteenth Amendment to the Constitution is not confined to the protec- tion of citizens" and judged all persons "without regard to any differences of race, of color, or of nationality" within the scope of the provision. He also emphasized that the "unequal and oppressive" application of the law produced racial bias: Chinese laundrymen faced punishment for an occupation that was lawfully permitted to all others. In *Yick Wo*'s most famous passage, Matthews proclaimed that while the ordinance carried race-neutral language, its discriminatory enforcement violated equal protection: "Though the law itself be fair on its face and impartial in appearance, yet if it is applied and administered by a public authority with an evil eye and an unequal hand, so as practically to make unjust and illegal discrimination between persons in similar circumstances, material to their rights, the denial of equal justice is still within the prohibition of the Constitution."[10]

Stunned commentators speculated on the potentially momentous implications of the *Yick Wo* ruling. The *San Francisco Bulletin* reported that "the decision will reach much further than the ordinance in question," but "how far it will reach cannot be definitively determined."[11] However, a series of failed Chinese test cases shortly after *Yick Wo*, including *Chae Chan Ping v. US* (1889), *Fong Yue Ting v. US* (1893), and *US v. Ju Toy* (1905), soon proved *Yick Wo* ineffective in the protection of Chinese immigrant rights. The rulings in these later Chinese cases gave the federal government broad-based, extraconstitutional plenary power over immigration control and the lives of noncitizens, and the holdings in *Chae Chan Ping* and *Fong Yue Ting* have never been overruled. One commentator observed that the "fundamental principles of American liberty have received...[no]...greater shock" than in the Supreme Court ruling in *Ju Toy*, which eliminated the right to judicial review for administrative immigration decisions.[12] Perplexed, the writer could not understand how the court reconciled this ruling with *Yick Wo*.

Despite *Yick Wo*'s anti-discriminatory statements, the Supreme Court rarely applied the ruling as a meaningful precedent in other equal protection cases from the era. In the decade after *Yick Wo*, the court remained undecided on how far it would enforce the "equal protection," "due process," and "privileges and immunities" clauses of the Fourteenth Amendment. Legal scholar Gabriel Chin goes so far as to challenge the idea of *Yick Wo* as a "race case" since it did not prohibit legal discrimination against African Americans and Chinese immigrants and neither was it applied to invalidate the "thousands of discriminatory prosecutions" against racial minorities brought before federal courts.[13] Instead, later applications of *Yick Wo* expanded the Fourteenth Amendment's protection of economic rights for white men and corporations, such as the right to buy and sell property or to run a business. By the end of the century, the Fourteenth Amendment did not protect a Black citizen from segregation or disfranchisement, but it did protect a corporation's right to contract.[14]

In the 1890s, *Yick Wo* made its way into Black voting rights test cases, but the ruling was often invoked by jurists to either refute or dismiss legitimate claims of racial bias. These legal challenges resulted in decisions that maintained racial inequality and extended constitutional sanction to anti-Black discrimination. By 1900, when Pauline E. Hopkins published her first novel, *Contending Forces*, it had become apropos of the era for her noble race-man Will Smith to proclaim, "Constitutional amendments are dead letters; the ballot box is nil."[15] In numerous test cases, including *Williams v. Mississippi* (1898), the Supreme Court decisively shifted the *Yick Wo* precedent away from the federal protection of Black citizens and toward the expansion of corporate power.

Across the final decades of the nineteenth century, as the federal government abandoned Reconstruction, southern states nullified the postwar amendments through new laws aimed at the DISFRANCHISEMENT of Black voters. In these former Confederate states, voting qualifications such as literacy tests, understanding clauses, property requirements, and poll taxes served as racial proxies, and registrars had an almost limitless authority over the registration process. In *Mills v. Green* (1895), Laurence Mills brought a lawsuit against the South Carolina registrar who denied him voter registration. It became one of the earliest cases challenging Black disfranchisement to come before the Supreme Court. Public commentary at the time speculated on the decisive bearing of *Yick Wo* on the Mills case. As the *Nation* magazine insisted, the *Yick Wo* doctrine affirmed "the power to investigate the workings of any local law, and to interfere for the protection of a citizen against the unjust administration of any statute."[16] However, the Supreme Court, unwilling to interfere with state elections or state constitutions, dismissed Mills's suit on a technicality.

Three years later, the plaintiff's attorney in *Williams v. Mississippi* extensively cited *Yick Wo* in its effort to challenge Black disfranchisement through the equal protection clause. In the case, a jury of white men had found a Black man named Henry Williams guilty of murder. The all-white jury had been selected from electors registered through a provision of the 1890 Mississippi Constitution, which included restrictive measures designed to disfranchise Black voters and remove them from jury service. Facing a death sentence, Williams appealed his conviction, claiming that his right to a fair trial and equal protection of the law had been violated.[17]

In the brief filed for Williams, his attorney noted that the law challenged in *Yick Wo* was deemed unconstitutional because it permitted "a discretion which could be used by the administrative authorities, to the discrimination of a class of persons, and the proof being that it was used to the discrimination of the China race," even though "the law did not disclose any obnoxious provisions upon its face."[18] Similarly, Williams argued, "the enforcement of this [Mississippi] law as provided, though apparently fair upon its face; has resulted in the denial of [Black] suffrage."[19] The court unanimously disagreed. Marshaling a theory of equal application, the court reasoned that the Mississippi constitution and statutes were neutral in regards to race since they equally disadvantaged white and Black men, making them formally equal before the law. Delivering the court's opinion, Justice Joseph McKenna insisted: "the operation of the Constitution and laws is not limited by their language or effects to one race. They reach weak and vicious white men as well as weak and vicious black men."[20] He refused to acknowledge the evidence of discriminatory intent or administration in the state constitution and registration laws.

Yick Wo had seemed to strengthen equal protection standards by suggesting that discriminatory application and effects were sufficient to invalidate a law. As historian Volney Riser argues, "Mississippi's 1890 constitution produced a discrimination, one that certainly seemed to fail the *Yick Wo* test for constitutionality, but the court found that the California case presented clear evidence of discrimination while the Mississippi case did not."[21] Forced to respond to the *Yick Wo* precedent, McKenna provided a detailed summary of the ruling in order to dismiss its applicability in Williams's case. The Mississippi suffrage provisions, McKenna declared, "do not on their face discriminate between the races, and it has not been shown that their actual administration was evil; only that evil was possible under them."[22] *Williams* was the last of three major nineteenth-century Black disfranchisement test cases, which included *Gibson v. Mississippi* (1896) and *Smith v. Mississippi* (1896). In ruling after ruling, the court held that "there was no ambiguity in the language employed and the Negro was not directly named" and refused "to find a meaning which discriminated against the colored voter," as Chesnutt denounced.[23] The *Williams* ruling confirmed that the Supreme Court of that era would not declare state-sponsored practices of Black disfranchisement to be unconstitutional or a "denial of...equal protection."

Two years earlier, Justice Henry Billings Brown had also found the segregated public accommodations in *Plessy v. Ferguson* "reasonable" and consistent with *Yick Wo*. The New Orleans Citizens' Committee helped orchestrate the test case challenging the Louisiana Separate Car Act. The law mandated "equal but separate accommodations for the white and colored races" on all passenger railways within the state.[24] In judging "equal but separate" as consistent with the Fourteenth Amendment, *Plessy* formally ushered in the era of racial segregation. It justified racial segregation in all aspects of public life until 1954, when the modern Supreme Court held in *Brown v. Board of Education* that segregated schools violated equal protection. In an empty show of judicial fairness, Justice Brown's *Plessy* ruling named *Yick Wo* as a glaring instance of a racially biased law directed not "in good faith for the promotion for the public good" but for the "oppression of a particular class," namely the Chinese.[25] However, his ruling refused to examine the racially discriminatory intent and impact of the Louisiana law in Plessy's case even as it affirmed *Yick Wo* as the standard for equal protection.

At century's close, the *Yick Wo* precedent had come to epitomize a widely accepted legal concept of formal but not substantive equality. Formal equality focuses on establishing rules or norms by which to govern society with no regard for group differences, whereas substantive equality takes into consideration lived differences among groups to ensure equitable outcomes and equal opportunity. These diverging approaches have shaped *Yick Wo*'s complex legacies. A frequent contributor to the *Albany Law Review*, New York lawyer B. Frank Dake observed that in *Yick Wo*, "Justice Matthews announced a general principle which it may be difficult to reconcile with more recent decisions of the court, which is clearly hostile to the spirit and administration of constitutional provisions and laws recently enacted by several of the States for the avowed purpose of practically suppressing the negro vote."[26] These rulings helped bring about the white oppression of Black life in what historian Rayford Logan has called the "nadir" of US race relations. Rather than substantive equality, *Yick Wo* heralded a new era of legal violence marked by the expansion of Jim Crow laws and Asian exclusion. In his 1904 article, Dake declared that the "world has come to realize that equality between negroes and Caucasians cannot be created by legislation."[27] In an echo of Hopkins's fictional Will Smith, Dake concluded, "the decisions of the Supreme Court...relating to the negro...[have turned]...the constitutional provisions and statutes enacted for him...[into]...dead letters."[28] Chesnutt went further in his condemnation. "[A]t present...no more disastrous course could be pursued by the colored race than to carry their wrongs to the Supreme Court," he cautioned. "They have rights, when they go there," but "when they leave, they are likely to have no rights at all."[29]

If, as this history teaches us, the Constitution has legal force only to the extent that courts invest it with meaning, then the *Yick Wo* case provides a useful vantage on the ever-evolving struggle for equality. In 1886, *Yick Wo* was decided by a federal judiciary reluctant to acknowledge how a majority-rule system put racial and ethnic minorities at risk. Our modern Supreme Court now recognizes *Yick Wo* as a landmark equal protection ruling. The legal reinvention of *Yick Wo* began after the formal end of immigration laws and policies that excluded and limited immigration from Asia. These changes coincided with the unprecedented expansion of civil rights, civil liberties, and federal power under Chief Justice Earl Warren's more liberal and activist Supreme Court. Since this era, the *Yick Wo* precedent has been used to strike down Jim Crow laws and other unfairly enforced state regulations related to disability rights, gender discrimination, and even gay marriage.

How we interpret equality continues to matter. Since the era of desegregation, the Supreme Court began subjecting modern equal protection challenges to a tiered framework of tests based on the nature of the rights affected by the contested law. Arguably, this hierarchical framework remains counterproductive to equality. The "rational basis" test is the most common and it has proven to be the most deferential form of equal protection review. It does not require a real analysis of the law, and contested laws and policies are often upheld. Laws that discriminate against "semi-suspect classifications," such as sex and gender, are subject to the "intermediate scrutiny" or "heightened scrutiny" test, while laws that discriminate against "suspect classifications," including race and national origin, or those involving certain fundamental rights are subject to the "strict scrutiny" test, the highest level of judicial scrutiny. These tests have narrowed the scope of constitutional discrimination claims and limited the judiciary's ability to use equal protection to remedy social inequities. It remains difficult to prove an equal protection violation when the law in question appears facially neutral. In the absence of discriminatory language or classifications, claimants must produce sufficient evidence that the law was motivated by discriminatory intent against a specific class of persons.

The history of *Yick Wo* demonstrates that equality must be understood as a substantive rather than formalistic concept. In the late twentieth and early twenty-first centuries, the most profound challenges to the meaning of equality and the hierarchal framework for equal protection review have come from women and LGBTQ communities. In numerous test cases involving discrimination on account of sex or sexual orientation, feminists and LGBTQ advocates have challenged federal courts to focus on the meaning of equality rather than on expanding the judicially created tiers of equal protection scrutiny. In these efforts, *Yick Wo* reminds us that equality considerations must address discriminatory impact and the effects of disparate treatment and life outcomes in our effort to achieve a more just and perfect union.

Notes

1. Jacob Howard, "Introduction of the Fourteenth Amendment," reprinted in Christopher Green, *Equal Citizenship, Civil Rights, and the Constitution: The Original Sense of the Privileges or Immunities Clause* (New York: Routledge, 2015), 156–159, 159.

2. Charles Chesnutt, "The Courts and the Negro" (c. 1908), in Joseph R. McElrath, Jr., Robert C. Leitz III, and Jesse C. Crisler, eds., *Charles W. Chesnutt: Essays and Speeches* (Stanford, CA: Stanford University Press, 1999), 262–270, 264.

3. John Hayakawa Torok, "Reconstruction and Racial Nativism: Chinese Immigrants and the Debates on the Thirteenth, Fourteenth, and Fifteenth Amendments and Civil Rights Law," *Asian American Law Journal* 3, no. 4 (January 1996): 55–103, 78.

4. Glenda Burke Slaymaker, "The Right of a Negro Litigant to a Trial by a Mixed Jury Under 'The Equal Protection of the Laws,'" *Albany Law Journal* (May 1903): 131–135, 132.

5. Nayan Shah, *Contagious Divides: Epidemics and Race in San Francisco's Chinatown* (Berkeley, CA: University of California Press, 2001), 66.

6. Cited in Marie A. Failinger, "*Yick Wo* at 125: Four Simple Lessons for the Contemporary Supreme Court," *Michigan Journal of Race Law* 17, no. 2 (Spring 2012): 217–268, 234.

7. Shah, *Contagious Divides*, 64.

8. Charles J. McClain, *In Search of Equality: The Chinese Struggle against Discrimination in Nineteenth-Century America* (Berkeley, CA: University of California Press, 1994), 104.

9. Ibid., 116.

10. United States Supreme Court, *Yick Wo v. Hopkins. United States Reports*, vol. 118, 10 May 1886, pp. 356–374, 373–374. *Library of Congress*, http://cdn.loc.gov/service/ll/usrep/usrep118/usrep118356/usrep118356.pdf.

11. "The Laundry Ordinance," *San Francisco Bulletin*, May 10, 1886, 2.

12. B. Frank Dake, "The Chinaman Before the Supreme Court," *Albany Law Journal* (September 1905): 258–267, 266.

13. Gabriel J. Chin, "Unexplainable on Grounds of Race: Doubts about *Yick Wo*," *University of Illinois Law Review* 2008, no. 5 (August 2008): 1359–1392, 1361.

14. Thomas W. Joo, "*Yick Wo* Re-Revisited: Nonblack Nonwhites and Fourteenth Amendment History," *University of Illinois Law Review* 2008, no. 5 (August 2008): 1427–1440, 1428.

15. Pauline Hopkins, *Contending Forces: A Romance Illustrative of Negro Life North and South* (New York: Oxford University Press, 1988), 297.

16. "The Case of Yick Wo," *The Nation*, vol. 60, no. 1562 (6 June 1895): 438–439, 439.

17. Michael Perman, *Struggle for Mastery: Disenfranchisement in the South, 1888–1908* (Chapel Hill, NC: University of North Carolina Press, 2001), 121.

18. Cornelius Jones, "In Error to the Supreme Court of the United States from the Supreme Court of Mississippi. Henry Williams vs. the State of Mississippi," in *Transcript of Record. Supreme Court of the United States. October Term, 1897. No. 531* (Filed December 1897), 15.

19. Ibid., 16.

20. United States Supreme Court, *Williams v. Mississippi. United States Reports*, vol. 170, 25 April 1898, pp. 213–225, 222, *Library of Congress*, http://cdn.loc.gov/service/ll/usrep/usrep170/usrep170213/usrep170213.pdf.

21. R. Volney Riser, *Defying Disenfranchisement: Black Voting Rights Activism in the Jim Crow South, 1890–1908* (Baton Rouge, LA: Louisiana State University Press, 2010), 71.

22. United States Supreme Court, *Williams v. Mississippi. United States Reports*, 225.

23. Chesnutt, "The Disfranchisement of the Negro," *Charles W. Chesnutt*, 181.

24. Charles Lofgren, *The Plessy Case: A Legal-Historical Interpretation* (New York: Oxford University Press, 1988), 191.

25. Brook Thomas, ed., *Plessy v. Ferguson: A Brief History with Documents* (Boston, MA: Bedford/St. Martin's Press, 1997), 48–49.

26. B. Frank Dake, "The Negro Before the Supreme Court," *Albany Law Journal* (August 1904): 238–247, 241.

27. Ibid., 238.

28. Ibid., 246, 247.

29. Chesnutt, "Liberty and the Franchise," *Charles W. Chesnutt*, 106.

Further Reading

Unlike the extensive literature on African American political struggle, the study of Asian Americans in the development of equal protection jurisprudence dates from the 1990s, when scholars began to recover, document, and discuss the thousands of cases that Chinese immigrants brought before federal courts to challenge admission and deportation decisions and infringements of their constitutional rights. See Erika Lee, *Making of Asian American History* (New York: Simon & Schuster, 2015) and *At America's Gates* (Chapel Hill, NC: University of North Carolina Press, 2004), Lucy Salyer, *Laws Harsh As Tigers* (Chapel Hill, NC: University of North Carolina

Press, 1995), and Charles McClain, *In Search of Equality* (Berkeley, CA: University of California Press, 1994) for detailed examinations of early sources; Brook Thomas, *The Literature of Reconstruction* (Baltimore, MD: Johns Hopkins University Press, 2017) for literary treatments of these cases; and Charles Postel, *Equality* (New York: Farrar, Straus, and Giroux, 2019), Mae Ngai, *Impossible Subjects* (Princeton, NJ: Princeton University Press, 2004), and Gerald Neuman, *Strangers to the Constitution* (Princeton, NJ: Princeton University Press, 1996) for broader engagements with US citizenship, immigration policy, and equality movements.

4

Scale
(or, Democracy in *las Américas*)

James E. Sanders

"Here is a word that everyone pronounces, it is the favorite theme of every orator. There are not gatherings, nor meetings, nor discussions in which you do not hear...the word 'Democracy.'"[1] Thus opined the politician and poet Vicente Paz in 1876, writing in the newspaper *El Montañes* from the coastal Pacific town of Barbacoas, Colombia. Yet how we, and Paz and his readers, understand democracy and its history critically relies on scale—geographic scale across the Americas, class scale within societies, and chronological scale through time. Democracy, in all of its incarnations, had different meanings and practices depending on where, which, and when historical actors thought over, spoke about, wrote on, and struggled for contested notions of democracy.

This volume, *Democracies in America*, explores the myriad relationships between "democracy" and "America"—the latter term usually meaning the United States. However, for so long the assertion that democracy is peculiarly American has *only* meant the United States, reeking of an exceptionalism the historical record does not support, instead of the broader *Americas*. To understand the history of democracy in the Americas, we must break the Eurocentric and Anglocentric prejudices that have informed its study for so long. The United States was the first but hardly the only republic in the Americas, and an identity of being "American" or "americano" accelerated across the hemisphere during anticolonial wars for independence. Indeed, save for Brazil (an empire) and some Caribbean islands that remained colonies, from Chile and Argentina to Mexico, all the states of South and Central America became republics after independence (in the 1820s). Latin American

James E. Sanders, *Scale (or, Democracy in* las Américas*)* In: *Democracies in America: Keywords for the Nineteenth Century and Today.* Edited by: D. Berton Emerson and Gregory Laski, Oxford University Press.
© D. Berton Emerson and Gregory Laski 2023. DOI: 10.1093/oso/9780198865698.003.0005

states also surpassed the United States in democratizing their republics, especially in regard to race, which was almost never directly used to restrict citizenship. Beyond institutional citizenship, a rich political culture emerged in which popular groups appropriated a wide-ranging repertoire of democratic and republican politics—voting, petitioning, marching in demonstrations, serving in citizen militias, pressuring legislators from galleries, participating in local councils, attending political clubs, and generally debating the political issues of the day, thereby creating a democratic public sphere in town squares, village markets, churches, cockfighting pits, and taverns. Both institutionally and culturally, democracy flourished in the mid-nineteenth century. Democracy's history is an American story, but American in the sense of the Americas, not just the United States: the majority of the world's democratic republics in the nineteenth century were in Latin America. Their history, so long derided, insists that the origins and development of democracy happened as much in Haiti, Colombia, and Mexico as in England, France, and the United States.

Certainly, Latin Americans themselves thought democracy was a peculiarly American practice, in comparison to Europe. The Mexican paper *El Monitor Republicano* declared, "The democratic republic is the natural government of America, just as monarchy is natural to Europe."[2] As the French invaded Mexico, another paper argued in 1862 that Mexico "represents the interests of the New World, land of democracy, combating the interests of the Old World, land of tyranny and human degradation."[3] Indeed, some Latin Americans assumed their societies surpassed the United States in democratic accomplishment, as they had first abolished slavery and first established equality of citizenship for all men (seen as central to democracy), regardless of race. Colombian President José María Obando celebrated the 1853 Constitution, which enacted universal adult male suffrage, as "the most democratic code that has governed any pueblo."[4] In Mexico, *El Globo* asserted, "Our Republic is the model for democracies...giving a lesson of progress to her powerful neighbor to the North, since she does not organize her social rankings according to tints of color nor racial distinctions."[5] Rethinking the scale of democracy demands the United States be viewed as it was: one American republic among many, all facing the same issues and conundrums—how to grapple with slavery, racial and cultural heterogeneity, inequality, and popular sovereignty.

In addition to geographic scale, rethinking democracy's history means recovering the voices and popular intellectual history of the poor, the

Indigenous, the recently freed—it demands attention to social class within societies. Although constantly invoked, democracy was rarely directly defined in the political discourse of nineteenth-century Latin America. There was no one definition of democracy; it meant very different things to different people, existing as a contested term (along with republicanism, citizen, liberty, EQUALITY, and liberalism), embraced by many Liberals and rejected by some Conservatives, and interpreted quite differently by popular groups versus educated elites. Almost all studies of democracy's intellectual history in Latin America have focused on those elites and the easily accessible (and often translated) formal writings they left behind, yet if we look at popular and quotidian political discourse in the public sphere—in petitions, speeches, newspapers, and festivals—significantly different visions of democracy emerge.

How did "democracy" appear in the public sphere? In political speeches and newspaper essays it was mostly used as a synonym for republicanism (which was more frequently utilized) or combined with it as the "democratic republic," although at times the two were contrasted (and even seen as contradictory).[6] In general, democracy was defined in opposition to monarchy, colonialism, and rule by the few over the many. By midcentury, the contrast of democracy with aristocracy and oligarchy was constant. Mexico's *El Republicano* opposed the formation of a "detestable oligarchy" so that "our republic will be essentially democratic."[7] The paper argued that if CITIZENSHIP were too restricted by property or literacy, the "government then resembles more aristocracy than democracy," arguments echoed by popular actors.[8]

For many Latin American Liberals, both popular and elite, democracy meant society's transformation. By the 1850s, Colombia had been a republic for decades, but for many it took a "social revolution" of liberal reforms—the abolition of slavery, freedom of the press, eradicating monopolies, ending the death penalty, a jury system, a reduced permanent army, expanded citizenship—to truly remake society, a revolution carried out by the poor and dispossessed who "contributed to the triumph of Democracy."[9] A Mexican Independence Day speaker celebrated replacing monarchies with "popular governments, the democratic Republics" that had brought justice to Indians and ended African slavery.[10] Luis de la Rosa, in another Independence Day speech, celebrated the "democratic instincts" of this racially mixed pueblo; the same pueblo had fought for independence, for "the triumph of the people over the privileged classes, the victory, perhaps bloody, but inevitable, of democracy over aristocracy." If one definition of democracy was evident in the nineteenth-century public sphere, it involved, in Rosa's words, "the eminently democratic principle of the sovereignty of the pueblo."[11] For the early United States, as Danielle Allen suggests in Chapter 1 of this volume, democracy was most often defined by the level of popular influence and the idea of popular sovereignty in contrast to aristocracies.

Yet many elites, especially Conservatives, viewed democracy negatively. In Mexico, elites lamented how an ignorant pueblo, under "democratic institutions," would elect unqualified men, leading to anarchy.[12] In general, for Conservatives and some disenchanted elite Liberals, democracy meant mob rule, attacks on property, and demands for social equality, evocatively denominated as "savage democracy."[13] The fear of racial equality that many popular Liberals thought democracy promised loomed large for many Conservatives. In 1849, *Ariete* argued those who believe in "democracy" wanted complete equality, but such equality was "absurd" as men were inherently unequal by abilities, intelligence, and race.[14]

A quick comparison of how popular classes understood democracy compared to wealthy Conservatives reveals how social class must be considered when studying democracy. For popular actors, bargaining—the expectation that their political support would merit some redress for their concerns—lay at the heart of democratic republicanism. Popular groups' basic assumption about democracy, often revealed through their petitions, was that a democratic government would hear their voice, as citizens, and respond to their demands (in other words, popular sovereignty). Indians from Mocondino, Colombia, wrote in 1866 to the state president to ask that their communal landholdings not be divided into individual private property: "we do not believe that an essentially democratic government that has proclaimed such beautiful principles" would ignore their wishes.[15] Another Indigenous village, Yumbo, also petitioned to protect their landholdings, arguing that an "enlightened, free and democratic municipal government" should help them.[16] Sebastiana Silva petitioned in 1874 for help in the return of her son, who had been forced to work for a family as a domestic servant. She demanded his return but the family had refused, "as if we still were in the barbarous times in which the government allowed the slavery of men. Today, thankfully, we have a republican and democratic government that will not allow such monstrosities."[17] Silva was poor, probably Afro-Colombian, and a woman, yet she still expected a democratic government to hear her voice and enforce her rights.

Popular groups did not tend to use the word "democracy" directly but instead focused on the elements of democracy as broadly understood in the public sphere, especially popular sovereignty and citizenship, often in pursuit of equality, rights, and social transformation (as Silva's petition suggests). Cali's Democratic Society, whose membership included many Afro-Colombians and other poor farmers, petitioned the state president to abrogate a new tax on liquor production. They acknowledged he had no legal authority to do so, yet urged him to act anyway, as "popular will" demanded the law's derogation. The Democratic Society argued that in "republican countries" the executive must act in moments when the pueblo demanded succor, and the state president needed to prove he was a "magistrate fit to lead a free people." If the legislature expressed outrage at his bypassing its authority, he could comfort himself knowing he enjoyed "an approbation that is more valuable, that of the sovereign pueblo."[18] In this case, the democracy of the pueblo's sovereignty overrode legal niceties or republican separation of powers.

Popular visions of citizenship also differed from those of elites. In 1877 the members of Cali's Democratic Society, after having just defeated the Conservatives in the 1876–7 civil war, demanded their backpay and pensions and, most importantly, the distribution of land as a reward for service. The veterans claimed they had fought for "liberty" against the Conservatives who saw them as the "slaves of these so-called feudal lords." This war had pitted those who enjoyed "great wealth and immense landholdings" against "the poor masses." Now soldiers demanded payment from a Liberal state that claimed to rule in the name of republican democracy. They demanded land so that they could fully be "citizens of a free people."[19] Citizenship, in a democratic republic, was thus contrasted with feudalism; however, the soldiers were legally citizens already. For them, democratic citizenship also meant a social transformation toward greater equality, especially owning land, for citizenship to be truly meaningful. While equality was often simply a legal question for elites, for popular groups equality, central to their visions of democracy, involved the social and economic realms as well.

An 1852 petition from the San Pedro Democratic Society in Buga, Colombia, sums up our themes. The Society petitioned the president to allow them to maintain the provincial capital against plans to move it to

Cartago. They claimed Cartago was full of "oligarchs" who had supported the Conservatives in the last civil war. However, Buga had fought for "the emancipation of the masses" and the "cause of the pueblo." They supported "the fruits of republicanism," while Cartago had opposed "democratic opinion."[20] Ultimately, democracy, however ill defined, was the popular against the powerful, the rights of the pueblo against the oligarchs, and the hope that "democratic opinion" would influence the state to work to transform society. While elites often looked askance at democracy (and today's scholars debate democracy's efficacy, especially its limitations and effectiveness at representing and including the poor and minority groups), popular actors in the Americas—Indians, African Americans, poor campesinos—insisted democracy (and its handmaidens citizenship and equality) had meaning and value. Across the Americas, including the United States, as other entries in this volume attest, different social groups imagined citizenship, equality, rights, and popular sovereignty distinctly. People across different classes in society tended to understand, and value, democracy quite differently, and this scale must always be kept in mind.

While thinking about or defining democracy in the long nineteenth century, *when* in the time period of that era must also be carefully considered: democracy's meanings, practices, and valorization would change dramatically over that century. Historians and political scientists have long noted how democracy has not advanced in a linear, even fashion, but instead developed rapidly in waves of democratization, often followed by reverse waves that roll back democratic gains. The famous political scientist Samuel Huntington pioneered this approach in his book *The Third Wave*; however, for the nineteenth century, his argument has three decided weaknesses: first, it ignores democratic developments in Latin America during his first wave of democratization (1828–1926), only focusing on the United States and Europe, in spite of many Latin American states meeting the institutional requirements for being declared democracies; second, it focuses almost completely on institutions, with little weight given to how societies actually valorized democracy; and third, it elides distinct waves of democracy within the long nineteenth century.[21] However, if these shortcomings are corrected, the concept of waves of democracy is very useful for highlighting chronological scale: how democracy changed over the course of the nineteenth century, instead of homogenizing the era.

Of course, the first great wave of democratization began in the Age of Revolution—led by the United States and Haiti, and eventually followed by the Spanish American republics (which coincided with the expansion of suffrage beyond a restricted property-owning elite in the United States), even if, in the early republics, democracy was often viewed with suspicion. This wave crested in the 1860s and early 1870s—a high-water mark for democracy across the Americas. In Mexico, republicans defeated the invading Emperor Maximillian, his French army, and monarchical Mexican Conservatives, reestablishing a republic and the democratic reforms of Benito Juárez. In Colombia, Afro-Colombians and Indigenous peoples enjoyed full citizenship rights and regularly entered the political arena. Cuban patriots, beginning to forge a pan-racial alliance, challenged Spanish rule and slavery. In the United States, slavery was belatedly abolished (compared to the rest of the Spanish American republics), freedmen claimed constitutional rights, the Conservative and aristocratic slavocracy fell, and women, for a moment, glimpsed the possibility of obtaining political rights. Across the Americas there was a sense that the forces of democracy, liberty, and equality had confronted slave-owners, aristocrats, monarchists, and imperialists and emerged triumphant. Examining these events, a Mexican newspaper declared in 1866 that, "Any attempt to compromise the development of the free peoples of the Americas will now be useless and sterile."[22] Many thought this wave of democracy would roll across the Atlantic to revolutionize Europe. A Chilean writer argued the influence of America would spread to Europe, as "democracy will destroy current European society," referring both to monarchy and the vast inequalities of wealth.[23] Manuel Merino in an Independence Day speech declared that "the Eagles of American democracy, crossing the Atlantic, will import into the Old World the modern doctrines of political association, thereby emancipating those peoples."[24] Democracy was American and modern, while monarchies were European and backward—the Americas, North and South, represented humanity's future.

This future was not to be. The democratic successes inspired a conservative (or perhaps classically liberal reaction), as politicians and capitalists acted to roll back past democratic gains. Across Spanish America a sense of falling behind the industrial United States emerged. In this vision, citizens must forget their democratic past and face a future defined by the hard realities of capitalist development: "The disrepute of the old revolutionary utopias increases daily. Those who still pursue an unrealizable democracy, fight with arms whose point has been broken by the iron-plated armor of reality."[25] Democracy, once declared an imprimatur of modernity, was now seen as allowing dangerous plebeians to create disorder and challenge property rights, preventing capitalist development. In Mexico, Justo Sierra argued that by establishing a utopian democracy, "democracy without limits," Mexico had not "maintained public security in order to attract foreign immigrants or capital."[26] Throughout the Americas, constitutions were changed to limit citizenship by class (but not openly by race, except in the United States). Dictatorships emerged, exemplified by Mexico's Porfiriato (1876–1911), which kept up a pretense of republicanism but in which one man ruled for decades, with the open desire to restrict democracy to encourage development. Eliseo Payán, a once-fervent democrat who would abandon his former beliefs when he became president of Colombia, declared in 1880 that because of chronic instability and "the violent attack on property" Colombia had suffered, "capital had fled or is hidden," while "industry is annihilated"; therefore, to correct these evils, "the path of dictatorship is considered justifiable as the way to obtain order and peace."[27] From celebrating the most democratic constitution in the world in the 1850s, elite Colombians now pondered dictatorship as a way to control demanding plebeians. Another Colombian politician, demanding restrictions on popular political participation, argued "there is much work to be done in order to make the masses understand what real and true liberty and democracy are."[28] The problem, of course, was that popular actors had long understood democracy, just not in ways that elite politicians appreciated. Without attention to scale, only looking at elites and only examining developments late in the nineteenth century, one could erroneously assume democracy had always failed in Latin America.

The United States would at first seem an outlier here, but the 1870s and 1880s also marked severe reversals in US democratic culture. The most important was the defeat of Radical Reconstruction and the removal of effective citizenship from African American males via DISFRANCHISEMENT. While led by Southerners, Reconstruction's defeat was also enabled by the suspicion of many Northerners that supporting the freedmen's efforts for citizenship and equality only emboldened their own working classes to make further demands. The notion that the state must take its citizens' demands seriously—a notion at the heart of popular visions of democracy—was crushed by Supreme Court legal decisions eviscerating the labor movement and federal and state government action to violently quell strikes and suppress Native American sovereignty via the processes of SETTLEMENT. H. W. Brands argues that there was a powerful sense among common people in the late-nineteenth-century United States "that the money power had gutted America's traditional values."[29] Corporate economic power, not popular sovereignty, was obviously supreme by the 1880s.

Yet these reversals do not invalidate past accomplishments in nourishing democracy across the Americas. If we only examine one part of the Americas, or one social class, or one time period, we can too easily mask the complexities of historical actors' lived experiences of democratic political culture.

Notes

1. *El Montañes* (Barbacoas), February 1, 1876. All translations mine.
2. *El Monitor Republicano* (México), July 1, 1867.
3. *La Alianza de la Frontera—Suplemento* (Chihuahua), July 29, 1862.
4. José M. Obando, "Mensaje del Presidente," Bogotá, February 1, 1854, Archivo General de la Nación, Bogotá, Colombia (hereafter AGNC), Fondo Archivo Histórico Legislativo Congreso de la República, 1854, Cámara, Correspondencia Oficial IV, 2.
5. *El Globo* (México), July 5, 1867.
6. *El Caucano* (Cali), August 6, 1863.
7. *El Republicano* (México), March 1, 1846.
8. *El Republicano* (México), April 3, 1846.
9. Ramón Mercado, *Memorias sobre los acontecimientos del Sur* (Cali: Centro de Estudios Históricos y Sociales "Santiago de Cali," 1996 [originally published 1853]), xviii, xcv.
10. Speech of Roque J. Morón, Chihuahua, September 16, 1862, *La Alianza de la Frontera* (Chihuahua), September 25, 1862.
11. Speech of Luis de la Rosa, México, December 16, 1846, *El Monitor Republicano* (México), September 19, 20, and 23, 1846.
12. *El Siglo Diez y Nueve* (México), June 23, 1848.
13. Vicente Cárdenas to Sergio Arboleda, Quito, November 19, 1878, Archivo Central del Cauca, Popayán, Colombia (hereafter ACC), Fondo Arboleda, Signatura 1,506.
14. *Ariete* (Cali), October 20, 1849.
15. The pequeño cabildo de indígenas of Mocondino to State President, Pasto, February 18, 1866, ACC, Archivo Muerto, paquete 94, legajo 54.
16. The pequeño cabildo de indígenas of Yumbo to President of the Municipality, Yumbo, June 9, 1869, Archivo Histórico Municipal de Cali, Colombia, tomo 156, p. 161.
17. Sebastiana Silva to Jefe Municipal, Popayán, October 13, 1874, ACC, Archivo Muerto, paquete 129, legajo 39.

18. The undersigned members of the Democratic Society to State President, Cali, October 14, 1866, ACC, Archivo Muerto, paquete 65, legajo 67.

19. The Democratic Society to Citizen President of the State, Cali, June 1, 1877, ACC, Archivo Muerto, paquete 137, legajo 7.

20. San Pedro Democratic Society to President José Hilario López, San Pedro, March 21, 1852, AGNC, Fondo Archivo Histórico Legislativo Congreso de la República, Cámara, 1852, Proyectos de Ley Negados, p. 47.

21. Samuel P. Huntington, *The Third Wave: Democratization in the Late Twentieth Century* (Norman, OK: University of Oklahoma Press, 1991).

22. *La República* (Chihuahua), February 15, 1867.

23. *El Ferrocarril* (Santiago) reprinted in *La Nación* (Montevideo), December 19, 1860.

24. Speech of Manuel Merino, Chihuahua, September 15, 1868, *La República* (Chihuahua), September 18, 1868.

25. *La Libertad* (México), December 27, 1884.

26. Justo Sierra, "Reorganización de la República: Las revoluciones," *La Libertad* (México), December 18, 1878–March 13, 1879, in Justo Sierra, *Obras completas del Maestro Justo Sierra, v. 4: Periodismo político* (Mexico City: UNAM, 1948), 174.

27. Speech of Eliseo Payán to Congress, Bogotá, April 8, 1880, *Rejistro Oficial* (Popayán), May 1, 1880.

28. Juan E. Ulloa to Salvador Camacho Roldán, Palmira, June 19, 1879, AGNC, Sección Academia Colombiana de Historia, Fondo Salvador Camacho Roldán, caja 13, carpeta 166, 6.

29. H. W. Brands, *American Colossus: The Triumph of Capitalism, 1865–1900* (New York: Anchor Books, 2010), 505–506.

Further Reading

There has been a massive reconsideration of democracy's history in Latin America. The best overviews are Hilda Sabato, *Republics of the New World* (Princeton, NJ: Princeton University Press, 2018) and two edited volumes: Javier Fernández Sebastián, ed., *Diccionario político y social del mundo iberoamericano*, 2 vols. (Madrid: Centro de Estudios Políticos y Constitucionales, 2009 and 2014) and José Antonio Aguilar and Rafael Rojas, eds., *El republicanismo en Hispanoamérica* (Mexico City: Fondo de Cultura Económica, 2002). For the importance of democracy in Americans' political culture, see James E. Sanders, *The Vanguard of the Atlantic World* (Durham, NC: Duke University Press, 2014). For Mexico, see Elisa Cárdenas Ayala, "La escurridiza democracia mexicana," *Alcores* 9 (2010) and José Antonio Aguilar Rivera, "La redención democrática," *Historia Mexicana* 69, no. 1 (2019). For Colombia, see Isidro Vanegas Useche, *Todas son iguales* (Bogotá: Universidad Externado de Colombia, 2010). For the public sphere, see Carlos A. Forment, *Democracy in Latin*

America, 1760–1900 (Chicago, IL: University of Chicago Press, 2003). Lucía Sala de Touron, "Democracia en América Latina," *Secuencia* 61 (2005), explores artisans' democratic engagement.

The historiography on popular participation in nineteenth-century politics has grown too vast to cite comprehensively. Florencia Mallon, *Peasant and Nation* (Berkeley, CA: University of California Press, 1995) pioneered reconsiderations of popular politics. Alejandro de la Fuente and George Reid Andrews, eds., *Afro-Latin American Studies* (New York: Cambridge University Press, 2018) provides an excellent overview of Afro-Latin American politics. For Peru, see Cecilia Méndez, *The Plebeian Republic* (Durham, NC: Duke University Press, 2005) and Mark Thurner, *From Two Republics to One Divided* (Durham, NC: Duke University Press, 1997). For Mexico, see Karen D. Caplan, *Indigenous Citizens* (Stanford, CA: Stanford University Press, 2010), Peter Guardino, *The Time of Liberty* (Durham, NC: Duke University Press, 2005), and Brian F. Connaughton, *Prácticas populares, cultura política y poder en México, siglo XIX* (Mexico City: Casa Juan Pablos, 2008). For Colombia, see Marixa Lasso, *Myths of Harmony* (Pittsburgh, PA: University of Pittsburgh Press, 2007), which has an excellent analysis of equality, and James E. Sanders, *Contentious Republicans* (Durham, NC: Duke University Press, 2004). For Bolivia, see Rossana Barragán, Dora Cajías and Seemin Qayum, eds., *El siglo XIX* (La Paz: Muela del Diablo Editores, 1997). For Argentina, see Gabriel Di Meglio, *¡Viva el bajo pueblo!* (Buenos Aires: Prometeo Libros, 2013) and Ariel de la Fuente, *Children of Facundo* (Durham, NC: Duke University Press, 2000). For Chile, see James A. Wood, *The Society of Equality* (Albuquerque, NM: University of New Mexico Press, 2011).

For waves of democracy, see Samuel P. Huntington, *The Third Wave* (Norman, OK: University of Oklahoma Press, 1991) and John Markoff, *Waves of Democracy* (New York: Sage Publications, 1996).

PART

II

Institutions and
Arrangements

We have frequently printed the word Democracy. Yet I cannot too often repeat that it is a word the real gist of which still sleeps .... It is a great word, whose history, I suppose, remains unwritten, because that history has yet to be enacted.

Walt Whitman, *Democratic Vistas* (1870)[1]

Democracy is difficult to convert from abstract idea into real, lived experience. It's not simply that creating democratic institutions requires the hard work and continuous commitment of the people—it certainly does. But official and often bureaucratic structures, while necessary for this political system to function and thrive in the real world, simultaneously limit the creative and energizing power of the demos. It is for this reason that the contemporary political theorist Sheldon Wolin argues that democracy is "fugitive," continually escaping and resisting expression in institutions and other static forms.[2] More recently, Wendy Brown has wondered whether democracy might more accurately refer not to a "form of governance" but to a "politics of resistance."[3]

The keywords in Part II draw this fundamental dilemma into focus. As you read and think about CONSTITUTION, REPRESENTATION, ANTI-BLACK VIOLENCE, CITIZENSHIP, WOMEN'S SUFFRAGE, and THE TOWN HALL MEETING, ask yourself: In what ways do the foundational commitments of democracy get enacted via institutional forms such as Congress, the franchise, and the Constitution itself? How do these various structures interact to secure both PERSONAL LIBERTY and EQUALITY, two keywords from Part I? How do other kinds of structures, such as town hall meetings, journalistic exposé, and the theater, work to actualize democracy, perhaps in different and better ways? How do people's individual and collective identities shape these structures? Who gets to be a citizen? How does this legal designation interact with other markers of status and identity—racial, gender, sexual, class? Is citizenship necessary for democracy to exist? How do these various modes of recognizing and representing people contribute to patterns of exclusion and inclusion? And what can we do when such patterns become institutions themselves, persisting across centuries and through generations?

The long nineteenth century provides a rich testing ground for thinking through these and other conceptual questions. In the following pages, you will find that not all women of the era wanted to vote; although many women fought for the right that would ultimately become enshrined in the Nineteenth Amendment to the Constitution, others believed that they could exercise democratic powers more effectively through non-institutional pathways. The debate turned in part on what it meant to be a *citizen*. In its original form, the Constitution had little to say on that score, but that did not stop African Americans, to take one example, from laying claim to that designation through practices including theatrical performances and organizing work such as the Colored Conventions—and, for some free Black men in the early 1800s at least, through voting. After the Civil War, the Fourteenth Amendment clarified that citizenship was a birthright (and helped to establish what we today hold as the commonsense association of "rights" and the "Constitution"). African Americans were formally contained within this legal designation. However, often they were citizens in name only. Resisting the terror of the lynch mob, and shut out from the franchise to which Black men had a legal right by the force of the Fifteenth Amendment, these citizens had to turn to alternative channels to gain representation in the public domain and—once again—fight against the dynamics of exclusion that kept them from full flourishing. For some activists, structures such as the town hall meeting and investigative journalism recommended themselves as a medium to materialize democracy. For Native Americans, on the other hand, the very prospect of being represented by the US democratic state upturned longstanding Indigenous political arrangements.

These intersecting yet divergent histories invite consideration of a fundamental dilemma with which our present democracy must contend: Through what channels and structures does democracy awaken, coming into being as both word and fact? And how can we configure these various structures to produce the democracy we want? As you consider the language that the long nineteenth century developed in response to this question, consider the twenty-first-century movements for Black lives and against mass incarceration, as well as protests at Standing Rock and #MeToo resistance. To borrow from Whitman, has democracy yet been enacted in these ways?

Notes

1. Walt Whitman, *Democratic Vistas*, ed. Ed Folsom (1871; repr., Iowa City, IA: University of Iowa Press, 2010), 37.
2. Sheldon Wolin, *Fugitive Democracy and Other Essays*, ed. Nicholas Xenos (Princeton, NJ: Princeton University Press, 2016).
3. Wendy Brown, " 'We Are All Democrats Now...,' " in *Democracy in What State?* (New York: Columbia University Press, 2011), 56.

5

Constitution

Jack Jackson

What is a constitution? Or more precisely for our purposes, how might we think of the US Constitution in the context of democracy in America?

In 1913, at the end of the long nineteenth century, historian Charles Beard approached this question in his iconoclastic text, *An Economic Interpretation of the Constitution of the United States*. It caused a stir, in part, by challenging the then-popular view of the origins of the Constitution. That view "may be stated in the following manner: The Constitution proceeds from the whole people; the people are the original source of all political authority exercised under it; it is founded on broad general principles of liberty and government entertained, for some reason, by the whole people and having no reference to the interest of or advantage of any particular class."[1] Against the fantasy of a unified people pursuing abstract universal justice, Beard began his inquiry by placing both political divisions and economic inequality at the heart of constitutional culture.

In a more recent exploration into the "Idea of a Constitution," political theorist Hanna Pitkin proposed that we eschew any search for an essential meaning of the concept. In much the same vein as Beard, Pitkin reminds us that the "'founding fathers' were men, not gods" and that constitutions "do not fall miraculously from the sky or grow naturally on the vine." Constitutions are born of politics, and thus they represent the "specific history of a particular people, and a political struggle in which some win and others lose."[2]

What is a constitution? Answering that question demands engagement with some of the primary conflicts and political struggles that irrigate, contour, and *constitute* the US Constitution.

Jack Jackson, *Constitution* In: *Democracies in America: Keywords for the Nineteenth Century and Today*.
Edited by: D. Berton Emerson and Gregory Laski, Oxford University Press. © D. Berton Emerson and Gregory Laski 2023.
DOI: 10.1093/oso/9780198865698.003.0006

The Preamble to the Constitution begins with a declaration of authorship and statement of political purpose. It is worth encountering the familiar words in their entirety: "We the People of the United States, in Order to form a more perfect Union, establish Justice, insure domestic Tranquility, provide for the common defence, promote the general Welfare, and secure the Blessings of Liberty to ourselves and our Posterity, do ordain and establish this Constitution of the United States of America."[3] A site of dispute (and eventually, civil war) opens in the first sentence: Is "the United States" a singular or plural concept? Put another way, is the sovereign "We" conjuring a national "people" or is the "We" derived from independent and sovereign "States"?

A decisive answer remains elusive. John C. Calhoun, in an essay published shortly after his death in 1850, advanced the view that the states are the primary locale of sovereignty. The "people are the source of all power" but the people have never been a "mere mass of individuals, without any organic arrangements to express their sovereign will."[4] The people of "We the People" are "the people of the several States." Again, Calhoun: "There is, indeed, no such community, *politically* speaking, as the people of the United States, regarded in the light of, and as constituting one people or nation... The whole, taken together, form a federal community—a community composed of States united by a political compact—and not a nation composed of individuals united by, what is called, a social compact."[5] Calhoun's position rested upon solid textual ground. One constitutional provision in particular buttresses the states-centric theory of sovereignty. Article V of the Constitution, the article setting forth the mechanisms of formally amending the Constitution, places the states at the center of this sovereign practice. No amendment may become part of the fundamental law unless it is "ratified by the Legislatures of three fourths of the several States." In addition, the one timeless prohibition of Article V secures equality between the states in the Senate. Article V is clear in its limitation: "no State, without its Consent, shall be deprived of its equal Suffrage in the Senate."[6]

In contrast, a long line of politicians and theorists have understood the Constitution to constitute, as it were, the nation. What perhaps began as the sovereignty of states turned into the sovereignty of a people in the act of constituting. Along these lines, political theorist Jason Frank argues that "self-authorized claims to speak in the people's name can only be retrospectively vindicated."[7] President Andrew Jackson leaned upon the second clause of the Constitution's Preamble to define and vindicate the people. In an 1832 public proclamation on the nullification crisis, Jackson explained that the Constitution "was formed for important objects that are announced in the preamble made in the name and by the authority of the people ... [t]he most important among these objects, that which is placed first in rank, on which all others rest, is 'to form a more perfect Union.'" In reply to the secessionist challenge, Jackson offered this rejoinder: the states may have some reserved rights, but the "States are not sovereign." In the act of bringing the Constitution into being, a nation was born. At the moment of ratification, each state "expressly parted with so many powers as to constitute jointly with the other States a single nation." Citizens were no longer primarily citizens of Virginia or South Carolina; "they became American citizens."[8]

Since the mid-nineteenth century, a train of events retrospectively vindicated the singularity of the nation: the Civil War, the addition of the Thirteenth, Fourteenth, and Fifteenth Amendments (often referred to as the Civil War Amendments), the emergence of a truly national economy, the expansion of federal power in response to the Great Depression, the Second World War, and the civil rights revolution of the 1950s and 1960s. Nonetheless, a majority of the US Supreme Court in 2012 struck down a key section of the Affordable Care Act on the grounds that the federal law could not be allowed to "undermine the status of the States as independent sovereigns in our federal system."[9] Calhoun was defeated, but not banished.

If the precise location and limits of the people's sovereignty remained a matter of fierce debate, the sovereignty of the people appeared to generate something approaching a consensus. Even conservative voices expressed their assent. For example, in *Federalist* 49, James Madison avers that "the people are the only legitimate fountain of power, and it is from them that the constitutional charter, under which the several branches of government hold their power, is derived."[10] John C. Calhoun began his essay "A Discourse on the Constitution and Government of the United States" (published posthumously in 1851) with the acknowledgment that the government created by the Constitution was "democratic, in contradistinction to aristocracy and monarchy ... the whole system is, indeed, democratic throughout. It has for its fundamental principle, the great cardinal maxim, that the people are the source of all power."[11] At first glance, this widespread concession to the allegedly democratic character of American society and the democratic basis of the Constitution seems to confirm Alexis de

Tocqueville's conclusion that in the modern age the swell of democracy is such an irresistible force that any effort "to halt democracy would then appear [as] a fight against God himself."[12]

The original exclusion of particular categories of persons (e.g., women, African Americans, Native Americans) from "the people" is now widely understood as a failure of democratic vision and promise. But this concern raises an even more fundamental question. Even assuming complete inclusiveness, how democratic is the US Constitution? We should return to the root definition of democracy. Democracy means, quite simply, "people rule." If "rule" implies an ongoing activity and practice, is this the same as serving as a "source" or "fountain" of power? Might the paeans to the authority of the people rest alongside efforts to curb their rule? In the Revolutionary period, the monarchy represented TYRANNY and the rule of the people heralded its opposite. Democracy and freedom marched together. The Declaration of Independence began by indicting the king for having but one goal, "the Establishment of an absolute Tyranny over these States," and concluded with a declaration of freedom and independence in "the Name, and by the Authority of the Good People of these Colonies."[13] However, by the time of the Constitutional Convention, tyranny now frequently appeared as conjoined to the people and their rule.

Far from being a celebration of democracy, the Constitution sought to counter it. As the authors of *The Federalist Papers* explained, the Constitution is designed to defend "justice" against an onslaught from "the superior force of an interested and overbearing majority."[14] Power would be scattered, barriers around the majority would be erected, and rule by the people would be made deliberately difficult. Anti-Federalist critics of the Constitution (e.g., "Cato," "An Old Whig") worried that the size of the new body politic and the kaleidoscope of cultures constituting it created the raw material for the reemergence of tyranny in the form of a traditional tyrant. Advocates for the Constitution turned these imagined demerits into virtues because they saw incipient tyranny lurking primarily in the demos: "Extend the sphere and you take in a greater variety of parties and interests; you make it less probable that a majority of the whole will have a common motive to invade the rights of other citizens; or if such a motive exists, it will be more difficult for all who feel it to discover their own strength."[15]

Consider the myriad provisions designed to check the power of the people: not only did the Senate represent states (not equally populated) but also the people in the states were barred from directly electing Senators;[16] with staggered Senate terms, no national vote could repudiate and replace the federal legislature in a single election; Justices to the Supreme Court were appointed by the president and confirmed by the Senate rather than the House of Representatives (the Senate could better withstand the "impulse of sudden and violent passions" associated with the people and their Representatives in the House);[17] and Article V lodged a powerful minority veto in the amendment process so that only overwhelming supermajorities could alter the fundamental law. Today, a Mars landing has more probability of success than passage and ratification of a constitutional amendment.

This is by design. The people and their passions are imagined as a danger to justice in both their capacity as a legislative majority and as an active source of constitutional authority and power. One of the authors of *The Federalist Papers*, Alexander Hamilton, in an imaginative defense of Article III (judicial power), split the people into these two dimensions. The democratic people, the people of everyday rule (to the extent it existed), too rarely respected limits to their power and thus had to be checked by an unelected judiciary. However, when the judiciary strikes down a law as unconstitutional, it does so as "the people themselves" in their constitution-making capacity. Democratic value thus undergirds the least democratic branch. Further, Hamilton insisted that the people remained empowered to alter or amend the Constitution "by some solemn and authoritative act."[18] In *Federalist* 49, Madison reaffirmed this in theory: "it must be allowed to prove that a constitutional road to the decision of the people ought to be marked out and kept open."[19] But this should be an exceedingly rare occurrence. Stability supplants democracy as a primary political value, and therefore Article V tends to the cultivation of constitutional "veneration" rather than the facilitation of popular participation in constitutional decision-making. In 1787 there existed "an enthusiastic confidence of the people in their patriotic leaders," but in the future there could be no guarantee of such deference.[20] Thus, the road of democracy should be open but not well traveled.

The difficulty in forming legislative majorities and the even greater difficulty of amending the Constitution has, over time, shifted enormous power to the federal judiciary. It is why, in the mid-twentieth century, Justice Robert Jackson could say with some confidence, "We are not final because we are infallible, we are infallible only because we are final."[21] And the election of the presidents who nominate the Justices cannot alone vindicate this judicial power from the perspective of democracy. Currently, five Supreme Court Justices sit on the court as a result of being appointed by a president who first arrived in the White House after losing the popular vote.[22] This too is a feature of the Constitution: the electoral college. Today, some celebrate such antidemocratic tendencies of the Constitution as being a centerpiece of its political genius; others "have become ever more despondent about many structural provisions of the Constitution that place almost insurmountable barriers in the way of any acceptable notion of democracy."[23]

The "main complaint against a democratic government as organized in the United States," Tocqueville wrote, "is not its weakness, as many Europeans claim, but rather its irresistible strength."[24] Minorities need protection from the tyranny of the majority. We usually think of minorities as those who are marginalized and without power in society or the political process— "discrete and insular minorities" in the language of constitutional law.[25] But the minority interests animating the anxieties of the founders rested very much at the center of power, and the Constitution was designed to protect them. In his famous theorization of "factions" in *Federalist* 10, Madison located the primary source of faction in private property. The "most common and durable source of faction has been the various and unequal distribution of property. Those who hold and those who are without property have ever formed distinct interests in society. Those who are creditors, and those who are debtors, fall under a like discrimination."[26] Justice, and the perpetual pall democracy cast over it, was conceived of in economic terms. The "improper or wicked" designs of the demos included a "rage for paper money, for an abolition of debts, for an equal division of property."[27]

In the latter part of the nineteenth century and into the early part of the twentieth, the Supreme Court would impose its own barriers around property. For example, constitutional "liberty" ensured a right of the employer and employee to contract without much democratic interference on behalf of the worker. Minimum-wage legislation, maximum-hour legislation, child labor laws—all were struck down by the Supreme Court as being inconsistent with the Constitution. Constitutionally speaking, "property" included not only land, manufacturing, labor, and finance; prior to the Thirteenth Amendment, it included human beings as well. In the infamous 1857 case of *Dred Scott v. Sandford*, the Supreme Court of the United States conceived of the plea for freedom by the enslaved Scott as being a revolt against property rights. The court came down on the side of property rights: "the right of property in a slave is distinctly and expressly affirmed in the Constitution."[28]

As this line should remind us, it is impossible to discuss the US Constitution without accounting for slavery and its enduring legacy. Notwithstanding the self-confident declaration of the court in *Dred Scott*, debates raged over whether the Constitution ensured slavery or offered a counter-vision to a polity swimming in human bondage. Textually, the so-called "3/5 compromise" shifted representational power to the slave states by figuring the enslaved as partial persons for purposes of political REPRE-SENTATION; at the same time, the Constitution did not consider the enslaved to be legal persons. Even more revealing, Article V's only other prohibition binding the sovereign people involved the slave trade (recall the other com-manded equal representation in the Senate): no amendment could be passed before 1808 if it "in any Manner affect[ed] the first and fourth Clauses in the Ninth Section of the first Article." Article I, Section 9, stipulated that "The Migration or Importation of such Persons as any of the States now existing shall think proper to admit, shall not be prohibited by the Congress prior to the Year one thousand eight hundred and eight."[29] Slavery thus served as a foundational element for the constitutional structure.

Yet others dissented. The great abolitionist Frederick Douglass offered a different reading of the Constitution. Noting that "neither slavery, slaveholding, nor slave can anywhere be found" in the Constitution, Douglass insisted that "the Constitution is a GLORIOUS LIBERTY DOCUMENT. Read its preamble, consider its purposes. Is slavery among them?"[30] Douglass argued that the Preamble speaks in the name of "We the People" rather than "We the White People."[31] It would take the Civil War and the Civil War Amendments to breathe potential life into that vision of the Constitution. But even with these amendments, this hope faltered in an era of DISFRANCHISEMENT and resurgent ANTI-BLACK VIOLENCE both inside and outside the law. As a result, "black America entered the twentieth cen-tury segregated, sundered from full and free participation in American life, and politically powerless to do much about it."[32] Recently, the Supreme Court has increasingly embraced a formally "colorblind" theory of the Constitution. Colorblindness in the law has coincided with an unprece-dented explosion in the rates of incarceration of African American men. Social critics, such as noted legal theorist Michelle Alexander, contend these two facts are linked and that we are in a period of "new Jim Crow" with racial discrimination infecting the discretionary practices of police, prosecu-tors, judges, and juries.[33] To paraphrase Tocqueville, one may change the face of the law without touching the customs it has produced.

Despite certain continuities across epochs, the destruction of the slaveo-cracy, defeat of the secessionist theory of state sovereignty, and passage of the Civil War Amendments fundamentally altered the Constitution. In addition to the formal abolition of slavery and the promise of equal protection of the law, the Civil War Amendments set the stage for the widespread understand-ing of the Constitution as being almost synonymous with "rights." Prior to the Civil War, the Supreme Court ruled in the 1833 case of *Barron v. Baltimore* that the Bill of Rights did not apply to state governments. The Fourteenth Amendment's due process clause served as the textual means by which the Supreme Court reversed course and gradually applied almost all of the Bill of Rights to the states. "Incorporation" (the term used to describe this process) mostly occurred in the twentieth century, but the logic was present from the outset in the Civil War Amendments: all of them guarantee national rights, check state power, and empower the federal government to enforce these rights.

But other forms of power and inequality endured. Over the vehement protests of women's rights activists, section 2 of the Fourteenth Amendment focused only on "male citizens," and the Fifteenth Amendment forbade the denial of franchise only on the basis of race, not gender. WOMEN'S SUFFRAGE would not become a constitutional right until the ratification of the Nineteenth Amendment in 1920, and the Supreme Court would not develop an equal protection analysis that challenged gender stereotypes and discrimination until the 1970s. A representative opinion of the nineteenth century's patriarchal constitutional order is found in the case of *Bradwell v. Illinois* (1873). The State of Illinois denied Myra Bradwell a license to prac-tice law because she was a woman. She challenged the constitutionality of the law. The Supreme Court ruled against her. In a concurring opinion, Justice Joseph Bradley wrote, "The Constitution of the family organization, which is founded in the divine ordinance as well as in the nature of things, indicates the domestic sphere as that which properly belongs to the domain and functions of womanhood."[34] We might say that this constitution of the private sphere itself constitutes the Constitution.

Karl Marx viewed this as the signature (and critical failure) of liberal "constitutions."[35] The naturalization of private power underwrites the lib-eral ideology of rights against public power, and public power works simul-taneously to secure the conditions of private power. Although the twentieth century witnessed constitutional transformations that began to break out of the logic Marx critiqued, the twenty-first century is increasingly a time when private power again enjoys renewed constitutional protection from democracy (e.g., the Supreme Court's protection of "corporate speech" in elections). Consequently, a turn back to the long nineteenth century can perhaps illuminate the pressing constitutional questions of our own time.

Notes

1. Charles A. Beard, *An Economic Interpretation of the Constitution of the United States* (New York: The Free Press, 1941), 10.
2. Hanna Pitkin, "The Idea of a Constitution," *Journal of Legal Education* 37, no. 2 (1987): 168.
3. US Constitution, https://www.law.cornell.edu/constitution/index.html.
4. John C. Calhoun, "A Discourse on the Constitution and Government of the United States," in Ross M. Lence, ed., *Union and Liberty: The Political Philosophy of John C. Calhoun* (Indianapolis, IN: Liberty Fund, 1992), 82, 136.
5. Ibid., 116.
6. US Constitution.
7. Jason Frank, *Constituent Moments: Enacting the People in Postrevolutionary America* (Durham, NC: Duke University Press, 2010), 32.
8. Andrew Jackson, "Proclamation Regarding Nullification," December 10, 1832, https://avalon.law.yale.edu/19th_century/jack01.asp.
9. *National Federation of Independent Business v. Sebelius*, 567 US 519 (2012).
10. *Federalist* 49, in Isaac Kramnick, ed., *The Federalist Papers* (London: Penguin Classics, 1987), 313.
11. Calhoun, *Union and Liberty*, 82.
12. Alexis de Tocqueville, *Democracy in America*, ed. Isaac Kramnick, trans. Gerald Bevan (London: Penguin Classics, 2003), 15.
13. "Declaration of Independence: A Transcription," https://www.archives.gov/founding-docs/declaration-transcript.
14. *Federalist* 10, *Federalist Papers*, 123.
15. Ibid., 127.
16. The Seventeenth Amendment (1913) provided for the popular election of Senators.
17. *Federalist* 62, *Federalist Papers*, 366.
18. *Federalist* 78, *Federalist Papers*, 440.
19. *Federalist* 49, *Federalist Papers*, 313.
20. Ibid., 313–314.
21. *Brown v. Allen*, 344 US 443, 540 (1953).
22. Justice Gorsuch, Justice Barrett, Justice Kavanaugh, Justice Alito, and Chief Justice Roberts.

23. Sanford Levinson, *Our Undemocratic Constitution: Where the Constitution Goes Wrong (And How We the People Can Correct It)* (New York: Oxford University Press, 2006), 6.

24. Tocqueville, *Democracy in America*, 294.

25. This phrase comes from the most famous footnote in US constitutional law, "FN 4" in *United States v. Carolene Products*, 304 US 144 (1938).

26. *Federalist* 10, *Federalist Papers*, 124.

27. Ibid., 128.

28. *Dred Scott v. Sandford*, 60 US 393, 451 (1857).

29. US Constitution.

30. Frederick Douglass, "What to the Slave Is the Fourth of July?" in John R. McKivigan, Julie Husband, and Heather L. Kaufman, eds., *The Speeches of Frederick Douglass* (New Haven, CT: Yale University Press, 2018), 88.

31. Douglass, "The American Constitution and the Slave," *Speeches*, 178.

32. W. Haywood Burns, "Law and Race in Early America," in David Kairys, ed., *The Politics of Law: A Progressive Critique,* rev. ed. (New York: Pantheon Books, 1990), 119.

33. Michelle Alexander, *The New Jim Crow: Mass Incarceration in the Age of Colorblindness*, rev. ed. (New York: The New Press, 2012).

34. *Bradwell v. Illinois*, 83 US 130 (1873).

35. Karl Marx, "On the Jewish Question," in Robert C. Tucker, ed., *The Marx-Engels Reader*, 2nd ed. (New York: Norton, 1978), 26–52.

Further Reading

Primary and canonical sources yield the biggest dividends. The starting point is surely James Madison, Alexander Hamilton, and John Jay, *The Federalist Papers* (London: Penguin Classics, 1987). One should recall that the proposed Constitution faced eloquent opposition, and thus the writings of the Anti-Federalists are indispensable; for a survey of the debates and representative writings of the Anti-Federalists, see John P. Kaminski and Richard Leffler, eds., *Federalist and Antifederalists: The Debate Over the Ratification of the Constitution* (Indianapolis, IN: Madison House Publishers, 1998). Ross M. Lence has provided a useful volume of John C. Calhoun's writings in *Union and Liberty: The Political Philosophy of John C. Calhoun* (Indianapolis, IN: Liberty Fund, 1992). To spend time with the thought of Frederick Douglass, see an excellent collection from John R. McKivigan, Julie Husband, and Heather L. Kaufman, eds., *The Speeches of Frederick Douglass: A Critical Edition* (New Haven, CT: Yale University Press, 2018). On the potential tensions between democracy and freedom, Alexis de Tocqueville's *Democracy in America* (London: Penguin Classics, 2003) provides unmatched theoretical depth; see especially volume 1 for commentary on democratic sovereignty and the Constitution. For contemporary scholarship on democracy and the Constitution, see Robert Dahl's *How Democratic Is the American Constitution?* (New Haven, CT: Yale University Press, 2003) and Sanford Levinson's *Our Undemocratic Constitution: Where the Constitution Goes Wrong (And How We the People Can Correct It)* (New York: Oxford University Press, 2008). For a panoramic view of constitutional history and politics, see generally Bruce Ackerman's *We the People, Vol. 1: Foundations* (Cambridge, MA: Harvard University Press, 1993) and *We the People, Vol. 2: Transformations* (Cambridge, MA: Harvard University Press, 2000); Linda K. Kerber's *No Constitutional Right to Be Ladies* (New York: Hill and Wang, 1998); and Derrick A. Bell's *Race, Racism, and American Law*, 6th ed. (New York: Wolters Kluwer Aspen Publishers, 2008).

6

Representation

Elizabeth Maddock Dillon

On the day before his death, Alexander Hamilton wrote, "Our real dis-ease...is Democracy."[1] These are perhaps surprising words from a man who is celebrated today as a champion of democracy and inclusion. Yet Hamilton, like many of his fellow founders, was superbly anxious about the nature of "the people." He believed many people (most especially those without wealth or commercial interests) were not capable of effective self-government. Hamilton worried that white men without sufficient property and education would have too strong a say in the ruling of the country; most white women, Blacks, and Native Americans, in turn, were not considered part of "the people" at all. The question as to the limits of the people—who should be allowed representation, and even who counts as a person—is embedded in US democracy and debates over its implementation from its inception. Whose voices should count in representations of the people? Conjoined with this question is another less visible but perhaps thornier issue: *How* should the people represent themselves? What *forms* of representation will be granted legal or de facto authority and political legitimacy?

In order for the people to govern, their collective ideas and wishes must be represented, but how this representation takes place is no simple matter. We are accustomed to thinking of democratic representation in terms of voting: "one person, one vote." Yet both the history of the franchise and current debates about the electoral college point to the fact that US democracy has never been one of direct representation; further, the history of debates about how to structure indirect representation (such as those misgivings voiced by Hamilton above) places the question of *how* to represent "the people" squarely in our critical crosshairs.

Elizabeth Maddock Dillon, *Representation* In: *Democracies in America: Keywords for the Nineteenth Century and Today.* Edited by: D. Berton Emerson and Gregory Laski, Oxford University Press. © D. Berton Emerson and Gregory Laski 2023. DOI: 10.1093/oso/9780198865698.003.0007

Importantly, a focus on voting rights alone—while an essential dimension of representation—is also limiting because it fails to consider crucial ways in which the representation of the people occurs outside of formal political channels. Historically, the people appear through competing and divergent modes of representation, including not only the ballot box but also modes of writing (the print public sphere) and performance (the performative commons), whether at the theater or in the streets. This chapter explores the eighteenth- and nineteenth-century concept of the "people out of doors" and their modes of embodiment, as well as the relation between literacy and the enforced a-literacy of disfranchised (non)members of the people, including, historically, unpropertied white men, African American and Native American men, and women of all races.

The matter of representation in democracy is thus twofold: Who are the people who require or deserve representation, and what is the mechanism of representation? A lot of attention has been devoted to the first of part of this question (who the people are and who can vote). But if we drill a little deeper into the question of representation, it becomes clear that as a mechanism or process, representation is itself never direct: any representation *re*-presents what it aims to signify, thus introducing an irremediable layer of difference and distinction between the representation (what is signified) and the thing/idea itself. In these more conceptual terms, familiar from literary theory and linguistics, we can note that representation, as a process, necessarily preserves some aspects of what it represents, and it erases others. Further, a close look at divergent modes and mechanisms of representation brings into focus two aspects of representation that receive less critical attention than warranted: aesthetics and materiality. Exploring these two dimensions in turn enables us to appreciate the fundamental and enduring tensions that representation poses for US democracy.

The US Constitution laid out the rules of the US democratic nation, but it did not grant anyone the right to vote. States wrote their own suffrage laws, which remained unconstrained by federal law until the passage of the Fifteenth Amendment (ratified in 1870), which explicitly outlawed limiting franchisement on the basis of race. Even at that point, states continued to tinker (as they do today) with suffrage rules and procedures in order to disfranchise non-white men and women. US CITIZENSHIP did not, then, confer the right to vote, and suffrage rules varied widely across states, circumscribed on the basis of factors including property ownership, gender, race, and religion. At the same time, the Constitution described enslaved Blacks as three-fifths of a person for the purpose of determining the representational numbers of each state. This appalling calculus enabled slave states to both deny humanity to slaves and to wield the force of their numbers to represent enslavers' interests at the federal level. Since the nation's inception, even the definition of "the people" and the actual people who are able to represent themselves through the electoral process have not been congruent.

The legal right to vote is historically grounded in the ownership of property, not in citizenship. Government by the people of the commonwealth (in parliamentarian or republican form) was originally based upon and limited by property ownership, first in England and later in colonial and US state-based legal codes derived from English law. The original (feudal) logic informing this system held that ownership of property allows one to be independent of constraint (unconstrained by allegiance to one's "lord" or owner of the property one lived and worked on) and thus free to make decisions about governance based on reason rather than allegiance or compulsion. The famous English jurist William Blackstone explained: "The true reason of requiring any qualification, with regard to property, in voters, is to exclude such persons as are in so mean a situation that they are esteemed to have no will of their own."[2] A later, capitalist version of the logic limiting voting rights to property owners evolved in both England and the United States; this argument held that only property owners are stakeholders in the social order and thus fit to govern. A speaker at the Massachusetts state convention of 1779 succinctly stated that the unpropertied should not be allowed to vote because they will "pay less regards to the rights of Property because they have nothing to lose."[3] The unspoken premise of this claim is that private property ownership is fundamental to the existence of society. Following the founding era, a more pointedly racial capitalist version of the logic of property ownership as the basis of voting rights came into full flower in the mid-nineteenth century based on the implicit assertion that white masculinity is itself a form of property—one that entitles only white men (whether owners of real property or not) to be fit stakeholders capable of self-government and worthy of suffrage rights in the United States.[4]

It is worth pausing here to note that in the United States, property ownership has been decisively shaped by the history of settler colonialism (appropriation of Indigenous lands) and race slavery (appropriation of non-white labor and life), far more so than in the English law from which US legal systems emerged. Indeed, we could briefly summarize the divergence of the US history of suffrage from an English history by noting that in the United States, racial categories came to replace class categories as the point of division between franchised and disfranchised men in England. As K-Sue Park points out, in the United States, both the reality of how property was accumulated and who accumulated it, as well as the legal and social systems supporting this system of accumulation, were based in settler colonialism and race slavery: "Over centuries, laws and legal institutions facilitated the production of the two commodities, or forms of property, upon which the colonial economy and the United States came to depend above all others: enclosures of Native nations' land and enslaved people."[5] The commodification and theft of Indigenous lands and the commodification of enslaved men and women as chattel property were tools used by white men to acquire and retain capital. By extension, then, these tools secured the status of white male property-holders as voting members of the US polis and defined the United States as a society of property owners.

Given the historical centrality of property ownership to electoral representation, political theorists Michael Hardt and Antonio Negri argue that the radical democratic possibilities of the republican revolutions of the eighteenth century, including those in the United States, were curtailed by their imbrication within capitalism, such that the rights of property took precedence over those of people. According to Hardt and Negri, "the establishment of the constitutional order and the rule of law served to defend and legitimate private property," and as a result the people were fundamentally not represented: rather, " 'a people of property' faced off against 'a multitude of the poor.' "[6] While Hardt and Negri focus on the ways in which capitalism and property ownership distort the politics of representation, they omit the even messier dimensions of racial capitalism that had particular salience in the United States. Between 1790 and 1850, the laws on voting rights transformed on a state-by-state basis such that property requirements were fully eliminated in every state save for one.[7] However, as the United States moved toward what has been incorrectly called "universal suffrage" by many historians in eras past, the same laws that abolished property requirements for white men created new restrictions in terms of race and gender, enforcing the implicit premise that independence of mind and capacity for self-governance were fundamentally linked to whiteness and maleness. By 1840, only four states allowed free Black men to vote; in states such as New Jersey, where propertied white women had once been allowed to vote, new "universal [white male] suffrage" laws eliminated women's right to vote.[8] The reorganization of suffrage around white masculinity cemented a cultural imaginary that excluded Blacks from all forms of citizenship and political belonging. As Derrick Spires has argued, "The loss of the franchise became foundational to further state-sanctioned stripping of black civil rights and symbolized a forcible removal of black citizens from the civic imaginary itself."[9]

The term "civic imaginary" points to a far broader arena of representational play at stake in the politics of government by the "people" than that of ballot-casting alone. Despite (and indeed perhaps because of) the history of white male supremacy embedded within US voting rights, other forms of representing the people—and means of contesting the limits of the people—have been crucial. From the moment the CONSTITUTION was being drafted, the framers recognized that a large portion of the "people" remained outside of formal representation. Indeed, cohorts of the people who were excluded from electoral representation took concrete shape in early America in the form of what was known as "the people out of doors." The phrase was often used in the late eighteenth century to describe the public that was literally outside the doors behind which elected officials deliberated. Newspaper reports at the time regularly describe and debate, for instance, the mechanisms by which information from the Continental Congress, state assemblies, and other representative bodies is conveyed to the "people out of doors" in late-eighteenth-century North America. As one example, the *New-York Daily Gazette* reported in 1790 on the deliberations of the first US House of Representatives, at which James Jackson (of Georgia) argued "that printing reports and bills was generally advantageous; it gave the members an opportunity of obtaining an opinion of the *people out of doors* and he was ever inclined to pursue measures the best calculated for acquiring full and complete information on every subject that came before them, whether it arose within or without the walls of the house."[10] Although many people were unable to vote at the time, as this newspaper account indicates, they were not entirely absent from political conversations; rather, the nature of their political "voice" was by no means formalized or guaranteed but was often spontaneously organized in forms of public assembly.

The people excluded from electoral representation *performed* their presence and their political convictions in ways that rose to visibility and efficacy. As the historian Benjamin Irvin explains, "The people out of doors articulated their political will through the vernacular of folk ritual. They hanged and burned effigies and buried them in mock funerals; they assaulted houses and public buildings; they carted offenders about town to the discordant rhythms of 'rough music'; and they paraded mock heroes, often persons of low social standing, in saturnine parody of their 'betters.' "[11] Irvin here describes persons who were not represented by the Continental Congress at the close of the eighteenth century in North America, but we might apply this description more broadly, as well, to a range of historical performances in the United States—theatrical, visual, and sonic—among recognized and non-recognized members of the people. Significantly, then, performance has been a key category through which the people—a term itself up for debate—achieve visibility and provoke change within existing regimes of representation.

Given the centrality of the people's will to democratic rule, the physical body of the public gathered at sites such as the theater acquired new meaning and political importance in the eighteenth century. Throngs of people in the streets as well as the robust crowds that gathered within commercial theaters created new locations at which THE COMMONS—the sovereignty of the people—was performatively articulated. These scenes of collective performance constitute what I have described as the "performative commons"— that is, commoning practices that wield democratic representational force through a politics of popular assembly.[12] In a configuration far different from that which obtains in today's theater, audience members assumed an extraordinarily active status in nineteenth-century theaters in the United States, attending the theater as much to represent themselves as to watch a play unfold before them on the stage. Voluble and volatile, audiences might, for instance, demand that a given song within a play be performed multiple times in succession should it particularly please them; or pelt the stage and one another with apples, nuts, and epithets; or join the actors onstage in moments of heightened excitement; or, indeed, mount a full-blown riot to express their displeasure with a manager's misbegotten casting of a given actor in a given role. Consider, for example, the following scene: in the closing sword fight of *Richard III* as performed at the Bowery Theater in New York City in 1832, more than 300 audience members joined the actors onstage to assist in the successful slaying of the tyrannical king.[13] And although it was officially illegal for African Americans (free or enslaved) to attend the theater in late-eighteenth-century Charleston, South Carolina, newspaper evidence shows that significant numbers of African Americans regularly attended and were considered an important component of the audience by the performers onstage. They did not attend the theater to sit in the dark and silently watch what occurred onstage: rather, they sought to display and represent themselves *in* public and represent themselves *as* a public. Far more so than the voting booth, the theater was a place where people of many different classes, races, and religions—including African Americans, Native Americans, Jews, Muslims, working-class whites, and immigrant Irishmen—appeared onstage and often in the audience as well.

Public assembly—including riots, theater performances, and parades—thus shaped the civic imaginary in important ways, as did literature, newspapers, and journals, although performance venues enabled the participation of non-English speakers and those who had been forcibly excluded from access to print, such as enslaved people for whom literacy was criminalized. Recent research on the vitality and significance of the Colored Conventions—state and national conventions held by and for Black people in the nineteenth century, organized in response to electoral DISFRANCHISEMENT—demonstrates how the performance of citizenship and personhood in print and in person contested and reshaped existing political discourse and belonging. Black state conventions, as Spires has shown, were "unofficial modes of participatory politics" that provided "viable, visible, and potentially revolutionary modes of direct intervention in [the] civic sphere."[14] The performative and imaginative dimensions of the conventions, which produced print artifacts to document and promote their work, were especially significant. As Spires has demonstrated, "This proliferation of documents, a veritable cacophony of voices, and constant agitation created a politicized space—different from a periodical, pamphlet, fair, or other form of publicity, yet combining elements of each—that resonated with recognizable events ranging from the Continental Congress and the US Declaration of Independence to contemporaneous states' conventions." The Black conventions served to create a "synergy between staging, print practices, and political participation in offering an alternative mode of citizenship practice even as official channels continued to close."[15]

While the work of Black writers and organizers aimed to bring to the fore the necessity of including non-white men and women in the realm of citizenship and recognition from the state, the effort to achieve representation must always also raise questions about the kinds of erasures associated with it. Indeed, perhaps surprisingly, a model of inclusive citizenship can serve to erase forms of Native American, non-US state political organization and belonging that preceded the establishment of the United States and continue to endure under colonial SETTLEMENT. As the anthropologist Audra Simpson has shown, the very concept of recognition by the settler state of the United States is predicated on the prior erasure of Indigenous possession of the land, and in this sense the representation offered by suffrage/electoral politics is also a form of acceding to the authority of this state and to the erasure of Indigeneity. Simpson notes that the "law in colonial contexts enforced Indigenous dispossession and then granted freedom through the legal tricks of consent and citizenship. For Native people, this ruse of consent marks the inherent impossibility of that freedom after dispossession, a freedom [that] is actually theft." "Recognition," Simpson argues, should not be considered "the only political game in town" because it comes at the cost of adhering to the settler protocols of private property ownership and Native dispossession that have been deeply destructive of Native sovereignty. In short, in this instance, representation—presumably a desirable, even necessary element of democracy—clearly functions as a means of erasing the social and political vitality of Indigenous tribal nations. Simpson, accordingly, advocates a stance of "refusal" of state recognition as "a possibility . . . for thinking beyond the recognition paradigm."[16]

Is there a strategy of representation that corresponds to a refusal of settler sovereignty? The notion of refusal points to the need to not only increase or widen representation in the interests of democratic representation but also to reimagine the forms of representation that are available and possible for those excluded from or erased by current forms of democratic representation. Two key aspects of contesting modes of representation include aesthetics (exploring new ways in which the civic imaginary can and might take shape) and materiality (the resistant presence of people who refuse to be erased by current regimes of representation). Any popular assembly has an important aesthetic dimension as well as a material one that involves the sheer embodiment of space and bodies. The sensate and physical resource of materiality can serve as a disruptive presence in relation to the mechanisms of erasure that occur in "representative" form. In this sense, the materiality of theater and performance, such as that of African Americans physically present on the stage and in the audience—performing themselves as members of the people—both in South Carolina theaters and at African American conventions in the nineteenth century, is once again particularly significant. Important contemporary social movements take part in both aesthetic, imaginative engagement and insistent materialism: consider, for instance, the movement for Indigenous land rights staged at Standing Rock, as well as the Black Lives Matter (BLM) movement. Both involve insisting on a presence, as well as the performance of a political collective that demands recognition in new terms. Indeed, BLM points to the materiality—the *matter*—of Black lives that are far too often viewed as immaterial and disposable with respect to human rights and political belonging. Standing Rock Sioux water protectors *stood*, ineradicably, on their land in order to speak to the relation of Indigenous people to the land and the water which the Dakota Access Pipeline threatened to destroy. In even more material terms, political debates now being waged in state legislatures concern the question of how votes are literally cast (remotely, in person, by mail, on Sundays) and counted (by computer, by hand): these kinds of gerrymandering laws hinge on crucial aspects of the materiality of representation.

As the political theorist Jason Frank writes, "At the heart of modern democracy's fantasy space lies its enigmatic constituent subject: the people."[17] The people, we might say, are always something of a phantasm—an entity constructed and reconstructed through competing modes of representation. The people do not preexist representation but come to exist through divergent modes of representation. Ultimately, then, matters of representation—including aesthetics, literature, imagination, materiality, and performance—are far more central to democracy and its history than is often assumed.

Notes

1. Alexander Hamilton to Theodore Sedgwick, July 10, 1804, Massachusetts Historical Society Collections Online, https://www.masshist.org/database/207#:~:text=Alexander%20Hamilton's%20Last%20Letter&text=Hamilton%20writes%3A%20%22...,and%20consequently%20the%20more%20virulent.%22.
2. Quoted in Alexander Keyssar, *The Right to Vote: The Contested History of Democracy in the United States*, rev. ed. (New York: Basic Books, 2009), 8.
3. Ibid., 16.
4. On the history of whiteness as a form of property, see Cheryl I. Harris, "Whiteness as Property," *Harvard Law Review* 106, no. 8 (1993): 1707–1791.
5. K-Sue Park, "The History Wars and Property Law: Conquest and Slavery as Foundational to the Field," *Yale Law Journal* 131 (February 22, 2021). Georgetown Law Faculty Publications and Other Works. 2361, available at SSRN: https://ssrn.com/abstract=3793972, 1.

6. Michael Hardt and Antonio Negri, *Commonwealth* (Cambridge, MA: Harvard University Press, 2009), 9.

7. Keyssar, *The Right to Vote*, 24.

8. Rogers M. Smith, *Civic Ideals: Conflicting Visions of Citizenship in US History* (New Haven, CT: Yale University Press, 1997), 257–258.

9. Derrick R. Spires, *The Practice of Citizenship: Black Politics and Print Culture in the Early United States* (Philadelphia, PA: University of Pennsylvania Press, 2019), 84.

10. *New-York Daily Gazette*, December 15, 1790; emphasis added.

11. Benjamin Irvin, *Clothed in Robes of Sovereignty: The Continental Congress and the People Out of Doors* (New York: Oxford University Press, 2011), 14.

12. Elizabeth Maddock Dillon, *New World Drama: The Performative Commons in the Atlantic World, 1659–1859* (Durham, NC: Duke University Press, 2014).

13. *New York Mirror*, December 29, 1832.

14. Derrick R. Spires, "Imagining a Nation of Fellow Citizens: Early African American Politics of Publicity," in Lara L. Cohen and Jordan A. Stein, eds., *Early African American Print Culture* (Philadelphia, PA: University of Pennsylvania Press, 2012), 275.

15. Spires, *The Practice of Citizenship*, 87, 90.

16. Audra Simpson, "The Ruse of Consent and the Anatomy of 'Refusal': Cases from Indigenous North America and Australia," *Postcolonial Studies* 20, no. 1 (2017): 20.

17. Jason Frank, *The Democratic Sublime: On Aesthetics and Popular Assembly* (New York: Oxford University Press, 2021), 14.

Further Reading

On the imaginative and literary horizons of citizenship and popular sovereignty in the nineteenth-century United States, see Carrie Hyde, *Civic Longing: The Speculative Origins of US Citizenship* (Cambridge, MA: Harvard University Press, 2018) and Jennifer Greiman, *Democracy's Spectacle: Sovereignty and Public Life in Antebellum American Writing* (New York: Fordham University Press, 2010). On popular political performance in the early United States, see David Waldstreicher, *In the Midst of Perpetual Fetes: The Making of American Nationalism, 1776–1820* (Chapel Hill, NC: University of North Carolina Press, 1997), Simon P. Newman, *Parades and the Politics of the Street: Festive Culture in the Early American Republic* (Philadelphia, PA: University of Pennsylvania Press, 1997), and Susan G. Davis, *Parades and Power: Street Theatre in Nineteenth-Century Philadelphia* (Berkeley, CA: University of California Press, 1988). On democracy and the politics of the theater in the early United States, see Dillon and Richard Butsch, *The Making of American Audiences: From Stage to Television, 1750–1990* (New York: Cambridge University Press, 2011). On nineteenth-century African American performance and politics, see Shane White, *Stories of Freedom in*

Black New York (Cambridge, MA: Harvard University Press, 2002) and Daphne Brooks, *Bodies in Dissent: Spectacular Performances of Race and Freedom, 1850–1910* (Durham, NC: Duke University Press, 2006). On the robust Colored Conventions movement, in addition to Spires, see P. Gabrielle Foreman, Jim Casey, and Sarah Lynn Patterson, *The Colored Conventions Movement: Black Organizing in the Nineteenth Century* (Chapel Hill, NC: University of North Carolina Press, 2021). On Native American sovereignty and the politics of refusal, see Simpson as well as Glenn Sean Clouthard, *Red Skin, White Masks: Rejecting the Colonial Politics of Recognition* (Minneapolis, MN: University of Minnesota Press, 2014).

7

Citizenship

Padraig Riley

From the outset, citizenship in the United States has been a contested concept, constantly invoked yet difficult to define. Until the Civil Rights Act of 1866, no national law explained how those born in the United States acquired citizenship, let alone what rights they might possess by virtue of their political status. The CONSTITUTION was remarkably vague. It required that any member of the House of Representatives or Senate be a "Citizen of the United States," while the president had to be a "natural born citizen or a Citizen of the United States, at the time of the adoption of this Constitution."[1] But what made one a "Citizen of the United States" in the first place? The Constitution did not say.

The meaning of "citizenship" only became more confusing in Article III, which explained that the Supreme Court's jurisdiction included cases "between a State and Citizens of another State" and "between Citizens of different States." Later modified by the Eleventh Amendment, this clause suggested that one could be both a "Citizen of the United States" and a citizen of a particular state at the same time. But what was the relationship between these two statuses? Was every citizen of the United States a citizen of a state, and vice versa? Article IV offered a possible resolution of this dilemma through what came to be known as the comity clause: "the Citizens of each State shall be entitled to all Privileges and Immunities of Citizens in the several States."[2] Yet what precise rights might be included under said "Privileges and Immunities"? Again, the Constitution was silent.

Given the limited and opaque discussion of citizenship in the Constitution, some scholars have claimed that national citizenship was relatively unimportant before the Civil War. While such arguments should caution us from reading a modern concept of citizenship back into the early nineteenth

Padraig Riley, *Citizenship* In: *Democracies in America: Keywords for the Nineteenth Century and Today.*
Edited by: D. Berton Emerson and Gregory Laski, Oxford University Press. © D. Berton Emerson and Gregory Laski 2023.
DOI: 10.1093/oso/9780198865698.003.0008

century, we should be careful not to minimize the importance of citizenship in early American politics. Indeed, the very ambiguity of national citizenship made it subject to ongoing contestation, as different groups sought to impose their own visions, both legal and ideological, of who might be included in the American political community. The result was a contradictory citizenship regime, on the one hand animated by the ideal of consensual membership and on the other hand governed by hierarchies of race, class, and gender.

Citizenship debates point to a fundamental problem in democratic governance: "we the people" claimed the right to rule themselves, but courts and legislatures determined who might become one of the people, and who among them had access to crucial political and civil rights. In theory and practice, citizenship thus became a means to exclude and harm as well as to incorporate and protect. This essay examines these dilemmas of democratic belonging by looking at two key questions animating early American citizenship politics: One, how should the federal government regulate naturalization (the process by which immigrants became citizens)? And two, were free African Americans citizens of the United States? Conflicting answers to these questions created a citizenship regime torn between consent and exclusion: white immigrants became citizens by volition, while slaveholders sought to limit citizenship by race, effectively alienating native-born free African Americans from the republic. To defend themselves against white supremacy, Black activists claimed birthright citizenship, anticipating the transformative politics of Reconstruction, when the ratification of the Fourteenth Amendment (1868) added a clear definition of national citizenship to the Constitution. But earlier conflicts over race and belonging returned in new forms, ensuring that citizenship would remain a battleground into the twentieth and twenty-first centuries.

During the Revolution, as James Kettner has argued, Americans began to develop a concept of "volitional allegiance" as "citizens" in contrast to their former status as subjects of the British empire. As South Carolina's David Ramsay claimed in 1789, that transformation was "immense." "Subjects look up to a master," he explained, "but citizens are so far equal, that none have hereditary rights superior to others. Each citizen of a free state contains, within himself, by nature and the constitution, as much of the common sovereignty as another."[3]

By the precedent of *Calvin's Case* (1608), anyone born in British territory became a subject owing perpetual allegiance to the monarch. Because they rejected monarchical authority, the American states had to determine a new rule of political membership for their inhabitants. In contrast to the birth-right obligations of British subjects, American citizens, in theory, chose membership in the republic. Consent might be expressed actively, through swearing an oath of allegiance to one of the new states, for example; or tacitly, through choosing to remain under a new state's legal authority. The concept of volitional allegiance thus helped Americans resolve the practical problem of political membership. It also helped define the legitimacy of the United States as a regime founded on the consent of its people.

In practice, however, American courts tended to adopt *Calvin's Case* to explain the transmission of citizenship from one generation to the next—children became citizens simply by the fact of birth on American soil. Yet volitional allegiance remained a critical idea in the early nineteenth century, as Americans confronted the problem of immigration into their new political community. Disagreements over immigration were obvious at the Constitutional Convention, where some members pushed long residency requirements (and, at the extreme, native birth) for holding federal office. In the 1790s, immigration politics helped define the first party system, as Federalists and Jeffersonian Democratic-Republicans fought over how to transform immigrant outsiders into citizens.

Both Federalists and Republicans understood immigration as a national problem, albeit one that played out in states and localities, since the Constitution gave Congress the power "to establish an uniform Rule of Naturalization."[4] Congress duly passed a Naturalization Act in 1790 that allowed "any alien, being a free white person" to apply for citizenship to any "common law court of record" after two years' residency in the United States and one year in a particular state. Once applicants proved their good character before the court and took an oath to support the US Constitution, they could become citizens.[5]

Such terms suggested a liberal regime of consensual membership, but the law also drew strict racial lines around who might claim citizenship through immigration—only "free white persons" need apply. The 1790 Act thus codified a divided citizenship policy: admitting white migrants on liberal terms promoted the United States as an "asylum of liberty" for the oppressed subjects of European states. Restricting naturalization by race sought to keep people of color out of that asylum, and it was likely intended to prevent free African Americans from claiming equal citizenship in an era of rising emancipation.

Neither side of this citizenship regime—liberal for white immigrants, restrictive for free Black people—was uncontested. During the 1790s, members of the Federalist party sought to constrain the more radical implications of volitional allegiance by extolling nativity and insisting on long residency requirements for admission to political membership. In House debates over the 1790 Naturalization Act, Massachusetts Federalist Theodore Sedgwick claimed that he did not wish to admit the "outcasts of Europe." His Republican counterpart in the Senate, Pennsylvania's William Maclay, was incensed at New England xenophobia: "We Pennsylvanians act as if we believed that God made of one blood all families of the earth," he wrote in his diary, "but the eastern people seem to think that he made none but New England folks."[6]

PARTISAN politics intensified throughout the 1790s as the United States confronted the aftermath of the French Revolution. Immigration became a critical issue in this wider debate over democracy and transatlantic politics. In 1795, Federalists pushed for longer residency requirements and more rigorous examination of an immigrant's "moral character." Sedgwick worried that the United States would be overrun by "the discontented, the ambitious, and the avaricious of every country"; he particularly hoped to exclude anyone driven by the "fierce and unrelenting passions" of the French revolutionary wars.[7] The resulting Naturalization Act of 1795 specified federal control over naturalization and required all applicants to swear to support the US Constitution as well as renounce any foreign allegiance and title of nobility (a Republican demand). The required period of residency was increased to five years.[8]

Partisan rancor increased during the "Quasi-War" with France (1798–1800), and Federalists sought to suppress Republican dissent through the Alien and Sedition Acts and the new Naturalization Act of 1798, which required a fourteen-year waiting period for immigrants to obtain citizenship.[9] Federalists were especially concerned about Irish immigrants, a group that included a number of political exiles who fought for Ireland's independence in the 1790s. As Massachusetts Federalist Harrison Gray Otis told the House in 1797, he did "not wish to invite hoards of wild Irishmen, nor the turbulent and disorderly of all parts of the world, to come here with a view to disturb our tranquility, after having succeeded in the overthrow of their own governments." In debates over the 1798 Act, Otis sought to deny all aliens access to federal office, while Federalist Robert Goodloe Harper "believed the time was now come when it would be proper to declare, that nothing but birth should entitle a man to citizenship in this country."[10] Under such rules, citizenship by consent would give way to nativist exclusion.

But after the Jeffersonian "revolution" of 1800—thanks in part to support from "wild Irishmen" like William Duane, editor of the Philadelphia newspaper *Aurora General Advertiser*—Republicans overturned Federalist naturalization policy and restored a volitional sense of American citizenship: political belonging, they argued, should be a matter of choice, not nativity. As British immigrant and Sedition Act victim Thomas Cooper contended in the *Aurora*, "the birth-duty of allegiance is a fraud upon infancy."[11] Duane's counterpart, John Binns, editor of the Jeffersonian *Democratic Press*, exemplified the principle of volitional allegiance. Soon after arriving in the United States in 1801, Binns watched a Pennsylvania militia company at drill and felt so moved that, "without the adoption of any form or words, I took my first oath of allegiance and fidelity to the United States."[12] He chose to become an American—an autonomous act that grew out of his commitment to republican political principles.

Binns could formally become an American once he took a verbal oath to support the US Constitution, per the Democratic-Republican Naturalization Act of 1802, which effectively returned to the terms of the 1795 Act.[13] In the years to come, the defense of immigrant citizenship remained a crucial issue for Jeffersonians. In debates over impressment leading up to the War of 1812, Republicans contested British claims that their subjects owed perpetual allegiance to the monarch and that therefore immigrant seamen who considered themselves American citizens (but who were born as British subjects) could be impressed into the British Navy. During the war itself, the United States defended immigrant prisoners of war whom the British had captured and threatened to execute as British subjects guilty of treason. Jeffersonians fought to secure their vision of volitional allegiance.

Nativism did not die out, and at the Hartford Convention of 1814 Federalists proposed amending the Constitution to bar all subsequently naturalized immigrants from federal office. But the Jeffersonians survived the War of 1812 and prevailed on the ideological battlefield of American politics. Despite the return of nativism in the antebellum years, the Naturalization Act of 1802 remained the fundamental law of the land, with minor alterations, until after the Civil War. For European immigrants, citizenship in the United States would be defined by consent rather than birth. And the figure of the immigrant as volitional agent, choosing the American republic, remained central to ideological constructions of the American state as a consensual regime, founded on universalist principles.

Yet Jeffersonians also maintained the "free white person" clause in the 1802 Naturalization Act, thus defining citizenship in ascriptive racial terms. Immigrants who could not claim whiteness could not become citizens. Clauses limiting naturalization to "free white persons" were first developed by Southern states during and after the Revolution, and the restriction apparently made its way into the 1790 Act with little debate. The "free white person" restriction was retained until 1870, when the Reconstruction Congress passed a new Naturalization Act that said explicitly "that the naturalization laws are hereby extended to aliens of African nativity and to persons of African descent."[14]

However, it would be misleading to read the "free white person" clause as indicative of a unified white supremacist polity. Naturalization policy only controlled the ability of immigrants to access citizenship. It said nothing at all about the citizenship status of individuals who were born in the United States. By way of *Calvin's Case*, an American child gained citizenship by the right of the soil (*jus soli*)—in other words, by being born within one of the United States—rather than by the right of blood (*jus sanguinis*)—that is, by being born to parents who held American citizenship. While Congress and the courts generally agreed that enslaved people were not citizens, the status of free African Americans was far less clear. In that space of uncertainty, free Black people made claims to political belonging that threatened the power of American slaveholders and the racial regime on which they relied.

The question of Black citizenship repeatedly came before Congress and incited sectional conflict. African Americans petitioned Congress in 1797 and 1800, asking for redress because of the operation of the Fugitive Slave Act of 1793, which led to debates about whether Black Americans enjoyed the right of petition; in 1800, Black petitioners described themselves as "a class of citizens." Slaveholders opposed both petitions insofar as they threatened their political control over slavery, and the 1797 petition was rejected outright. But Northern members came to the defense of the petitioners and parts of the 1800 petition were accepted by the House, suggesting a limited recognition of Black political standing at the federal level.[15]

Such recognition persisted in subsequent debates. In 1803, a House committee proposed a $1,000 fine for any ship captain who brought "any negro, mulatto, or person of color" into a state that prohibited their entry, in order to mollify North Carolinians anxious about migrants from the French Caribbean. Massachusetts Republican John Bacon found the bill "exceptionable": he contended that free African Americans were "citizens of the United States; they were such previous to the time of forming the Constitution, and actually had a voice in that solemn compact." The bill thus violated the privileges and immunities clause (Article IV, Section 2) because it threatened to deprive Black Americans of "the common rights of citizens," such as the right to travel where they saw fit or work for whom they chose. An amended bill specified that it would not apply to "a native, a citizen, or registered seaman of the United States" in order to protect free African American sailors. Black rights—and, at least in Bacon's mind, Black citizenship—commanded a degree of respect.[16]

But Black political standing remained imperiled by the politics of slavery. By the early nineteenth century, multiple Southern states either directly outlawed the in-migration of free African Americans or else required free migrants to post a prohibitively high bond in order to enter. In 1806, Virginia demanded that anyone freed from slavery leave the state within a year, under threat of being re-enslaved. In Congress, Southerners expressed deep hostility to Black freedom. During debates in 1807 over ending the international slave trade, Georgian Peter Early opposed liberating any enslaved people captured through federal interdiction: "Wherever people of color are found in a state of freedom," he claimed, "they are considered as the instruments of murder, theft, and conflagration." If free Black people were introduced into the South, Early warned, "we must in self-defence—gentlemen will understand me—get rid of them in some way."[17]

Northerners in Congress were more inclined to support a limited version of Black freedom—they opposed Early in 1807 and resisted Southern demands for stronger fugitive slave laws in 1802 and 1818. Yet at the same time, Northern state governments acted decisively to constrain the rights of free Black people. By the antebellum period, New Jersey (1807), Connecticut (1821), and Pennsylvania (1838) had denied Black men the right to vote, while New York (1821) had imposed a $250 property qualification exclusively on Black male voters. Northern states innovated regimes of segregation in public life, both formal and informal, that kept free Black people in a state of political vulnerability. Without equal civic standing, free African Americans were less able to challenge the long reach of slavery, which posed a direct threat through the prospect of kidnapping and sale into the domestic slave trade.

The rise of the American Colonization Society after the War of 1812 posed a new threat to free Black life, as slaveholders and white Northerners joined together to resettle Black Americans in Africa. Colonization emphasized the divided citizenship regime of the early nation: while Jeffersonian Republicans embraced the immigrant citizen as a consensual member of the body politic, many whites came to view free African Americans—most of whom had been born in the American colonies or the United States—as internal aliens who could never be granted full membership in the republic. During the last phase of the Missouri Crisis of 1819–21, Southerners made precisely this point. After slaveholders and their Northern allies won Missouri's admission as a slave state, Missourians proposed to exclude all free African Americans from entry. Northern congressmen objected, claiming that free Black people were citizens, and that such exclusion would violate Article IV of the Constitution. Southerners denied that Black people were equal members of the American polity. They argued that the United States was in origin and purpose a community of white people and that "the Negro," as Virginian Alexander Smyth put it, was a "perpetual alien to the white man."[18] Southerners inverted consensual theories of citizenship: instead of immigrants claiming membership through choosing the United States, the existing political community claimed the power to deny full membership to those born free within its boundaries.

In the face of such racist hostility, free African Americans fought to defend themselves from white supremacy and claim political standing as Americans. In doing so, they advanced a new vision of birthright citizenship. Throughout the Northern states, Black people contested colonization and argued for Black political belonging. At a pivotal January 1817 meeting chaired by James Forten, Black Philadelphians resoundingly rejected any project "to exile us from the land of our nativity" and made plain their ongoing commitment to abolish slavery in the United States.[19]

In effect, Black resistance to colonization laid the groundwork for a radical politics of nativity. As David Walker put it in his *Appeal to the Coloured Citizens of the World* (1829), "America is more our country, than it is the whites—we have enriched it with our *blood and tears*."[20] Such claims challenged the racist citizenship regime proposed by slaveholders like Smyth, later given definitive expression in *Dred Scott v. Sandford* (1857), where Roger B. Taney argued that Black people "are not included, and were not intended to be included, under the word 'citizens' in the

Constitution and can therefore claim none of the rights and privileges which that instrument provides for and secures to citizens of the United States."[21]

Taney's views were emphatically overturned by the Civil Rights Act of 1866 and by the Fourteenth Amendment, which finally established a definition of citizenship in the US Constitution: "All persons born or naturalized in the United States, and subject to the jurisdiction thereof, are citizens of the United States and of the state wherein they reside." While echoing the common-law understanding of birthright status taken from *Calvin's Case*, the Amendment's theory of citizenship evoked the vision of Black abolitionists like Walker: all those born in the United States had a claim of belonging and rights worthy of respect.

The Fourteenth Amendment transformed the American political order, placing national citizenship over state citizenship and promising federal power to protect the rights of citizens. But it obviously did not end conflict over citizenship; long after its passage, African Americans and other citizens by birth struggled to secure basic civil and political rights in the United States. Meanwhile, although Congress modified the Naturalization Act to include persons of African descent in 1870, it refused to entirely remove the restriction of naturalization to "free white persons," despite an eloquent appeal by Charles Sumner. This ensured that immigrants deemed to be neither white nor of African descent would be denied access to citizenship well into the twentieth century, even as their native-born children gained citizenship through the Fourteenth Amendment.[22] Congress did not abandon the racial restrictions in naturalization policy until 1952.

In the twenty-first century, Americans continue to fight over citizenship. Some conservatives seek to limit the scope of the Fourteenth Amendment, arguing that it should not apply to children of undocumented migrants, despite a long record of judicial interpretation to the contrary. Contemporary nativists seek to exclude foreigners deemed dangerous to the republic, now migrants from Latin America rather than the "wild Irishmen" of the early nineteenth century. At the same time, undocumented people who arrived in the United States as children and who have lived most of their lives within its borders seek a new vision of citizenship, one that will acknowledge their rightful place in the American polity and provide a defense against deportation and exclusion. Despite being defined in the Constitution, citizenship remains contested.

Notes

1. US Constitution, https://constitution.congress.gov/constitution.
2. Ibid.
3. David Ramsay, *A Dissertation on the Manner of Acquiring the Character and Privileges of a Citizen of the United States* (Charleston, SC, 1789), 3.
4. US Constitution.
5. Act of March 26, 1790, 1 *Stat.* 103.
6. *Annals of Congress (AC)*, 1st Cong., 2nd Sess., 1155–1156; *The Journal of William Maclay* (New York: Albert & Charles Boni, 1927), 205; Frank George Franklin, *The Legislative History of Naturalization in the United States* (Chicago, IL: University of Chicago Press, 1906), 41–44.
7. *AC*, 3rd Cong., 2nd Sess., 1005–1009.
8. Act of January 29, 1795, 1 *Stat.* 414.
9. Act of June 18, 1798, 1 *Stat.* 566.
10. *AC*, 5th Cong., 1st Sess, 429–430; 5th Cong., 2nd Sess., 1567.
11. *Aurora General Advertiser*, January 24 and 25, 1800; I-Mien Tsiang, *The Question of Expatriation in America Prior to 1907* (Baltimore, MD: Johns Hopkins University Press, 1942), 35.
12. John Binns, *Recollections of the Life of John Binns* (Philadelphia, PA: Binns, Parry and M'Millan, 1854), 173.
13. Act of April 14, 1802, 2 *Stat.* 153–155.
14. Act of July 14, 1870, 16 *Stat.* 254.
15. Nicholas Wood, "A 'Class of Citizens': The Earliest Black Petitioners to Congress and Their Quaker Allies," *William and Mary Quarterly* 74, no. 1 (January 2017): 109–144.
16. *AC*, 7th Cong. 2nd Sess., 385–386; 423–424; 464–472; 1564–1565.
17. *AC*, 9th Cong., 2nd Sess., 174.
18. *AC*, 16th Cong., 2nd Sess., 557.
19. William Lloyd Garrison, *Thoughts on African Colonization, Part II* (Boston, MA: Garrison and Knappy, 1832), 9–13.
20. David Walker, *Walker's Appeal . . . to the Coloured Citizens of the World*, 3rd ed. (Boston, MA: David Walker, 1830), 73.
21. *Scott v. Sandford*, 60 US 393 (1857), 404.
22. Wang Xi, *Trial of Democracy: Black Suffrage and Northern Republicans, 1860–1910* (Athens, GA: University of Georgia Press, 1997), 68–78.

Further Reading

For more on citizenship, see James Kettner, *The Development of American Citizenship* (Chapel Hill, NC: University of North Carolina Press, 1978); Rogers Smith, *Civic Ideals: Conflicting Visions of Citizenship in US History* (New Haven, CT: Yale

University Press, 1997); Kunal Parker, *Making Foreigners: Immigration and Citizenship Law in America, 1600–2000* (New York: Cambridge University Press, 2015); Andrew Diemer, *The Politics of Black Citizenship: Free African Americans in the Mid-Atlantic Borderland, 1817–1863* (Athens, GA: University of Georgia Press, 2016); Martha S. Jones, *Birthright Citizens: A History of Race and Rights in Antebellum America* (New York: Cambridge University Press, 2018); Christopher James Bonner, *Remaking the Republic: Black Politics and the Creation of American Citizenship* (Philadelphia, PA: University of Pennsylvania Press, 2020); and Kate Masur, *Until Justice Be Done: America's First Civil Rights Movement, from the Revolution to Reconstruction* (New York: Norton, 2021).

8

Anti–Black Violence

Ariel Elizabeth Seay-Howard

On August 29, 2014, an African American high school student named Lennon Lacy was found dead. With a noose around his neck, Lacy was hanging from the frame of a swing set in the center of a North Carolina mobile home community. The state's chief medical examiner initially declared the death a suicide, but Lacy's family believed he had been lynched. Investigators uncovered that Lacy had been part of an interracial romantic relationship. Lacy's girlfriend also believes his death was a murder; white male neighbors had warned the couple that relationships across the color line were not acceptable. Soon after, Lacy was found dead, and the neighbors had moved out of the community. But this suspicious timing did not motivate the police to look into the neighbors' impromptu move. In June 2016, the FBI concluded their investigation, declaring they had found insufficient evidence to pursue federal criminal or civil rights charges. Lacy's case was closed.[1] And yet Lacy's story is not truly closed. For it is part and parcel of the violence African Americans have suffered for centuries within a nation that is populated largely by people who consider its government to be a system where the citizens choose their representatives and, in this way, grant them authority to make law.

The cold case of Lennon Lacy illuminates the way in which decades after the vast DISFRANCHISEMENT of African Americans in the Jim Crow era, which legally ended in 1965, Black citizens remain excluded from a system that promises liberty and EQUALITY for all. Violence, in the form of both extrajudicial violence by whites and an inequitable judicial system that sustains oppression and legitimizes violence, has been a primary method for enforcing and sustaining this exclusion across centuries. The US judicial system features an overwhelming number of cases of white violence toward the African

Ariel Elizabeth Seay-Howard, *Anti-Black Violence* In: *Democracies in America: Keywords for the Nineteenth Century and Today.*
Edited by: D. Berton Emerson and Gregory Laski, Oxford University Press. © D. Berton Emerson and Gregory Laski 2023.
DOI: 10.1093/oso/9780198865698.003.0009

American community. However, as with Lacy, more often than not African American victims rarely see justice. This state of affairs has forced Americans of African descent to treat claims about a "democratic" society with suspicion, even as they have fiercely fought for the freedom of speech, the right to vote, and even the right to live.

Indeed, across the long nineteenth century, African Americans have engaged in this fight in and through the public sphere. German philosopher Jürgen Habermas defines the public sphere as an area of social life where individuals can come together to freely discuss and identify societal problems and, through debate, influence political action.[2] Acts of anti-Black violence have functioned to enforce a notion of the dominant public sphere that bars the Black community from participation. As a consequence, counter-publics have arisen in response. Organizations and movements, such as the National Association for the Advancement of Colored People (NAACP), the Black Panthers, and, more recently, Black Lives Matter, have created their own public spaces to fight against white force.

Sometimes Black Americans have turned to acts of physical violence to resist white force and defeat white perpetrators. Nat Turner is one person who used such force to fight against white oppressors in the slave rebellion he led in Southampton County, Virginia, in August 1831. Although some may think it counterproductive to use violent force to fight against violence, in the second half of the 1850s Black abolitionist James McCune Smith became frustrated with the direction in which national and state politics were heading and gave up his faith in the power of words. Through his frustrations he began to realize that "our white brethren cannot understand us unless we speak to them in their own language; they recognize only the philosophy of force."[3] Although this sentiment may have been true, it wasn't always effective or possible as a strategy, as African Americans didn't have access to the same store of weapons as did whites. Moreover, for many, democracy promises an outlet for negotiating difference and disagreement without resorting to physical violence. Yet, if this is true, then a question arises: How does a group that was once excluded from CITIZENSHIP and later recognized by birthright as citizens and ensured equal protection under the law—all the while suffering nearly unstinting acts of legal and extralegal violence—become fully fledged members of a democratic society in theory as well as practice?

As one response, Black abolitionists and freedom fighters such as Ida B. Wells have worked tirelessly to protect the Black community from violence by using their voices as tools to deconstruct white violence, create better representation of the Black community, and illuminate the short-comings of the US democratic society. As the rhetorical scholar Catherine Squires has argued, Blacks gained better representation with the emergence of the national Black press founded in 1827; along with Wells came other journalists and editors who created their own space to express their opinions, ideas, and issues their community faced.[4] This history reveals the way in which African Americans have turned to counter-publics to do the democratic work of centering themselves and to challenge racial exclusions that limit them from full inclusion in a so-called "democratic nation"—meeting violence with nonviolent tools rather than more acts of physical force. As we will see, their voices were often the most powerful weapons to fight against white force, specifically lynching. Despite the success of this work, the case of Lacy shows us that it remains to be seen what a more fully democratic United States would look like once this counter-public work is done, and when a group of people once deemed on the outside become fully integrated into the democratic society on the inside and the problem of violence as a long-running presence within US democratic society becomes moot.

To comprehend why these counter-spaces formed in the first place, we need to understand how violence toward the African American community developed as a form of surveillance. The most common practice of surveillance is policing, which emerged as an institution in the 1800s as a way of controlling enslaved people. The white individuals who served in this role were often called "night watch" or "slave patrols." After the Civil War, and the legal abolition of slavery, modern policing filled the place of slave patrols and became the dominant tool used to regulate African American freedom. For that reason, policing took on a more contemporary form of being used as a surveillance mechanism. As policing progressed into a more "suitable" form of white control, white police officials used violent acts such as lynching to keep the Black community in order and under control. After the legal end of slavery, other acts of mob violence were perpetrated upon freed Black people, most famously by members from the Ku Klux Klan. During the Reconstruction era, and into the Jim Crow period of the late nineteenth and early twentieth centuries, lynching was a prevalent form of violence used to terrorize African Americans.

Consider the murders of three Black men, who were found shot to death in an old field in Tennessee. In March 1892, in a mixed-race neighborhood located just outside of Memphis called the Curve, near Mississippi Boulevard and Walker Avenue, a white grocer named William Barrett found his business shrinking because of the success of a grocery store nearby run by three Black men: Will Stewart, Tommie Moss, and Calvin McDowell. False rumors and accusations against the three Black men drove a large group of armed white men into the Curve, where gunshots were traded and several white men were injured. The Black grocers were arrested and jailed. Three days later, the downtown jail was stormed, and Stewart, Moss, and McDowell were dragged out and taken to the nearby railroad yard. The three men fought back, but eventually McDowell was shot. Stewart resisted until he was shot in the neck. And before he was killed, Moss was asked if he had any final words. He said, "Tell my people to go West. There is no justice for them here." He was shot and left with the others under a pile of brush.[5]

Although the families of the three men never received justice for their murders, each death struck a personal chord within their good friend Ida B. Wells. Wells, a historical pioneer, activist, and journalist, founded the anti-lynching campaign in response to the Curve killings. Wells was one of the prominent activists who fought to end lynching. She was born to enslaved parents in Holly Springs, Mississippi, and educated at Rust University, a high school and industrial school for former slaves established in Holly Springs in 1866. As part of her anti-lynching campaign, she helped co-found the NAACP in 1909 and became the co-owner and editor of the *Memphis Free Speech and Headlight* in 1910. She worked hard to end lynching by visiting places where African Americans had been hanged, shot, beaten, burned alive, drowned, or mutilated. She examined photos of victims hanging from trees, she took sworn statements from eyewitnesses, and she even hired private investigators to dig deeper into unsolved lynchings. Her dedication to bring justice to the falsely accused Black victims and expose the truth behind the under-investigated crimes became her life mission. Wells argues in her acclaimed 1895 book *The Red Record* that "ten thousand Negroes have been killed in cold blood, [through lynching] without the formality of judicial trial and legal execution. The government which had made the Negro a citizen found itself unable to protect him."[6] Since the government had failed to protect the Black community, Wells made it her mission to do so. She did this by traveling to different parts of the South, using her voice as a form of activism and resistance against the lynchings plaguing the Black community.

Throughout her travels she saw and learned of different murders that African Americans had suffered. She also realized that by no means were African Americans exempt from lynching because of gender, pregnancy, age, or sex, as the 1918 lynching of Mary Turner demonstrated. In Lowndes County, Georgia, the pregnant Turner was lynched because she fought against the false accusations that her husband, Hazel Hayes-Turner, had murdered a white farmer. Additionally, in May 1918, Hampton Smith, a thirty-one-year-old white plantation owner in Brooks County, Georgia, was shot and killed by one of his Black workers named Sydney Johnson. During the manhunt to find Smith's killer more than thirteen African American men were killed; Turner's husband was among the falsely accused Black male victims. When Turner vowed to press charges against her husband's killers, she too fell victim to a mob. The mob hung Turner upside down by her ankles; they were not disturbed by the fact that she was less than a month away from giving birth. They covered her clothes with gasoline and burned them on her body. Then, using a hunting knife, they cut the unborn baby from her womb. Upon hitting the ground, the baby was killed, but still the mob was not satisfied. They shot hundreds of bullets into the dead fetus and body of Mary Turner.[7]

The killers of Hazel Hayes-Turner, Mary Turner, and their unborn baby were never brought to justice. The injustice the Turner family faced is not uncommon for Black lynching victims. Historically, the violent act of lynching has been defended as a necessary activity on a violent frontier. Many lynch victims never received a proper burial, and most victims were lynched before being given a fair legal trial to defend themselves. In addition, if an individual was granted a trial, most of the time insufficient evidence was given to the court to prove that the victim was innocent.

Wells saw how her so-called "democratic society" was failing to protect the rights of the Black community, and by 1892 her anti-lynching movement began to flourish. Specifically, Wells altered the mainstream narratives that suggested lynching victims were criminals, often the rapists of white women. Newspapers such as the *New York Age* had framed certain lynchings in a villain/hero narrative, such as this 1919 headline: "Negro was lynched to save white woman's secret lover."[8] Wells actively expressed how dangerous this kind of framing was for the Black community.

In her 1893 speech "Lynch Law in All Its Phases," Wells explains how the overplayed narrative of Black men raping white women was toxic for the Black community. She declared:

Nobody in this section of the country believes the old threadbare lie that negro men rape white women. If Southern white men are not careful, they will overreach themselves, and public sentiment will have a reaction. A conclusion will then be reached which will be very damaging to the moral reputation of their women.[9]

Predicting a karma-like effect that this false narrative would have on the white community, Wells constructed a platform through the Black press for future activism from the NAACP, which made anti-lynching a priority, and drew Black and white women into its anti-lynching campaign.

By the 1920s, women's anti-lynching activity had become essential to the NAACP's campaign for passage of the Dyer Bill, a federal anti-lynching bill that was first introduced into Congress in 1918. Surprisingly, from our contemporary vantage point, the NAACP had doubts about supporting the passage of this bill. The group initially argued that the bill was unconstitutional based on the recommendations of Moorfield Storey, a lawyer and the first president of the NAACP. Although believing the legislation was desirable, Storey expressed fears about the larger stakes of the bill: "As great as that evil [lynching] is, it would not, however, equal that which would follow the usurpation by the Congress of the United States of power it does not possess under the Constitution."[10] In other words, Storey saw the possibility of Congress further extending and taking power over the African American community if the bill were to pass. In time, Storey reversed his position, and from 1919 onward the NAACP supported Dyer's anti-lynching legislation.

Wells had led the way in developing a space, through the press, for the disfranchised to expose the truth of how the Black community had been most affected by lynching. Confronting exploitation and exclusion, she created a Black counter-public to do her democratic work; she forged a space where Black community members could voice their opinions, educate themselves, and work together to protect one another and reshape the lynching laws. Recognizing the need for such a space, the NAACP developed their mission statement to "ensure a society in which all individuals have equal rights without discrimination based on race."[11] The mission statement is a reflection of the inclusive space the association has built for the African American community and for allies in support of the African American community. The protected space points the community toward a place free from discrimination and murder: a democratic counter-space. Wells and other African Americans have known first-hand how crucial such spaces are for surviving and thriving in the United States.

When the Dyer Bill passed in the House of Representatives on January 26, 1922, the African American community felt as if they were making substantial progress toward political freedom. But the legislation languished in the Senate, where the struggle extends into the twenty-first century. The Justice for Victims of Lynching Act was introduced by the Senate in June 2018 and passed in December 2018. However, the bill died because it was not passed by the House before the 115th Congress ended in January 2019. Efforts to pass an anti-lynching bill continued, and on February 26, 2020, the Emmett Till Antilynching Act was introduced as a revised version of the Justice for Victims of Lynching Act. This version passed the House two years later, in February 2022, with a vote of 422–3. After briefly being held up in the Senate by Senator Rand Paul from Kentucky, who expressed concern that a convicted criminal could face "a new 10-year penalty for minor bruising," the bill was finally approved by the Senate and signed into law in March 2022.[12]

Throughout this long process, members of the Black community have continuously felt unsafe and unfree from violence. This long-term failure once again illuminates how the systematic design of this US "democratic" society has been built upon the exclusion of the African American community. Not only has it withheld their rights, but it has repeatedly demonstrated that the priority of this democracy is not to protect the Black community, but to uphold a racist ideology underwritten by physical violence. The Declaration of Independence promises that "all men are created equal, that they are endowed by their Creator with certain unalienable Rights, that among these are Life, Liberty and the Pursuit of Happiness." In contrast, as four centuries of historical record and the current moment show, African American citizens are still subjected to violence; therefore, life, liberty, and the pursuit of happiness—the supposed bedrock of US democratic society— does not apply to all American citizens.

The systematic violence that continues to plague the Black community has affected not only victims such as Tommy Moss, Calvin McDowell, Will Stewart, and the Turner family, but also present-day victims, such as the innocent, young, and in-love seventeen-year-old Lennon Lacy, who never had a chance to fight for his own justice or give a compassionate goodbye to his mother and brother, and even more recent victims: Eric Garner, Sandra Bland, Ahmaud Arbery, Breonna Taylor, George Floyd, and Robert L. Fuller. Garner was killed on July 17, 2014, by a New York City police officer. The officer approached Garner on the suspicion that he was selling single cigarettes from packs without tax stamps. After Garner told the officer that he was tired of being harassed and that he was not selling cigarettes, the officer attempted to arrest Garner by using the chokehold method, which resulted in Garner's death. Bland, a twenty-eight-year-old African American woman, was found hanged in a jail cell in Waller County, Texas, on July 13, 2015, three days after being arrested for a minor traffic violation; Bland's death was ruled a suicide. Arbery was shot dead by two white men while taking a jog in a South Georgia neighborhood on February 23, 2020. Taylor was killed by Louisville, Kentucky, police officers while sleeping in her own home on March 13, 2020; the police wrongly thought she was a suspect in an investigation. Floyd was killed on May 25, 2020, by a Minneapolis police officer who held his knee on Floyd's neck for roughly nine minutes. Fuller was a twenty-four-year-old African American man who was found on June 10, 2020, at 3 AM hanging from a tree in front of the City Hall in Palmdale, California. His death was ruled a suicide by the Los Angeles County Sheriff's Department.

The loss of life of these victims—even those whose killings were prosecuted successfully under the court system, as in the Floyd and Arbery cases—expose the painfully lethargic process of the judicial system. Thus, investigating the tragedies of these and other Black victims underscores the suffering, inequality, and injustices the Black community endures both in the gruesome past and in the bloody present. If the people of the United States of America are going to continue to consider the nation a democratic society where all citizens are protected by the law and the judicial system against unjust acts of violence, then we as a country need to protect all citizens regardless of their race, not to mention their gender and sexual orientation. Ida B. Wells and the NAACP created a foundation to do democratic counter-public sphere work, and their legacy continues in the form of the Black Lives Matter movement and through organizations such as the Equal Justice Initiative, founded by Bryan Stevenson. Understanding these groups' methods to make positive change can help rising generations create a safer future for the African American community in the United States of America.

Notes

1. *Always in Season*, dir. Jacqueline Olive (Brooklyn, NY: Multitude Films, 2019).
2. Jürgen Habermas, *The Structural Transformation of the Public Sphere: An Inquiry into a Category of Bourgeois Society*, trans. Thomas Burger (Cambridge, MA: MIT Press, 1991), 8.

3. James McCune Smith, *The Works of James McCune Smith: Black Intellectual and Abolitionist* (New York: Oxford University Press, 206), 141, quoted in Kellie Carter Jackson, *Force and Freedom: Black Abolitionists and the Politics of Violence* (Philadelphia, PA: University of Pennsylvania Press, 2019), 2.

4. Catherine Squires, "The Black Press and the State," in Robert Asen and Daniel C. Brouwer, eds., *Counterpublics and the State* (Albany, NY: SUNY Press, 2001), 111–136.

5. "The People's Grocery Lynchings (Thomas Moss, Will Stewart, Calvin McDowell)," Lynching Site Projects, Memphis, https://lynchingsitesmem.org/lynching/peoples-grocery-lynchings-thomas-moss-will-stewart-calvin-mcdowell.

6. Ida B. Wells-Barnett, *The Red Record* (Frankfurt am Main: Outlook Verlag, 2018), 4.

7. See Julie Buckner Armstrong, *Mary Turner and the Memory of Lynching* (Athens, GA: University of Georgia Press, 2011).

8. Quoted in Ralph Ginzburg, *100 Years of Lynching* (Baltimore, MD: Black Classic Press, 1988), 121.

9. Ida B. Wells-Barnett, *Southern Horrors: Lynch Law in All Its Phases* (Frankfurt am Main: Outlook Verlag, 2018), 5.

10. William B. Hixson, "Moorfield Storey and the Defense of the Dyer Anti-Lynching Bill," *New England Quarterly* 42, no. 1 (1969): 79.

11. "NAACP History: Dyer Anti-Lynching Bill," NAACP, https://naacp.org/naacp-history-dyer-anti-lynching-bill.

12. "Sen. Paul acknowledges holding up anti-lynching bill, says he fears it would be wrongly applied," *The Washington Post*, June 3, 2020, https://www.washingtonpost.com/powerpost/sen-paul-acknowledges-holding-up-anti-lynching-bill-says-he-fears-it-would-be-wrongly-applied/2020/06/03/29b97330-a5bf-11ea-b619-3f9133bbb482_story.html#comments-wrapper.

Further Reading

The keyword *violence* crosses multiple fields and is often closely aligned with lynching. The work of Collins Winfiel Hazlitt is an important starting place; see *The Truth about Lynching and the Negro in the South* (New York: Neale Publishing Company, 2006). *Southern Horrors and Other Writings: The Anti-Lynching Campaign of Ida B. Wells 1892–1900*, ed. Jacqueline Jones Royster (New York: Bedford/St. Martin's, 2016) and *The Works of James McCune Smith: Black Intellectual and Abolitionist*, ed. John Stauffer (New York: Oxford University Press, 2006) are good primary sources. For a history of African American responses to white violence across the nineteenth century, see Kidada E. Williams, *They Left Great Marks on Me: African American Testimonies of Racial Violence from Emancipation to World War I* (New York: New York University

Press, 2012). The concept of surveillance is another closely linked topic; see Victor E. Kappeler's "A Brief History of Slavery and the Origins of American Policing" (Eastern Kentucky University Police Studies, https://plsonline.eku.edu/insidelook/brief-history-slavery-and-origins-american-policing); Charles Sackett Sydnor, "A Slave Owner and His Overseers," *The North Carolina Historical Review* 14, no. 1 (1937): 31–38; and Simone Brown, *Dark Matters: On the Surveillance of Blackness* (Durham, NC: Duke University Press, 2015). On the rhetoric of publics and counter-publics, see Robert Asen and Daniel C. Brouwer, eds., *Counterpublics and the State* (Albany, NY: SUNY Press, 2001) and Gerard A. Hauser and Thomas W. Benson, *Vernacular Voices: The Rhetoric of Publics and Public Spheres* (Columbia, SC: University of South Carolina Press, 1999). To learn more about the Nat Turner slave rebellion, consult Herbert Aptheker, *Nat Turner's Slave Rebellion Including the 1831 "Confessions"* (Mineola, NY: Dover, 2006). Finally, on the lynching crusader Ida B. Wells, see *Crusade for Justice: The Autobiography of Ida B. Wells*, 2nd ed., ed. Alfreda M. Duster (Chicago, IL: University of Chicago Press, 2020).

9

Women's Suffrage

David Gold

In 2020, the United States marked the one hundredth anniversary of one of its most celebrated democratic achievements, the ratification of the Nineteenth Amendment to the Constitution, granting women the right to vote. From a contemporary perspective, it may seem obvious, perhaps even inevitable, that women would unite in support of this cause. Today, we see voting as a fundamental right of citizenship, and suffrage advocates held that the franchise was not just key to securing basic political REPRESENTATION but the only way for women to achieve "equal protection" under the law, as promised by the Fourteenth Amendment. Yet there were serious obstacles to this goal. Not only were women denied suffrage; it was also widely argued that they did not require suffrage, since they were effectively represented by male family members. Moreover, gendered conceptions of citizenship in the period held that women's sphere of duty was in the home, so that even advocating for suffrage in the public sphere could be seen as a violation of the social order. Indeed, not all women in the long nineteenth century saw suffrage as necessary to the exercise of citizenship, believing they could participate in civic life by using their moral influence as protectors of public virtue.

The most prominent anti-suffrage organizations were led by women; while many wished to preserve economic and racial privilege for upper- and middle-class white women, others were civic reformers who maintained they could have greater impact in the public sphere by refraining from PARTISAN politics in which there was no moral high ground. Suffrage organizations themselves were divided along ideological and strategic lines, debating not just how to achieve suffrage but also who should benefit from it, sometimes "exchanging principle for expediency."[1] For many white

David Gold, *Women's Suffrage* In: *Democracies in America: Keywords for the Nineteenth Century and Today.*
Edited by: D. Berton Emerson and Gregory Laski, Oxford University Press. © D. Berton Emerson and Gregory Laski 2023.
DOI: 10.1093/oso/9780198865698.003.0010

women, citizenship was tied to racial identity, and even suffrage advocates were inconsistent in their support for universal suffrage that included women of color, fracturing potential cross-racial alliances. For many Black women and men, meanwhile, women's suffrage was inseparable from racial justice.

Women's suffrage thus has not been stable or meant the same thing to all constituencies. The shifting terrain that paved the road to the Nineteenth Amendment illuminates the conflicts that emerge among competing claims as to what counts as democratic inclusion, and points as well to the divides that still challenge the contemporary struggle for gender equality as one dimension of the promise of EQUALITY required for a democracy.

Though the United States is often seen as a bastion of representative democracy, for much of its history most of its inhabitants did not have full CITIZEN-SHIP rights. When women began to organize for suffrage in the 1840s and 1850s, in most locales they lacked not only the right to vote but other basic rights of citizenship too, including the right to independently own property, choose their marriage partners, or have autonomy over their own bodies. Perhaps not surprisingly, early women's rights activists found common cause with abolitionists advocating for Black civil rights. Indeed, many women in the early suffrage movement began as abolitionists, turning to women's rights activism as they experienced not just harsh public criticism for their activities but also unequal treatment within the movement.

Across the nineteenth century, suffrage advocates developed two main lines of argument: one based on the presumed similarity of women to men, sometimes termed "justice" or "equality" arguments, and one based on presumed differences, sometimes termed "expediency" arguments.[2] In using the trope of justice, suffrage advocates appealed to widely shared beliefs in both constitutional and religious principles of equality, arguing that women possessed the same intellectual abilities, natural rights, and spiritual capacities as men and thus were equally entitled to the franchise and full participation in the public sphere. In using the trope of expediency, suffrage advocates appealed to equally widespread beliefs about women's ostensible differences, arguing that women's nurturing abilities and "purer" nature particularly fit them to participate in the public sphere and that granting women the franchise would allow them to both advocate for their own rights and improve politics overall.

In the early decades of the movement, suffrage advocates, inspired by abolitionist activism, tended to make heavier use of justice arguments. The

Declaration of Sentiments signed by delegates at the 1848 Seneca Falls Woman's Rights Convention famously drew on the language of the Declaration of Independence, proclaiming, "We hold these truths to be self-evident: that all men and women are created equal."[3] In the latter half of the nineteenth century, suffrage advocates increasingly shifted from justice to expediency arguments, though both would be used throughout the suffrage struggle, often in concert. Speaking in 1860, Elizabeth Cady Stanton declared that women had "all the duties and responsibilities of the citizen" but none of "the rights and privileges." At the same time, she argued that women were more fit for the franchise than "the ignorant alien, the gambler, the drunkard, the prize-fighter, the licentious profligate, the silly stripling of twenty-one, the fool, the villain."[4] This dichotomy between arguing that all citizens were worthy of the franchise while maintaining that some (white female) citizens were worthier than others would increasingly expose tensions in the movement as the century progressed.

Founded in 1866 after the Civil War, the American Equal Rights Association (AERA), the first national suffrage organization, sought to "secure Equal Rights to all American citizens, especially the Right of Suffrage, irrespective of race, color or sex."[5] It included among its members many prominent advocates for abolition and Black civil rights, both white and Black, male and female, among them Henry Blackwell, Frederick Douglass, Frances Ellen Watkins Harper, Lucretia Mott, Lucy Stone, and Sojourner Truth, as well as the two women who would become most associated with the suffrage movement in public memory, Susan B. Anthony and Elizabeth Cady Stanton.

Yet from the organization's start, conflicts emerged among these respective constituencies. With the imminent passage of the Fifteenth Amendment—which guaranteed male citizens the right of suffrage regardless of "race, color, or previous condition of servitude"—the fragile coalition between women's rights and Black civil rights activists fractured.[6] At the 1869 AERA convention, Elizabeth Cady Stanton bristled against the Amendment, arguing that she "did not believe in allowing ignorant negroes and foreigners to make laws for her to obey." Susan B. Anthony likewise argued, "If you will not give the whole loaf of suffrage to the entire people, give it to the most intelligent first. If intelligence, justice, and morality are to have precedence in the Government, let the question of woman be brought first and that of the negro last." Frederick Douglass, while maintaining support for women's suffrage, urged support for the Amendment, asking his audience to consider the daily threat of state-sanctioned ANTI-BLACK VIOLENCE under which African Americans lived: "With us, the matter is a question of life and death." Lucy Stone, though disappointed at women's exclusion from the Amendment, also argued for its necessity: "Woman has an ocean of wrongs too deep for any plummet, and the negro, too, has an ocean of wrongs that can not be fathomed.... I will be thankful in my soul if *any* body can get out of the terrible pit." Frances Harper expressed her support for the Amendment, further questioning whether white suffragists' commitment to women's rights "was broad enough to take colored women."[7]

The AERA soon dissolved. In its wake, Stanton and Anthony founded the National Woman Suffrage Association (NWSA), which opposed the Fifteenth Amendment, limited male membership, and worked toward a federal suffrage amendment; later that year, Stone, her husband Henry Blackwell, and other former abolitionists founded the American Woman Suffrage Association (AWSA), which supported the Fifteenth Amendment, welcomed men to its membership, and supported a strategy to enact suffrage state by state. The two groups would merge in 1890 as the National American Woman Suffrage Association (NAWSA), but the racial tensions that underlay the AERA's demise would remain.

Through the end of the century, debate over suffrage would become increasingly racialized. Southern whites, both men and women, who still saw the Fifteenth Amendment as an affront, often opposed suffrage on the grounds that it would enfranchise Black women. In order to gain Southern support, white suffragists in the North were often willing to sacrifice the rights of their Black sisters; this ranged from excluding Black women from suffrage activities where Southern sensibilities might be offended to openly abandoning the principle of universal suffrage in favor of "educated suffrage," by which Southern states could presumably ensure continued white dominance. White suffragists also often used racial appeals in advocating for suffrage, arguing the injustice of presumably unqualified Black and foreign-born men having the vote while "virtuous" white mothers, wives, and daughters did not.

It was not merely racial animus or cold political calculation that underlay these actions; in much of the nineteenth century the notion of citizenship itself was marked as white, the presumed natural inheritance of the white Northern European forebears who founded the republic, in contrast to the putative noncitizen state of Black Americans, Natives, and the foreign-born.

In advocating for women's role in nation building and the particular civiliz-ing influence of women in the public sphere, white suffragists also advanced a notion of the nation state based on white purity and power.

For their part, Black Americans often saw women's suffrage as tied to racial uplift. Black women activists, though disappointed in the exclusion of women from the Fourteenth and Fifteenth Amendments, supported their passage, seeing them as at least partial victories for racial equality. In advo-cating for women's suffrage, Black suffragists had to argue not only for women's equality writ large but also for the rights of Black citizens against a political and cultural milieu that constructed citizenship as white and a suffrage discourse that frequently relied on racist arguments both for and against suffrage. Black women activists, suffering both racial and sexual dis-crimination, also did not have the luxury of advocating for a single cause; most suffrage advocates, such as Frances Harper, Ida B. Wells, Mary Church Terrell, and Nannie Helen Burroughs, also worked on educational, eco-nomic, social, and civil rights reform. Although Black suffrage activists worked with white-dominated suffrage organizations such as NAWSA, the discrimination they experienced led them to form their own coalitions; particularly important to these efforts were Black educational institutions, women's clubs, periodicals, and civil rights organizations.

One such organization, the National Association for the Advancement of Colored People (NAACP), advocated for suffrage through its journal *Crisis*, under the leadership of editor W. E. B. Du Bois. In perhaps its most notable moment of suffrage advocacy, in August 1915 the journal published a "Votes for Women" symposium, featuring twenty-six writers, eleven men and fif-teen women, comprising a wide range of activists, educators, writers, and religious, business, and civic leaders. These writers faced a daunting rhetor-ical challenge, addressing not just traditional gendered and racialized argu-ments against suffrage but also racialized arguments in *favor* of suffrage, both from Southern suffragists who saw voting as a vehicle for maintaining white supremacy and from Northern suffragists who maintained that the DISFRAN-CHISEMENT of Black women was not a suffrage concern. In drawing upon traditional justice and expediency arguments, they were also sensitive to the ways in which these arguments had been used against them and sought to counter these moves in the pursuit of equality.

Particularly striking is the gendered rhetorical strategies the contributors employed. All of the men made justice arguments, emphasizing women's intellectual and moral parity and invoking logical, democratic, and religious principles in arguing for women's suffrage. Francis J. Grimke offered a straightforward case for giving women the ballot: "The average woman is just as well qualified to form an opinion as to the character and qualifications of those who are to be entrusted with power as the average man.... To deprive her of the right to vote is to govern her without her consent, which is contrary to the fundamental principle of democracy."[8] These writers were also aware of the ways in which suffrage discourse had been racialized, and a majority either argued for the specific need for Black citizens to obtain the vote or drew parallels between women's rights and civil rights. Robert H. Terrell emphatically declared that "the Negro should be most ardently in favor of woman suffrage, for above all others, he knows what a denial of the ballot means to a people."[9]

While the women contributors also made justice claims, two-thirds argued primarily from expediency, asserting that women either had particular need of the ballot or would bring special talents to it, calling attention, for example, to the exigencies of working women, mothers, and teachers. Anna H. Jones argued for the ballot as a means of expanding women's sphere: "Of the four great institutions of human uplift—the home, the school, the church, and the State, woman has a direct controlling force in the first three.... Should she not have the legal means—the ballot—to widen and deepen her work?"[10] While both the men and women rhetors forged parallels between the experiences of women and African Americans as disfranchised citizens, the women were more likely to ground their claims in embodied racial experience. Josephine St. Pierre Ruffin, challenging the notion that suffrage was white women's concern, argued that "equality of the sexes means more progress toward equality of the races," while Nannie Helen Burroughs advocated for the ballot as a "weapon of moral defence" for the Black woman, who "needs the ballot to reckon with men who place no value upon her virtue, and to mould healthy public sentiment in favor of her own protection."[11]

This divergence speaks to the different embodied experiences Black men and women brought to suffrage discourse, even as they suffered from similar racial injustice. The connection these writers drew between women's suffrage and Black civil rights further suggests that in their view the struggles were linked. Suffrage was not simply a "woman's" issue.

Nor was suffrage simply a battle between men and women; indeed, the most powerful and consistent organized resistance to suffrage would largely come from women. The Women's Anti-Suffrage Association of Massachusetts, founded in 1895, had registered nearly 37,000 women members by 1916 and would be instrumental in helping to defeat a state suffrage referendum in 1915.[12] The National Association Opposed to Woman Suffrage, founded in 1911, had as many as 350,000 members by 1916. Though anti-suffrage organizations claimed a broad coalition of support, they drew their ranks largely from middle- and upper-class women. The movement, moreover, was exclusively white.

Though anti-suffragists have been portrayed as politically reactionary and anti-feminist, the reality was more complicated. Certainly many wanted to preserve their power, privilege, and prestige. Some were motivated by supremacist or nativist beliefs or what they saw as threats to the social order; the Nebraska Association Opposed to Woman Suffrage decried "the alliance of suffrage with socialism which advocates free love and institutional life for children," while the Georgia Association Opposed to Woman Suffrage warned of "the danger to farmers' families if negro men vote in addition to 2,000,000 negro women," arguing that "White Supremacy must be maintained."[13]

Yet anti-suffragists were not uniformly opposed to women's rights and many labored alongside their suffragist sisters for progressive causes such as better labor conditions, equal pay, and access to higher education, even belonging to the same reform organizations. The eighteen women who contributed to the 1916 *Anti-Suffrage Essays by Massachusetts Women* were active in both professional and public life and supported women's participation in the public sphere. Where they departed from the suffrage cause was on the nature of that participation; many anti-suffragists maintained that women could most effectively participate in public affairs *without* the franchise, which by rendering them into affiliates of various political parties would only weaken their effectiveness as nonpartisan advocates for the public good.

To make their case, anti-suffragists argued that suffrage was not a precondition for citizenship; indeed, many saw the ballot as a relatively weak means of promoting the public welfare. Various contributors to *Anti-Suffrage Essays* exhaustively delineated the accomplishments of public-minded women absent the ballot in the areas of social, health, educational, and labor reform, while others noted the failure of progressive reform and the lack of women's political participation in states where women's suffrage had been achieved. Several argued that suffrage would *lessen* women's political power

by diluting their heretofore unquestioned "moral influence." Wrote
Margaret C. Robinson, "The possession of this unprejudiced, unrestricted
power is something which anti-suffragists value so highly that the threat of
the suffragists to destroy it is a very serious grievance."[14] Some even argued
that it was suffragists, with their single-minded and narrow advocacy, who
were acting in an anti-feminist fashion. Suffragism, wrote Dorothy Godfrey
Wayman, was complicit in "destroying the power of that great, womanly
contribution towards the solving of the vexed questions of the day made by
the disinterested, because disfranchised citizenness."[15]

Many anti-suffragists were unable to imagine the struggles of women not
in their social or economic class. Contributors to the volume repeatedly
affirmed that men could be trusted to manage political affairs, downplayed
their own political capabilities, and questioned the womanliness and sincer-
ity of suffrage advocates. Even as they acknowledged the seeming dichotomy of their actions, they were sincere in their desire for participation in
civic life. "We antisuffragists have taken part in a political campaign to keep
ourselves out of politics for the rest of our lives," wrote Alice Ranney Allen,
"but we know that in a proper division of duty we have better work to do
along civic, sanitary, and philanthropic lines."[16] Even as anti-suffragists
sought political influence for women, however, their conception of citizenship excluded those who did not share their race and class privileges. In
advocating for a gendered public sphere, marking the limits of the franchise
in advancing political equity, and calling attention to widespread political
indifference among women, anti-suffrage activists highlighted the great
challenge suffragists faced in persuading their fellow citizens of the need for
constitutional reform granting women the franchise. Their legacy also
reminds us that voting is but one tool available to citizens seeking to mobilize for greater equality.

In the final years before the passage of the Nineteenth Amendment, a new
line of suffrage advocacy developed: "earned rights" arguments.[17] As women
increasingly entered professional and public life, there was growing accept-
ance of their participation in these arenas. By 1920, nearly one-quarter of
women were in the workforce, challenging conventional assumptions about
women's roles. Women's participation in the First World War, from factory
and volunteer work at home to military support roles abroad, also persuaded
many that women deserved the franchise. In her 1916 NAWSA presidential
address, Carrie Chapman Catt detailed the social transformations taking

place around the world as a result of the war: "In all the belligerent lands, women have found their way to high posts of administration where no women would have been trusted two years ago." Such changes, she declared, were "bound to bring political liberty" after the war, and she urged her audience to "arise: demand the vote!"[18]

As women increasingly mobilized to secure suffrage, their efforts became bolder. In 1917, the National Woman's Party (NWP) picketed the White House in silent protest, with activists holding banners that pointed out the dichotomy between America fighting "a world war so that democracies may survive" while "twenty million American Women are denied the right to vote."[19] Though they suffered violent arrests and public mockery, their efforts paid off when President Woodrow Wilson publicly endorsed suffrage in 1918.

The subsequent passage of the Nineteenth Amendment by Congress on June 4, 1919, and ratification by the states on August 18, 1920, did not resolve the question of women's place in the public sphere. NAWSA would give rise to the League of Women Voters in 1920, which pursued nonpartisan efforts aimed at social and civic reform. In 1923, Alice Paul and the NWP drafted an Equal Rights Amendment, beginning an activist effort that is still ongoing. Meanwhile, conservative women's organizations such as the Daughters of the American Revolution used traditional maternal tropes to mobilize against what they considered the anti-Americanism of feminist and progressive ideals, calling into question the gender-based unity that had undergirded the suffrage movement, even as they made use of the franchise. This living history confirms that suffrage is but one component of citizenship and that the fight for women's suffrage is but one part of a larger, ongoing struggle for equality in the United States.

Notes

1. Lisa Tetrault, *The Myth of Seneca Falls: Memory and the Women's Suffrage Movement, 1848–1898* (Chapel Hill, NC: University of North Carolina Press, 2014), 170.
2. Aileen S. Kraditor, *The Ideas of the Woman Suffrage Movement, 1890–1920* (1965; New York: Norton, 1981), 43–74.
3. Elizabeth Cady Stanton, Susan B. Anthony, and Matilda Joslyn Gage, eds., *History of Woman Suffrage, Vol. I, 1848–1861* (Rochester, NY: Charles Mann, 1881), 70.
4. Faye E. Dudden, *Fighting Chance: The Struggle over Woman Suffrage and Black Suffrage in Reconstruction America* (New York: Oxford University Press, 2011), 44.

5. American Equal Rights Association, *Proceedings of the First Anniversary of the American Equal Rights Association* (New York: Robert J. Johnston, 1867), 3.

6. "15th Amendment to the US Constitution," Library of Congress, https://guides.loc.gov/15th-amendment.

7. Stanton, Anthony, and Gage, eds., *History of Woman Suffrage, Vol. II, 1861–1876* (Rochester, NY: Charles Mann, 1887), 382–384, 391–392; see also Dudden, 176–182.

8. Francis J. Grimke, "The Logic of Woman Suffrage," in "Votes for Women: A Symposium by Leading Thinkers of Colored America," *Crisis*, August 1915, 178.

9. Robert H. Terrell, "Our Debt to Suffragists," in "Votes for Women," 181.

10. Anna H. Jones, "Woman Suffrage and Social Reform," in "Votes for Women," 189.

11. Josephine St. Pierre Ruffin, "Trust the Women!" in "Votes for Women," 188; Nannie Helen Burroughs, "Black Women and Reform," in "Votes for Women," 187.

12. *Anti-Suffrage Essays by Massachusetts Women* (Boston, MA: Forum Publications, 1916), 21.

13. Nebraska Association Opposed to Woman Suffrage, "Why We Do Not Approve of Woman Suffrage," Claremont Colleges Digital Library, https://ccdl.claremont.edu/digital/collection/p15831coll5/id/0; Georgia Association Opposed to Woman Suffrage Card (c. 1915), DocsTeach, National Archives, https://www.docsteach.org/documents/document/ga-opposed-woman-suffrage-card.

14. Margaret C. Robinson, "Woman Suffrage a Menace to Social Reform," *Anti-Suffrage Essays*, 99.

15. Dorothy Godfrey Wayman, "Suffrage and the Social Worker," *Anti-Suffrage Essays*, 97.

16. Alice Ranney Allen, "Woman Suffrage vs. Womanliness," *Anti-Suffrage Essays*, 77–78.

17. Tiffany Lewis, "Winning Woman Suffrage in the Masculine West: Abigail Scott Duniway's Frontier Myth," *Western Journal of Communication* 75, no. 2 (2011): 127–147.

18. Terry Desch Croy, "The Crisis: A Complete Critical Edition of Carrie Chapman Catt's 1916 Presidential Address to the National American Woman Suffrage Association," *Rhetoric Society Quarterly* 28, no. 3 (1998): 54, 56, 72.

19. Belinda A. Stillion Southard, *Militant Citizenship: Rhetorical Strategies of the National Woman's Party, 1913–1920* (College Station, TX: Texas A&M University Press, 2011), 142.

Further Reading

For a popular treatment of women's suffrage, see Elaine Weiss, *The Woman's Hour: The Great Fight to Win the Vote* (New York: Penguin, 2018). For scholarly treatments of the themes in this chapter, see Jean H. Baker, ed., *Votes for Women: The Struggle for Suffrage Revisited* (New York: Oxford University Press, 2002); Alexander Keyssar, *The Right to Vote: The Contested History of Democracy in the United States*, rev. ed.

(New York: Basic Books, 2009); Lisa Tetrault, *The Myth of Seneca Falls: Memory and the Women's Suffrage Movement, 1848–1898* (Chapel Hill, NC: University of North Carolina Press, 2014); and Marjorie Spruill Wheeler, ed., *One Woman, One Vote: Rediscovering the Women's Suffrage Movement* (Troutdale, OR: NewSage, 1995). On suffrage activism by Black women and women of color, see Cathleen D. Cahill, *Recasting the Vote: How Women of Color Transformed the Suffrage Movement* (Chapel Hill, NC: University of North Carolina Press, 2020); Ann D. Gordon, with Bettye Collier-Thomas, John H. Bracey, Arlene Voski Avakian, and Joyce Avrech Berkman, eds., *African American Women and the Vote, 1837–1965* (Amherst, MA: University of Massachusetts Press, 1997); Martha S. Jones, *All Bound Up Together: The Woman Question in African American Public Culture, 1830–1900* (Chapel Hill, NC: University of North Carolina Press, 2007); Martha S. Jones, *Vanguard: How Black Women Broke Barriers, Won the Vote, and Insisted on Equality for All* (New York: Basic Books, 2020); and Rosalyn Terborg-Penn, *African American Women in the Struggle for the Vote, 1850–1920* (Bloomington, IN: Indiana University Press, 1998). For anti-suffragism and the role of race in the suffrage movement, see Faye E. Dudden, *Fighting Chance: The Struggle over Woman Suffrage and Black Suffrage in Reconstruction America* (New York: Oxford University Press, 2011); Susan E. Marshall, *Splintered Sisterhood: Gender and Class in the Campaign against Woman Suffrage* (Madison, WI: University of Wisconsin Press, 1997); and Louise Michele Newman, *White Women's Rights: The Racial Origins of Feminism in the United States* (New York: Oxford University Press, 1999).

10

The Town Hall Meeting

Sandra M. Gustafson

The town hall meeting, or simply the town meeting, has long been celebrated as both an effective model of self-governance and a school for
democratic CITIZENSHIP extending to state, national, and even global levels.
Historically associated with the New England region, in its most fully realized form the town meeting fosters the cognitive and expressive skills
required for the coalition-building and problem-solving that are central to
democracy, while engaging participants in consequential decision-making
that directly impacts the public domain and contributes to the experience
of communal life.

The philosopher and progressive educator John Dewey, himself a product
of a New England township, reflected on the significance of the town meeting in his classic analysis of *The Public and Its Problems* (1927). According to
Dewey, "American democratic polity was developed out of genuine community life, that is, association in local and small centres where industry was
mainly agricultural and where production was carried on mainly with hand
tools. It took form when English political habits and legal institutions
worked under pioneer conditions."[1] Dewey described the national state as
the sum of these decentralized institutions, and he proceeded to consider
the stresses on democratic public life produced by territorial expansion,
industrialization, population growth, and new technologies. *The Public and
Its Problems* focuses on matters of SCALE and on the consequences of immigration after the American Civil War.

Dewey chose to skirt the relationship between racial diversity and the
town meeting ideal, but he need not have: there is a history to the idea that
the town meeting could be used to dismantle the legacy of slavery and create a racially integrated society. A leading proponent of this view was Albion

Sandra M. Gustafson, *The Town Hall Meeting* In: *Democracies in America: Keywords for the Nineteenth Century and Today.*
Edited by: D. Berton Emerson and Gregory Laski, Oxford University Press. © D. Berton Emerson and Gregory Laski 2023.
DOI: 10.1093/oso/9780198865698.003.0011

Tourgée, a Radical Republican and Civil War veteran, man of letters, and influential civil rights lawyer. Tourgée came from the Western Reserve in Ohio, a region settled by New England migrants. After the war he moved to North Carolina, seeking to "aid in transmuting an oligarchy based on race and caste into a democratic republic."[2] He was a "carpetbagger," a type of Northerner disdained by many white Southerners as an agent of a hostile regime. In North Carolina—a state long run by a white planter oligarchy—he farmed and practiced law, founded a school, and helped his African American neighbors acquire land and achieve economic self-sufficiency.

In 1868, Tourgée played a leading role in the state constitutional convention, helping to create self-governing townships throughout North Carolina.[3] He believed that the racial and class inequities of the South would only be resolved through the exercise of democratic self-rule rooted in the township system. His hopes were dashed when the Reconstruction era came to an end, following a wave of white supremacist reaction exemplified by the rise of the Ku Klux Klan. The backlash led to the restoration of oligarchy, with the governor and state legislature taking responsibility for all official appointments. Tourgée left the South forever in 1879. His political aspirations had been upended, his life had been threatened, and his lofty goals had crumbled.

A few months later he published *A Fool's Errand* (1879), which drew comparisons to Harriet Beecher Stowe's *Uncle Tom's Cabin* (1852) and achieved similarly explosive sales and international circulation. *A Fool's Errand* highlights white efforts to transform the legacy of slavery as well as white Southern reaction against the efforts of Northerners like Tourgée. The novel ends with a plea for a national system of education: "Let the Nation educate the colored man and the poor-white man *because* the Nation held them in bondage, and is responsible for their education: educate the voter *because* the Nation can not afford that he should be ignorant."[4] This emphasis on education also appears in *Bricks without Straw* (1880), Tourgée's second Reconstruction novel, which gives greater scope to the experiences of formerly enslaved people. Here Tourgée proposes the town hall meeting as a means to reconcile Black and poor white Southerners. Two of the novel's central characters, Nimbus (who uses a single name) and Eliab Hill, exemplify the freed people's aspirations toward self-sufficiency and citizenship. Together these men build a thriving African American community based on Nimbus's agricultural skill and business acumen and Hill's spiritual leadership. They are aided by Mollie Ainslee, a young white woman from Massachusetts, who sets up a school in the community's church. Trouble arises when a request to have a polling station in the settlement is rejected. Any sign of civic agency among former slaves is taken as a threat by local whites. Terrorized by the Klan, the once-thriving free Black community falls apart.

Even as the town organized by Nimbus and Hill collapses, Northern and Southern whites reconcile through the marriage of Ainslee to Hesden Le Moyne, a plantation owner with an ambivalent relationship to his heritage. It is Le Moyne who becomes the mouthpiece for "the success and glory of the great republic" (322)—which he, like Tourgée, believes to reside in the South's adoption of the New England township system and town meeting. Le Moyne champions the town meeting as a crucial institution for bringing the South into line with Northern democratic values. "I venture to say," Le Moyne asserts to a skeptical Northern congressman, "that the presence and absence of the town-meeting—the township system or its equivalent—in the North and in the South, constituted a difference not less vital and important than that of slavery itself. In fact, sir," he continues, "I sincerely believe that it is to the township system that the North owes the fact that it is not to-day as much slave territory as the South was before the war" (422). The South, by contrast, "is to-day and always has been a stranger to local self-government" (425). Southern officials are appointed by "some central power in the county" rather than by popular election (425). Le Moyne goes on to attribute New England's early abolition of slavery, high levels of education, and greater per capita wealth to the influence of the town meeting. He calls for a federally funded educational system that would alleviate lasting tensions between North and South by proving to Southern whites that the North's aim was not to dominate them but to end racial injustice. Such a system would also help create the conditions for self-government in a racially diverse community. The township system, Le Moyne argues, has proven to be "an essential concomitant of political equality" as well as "a vital element of American liberty" (423). Citing Alexis de Tocqueville, he traces the town meeting to "the little colony upon the Mayflower" (426) and makes a case for republican self-government.

When Tourgée proposed the town meeting as a solution to deep-rooted social problems, he was building on foundations dating back to colonial times. The modern republic shared with its classical ancestors a fundamental commitment to popular sovereignty, but it differed in size (the extended republic replaced the city-state), economy (commerce and later industry became more important than agriculture), and makeup (movements of people and contests for rights gradually produced a greatly diversified body of citizens). REPRESENTATION provided the formal mechanism for expanding classical republican practices of face-to-face deliberation to large territories. Instead of meeting to discuss and debate at the state and national levels, citizens sent their elected officials to deliberate for them. Continued experiences of self-governance at the local level enabled citizens to remain connected to the deliberations in these representative bodies.

As early as 1788, the Reverend William Gordon identified the town meeting as foundational to the polity then taking shape. In his four-volume *History of the Rise, Progress, and Establishment of the Independence of the United States of America*, Gordon described the structures of self-governance in the region:

> Every town is an incorporated republic. The selectmen, by their own authority, or upon the application of a certain number of townsmen, issue a warrant for the calling of a town-meeting. The warrant mentions the business to be engaged in, and no other can be legally executed. The inhabitants are warned to attend... They choose a president by the name of moderator, who regulates the proceedings of the meeting. Each individual has an equal liberty of delivering his opinion, and is not liable to be silenced or brow-beaten by a richer or greater townsman than himself. Every freeman, or freeholder, gives his own vote or not, and for or against, as he pleases; and each vote weighs equally, whether that of the highest or lowest inhabitant.[5]

Gordon's description captures the way in which republican ideals were connected with the town meeting.

This New England-based origin story for what Tocqueville termed democratic republicanism had wide purchase. In *Democracy in America* (1835, 1840), Tocqueville similarly emphasized that town meetings embodied the local tradition of self-governance that laid the groundwork for the federal republic. *Democracy in America* in turn had a substantial impact on John Stuart Mill's understanding of the role that local deliberative bodies can play in representative governments. Tocqueville also emphasized the place of voluntary associations, which extended the town meeting tradition in new directions. Mimicking the forms of state with their constitutions, debates, and parliamentary procedures, voluntary associations were organized to solve social problems through economic development (agricultural societies and working men's groups), institution-building (Bible societies and churches), moral reform and self-culture (temperance, the lyceum movement), and social reform (colonization societies and mission societies). George Bancroft's ten-volume *History of the United States* (1834–74) amplified the theory that American democracy originated with the Puritans and their town meetings. Taking up ideas that he learned during his studies in Germany, he developed a form of Romantic historiography that put the growth and spread of democracy at the heart of the history of the United States.

Historian Arthur May Mowry presented a similar understanding of the town meeting in an essay on "The Influence of John Calvin on the New England Town Meeting" (1890) that appeared in the *New England Magazine*. Explicitly building on Bancroft's claims, Mowry notes that "the town-meeting of the seventeenth century has been declared to be most precious by such men as John Stuart Mill, De Tocqueville, John Adams, Samuel Adams, and Ralph Waldo Emerson."[6] Mowry also cites the Unitarian minister George Batchelor and the British liberal historian James Bryce on what is sometimes called the "Teutonic germ theory"—that is, the theory that the town meeting descended from Germanic traditions of self-governance known as folk-motes (a view that Tourgée alludes to as well in *Bricks without Straw*). There is an Anglo-Saxonist bias behind this theory of Germanic origins, evident when Mowry writes: "What is the present condition of the town and the town-meeting? What is to be its future? The growth of the towns and the necessity of making them into cities is one cause of change. The increase of foreigners, i.e. of those who are not of Anglo-Saxon ancestry, and have not as yet imbibed fully the principles that lie back of a proper conducting of town and town-meeting, furnishes another cause of change." Mowry closes with a passage from a biography of Sam Adams: "Certainly it is well to hold the town-meeting in memory; to give it new life if possible wherever it exists, and to reproduce some semblance of it, however faint, in the regions to which it is unknown."[7]

While Mowry focuses mainly on the town meeting's past, the essay immediately preceding his article addresses its potential impact on the future. Titled "The Chautauqua as a New Factor in American Life" and written by the scholar Frederick Perry Noble, the essay employs the same language of the Teutonic germ theory as Mowry to describe what was sometimes termed "the Chautauqua phenomenon."[8] The vagueness of the phrase reflects the multifaceted nature of the Chautauqua movement. Established in 1874 as a Methodist camp meeting, Chautauqua Institution quickly expanded its mission to include interfaith dialogue as well as educational and cultural activities. It also developed a large correspondence learning program with national and international reach, and it spun off numerous regional and traveling Chautauquas that featured lectures and entertainment. A descendant of the lyceum circuit, which historian Carl Bode called "the town meeting of the mind," the Chautauqua was a major force in American life from roughly 1880 to 1920.[9]

Scholars have connected the Chautauqua phenomenon to the deliberative traditions of town meetings. They note that by bringing people together to discuss cultural events, lectures, and shared readings, the "mother Chautauqua" (as the original site was known) and its offspring helped create frames of reference and nurtured habits of civil discourse. Noble stated the impact of Chautauqua expansively:

> Chautauqua is a power in the upbuilding of that real democracy wherein character and culture shall be ranked above the wealth and pride of blood and social forms that warp even this republic . . . Bringing people together, putting the more scholarly in touch with the less scholarly, enlarging for the community its stock of ideas and common sympathies, Chautauqua leads all sorts and conditions of men into some understanding of each other. As organized feeling, Chautauqua is a social force from whose reserves humanitarian and reformatory movements may draw supplies of power.[10]

The idea of Chautauqua as "organized feeling" is suggestive in connection with three elements that characterize Noble's essay as a whole: he highlights the importance to women of the educational, cultural, and social resources that Chautauqua made available; alludes to the hope that the Chautauqua phenomenon could help defuse class conflict; and fails to mention race, despite the fact that he had a long-standing concern with racial justice. Indeed, not long after publishing this essay Noble collaborated with Albion Tourgée over the representation of Africa at the Columbian Exposition in Chicago. A central reality of the town meeting as it was promoted by the Chautauqua system is captured in Noble's silence on race.

It did not have to be this way.

In 1881, Tourgée had purchased a home in Mayville, New York, less than five miles from Chautauqua Institution. From that remote yet oddly central location, midway between New York City and the exploding metropolis of Chicago, Tourgée remained active in the cause of racial justice. He pursued that goal through a variety of cultural and legal endeavors, writing on the subject for *The Chicago Inter-Ocean* and pursuing his own literary and publishing projects, which included support for African American writers, notably Charles Chesnutt. He occasionally lectured at Chautauqua and advertised his works in its publications. Mayville remained his main residence when he agreed to represent Homer Plessy in the watershed case that became *Plessy v. Ferguson*. Despite his efforts, in its 1896 decision the Supreme Court fashioned the "separate but equal" policy that established racial segregation as the legal norm throughout the United States. Tourgée felt this failure keenly. He later moved to France, serving as US consul in Bordeaux. After his death in 1905, his body was returned to Mayville for burial.

Though Tourgée appeared at Chautauqua Institution, the absence of a strong affiliation points to the limits of the Chautauqua phenomenon. Opening avenues for women and cautiously advancing religious diversity, the Chautauqua network had an ambiguous impact on race relations. African American performers and speakers presented at the Institution and toured on the Chautauqua circuit, sometimes in exoticized roles. Even so, racial injustice was rarely if ever a major theme. Southern venues were often less than welcoming, and in some locales independent Chautauquas were established to serve the African American community. The kinds of issues that Tourgée and Noble confronted in getting respectful representation of African and African American people at the Columbian Exposition in Chicago were also issues affecting the Chautauqua system. In this regard, the Chautauqua phenomenon indexes the historic limits of the town meeting ideal as a model for American democracy.

The ambiguous legacy of the Chautauqua movement is part of a larger narrative of faltering democratic reform in the United States that includes the failure of Tourgée's political reconstruction and the social transformations addressed in Dewey's *The Public and Its Problems*. In its hopeful moments, this narrative points to two distinct lines of potential development for the town meeting: the more robust use of local governments to address racial disparities and the adaptation of the town meeting to emerging media, notably radio and television.

During the middle decades of the twentieth century, Dewey's diagnosis of the challenges besetting American democracy helped catalyze efforts to reclaim the town meeting as a political form by adapting it to the new social and media environment. Among these efforts was *America's Town Meeting of the Air*, an innovative NBC radio program that was broadcast between 1935 and 1956. The program featured experts representing opposing views who debated the issue of the week. Audience members were given an opportunity to make statements and pose questions to the experts in a format that was later used for television talk shows. Among the topics covered were labor relations and the place of communism, the war effort, the nature of democracy, and racial and religious differences. One program asked, "Should We Ignore Racial Differences?" while another explored "Public Opinion and the Town Meeting Idea."

More recently, the televised town hall became a staple of presidential politics during the 1992 election, when Bill Clinton staged several campaign events that were styled "town meetings." This format—typically involving a representative audience, a moderator, and candidates or experts who field questions—has become a familiar element of the political coverage on national television. In 1997, President Clinton took the format in a fresh direction when he pursued a "race initiative" involving town meeting-style gatherings.

More than fifteen years later, two high-profile adaptations of the televised town meeting addressed the persistent racial divide in the United States, when PBS aired town meetings in response to acts of ANTI-BLACK VIOLENCE in Ferguson, Missouri, and Charleston, South Carolina. *America after Ferguson* (2014) and *America after Charleston* (2015) used the televised town meeting format to engage public figures and typical citizens on race in the United States. Then in July 2016, President Barack Obama participated in a town meeting on the topics of race and policing, which was broadcast on ABC News. The aim of these events was to create a forum for civil dialogue on emotional issues that involve enduringly separate historical experiences and narratives.

Colleges and universities—which often aspire to serve as incubators for a racially diverse polity—have also embraced the town meeting model for addressing identity-based conflicts. These heirs of the lyceum and Chautauqua systems, and of Dewey's progressive pedagogy, test the capacity of the town meeting to stretch in ways that accommodate very different kinds of issues from the maintenance of roads and the running of public schools for which it was originally designed.

If Albion Tourgée was alive today, he would find a startling paradox: the town meeting as a media event or campus forum has become a preferred model in the United States for addressing racial identity and its attendant conflicts; and yet the institution of the town meeting remains largely confined to its home region of New England, where racial diversity is relatively thin. The gap between these two ways of enacting the town meeting ideal is profound. Traditional town meetings are places where civic learning occurs in tandem with consequential decision-making. The meeting is not mainly an arena for airing opinions, sharing experiences, and narrating histories; it is a place for enacting measures that affect the life of the community. Lacking in pragmatic capacities for achieving concrete goals, arenas such as the televised town meeting or the campus forum can make important contributions to civil discourse, even as they carry a political deficit. While they may nurture expressive and listening skills, they fail to capture important benefits of democratic participation that remain central to the historical town meeting system.

Tourgée's BELIEF in the value of town meetings as pragmatic arenas for transcending the legacy of slavery has yet to be fully tested. Could a system such as he envisioned succeed on college and university campuses? Student populations are similar to the size of towns, and for many people higher education is their first—and possibly their greatest or even their last—experience of significant racial diversity. There are three distinct challenges involved in transforming the campus town hall from a largely symbolic exercise to an institution with a capacity to enhance democratic civic life. One challenge involves the nature and extent of free speech on college campuses. What sources of information should be consulted, and what, if any, boundaries should be established around the expression of views and beliefs? How should these choices be determined and the limits enforced? A second challenge requires giving student town meetings practical impact by strengthening connections to campus governance. Students would not only discuss sensitive issues such as race; they would then also work to craft and implement university policies building on those discussions. Students are only present on campus for a handful of years, however, and this limits their ability to enact policies and their understanding of obstacles and consequences. Some mechanism for involving recent graduates seems vital to the success of this educational paradigm. A third element of such a project would involve the creation of a university-to-society pipeline for enhancing graduate involvement in civic life. Town meetings are not the norm in most areas of the United States. What alternative outlets could graduates find for their new civic skills? These considerations need further exploration to determine whether the democratic potential that Tourgée saw in the town meeting ideal can eventually be achieved and what role the system of higher education can play in its realization.

Notes

1. John Dewey, *The Public and Its Problems: An Essay in Political Inquiry*, ed. Melvin Rogers (State College, PA: Pennsylvania State University Press, 2012), 101–102.
2. Albion W. Tourgée, *Bricks without Straw: A Novel*, ed. Carolyn L. Karcher (Durham, NC: Duke University Press, 2009), 8. Hereafter cited parenthetically.
3. Tourgée had been closely involved with introducing the township system and the town meeting into North Carolina's post-war Constitution. Daniel Farbman highlights Tourgée's role in "Reconstructing Local Government," *Vanderbilt Law Review* 70, no. 2 (March 2017): 413–497.
4. Albion W. Tourgée, *A Fool's Errand*, ed. John Hope Franklin (Cambridge, MA: Belknap Press of Harvard University Press, 1961), 387.
5. William Gordon, *The History of the Rise, Progress, and Establishment, of the Independence of the United States of America: Including an Account of the Late War; and of the Thirteen Colonies, from Their Origin to that Period*, vol. 1 (London: Printed for the author, 1788), 382.
6. Arthur May Mowry, "The Influence of John Calvin on the New England Town-Meeting," *New England Magazine* 2 (1890): 109.
7. Ibid.
8. Frederick Perry Noble, "The Chautauqua as a New Factor in American Life," *New England Magazine* 2 (1890): 90–101.
9. Carl Bode, *The American Lyceum: Town Meeting of the Mind* (New York: Oxford University Press, 1956).
10. Noble, "The Chautauqua as a New Factor in American Life," 99.

Further Reading

A previous generation of scholars explored the roots of modern republican thought in classical republicanism. More recently, Philip Pettit's *Republicanism: A Theory of Freedom and Government* (Oxford: Oxford University Press, 1997) provides the most sustained consideration of its contemporary relevance, including its ties to deliberative democracy theory, on which see James Fishkin's *Democracy When the People Are Thinking: Revitalizing Our Politics Through Public Deliberation* (Oxford: Oxford University Press, 2018). For biographical information on Tourgée, see Mark Elliott, *Color-Blind Justice: Albion Tourgée and the Quest for Racial Equality from the Civil War to Plessy v. Ferguson* (New York: Oxford University Press, 2006); Carolyn L. Karcher, *A Refugee from His Race: Albion W. Tourgée and His Fight Against White Supremacy* (Chapel Hill, NC: University of North Carolina Press, 2016); and Steve Luxenberg, *Separate: The Story of Plessy v. Ferguson, and America's Journey from Slavery to Segregation* (New York: Norton, 2019). Andrew Chamberlin Rieser's *The Chautauqua Moment: Protestants, Progressives, and the Culture of Modern Liberalism, 1874–1920* (New York:

Columbia University Press, 2003) provides a valuable general history, while Charlotte Canning addresses issues of race in *The Most American Thing in America: Circuit Chautauqua as Performance* (Iowa City, IA: University of Iowa Press, 2005). Carl Bode's *The American Lyceum: Town Meeting of the Mind* (New York: Oxford University Press, 1956) is still useful. On televised town halls, see Merrill Fabry, "This is how the town hall meeting became a campaign-season staple," *Time Magazine*, January 6, 2016, http://time.com/4190233/town-hall-meeting-history, and Jill Goldsmith, " 'America After Charleston' shapes model for next-generation town hall," *Current*, October 5, 2015, http://current.org/2015/10/america-after-charleston-shapes-model-for-next-generation-town-hall.

PART III

Feelings, Attitudes, and Interdependence

We are all bound up together in one great bundle of humanity, and society cannot trample on the weakest and feeblest of its members without receiving the curse in its own soul. . . . This grand and glorious revolution which has commenced, will fail to reach its climax of success, until throughout the length and breadth of the American Republic, the nation shall be so color-blind, as to know no man by the color of his skin or the curl of his hair. It will then have no privileged class, trampling upon and outraging the unprivileged classes, but will be then one great privileged nation, whose privilege will be to produce the loftiest manhood and womanhood that humanity can attain.

Frances Ellen Watkins Harper, "We Are All Bound Up Together" (1866)[1]

For some, politics operates in a particular realm that we can dissociate from other parts of social life. We often hear, for example, that it is wise to leave politics behind when we gather for a holiday meal with extended family if we hope to get along agreeably. Although much of democracy depends upon institutional procedures and legitimate practices, there is plenty from everyday life that must be considered if we are to imagine a democratic society from its definitional foundation: the "people rule." How do we decide what is worthy of belief, what is comfortable, what is disgusting? In many ways, these decisions are highly personal, but norms and customs set strong parameters that place boundaries around our opinion-making.

When individual choices encounter common customs, we inevitably reenter the world of politics. Indeed, the back-to-back positioning of Part II and the following Part III enacts yet another central, enduring dilemma for democracy: the constant collision of the personal and the political, and the manner in which democracy promises individual freedom, agency, and self-actualization but also elevates the collective in ways that impose limits on our personal choices.[2]

Essays in this Part on BELIEF, PUBLIC OPINION, CHARISMA, PARTISAN, DISGUST, MODERATION, and COMFORT invite you to ponder a set of intertangled questions: What does it mean to live in and with others in a democracy? How do citizens express their opinions, as individuals and as one "people"? What if the desires of the people violate a commitment to justice, an end that both founding documents—the Declaration of Independence and the Constitution—seek? What does it mean to behave democratically; that is, in manners, appearance, and attitudes? Can someone violate the law but still treat others justly? In seeking to actualize democracy, should citizens work within formal institutional arrangements? In what ways must they be unruly and agitate—shirking these structures? If the people no longer believe in the systems that give democracy life, what should they believe in? One another? A higher power?

Speaking at a National Women's Rights Convention in 1866, Frances Ellen Watkins Harper addressed her audience about women's right to vote. Just over one year since the surrender of Robert E. Lee to Ulysses S. Grant at Appomattox, and just one month following the passage of the Civil Rights Act (which required Congressional override of President Andrew Johnson's veto), Harper directed the conversation well beyond the procedural mechanisms of democracy and into the experience of everyday lives, emphasizing her position as a Black woman. She doubted that voting rights for women would cure all ills. In memorable words, she illustrated her point: "You white women speak here of rights. I speak of wrongs.... Let me go to-morrow morning and take my seat in one of your street cars...and the conductor will put up his hand and stop the car rather than let me ride."[3] Voting rights for all would not be enough to bring democracy to life. Regardless of federal legislation, racial and gender discrimination would always undermine the political efficacy of all people, the reality that the people are ruling.

If Harper is right (and we think she is), then what will make democracy real? How might one carry oneself among others, present oneself to others, determine oneself in front of others, raise issues pertaining to the individual self that might rule? And how can collective rule of free and equal individuals emerge from these conditions? Harper's speech makes one ask what democracy might look like, feel like, and taste like if it were to take on material qualities that our human senses might detect. In this Part we encounter matters more emotional and spiritual than rational and deliberative, conflicts arising between insiders and outsiders. Ultimately, democracy must operate in both realms, in the debate hall and at the dinner table. The tensions explored via these keywords seek to extend our conversations about democracy into the reaches of everyday living and experience.

Notes

1. Frances Ellen Watkins Harper, *A Brighter Coming Day: A Frances Ellen Watkins Harper Reader*, ed. Frances Smith Foster (New York: Feminist Press, 1990), 217–218.
2. On this dilemma, see Danielle S. Allen, *Talking to Strangers: Anxieties of Citizenship Since Brown v. Board of Education* (Chicago, IL: University of Chicago Press, 2004).
3. Harper, *A Brighter Coming Day*, 218.

II

Belief

Christopher Castiglia

Picture a purportedly democratic government that operates for the sole purpose of increasing the wealth of the already wealthy but disguises that interest behind claims to operate benevolently for the people's good, with many citizens accepting that rhetoric as truth. Consider a Congress nominally representing their diverse constituents, holding progress in check as they filibuster and hurl accusations at one another, choosing party loyalty over the people's best interests. Entertain the idea of an entire government operating through incivility, preferring aggressive, often nasty rhetorics pitched to appeal to people's baser instincts rather than seeking to rationally deliberate and educate. Envision a government that furthers its own interest—and that of the class it benefits—by vilifying the already vulnerable, perversely positioning the most threatened people as threats to national security and well-being. Ponder a populace that feels itself incapable of effecting change because the government has grown too large, too remote, too intransigent, and too corrupt, and where the local political spheres where individuals *might* effect change seem defeated before the fact by a judiciary that, serving the same interests as the government as a whole, appears to have lost the principles of compassion and justice. Picture an electorate grown so cynical that all of the above barely needs disguising behind democratic rhetorics. Imagine a citizenry that no longer believes in democracy at all, not really.

Given how similar the imagined picture of dysfunctional democracy set forth above is to the political situation many feel we live in today, it's striking that the former dates from over a century ago. In *Messages from George Washington; or, Government and the Future Life* (1873), the renowned American spiritualist John Worth Edmonds (1799–1874) recounts his communications

Christopher Castiglia, *Belief* In: *Democracies in America: Keywords for the Nineteenth Century and Today.*
Edited by: D. Berton Emerson and Gregory Laski, Oxford University Press. © D. Berton Emerson and Gregory Laski 2023.
DOI: 10.1093/oso/9780198865698.003.0012

with the spirit of the first president during private séances in West Roxbury, Massachusetts, in August 1854. Washington chose an informed medium in Edmonds, who had served as a member of the New York Senate and a Justice on the New York Supreme Court. Having been forced from the latter position by controversies over his spiritualist activities, Edmonds was receptive to the bitter lessons concerning democracy Washington would deliver to him through the transcriber, George T. Dexter. Washington, Edmonds reports, despairs that the spirit of freedom has been "buried beneath the load of oppression and selfishness which has grown up and overwhelmed us.... There is no perversion more firmly seated in the minds of my countrymen—none more injurious—none that is calculated to be more lasting in its effects, than that which attaches to the purposes of government the idea of augmenting wealth alone."[1] Washington's spirit makes the point more forcefully when he states,

> Appealing as that idea does to the selfish propensities of the human heart, binding man in subjection by the cords of corruption, it has been cherished, fostered, and propagated by those who, clothed with power, have ever cared to exercise it rather for themselves than others; and it has been the chief instrument of maintaining the fatal fabrics of absolutism.   (10)

Even when citizens have "leaped the foul barrier and moved abroad among men with cheering hope," Washington's spirit laments, "it has often been arrested in its progress, and turned aside from its high and holy purposes by this same appeal" to greed (10). Despite opposition, greed steals "silently, yet with the tenacity of death" and winds "its way into the very body of Freedom" (11). Rather than supporting a common weal, the government exists solely for "increasing material individual wealth," becoming in the process a system "of cruelty, and of intolerance" (12). Such a government deliberates only through "sarcasm and retort" (19).

Washington's spirit finds particularly grievous the government's exercise of its scandalous greed through slavery. "I regret the government was formed with such an element in it; so full of wretchedness, misery, cruelty, debauchery, and every wickedness that can curse both the oppressor and the oppressed," the spirit told a séance held by Isaac Post. "I can no longer counsel to harmony, if at the expense of liberty. I must now advise to the right, and leave the consequences to God, for it is better to carry out the principles of goodness, of love, and of justice, even if the bodily life is forfeited; as the inspired man said, for such to die bodily is gain, and of course, to live an oppressor is loss."[2] Going even further, the spirit counsels that if an individual's conscience comes into conflict with "Government or sects," that individual must stand against the government at peril of his soul, for "what man finds to be his duty as one of a sect, state, or nation," if it goes against the will of God, will haunt them through all eternity (37).

Washington's spirit did not come simply to condemn, however. The first president had suggestions for improvement. Seeming to endorse Congressional override, even impeachment, the spirit tells Edmonds that when someone, even a leader, breaks the laws of government or of self, he must be brought "to return to its pathway and keep its action within due bounds" (24), for "lying at the foundation of their [the spirits'] system of self-government [is] that each first learn to govern himself, and he who permits himself to lose self-control," according to the spirit, forfeits "the power of interfering in the government of others until a proper frame of mind is restored to him" (22). Espousing a belief close to what we today identify as a theory of THE COMMONS, Washington's spirit recommends living in communities comprising no more than twenty to fifty people, so the government and the governed can know each other's interests intimately, and each citizen will be surrounded "with the product of their combination, which is Heaven, wherever it may chance to be" (17).

About the structural arrangements of federal government, too, Washington had clear instructions based on the successful governance of the spirit world. If there is to be a Congress in this democracy, the terms of its members should be unlimited, although the actions of representatives must be made known to the governed who may recall their representative at any time. The Congress should include the old and the young, men and women, and be led by a person whose responsibility is "to preserve order and infuse regularity and system into their deliberations." Representatives are elected "by the free, open, unbiased voices of the whole community, male and female" (18), and no election should be held by a secret ballot, "which taints your earthly institutions, and which is as frequently the instrument of deception as it is the protection against oppression." Washington's spirit insists that "the great obligation is to exercise power for the good of others, and not for selfish purposes... temper[ing] justice with mercy" (19). Responsible representatives will be known by "the extreme deference they pay each other" (20), and "he who permits himself to lose self-control is at once deprived, and that in his own consciousness, of the power of interfering in the government of others until a proper frame of mind is restored to him" (22).

Ruled by such self-government, citizens "need no judiciary to inflict punishment for error or administer reward for rectitude. Each man bears the
court in his own bosom, aided and supported at times from without, but
always open and at work within" (25). And as to the citizenry, they too have
obligations: "He reaches out no hand for it beseechingly to his rulers, but
claims it as his due—lays hold upon it as his right—the more certainly and
the more effectively that he is at length free from the material appliances
which, on earth, so often stand between virtue and its reward" (25).

I have visited so long with Washington's spirit not to endorse belief in
ghosts, but to advocate for belief in belief. In what follows, I will argue that
the effective response to a prevailing cynicism is not the reassertion of tenets
of political theory but the reinvigoration of the capacity to believe. When I
refer to "democracy" here I mean the outcome of citizen-participation in
the broadest terms, but more specifically I mean participation to bring
about social change. That kind of participation in democracy is motivated
by belief in ideals, whether it's "justice," "equality," "fairness," "compassion,"
"neighborliness," or "the common weal." Citizens who promote social
change do so because they recognize that conditions as they currently exist
fall short of the ideal they imagine *could* exist. One may work for social
justice because one recognizes the unfairness of present conditions, but one
sees those conditions as wrong because one has a prior concept of what
"right" would look like. That "right" might be found in some other social
context, but more often it exists in the realm of an ideal. Democracy in the
United States is an aggregate of such abstractions ("liberty and justice for
all"). Right from its inception, American democracy relied on an ideal,
moving citizens toward ("in order to form") a concept ("a more perfect
union") against which British rule could be conceived as TYRANNY.
     While social change relies on ideals, however, that does not mean that
ideals necessarily produce participation. The people must *believe* in those
ideals, must feel some deep connection to them. Without that conviction,
we find it all too easy to walk away from democratic ideals. Suffering from
what Washington's spirit called "that alienation in the hearts of your people"
(7), we become cynical. Cynicism is one of the greatest threats to democracy today, as it was, judging from Washington's condemnation, in the middle of the nineteenth century. And the only way to counter cynicism, I
would argue, is by cultivating habits of belief, for belief is what holds people
to the ideals that animate their participation in a democracy.

How that will happen I won't pretend to prescribe. But it is clear that reckoning with belief in a secular democracy must be one of the first steps in our theorizing (itself a kind of idealism) of "democracies in America" today. Doing so will require that we—as intellectuals and activists—take belief seriously, not as something only ignorant or superstitious people have or that is confined to a religion. We need, furthermore, to focus less on what people believe *in* (the nature of their ideals) and more on understanding, encouraging, and fostering the experience of belief itself, belief for its own sake, belief *in* belief. It is that capacity that is missing in American democracy today, and in order to take that seriously we need to stop demeaning or dismissing what we should be taking most seriously.

So here I return to the séance table, one of the easiest sites of belief to dismiss as silly. But something serious happened at those tables, something related to the problems and needs I just discussed. Participants at séance tables were doubtless sometimes thrill-seekers, wishful-thinkers, and gullible dupes. But they were also often social reformers, whose dedication to causes such as abolition and relief for the impoverished made their time precious and their outlook on society anything but naïve. (Edmonds was himself a prison reformer who co-founded the Children's Village, which opened in 1853 as a haven for New York's growing number of homeless children.) Those reformers would have experienced Washington's spirit approaching them with criticism of and alternatives to slavery, the treatment of the poor, and government illegality as an affirmation—and from the highest of authorities—that what they were fighting for, *their* ideals, were worth the risks they took trying to bring them into existence. The fact that those ideals were represented by *spirits* made their articulations restorative not only because of what was said but also because adhering to the ideals spoken from the afterlife required performances of belief, which attached reformers to these ideals more powerfully than if they had simply read them in the tracts their own societies published. Belief made ideals come alive when they came from the dead. That irony invested believers with ways to retain their convictions and to develop resilience despite repeated discouragement and defeat. In sum, believers attended séances not only to receive particular messages, or even with the assurance that those messages would come or be encouraging. Rather, they came for the experience of belief itself. Attending séances affirmed participants' capacity to believe, which was a prerequisite to adherence to any ideal that might be presented in the séance or elsewhere.

I am proposing that séances like the one held by Edmonds were not occasions worthy of our ridicule, but rather models for where we might find and how we might consider experiences of belief. The reformers sitting at that séance table *believed* in democracy in America, but their capacity to believe, like ours today, needed to be revived and reinvigorated over and over to make their participation sustainable.

One of the difficulties in discussing belief as a *secular* practice is the term's association with adherence to tenets of a particular organized religion. Belief as a democratic phenomenon, if reduced to prescribed rules or practices, would be counterproductive to what I am describing here. Rather, I mean what John Dewey, distinguishing his concept of belief from that circumscribed by organized religion, somewhat awkwardly called *religiousness*. A state of mind or disposition, religiousness "denotes nothing in the way of a specifiable entity, either institutional or as a system of beliefs," Dewey writes; "it does not denote anything that can exist by itself or that can be organized into a particular and distinctive form of existence." Rather, religiousness is a *living* experience, an everyday possibility, "not so rare and infrequent as they are commonly supposed to be."[3]

Religiousness, in Dewey's account, remains an everyday occurrence for two reasons. First, belief is the outcome of human association, between what Dewey called "miscellaneous aggregates" of citizens, laborers, neighbors, and so on. Those associations (which, for Dewey, include the natural environment) "support and deepen the sense of values which carry one through periods of darkness and despair to such an extent that they lose their usual depressive character" (16). As that claim suggests, the second feature of religiousness involves what he called values or ideals. Far from one-size-fits-all moral codes, ideals in Dewey's sense are continuous creations, being "rooted in everyday life" where they continue to animate "the processes of living" (13). Religiousness, grounded in the everyday experiences of human association, is what Dewey describes as "the organic plentitude of our being" (16), which, for Dewey, is necessary to progressive action, since "the reality of ideal ends as ideals is vouched for by their undeniable power in action" (40). Religiousness, for Dewey, involves any activity "pursued in behalf of an ideal end against obstacles and in spite of threats of personal loss because of conviction of its general and enduring value" (26).

And since ideals are everyday creations, so too are the changes they effect, which "must take place, if at all, through continued cooperative effort."

Dewey continues, "There is at least enough impulse toward justice, kindliness, and order so that if [religiousness] were mobilized for action, not expecting abrupt and complete transformation to occur, the disorder, cruelty, and oppression that exist would be reduced" (44). "It is this *active* relation between ideal and actual," Dewey boldly states, "to which I would give the name 'God'" (47). But I think we might just as reasonably give it the name "democracy." If democracy can be considered a series of values negotiated by communities of citizens who accept that those values should be negotiated and adapted to the needs of the people, if we accept that the goal of democratic values is to keep human association vital, porous, and engaged in the realization of ideals, and if we agree that democracy lives in the everyday experiences of community members and not simply the vote for representatives who assume the work of creating, maintaining, and adjudicating those ideals, we can take Dewey's description of *religiousness* as a viable definition of what, with a nod to Dewey, we might call *democraticness*.

The difficult part of Dewey's theory comes not in his belief that ideals arise from human interaction and inspire action but in his insistence that those ideals exist primarily in the realm of imagination, a word rarely heard in discussions of democratic theory because of what Dewey calls "our frequent use of the word 'imagination' to denote fantasy and doubtful reality" (40). Correcting that assumption, Dewey insists, "An ideal is not an illusion because imagination is the organ through which it is apprehended. For *all* possibilities reach us through the imagination. In a definite sense the only meaning that can be assigned the term 'imagination' is that things unrealized in fact come home to us and have power to stir us" (40). Belief, Dewey argues, "is a kind of anticipatory vision of things that are now invisible because of the limitations of our finite and erring nature" (18). Dewey likened the imaginative infusion of the *real* with the *possible* to mystical experiences, which, he notes, "occur so frequently that they may be regarded as normal manifestations that take place at certain rhythmic points in the movement of experience" (35). And without imagination, Dewey believed, there is no progressive action, since "all endeavor for the better is moved by faith in what is possible, not by adherence to the actual" (22). Although the ideals given shape by imagination are not present, then, that does not mean they are disconnected from or have no implications for the lived world, for those ideals, Dewey writes, "are made out of the hard stuff of the world of physical and social experience" (45). Imagination, in that sense, negotiates between the actual and the possible, propelling the former toward the latter.

As it did for nineteenth-century reformers, belief comprises an "allegiance to inclusive ideal ends, which imagination presents to us and to which the human will responds as worthy of controlling our desires and choices" (31).

With Dewey in mind, we can return to the Edmonds séance, why its participants attended, and why it is significant that they contacted the spirit of George Washington. Although Dewey opposed belief centered on what he called supernatural beings (deities, angels, demons, and so on), he acknowledged that, when the ideals underpinning progressive imagination are too dangerous, they may temporarily be assigned to some purportedly supernatural entity, temporarily, for a kind of safekeeping. If so, the supernatural could be considered a placeholder for belief-under-siege. If Washington's spirit was one such space, we can deduce that the democratic ideals under threat in mid-nineteenth-century America included civility, local agency, individual adherence to principles of justice, and so on. Washington also gives us a picture of the forces that made a placeholder necessary: corruption, over-large political bodies, abstraction of human association into (un)representative government, greed.

Of course, there are editorials, political tracts, satires, and a host of other forms through which we could come to the same knowledge, as citizens did at the time. So what's the value added, as it were, by belief? My answer returns to the point that between a representation of the dangers of society *as it is* and values *as they should be* is the phenomenon of belief, the affective experience that adheres participants to the values *they* share and pushes them ahead into a world closer to democracy's imaginative possibilities. To continue their work as social reformers, séance participants needed a sense both of the values of human association (justice, decency, compassion) and of an imaginative picture of the possible world that resisted complacency and gave reformers a vision to struggle for, even though that vision might be ephemeral, even impossible. Perhaps more important than how spirits confirmed what reformers believed *in*, therefore, are the ways they became the occasion for collective experiences of belief for their own sake. Between the values of human association and the will to move forward toward an ideal world was what Dewey called *religiousness* and what I am calling belief. Sitting at the séance table, participants felt themselves in the act of believing, a preceding openness to and desire for the imaginative values they were about to hear described. Belief attached people *at the core of their being*, their daily dispositions, to the possibility of imaginative possibility, of ideals not as learned abstractions but as living revelation. Without their belief, I would contend, the reformers' efforts would have been unsustainable. It was belief in an imaginative future that made their collective efforts meaningful. Those who attended séances regenerated belief, not because they were dupes, but because they were believers who, sustaining imaginative ideals for the benefit of the demos, put the spirit back in democracy.

I choose reformers as the particular focus of my argument for a reason. In reading a defense of belief as a democratic force, one might point out that, especially in the twenty-first century, belief in atrocious falsehoods has posed one of the most immediate threats to democracy, with groups such as QAnon spreading misinformation about fair elections and anti-vaxxers trying to dissuade people from receiving necessary medical precautions. One way to understand this situation is through a groundbreaking Duke University study that finds distinctions between what it calls more and less "conscientious" citizens. The latter, lacking the impulse control necessary to goal-directed behavior, engage in political discourse in order to generate chaos, while the former engage it for constructive ends. This characterization does not necessitate an already-polarizing distinction between conservatives and liberals, but rather between more or less conscientious parties on both sides of the political spectrum.[4] Belief, I would argue, can be understood in these terms. A conscientious belief would be, as it was for many antebellum reformers, a desire to reconstruct society in more fair and equitable terms, whether or not reformers were progressives (wanting forward-looking change) or conservative (wanting change through a restoration of previous, now-degraded ways of life). While my focus has been on progressive believers, like those who conjured George Washington, I hold open the possibility that what makes for a constructive or destructive belief is not the political or social affiliation of those who hold it but the degree of conscientiousness with which they believe.

I propose that, as in the 1850s, the crisis of American democracy in the twenty-first century requires a return to habits of *conscientious* belief. We have allowed historic manifestations of experiences of belief to be dismissed, vilified, forgotten, or, worst of all, manipulated by the very interests Washington warned against, leaving the language of belief to organized (and usually fundamentalist) religions, which is precisely what Dewey believed belief wasn't. So, what kinds of belief might we marshal for contemporary political discourse in order to counter the cynicism and hopelessness that threaten to paralyze the citizenry? How can progressive secularists distinguish between doctrinal belief (of which secular progressives are themselves all too capable of worshipping) and something more imaginative, hopeful, and incentivizing; something not limited to material adjustments of present injustices, urgent as those are, but alive in a discourse of ideals that might transcend or inform particular political positions? Most importantly, how can we understand how to encourage belief in democracy while examining the social and individual dynamics of belief itself? Without an understanding of belief as a way to *feel* the values their communities might imagine, we are unlikely to convince people to participate in a democracy that realizes the ideals articulated by George Washington's ghost.

To be honest, I have more questions than answers. But I propose that a good place to start would be to suspend our rationalism, especially the version that plays out as cynicism provoked by destructive dishonesty on the part of democracy's enemies, such as those self-serving, class-invested, greedy, uncivil, dishonest, and ruthless political agents Washington's spirit condemned. Instead, we should allow ourselves to talk and write about topics too long dismissed as beside-the-point and utopian diversions. If we are to turn our critiques of injustice into viable initiatives, we ourselves, as citizens and intellectuals, must become mediums for imaginative value and belief. We might put the spirit back into democracy.

Notes

1. John Worth Edmonds, *Messages from George Washington; or, Government and the Future Life* (New York, 1873), 8. Hereafter cited parenthetically.
2. Isaac Post, *Voices from the Spirit World, Being Communication from Many Spirits* (Rochester, NY: Charles H. McDonell, 1852), 36, 37. Hereafter cited parenthetically.
3. John Dewey, *A Common Faith* (1934; repr., New Haven, CT: Yale University Press, 2013), 9. Hereafter cited parenthetically.
4. M. A. Lawson and H. Kakkar, "Of Pandemics, Politics, and Personality: The Role of Conscientiousness and Political Ideology in the Sharing of Fake News," *Journal of Experimental Psychology: General* 151, no. 5 (2022): 1154–1177.

Further Reading

For nineteenth-century accounts of spiritualism, see John Worth Edmonds, *Spiritualism* (New York: Partridge & Brittan, 1855). Although spiritualism had eminent defenders, such as Edmonds, it was also attacked as mere stagecraft by many skeptics. One of the most famous debates over spiritualism's validity was between Arthur Conan Doyle (*The History of Spiritualism* [New York: Cassell & Co., 1926]), author of the Sherlock Holmes mysteries, and the famous escape artist Harry Houdini (*A Magician Among the Spirits* [New York: Harper & Brothers, 1924]). Russ Castronovo has argued that the "spiritualization" of politics detrimentally deferred citizen activism from the here and now to the hereafter in *Necro Citizenship: Death, Eroticism, and the Public Sphere in the Nineteenth-Century United States* (Durham, NC: Duke University Press, 2001). Although he turned to the study of religion later in his career, John Dewey articulated his positions about democracy in his better-known writings on education such as *Democracy and Education: An Introduction to the Philosophy of Education* (New York: Macmillan, 1916).

12

Public Opinion

Mark Schmeller

A very model ruler for today
Whose fetish, if you peel it to the core
Public opinion is no more than this
What people think that other people think

Alfred Austin, *Prince Lucifer* (1887)

If public opinion is what people think that other people think, we know much more about it than our predecessors. Today an abundance of data about what other people think can be harvested from surveys, market research, social media, search engines, and the digital devices we carry. Collectors and interpreters of that data presume that public opinion is best understood as the distribution of opinions across a population. Popular interest in polling, exemplified by the website fivethirtyeight.com, reinforces such statistical conceptions of public opinion.

But disagreements about how that information should be understood persist among both experts and laypersons. Complaints that public opinion polls are skewed or even "fake" are commonplace. Moreover, the concept of public opinion contains a variety of meanings that cannot be expressed numerically. For example, "public opinion" is commonly used to distinguish expert opinion from lay opinion. We might use "public opinion" in the course of describing a contest between competing opinions, or to identify an area of widespread agreement. When we talk about public opinion we often talk about *power*, whether the power of "the people" to effect social or political change or a force that influences, compels, or even ostracizes individuals. Public opinion can refer to the opinion of everyone, or of a

Mark Schmeller, *Public Opinion* In: *Democracies in America: Keywords for the Nineteenth Century and Today.*
Edited by: D. Berton Emerson and Gregory Laski, Oxford University Press. © D. Berton Emerson and Gregory Laski 2023.
DOI: 10.1093/oso/9780198865698.003.0013

powerful few, or of a majority that marginalizes and even silences minority voices. Statements about public opinion can be descriptive as well as normative, ranging from prosaic compilations of statistical and anecdotal evidence to poetic appeals to ideals of publicity, reason, or deliberation. We talk about public opinion using the past tense, the present tense, and—most importantly—the future tense. The question of what the people will think often supplies the element of suspense that drives our political narratives.

Public opinion, then, is more than what other people think; it is *how* we think about what other people think, and *why* we think it matters. For these reasons, it is difficult to imagine democracy without public opinion. But we should be careful not to make public opinion synonymous with democracy. People do not usually talk about public opinion with some ethical ideal of democracy in mind. In most instances, they invoke it to serve an argument about something else, and define it in a way that best suits their purpose. Nineteenth-century Americans were no different. They deployed the concept of public opinion in three broadly defined but distinct ways that variously rejected, redeemed, or attempted to reassemble enduring democratic sensibilities. Politicians were the first to invoke public opinion, using the concept to define and legitimate political parties. Reformers came next to enlist public opinion in sundry projects of moral agitation and social transformation. Last came the social scientists, who redefined public opinion as a psychosocial phenomenon generated by mass communication and propaganda.

Across the long nineteenth century, public opinion traveled from politics to reform to social science. But the route neither progressed toward nor descended from democracy: the concept of public opinion is too rife with tensions to allow for such linear narratives. By examining those tensions, we can gain a better sense of how Americans have used the concept to understand their political world—and sometimes even to change it.

In modern English, "opinion" can be individual or collective, private or public, but it was not until the late eighteenth century that Anglophones began to speak of "public opinion" as a distinct and consequential political force. Before then, common proverbs and maxims attested to the power of opinion—"the world is ruled by opinion" was especially popular—but only to teach that worldly affairs were more often governed by appearances than realities. John Locke, the seventeenth-century English philosopher of politics and psychology, railed against "opinionaetry," complaining that "the floating of other men's opinions in our brains" undermined our autonomy and made us "not one jot more knowing."[1] Eighteenth-century philosophers took a more charitable view of opinion, discovering in its subtle operations the means by which the few could rule over the many without frequent resort to violence. David Hume, for example, marveled at the ease with which ordinary people resigned their sentiments to those of their rulers, a phenomenon he observed in political societies both free and despotic.[2]

By the mid-eighteenth century, "opinion" had become synonymous with order and public tranquility. So it is no surprise that Anglo-American radicals and revolutionaries seldom employed it in their arguments. Opinion was, in many respects, an obstacle to revolution: Thomas Paine appealed to "Common Sense" as the enemy of common opinion and the conventional wisdom that unreflectively esteemed monarchy and the British constitution. Paine's fellow American revolutionaries went to great lengths to persuade the public and mold its opinions, but they did not—as French revolutionaries would—invoke public opinion as an irresistible force of critical reason.

The political ideas that informed the American Revolution did not produce a revolutionary concept of public opinion. Americans practiced a politics of public opinion without a theory of public opinion. The concept rarely factored in the debates over the federal CONSTITUTION of 1787. It appeared only ten times in *The Federalist Papers*: when James Madison recited the truism that "all government rests on opinion," it was to illustrate that "frequent appeals" to the people "would, in great measure, deprive the government of that veneration which time bestows on everything" and upset "the public tranquility."[3]

Just four years later, Madison changed his tune: "public opinion sets bounds to every free government," he wrote in a 1791 essay, "and is the real sovereign in every free one."[4] Frequent appeals to the people, previously deemed a danger to public order, were now declared essential to the sovereign rule of public opinion. What accounts for this seeming reversal? Party politics explains much of it. Madison published his anonymous essay in the *National Gazette*, a newspaper recently established to oppose President George Washington's administration. Thomas Jefferson played a major, if secret, role in establishing the paper, and urged Madison to write for it. Both men had come to believe that the administration had departed from republican principles. Likeminded politicians and voters soon joined Jefferson and Madison to form the Democratic-Republican Party.

Democratic-Republicans believed that appeals to the public were necessary because the Washington administration and its Federalist supporters had managed to "counterfeit" public opinion through their own newspapers and the pernicious influence wielded by Secretary of the Treasury Alexander Hamilton's financial system. Indeed, Hamilton and his allies often likened public opinion to public credit: the general confidence in the ability of the government to fulfill its financial obligations. For Hamilton, credit was essentially a matter of opinion, and opinion was affected by "appearances as well as realities." By ensuring that the United States would repay its creditors in full, Hamilton hoped to instill public confidence in the newly created federal government and to secure the support of its wealthiest citizens. In this view, public opinion was a public resource that enabled the state to act with energy and dispatch. If it did not exist, the prudent politician should find a way to create it.

Democratic-Republicans regarded Federalist talk of "energetic government" with keen suspicion, and the concept of public opinion helped them to explain why. Where Federalists worried over the weakness of public opinion and its enervating effect on government and the economy, Madison and his allies saw a very different danger. In 1791, Madison wrote:

> The larger a country, the less easy for its real opinion to be ascertained, and the less difficult to be counterfeited; when ascertained or presumed, the more respectable it is in the eyes of individuals. This is favorable to the authority of government. For the same reason, the more extensive a country, the more insignificant is each individual in his own eyes. This may be unfavorable to liberty.[5]

For Democratic-Republicans, Federalists' "public opinion" was a "counterfeit" manufactured by Hamilton's financial system and a moneyed "paper aristocracy." But how could authentic public opinion be ascertained? For Democratic-Republicans, the answer soon became clear: through political organization, or parties. The ability of an energetic government or a powerful cabal of private individuals (or both) to counterfeit consensus necessitated the creation of a popular party organized at the "grassroots." This rationale for party organization persisted from the 1790s to the 1830s, when Andrew Jackson combatted the Bank of the United States and its efforts to "control" public opinion.

The dialogue of parties remained consistent until the eve of the Civil War: Democrats portrayed public opinion as a means of checking "aristocratic power" through party organization, and Federalists and their Whig successors identified it with public confidence and energetic government. The purpose of this dialogue was rather limited, even conservative, in nature. It allowed politicians to draw partisan distinctions, mouth edifying but inconsequential platitudes about popular sovereignty, and police the boundaries of constitutional government. As politicians jostled to claim a public opinion favorable to their agendas, they often did so in ways that marginalized dissent, forestalled deliberation, and cemented prejudices.

If we are looking for a concept of public opinion more congenial to enduring democratic sensibilities, we are unlikely to find it in the political thought of the "Founding Fathers" and their successors. From Washington to Jackson, American politicians paid tribute to the power of public opinion, but the great leader—the *statesman*—remained at the center of their imagined political order. They recognized that ordinary men and women could, through organization and persuasion, effectively agitate public opinion on a particular issue. But politicians generally regarded such campaigns as nuisances at best, and seditious conspiracies at worst. They were most troubled by campaigns that agitated on moral questions, especially the abolition of slavery.

A different understanding of public opinion motivated nineteenth-century reformers. Few among their ranks worried over the feebleness of public opinion or the ease with which it could be counterfeited. Most feared that public opinion had become *too* powerful. Along with contemporary European writers such as John Stuart Mill and Alexis de Tocqueville, they regarded public opinion as a tyrannizing force of conformity that often stifled free thought and silenced dissent. Worse still, they worried that public opinion tended to dull the conscience and corrupt the morals of ordinary women and men. But this did not discourage reformers. Beneath the hard shell of convention, prejudice, and PARTISAN allegiance that seemed to pass for public opinion, they envisioned a deep reservoir of benevolence and moral sentiment that, when properly roused, would effect great reforms.

This belief that moral suasion and public opinion could abolish deeply ingrained and long-existing evils may appear unusually naïve. But reformers drew inspiration from some vital and venerable traditions, and were emboldened by some auspicious social and technological developments. The moral philosophers and sentimental writers of the Enlightenment taught them that humans possessed an innate moral sense, and that its proper cultivation could promote social harmony and improvement in ways that reason, law, and interest could not. Evangelical Christianity, with its emphasis on spiritual rebirth and moral perfection, inspired many reformers to believe that the moral regeneration of society was both possible and an urgent necessity. Dramatic improvements in transportation and communication—postal systems and railroads, bridges and canals, steam-powered presses, telegraphy, and mass-circulation newspapers—convinced reformers great moral revolutions could be produced through public opinion.

Americans, as the prominent reformer Wendell Phillips declared in an 1852 speech, now lived in "a reading and thinking age" in which "the accumulated common sense of the people outweighs the greatest statesman or the most influential individual." Theirs was "a government of men—and morning newspapers," and the "penny papers of New York do more to govern the country than the White House at Washington." For Phillips, the recent history of the abolitionist movement demonstrated that the statesman was no longer "an integral element in the state." Just twenty years before, the nation's greatest statesmen had "pledged themselves not to talk about slavery." They had banned abolitionist literature from the mail, imposed a gag rule on abolitionist petitions to Congress, and formed national political parties that studiously avoided the issue. But the tireless efforts of abolitionists produced a "regeneration of public opinion" that eventually forced politicians to confront slavery.[6]

While this public opinion held more democratic potential than the public opinion imagined by the founders, it posed new threats to PERSONAL LIBERTY and freedom of thought. Phillips warned that government by public opinion could be "a dangerous thing under which to live." Individuals could become timid and submissive before the seeming omnipotence of public opinion. Newspaper editors might wield more influence than statesmen or clergymen, but they remained captive to the power of opinion: an editor "might as well shoot his reader with a bullet as with a new idea." Only the agitator could remedy this malady by raising questions that people were reluctant to hear and institutions reticent to address. "Republics," Phillips insisted, "exist only on the tenure of being constantly agitated."[7]

Agitators did more to provoke than to persuade, and the provoked often answered with violence. In 1835, the American Anti-Slavery Society took advantage of cheap postage and the recently introduced Hoe single-cylinder press to send 175,000 newspapers, pamphlets, and illustrated magazines to postmasters, businesses, public offices, and homes throughout the slave states. Southerners made bonfires of the mailings, burned prominent abolitionists in effigy, and demanded that Northerners suppress abolitionism by legal or extralegal means. Northern mobs complied, targeting abolitionists and their printing presses, and Northern politicians lent crucial and enthusiastic support to bans on anti-slavery petitions and mailings. While defending such measures, Northern anti-abolitionists deplored the harmful effects of agitation in ways that echoed eighteenth-century notions of opinion as a source of public order and tranquility. For Calvin Colton, a clergyman and Whig Party propagandist, abolitionist agitation was one of many "spurious and unhealthful excitements" inflicted upon the public by a cadre of "fanatics" espousing "wild projects of reformation."[8]

Southern defenders of slavery took these conservative notions of public opinion a step further, using them to explain how a society built on the racist exploitation of enslaved persons could be both harmonious and humane. In Southern society, Virginian George Fitzhugh explained, "public opinion unites with self-interest, domestic affection, and municipal law to protect the slave." A man "who maltreats the weak and dependent" would be "universally detested." Looking North, Fitzhugh saw no comparable protections. This "laxity of public opinion" also allowed sundry fanatics to "disturb the peace of society, threaten the security of property, offend the public sense of decency, assail religion, and invoke anarchy."[9]

The radical saw a fixed public opinion as morally deadening and perpetual agitation as a necessary remedy; the conservative craved fixed opinion and detested agitation. Between these two poles lay hopes that norms of civility and practices of deliberation could cultivate MODERATION. While laudable in theory, calls for civility and deliberation often had the practical effect of silencing the less privileged and deferring popular demands for action and justice. To the frequent complaints that abolitionists should "argue more and denounce less" and "persuade more and rebuke less," an exasperated Frederick Douglass insisted that the time for argument had passed: "where all is plain there is nothing to be argued."[10] Those who still refused to recognize the humanity of enslaved humans could not be persuaded; they could only be mocked, shamed, and ostracized. A rude democracy was still a democracy; a democracy that failed to recognize the equality of all persons was no democracy at all.

Abraham Lincoln proposed a more conventional remedy: party politics. "Public opinion," in his view, was "formed relative to a property basis," and the property interests of those who owned slaves would always overwhelm the indifference of those who did not. For this reason, public opinion favored slavery, and no amount of moral suasion or condemnation would change that. But beneath public opinion lay a "collective sense of right and wrong" that Lincoln called "public sentiment." By organizing the interests of voters, the newly created Republican Party "would mold public opinion to the fact" that slavery was wrong, and halt its extension. Public opinion would be brought into line with public sentiment, and Americans could once again "rest in the belief" that slavery was on course toward its "ultimate extinction."[11]

The success of Lincoln and his party in the election of 1860 failed to produce the promised soothing of the public mind. The resulting Civil War had little direct effect on the way Americans thought about public opinion. But in the half-century following the war, new concerns supplanted antebellum preoccupations with agitation and order. The idealism of the reformer gave way to the "realism" of the social scientist: the purported complexity of an industrializing and modernizing society encouraged an ascendant class of professionals and experts to bemoan the inability of the average citizen to comprehend public affairs. Politicians continued to invoke public opinion, and reformers still aimed to agitate it, but experts increasingly spoke of public opinion as a *problem* that neither political organization nor moral awakening could solve.

The problem began with newspapers. Improvements in printing and news-gathering, expanding circulation, and growing advertising revenues allowed the postwar press to emerge as a power in its own right—a "fourth estate." Editors and publishers defended their newspapers from political and legal challenges by emphasizing their custodianship over public opinion. Even critics of the newspaper press such as the influential journalist E. L. Godkin agreed that the "formation of public opinion" had been "left entirely to the press." Statesmen and clergymen, authors and educators, might still be heard, but the press appeared to command nearly constant and undivided public attention. Godkin also believed that "democratic public opinion in the modern world" was driven "as never before by economic, rather than religious, moral, or political considerations."[12] Arguments over tariffs, currency, corporations, trusts, and "the labor question" dominated late-nineteenth-century public discourse, and the economic and legal complexities of these issues amplified differences between the opinions of educated experts and those of untutored laypersons. For critics sympathetic to the former, such issues vividly exposed the mendacity of politicians, the venality of the press, the mean selfishness of the voter, and the futility of public discussion.

Progressive reformers and "muckraking" journalists roused public opinion with impressive compilations of facts and affecting stories of corruption and exploitation. But their professed faith in public opinion often mingled with sighs of despair over the gullibility and indifference of the public. Exposing political corruption, as Lincoln Steffens lamented in his *The Shame of the Cities* (1904), did nothing to stop it. The sighs turned to shouts in the aftermath of the Great War. The disturbing success of wartime propaganda—the ease with which governments and news media incited mass hatred and circulated falsehoods—led some to conclude that informed public opinion was a pipe dream. The press could not, as the political pundit Walter Lippmann asserted, "furnish from one edition to the next the amount of knowledge which the democratic theory of public opinion demands."[13] If reformers had seen public opinion as an instrument to expanding democracy, Lippmann saw public opinion as a danger to the continued existence of democracy. The problems of modern society demanded technical expertise, not partisan or moral agitation.

Social scientists and literary scholars saw a different path forward. The power of propaganda, they believed, lay in its use of evocative fictions, myths, and symbols. "Public opinion" was one such fiction, and critical analysis of the rhetorical strategies used to craft it could rob propagandists and political demagogues of their power. Rigorous empirical research into mass communications and opinion promised to do the same. For example, in his influential *The Process of Government* (1908), the political scientist Arthur Bentley promised to demystify public opinion by breaking it down into its social components, and found nothing more than a "differentiated group activity."[14] This desire to demystify and disaggregate drove the development of public opinion survey research in the mid-twentieth century. By collecting randomly selected individual opinions, pollsters such as George Gallup promised to discover a genuine public opinion that could guide experts and "air the smoke-filled rooms" of governments, corporate boards, and political parties. Critics of polling soon pointed out that the "public opinion" measured by polls did not involve a "public" at all; pollsters had merely replaced a rhetorical fiction with a statistical fiction. And the omnipresence of polls in contemporary life has made a parody of the reformist intentions of early opinion researchers. Political campaigns, special-interest lobbies, and corporations conduct and release polls for publicity purposes because they know that representations of public opinion can influence public opinion. Public opinion, in this respect, is what people think that other people think.

There is no model of "real" public opinion from some bygone era that we may hold up against the public opinion presented in polls today. Public opinion is a fiction, but it is also indispensable to modern politics. Understanding its history can help us to treat claims about public opinion with healthy skepticism, and to appreciate its complicated relationship to democracy in the past and present.

Notes

1. John Locke, *An Essay Concerning Human Understanding* (1689), ed. Peter Nidditch (Oxford: Oxford University Press, 1975), 101.
2. David Hume, "On the First Principles of Government" (1741), in Eugene Miller, ed., *Essays, Moral, Political, and Literary* (Indianapolis, IN: Liberty Fund, 1987), 32.
3. [James Madison], *Federalist* 49, in *The Federalist Papers*, ed. Clinton Rossiter (New York: Signet, 1961), 314–315.
4. [James Madison], "Public Opinion," *National Gazette*, December 19, 1791.
5. [James Madison], "Public Opinion," *National Gazette*, November 19, 1791.
6. Wendell Phillips, "Public Opinion" (1852), in Phillips, *Speeches, Lectures, and Writings* (Boston, MA: Lee and Shepherd, 1884), 38–39.
7. Ibid., 52–53.
8. A Protestant (Colton), *Protestant Jesuitism* (New York: Harper and Brothers, 1836), 204.
9. George Fitzhugh, *Cannibals All!* (1856), ed. C. Vann Woodward (Cambridge, MA: Harvard University Press, 1988), 131, 249.
10. Frederick Douglass, "What to the Slave is the Fourth of July?" (1852), in *The Frederick Douglass Papers*, ed. John Blassingame (New Haven, CT: Yale University Press), 2:370–371.
11. Abraham Lincoln, "Speech at Hartford, Connecticut" (1860), in Roy Basler, ed., *Collected Works of Abraham Lincoln* (New Brunswick, NJ: Rutgers University Press, 1953), 4:3–6; Abraham Lincoln, "Speech at Ottawa" (1858), in Paul M. Angle, ed., *The Complete Lincoln-Douglas Debates* (Chicago, IL: University of Chicago Press, 1991), 2:120.
12. E. L. Godkin, "Opinion-Moulding," *The Nation*, August 12, 1869, 126; Godkin, *Unforeseen Tendencies of Democracy* (New York: Houghton, Mifflin, and Company, 1898), 222.

152   DEMOCRACIES IN AMERICA

13. Walter Lippmann, *Public Opinion* (New York: Harcourt, Brace, and Company, 1922), 228.
14. Arthur Bentley, *The Process of Government: A Study of Social Pressures* (Chicago, IL: University of Chicago Press, 1908), 238–239.

Further Reading

Much of the scholarship on the history of public opinion is indebted to Jürgen Habermas, *The Structural Transformation of the Public Sphere* (Cambridge, MA: MIT Press, 1962). On the history of public opinion in America, see Mark Schmeller, *Invisible Sovereign: Imagining Public Opinion from Revolution to Reconstruction* (Baltimore, MD: Johns Hopkins University Press, 2016). Richard Brown, *The Strength of a People: The Idea of an Informed Citizenry in America, 1650–1870* (Chapel Hill, NC: University of North Carolina Press, 1997) helpfully expands on some of the themes discussed above. Colleen Sheehan, *James Madison and the Spirit of American Government* (New York: Cambridge University Press, 2009) analyzes the role of public opinion in the politics of the 1790s. Insightful discussions of agitation and reform appear in Kimberly Smith, *The Dominion of Voice: Riot, Reason, and Romance in Antebellum Politics* (Lawrence, KS: University of Kansas Press, 1999) and Manisha Sinha, *The Slave's Cause: A History of Abolition* (New Haven, CT: Yale University Press, 2016). On European liberals and public opinion, see Alan Kahan, *Aristocratic Liberalism: The Social and Political Thought of Jacob Burckhardt, John Stuart Mill, and Alexis de Tocqueville* (New York: Oxford University Press, 1992). On social science and the development of opinion polling, see Sarah Igo, *The Averaged American: Surveys, Citizens, and the Making of a Mass Public* (Cambridge, MA: Harvard University Press, 2008).

I3

Charisma

Vincent Lloyd

What form does political authority take in a democracy? If we must choose between the three options presented by the influential social theorist Max Weber in the early years of the twentieth century, we may be left stumped. Certainly democracy does not rely on traditional authority, deferring to people and practices of years gone by. While democracy may, for pragmatic reasons, employ bureaucracy and formalized processes for governance, locating authority in bureaucracy runs counter to core democratic commitments. Weber's final category in his typology of authority—charisma—at first seems the least aligned with democratic values. Charismatic authority entails deference to individuals with extraordinary abilities, seemingly gifted from beyond the world. Here we have rule of the exceptional one rather than rule of the mundane many.[1] But in fact charisma has close, though ambivalent, affinities with democracy, and particularly with American democracy. Think William Jennings Bryan or Teddy Roosevelt, for example.

The political import of charisma is characterized by paradox. On one hand, charisma is radically authoritarian. One individual receives deference, unmediated by history or institutional structures. On the other hand, charisma is radically democratic—perhaps frighteningly democratic. The people collectively decide to ignore precedent, to overturn legal and institutional structures, and to instantiate a new form of governance. Certainly the extraordinary abilities of a charismatic leader not only make possible but give shape to that new form of governance, but the charismatic leader only attracts followers if their abilities resonate with the desires of the people. The people's desires are to some extent inchoate and dynamic, of course, but a successful charismatic leader appeals to deep commitments and values,

Vincent Lloyd, *Charisma* In: *Democracies in America: Keywords for the Nineteenth Century and Today.*
Edited by: D. Berton Emerson and Gregory Laski, Oxford University Press. © D. Berton Emerson and Gregory Laski 2023.
DOI: 10.1093/oso/9780198865698.003.0014

articulating those commitments and values in a way that is recognizable to the people even if the people could not previously articulate them on their own. Yet a charismatic leader could also give shape to the people's desires in a way that advances their own interests, their claims only having a superficial resemblance to the people's commitments and values.

Concretely, charisma is found when democratic cultures are at their worst and when they are at their best: in populist, authoritarian leaders and in transformative social movements such as abolitionism and women's suffrage. Hitler and Idi Amin are charismatic, but so are Frederick Douglass and Emma Goldman. In the former cases, the charismatic leader shapes the desires of the people to further their personal interests; in the latter cases, the charismatic leader catalyzes a social movement by helping auditors break free of the authority of tradition and law. Those who hear Douglass, Goldman, or others respond with orientations toward justice and commitment to working collectively to advance justice. The charisma found in social movements—*animating* social movements—is contagious. Listeners catch the spirit, so to speak, enter the movement, and become leaders themselves. Of course, when we are looking beyond ideal types isolated in laboratory conditions, in the rich complexities of the world, charisma's two tendencies intermingle, with talented social movement leaders acquiring some authoritarian tendencies and authoritarian leaders unwittingly activating some anti-authoritarian tendencies in their listeners.

Another deep paradox of charisma is that it is at once a highly individual phenomenon, the exceptional abilities of one, and necessarily a collective phenomenon, with the existence of an audience among its conditions of possibility. Charismatic authority works when encountering it means encountering difference and similarity at once, someone who is like you in some ways but also dramatically unlike you, because of some extraordinary gift. This is closely related to a paradox of democratic politics, and particularly American democratic politics: appreciating individuality is essential but so is collective decision-making. Unlike other political cultures, American democratic culture lauds attending to the depths of the self, encouraging the rich plurality entailed in "the people" to flourish. At the same time, waves of collective feeling and action, "the people" in motion together, are also crucial features of American democratic culture.

The paradoxes associated with charisma produce less tension when we appreciate that charisma is a concept with two distinct histories, one very long, in Christian theology, and the other very short, as Weber's terminology migrated into popular discourse. The "gifts of the spirit" found in early Christian communities, depicted in the New Testament, are *charismata*: speaking in tongues, working miracles, and predicting the future, among others. More generally, charisma in theological contexts suggests the Holy Spirit filling humans with extraordinary abilities, the human channeling the divine and thus becoming a pointer to the true, the good, and the beautiful. Weber's sociological definition of charisma was inspired by his theologian colleagues but bracketed questions of value, instead focusing on the structure of authority that follows from an individual being perceived as having superhuman gifts.

When the term "charisma" circulates broadly and loosely today, its theological meaning and the accompanying sense that charisma is necessarily oriented to goodness, truth, and beauty is often forgotten. Christian theologians are well practiced at discerning between humans elevating themselves to the position of the divine, idolatry, and humans who are filled with the divine, filled with the Spirit. But if we are to draw on Christian theologians to understand charisma, it might seem as if charisma becomes incompatible with democracy. It becomes, instead, a practice associated with theocracy, overturning worldly laws and secular traditions in order to establish the rule of God through God's representatives on earth. But this is not the case if we associate charisma with a humanism founded on the notion that there is some aspect of each human being that transcends any worldly description—*who* I am beyond *what* I am. In that case, a charismatic individual simply displays the essence of their humanity, which appears extraordinary and superhuman because it exceeds the world. Auditors and viewers are attracted to charismatic individuals because seeing the extraordinary displayed in the ordinary reminds them of their own humanity—that they themselves are also more than the world's perception of them. With this realization, they are primed to organize against injustice, against all those worldly forces of domination that systematically suppress their humanity. Christians may want to add that the world-transcending nature of the human comes about because the human images the divine, but that claim is a contingent rather than necessary part of this account of charisma.

Understanding charisma in this way makes it easier to distinguish charisma from related concepts such as slickness and celebrity. Today, the term "charisma" is used loosely, including in a more or less pejorative sense for those who are good at attracting and holding an audience's attention. Indeed, there is a genre of self-help book that purports to offer its readers practical lessons on becoming more charismatic, by which these books mean becoming more authoritative by attracting and holding an audience's attention. But a slick performance, whether practiced or natural, conceals one's humanity with an overwrought mask rather than revealing it; charisma, in its most democratic sense, functions by revealing one's humanity, puzzlingly ordinary and extraordinary at once. Similarly, a celebrity may be venerated and treated as authoritative (at least as a consumer product adviser), but this is because of the role the celebrity occupies rather than because of some extraordinary gift. The charisma associated with a role, such as that of a CEO, a university president, or a bishop, is a particularly undemocratic form of charisma; indeed, it is more closely related to traditional or rational-bureaucratic authority than to charismatic authority.

Charisma is not a uniquely American phenomenon, but it is a typically American phenomenon. Charisma involves turning away from dusty authorities and encrusted procedures. It surprises. It brings into the world something unexpected, beyond what was thought to be the horizon of possibility. But charisma, at least in its most democratic sense, does not mean bringing down newly discovered truths from on high. Rather, it involves attending to the expansiveness of souls, in others and in ourselves. Charisma pairs suspicion of established authority with appreciation for individuality, too often crushed by authority. These two moments of charisma, suspicion and appreciation, are honed through collective discernment, a shared project—a national project.

As a phenomenon, something like charisma may be found across time and place, but the historian Jeremy C. Young has aptly labeled the nineteenth century in the United States the "age of charisma." At the time, the word "charisma" was rarely used, and when it was, it was found in Christian contexts. But technology and social conditions conspired during this period to produce numerous icons of charisma. Newspapers and railroads made it possible to establish sustainable lecture circuits. Listening to a charismatic orator involved an important element of entertainment and spectacle as well as information, argument, and motivation. The Second Great Awakening in the early decades of the century disseminated a repertoire of charismatic practices in the older, theological sense: Spirit-filled preachers prompting the faithful, or newly faithful, to speak in tongues and exhibit other extraordinary behaviors as they, too, became filled with the Spirit. While social movements in the later years of the nineteenth century (including the freethought movement, led by that towering figure of charisma Robert Ingersoll) did not foreground the workings of the Spirit, the charismatic scenario played out over and over again throughout the nation with new actors and new themes. Charisma traveled, but it also settled. In utopian community-making, Americans sought to infuse the ordinary with the extraordinary. There was a sense in which this describes every village and city, and the nation as a whole: instantiating the Puritans' aspirations to charity-filled, Spirit-filled community.

If charisma at its most democratic fits with a vision of humanism founded on humanity's excess, then inwardness—that within ourselves which is indescribable by the world—is at the heart of charisma. This is the diagnosis offered by cultural critic Philip Rieff, who draws less on Max Weber than on Søren Kierkegaard to conjure images of charisma at its noblest. Unfortunately, Rieff asserts, modernity quashes inwardness, leaving us only with what he labels "spray-on charisma."[2] We might extend Rieff's argument by finding in the nineteenth-century American novel a precipitate of the struggle between charisma and the forces of modernity—the drives to exhaustively explain, map, and control—that reject it. In particular, the novel showcases inwardness, and it attracts readers in the same way that the lecture circuit attracted auditors: with the promise of access to something extraordinary concealed within the ordinary that captures the attention and solicits from the reader or auditor a response from the soul, as it were. Put another way, in the context of long-nineteenth-century America, where ideologies of racial, class, gender, and settler-colonial domination were very much part of the culture, could charisma still hold the democratic promise of catalyzing anti-authoritarian movements?

To explore this question, and to probe the deformations of charisma that it implies, let us turn to an extraordinary novel: Herman Melville's *The Confidence Man*. Appearing in 1857, Melville's last published novel is barely recognizable as a novel. It does not have a single protagonist who grows and changes over time. Rather, it consists of a series of encounters between passengers on a boat and a confidence man (what today we would call a "con-man"). Taking on different appearances, this figure engages in dialogues with other passengers; these dialogues have as their primary aim the extraction of money, but they also open into extensive philosophical, religious, political, and historical ruminations.

On its surface, *The Confidence Man* is about persuasion. The shape-shifting protagonist attempts to elicit commitment, materialized in hard currency, from his fellow passengers. While he at times employs tools of the huckster in order to secure funds from others, his primary modus operandi is rather different. The novel takes place on a boat unsubtly named the *Fidèle*, faithful, and the protagonist leverages the self-image of his fellow passengers as creatures of faith. This faith is only incidentally Christian in the novel's depiction. It is really a primal faith in fellow humans, a belief held, despite some evidence that puts the belief in DOUBT, that people really are who they say they are. In a typical encounter, the confidence man asks for money, is rebuffed, accuses his interlocutor of lacking faith, and eventually secures the money.

The *Fidèle* is full of strangers displaying the varieties of humankind in America: "Natives of all sorts, and foreigners; men of business and men of pleasure; parlor men and backwoodsmen; farm-hunters and fame-hunters; heiress-hunters, gold-hunters, buffalo-hunters, bee-hunters, happiness-hunters, truth-hunters, and still keener hunters after all these hunters."[3] People of all nationalities mingle, but they share a desire for the hunt; they share a desire for something, some object in the world or beyond. What is expected of such a motley crew as they encounter each other? Are they to suspect one another, or are they to offer each other the benefit of the doubt, in charity? Or are they to seek out some path of prudence in between?

Just as an orator on the lecture circuit (or novelist) speaks to such a diverse audience, channeling audience members' desires either to complement their own or to aim beyond the world, beyond the options on the table, in the direction of justice, Melville's confidence man channels the varied desires he encounters into a particular form. The passengers on the *Fidèle* want to have confidence, to have faith in their fellows. This desire takes the form, repeatedly, of "philanthropy." Each passenger wants to love rightly, to be a lover of humankind. Indeed, the novel opens with the confidence man apparently deaf and dumb, writing on a chalkboard affirmations of charity: "Charity thinketh no evil," "Charity sufferith long, and is kind," "Charity believeth all things," "Charity never faileth" (3, 4).

In one sense, the confidence man is channeling an audience's desires in the direction of values that transcend the material, that push beyond the horizon of the world. What they really want, the word on the confidence man's chalkboard that is never erased, is "charity"—love that is inextricably coupled with faith. In a sense, this is a nostalgic desire. They now live in a pluralistic world, one that is full of strangers on the move, and yet they wish they could just love and have faith in each other as in the (imagined) days of yore. The confidence man exploits this ambivalence and longing, offering stories for the passengers to believe that put them at ease in trusting a stranger. This is the essence of charisma: telling stories that put an audience at ease deferring to the orator's authority. Amid uncertainty and instability, the charismatic speaker uses their extraordinary qualities to elicit commitment.

At the most basic level, Melville draws attention to the dangers of charisma, the risks that accompany deferring to another person as an authority. In nineteenth-century America, this risk was particularly salient. With a suspicion of tradition and legalism, and with a social and economic context that put varied people in close contact with each other, charisma found a natural home. And yet, then as now, charisma always brings with it the risk of authoritarianism, the possibility that a charismatic leader will channel desires to help their own self-interest. This sort of charisma captures and holds the attention of a listener, directing them to certain worldly actions that will really benefit the charismatic speaker (quite straightforwardly in *The Confidence Man*: handing over money). In contrast, charisma at its most democratic infects a listener, and together charismatic speaker and listener interrogate illegitimate worldly authorities while imagining what could be beyond the current horizon of possibility.

It is too simple to see the risk of charisma as enriching the charismatic leader. Ultimately the leader is of only incidental significance. Charisma's real risk is that, at its worst, it congeals oppressive structures rather than organizing social movements that challenge domination. The charismatic leader naturalizes racism, sexism, xenophobia, and homophobia, for example—or, as Kathryn Lofton demonstrates in her study of the extraordinary contemporary charismatic Oprah Winfrey, capitalism.[4] In such cases, charisma, celebrity, and slickness slide into each other. The apparent charisma of those who already occupy roles of authority functions to advance the status quo, the toxic values that are entangled with the systems that enable and perpetuate celebrity culture. The charismatic figure stokes an audience's desire for what it thinks it wants rather than provoking an audience to interrogate its own desires, hence the appearance of slickness.

Midway through *The Confidence Man* Melville offers a long philosophical meditation on the "metaphysics of Indian-hating" that probes this dynamic (201–212). This text is part of one of the protagonist's dialogues with his fellow passengers, but it is also a meditation on the dark underside of faithfulness, extending far beyond the personal enrichment of a huckster. In Indian-hating we have precisely the opposite of confidence and love: the

Indian represents infidelity and elicits hate. Even after years of apparent domestication, the Indian is still liable to break the promises of civilization and wildly attack the white man—so says Melville's narrative within a narrative. Because the Indian can never be trusted, the fitting response for the loving man, for the Christian man, is pure hatred directed at the Indian. To deny faithfulness is to deny humanity, rendering one unworthy of love. Not all men come to this realization, the narrative concludes. Indian-haters are likely to have had their parents or other relatives killed by Indian trickery. While the Indian's infidelity threatens the basis of community, the Indian's murderous duplicity literally disrupts inheritance. Together, this represents the origins of the "metaphysics" that is itself a faith, "not wholly without the efficacy of a devout sentiment" (135). The faith that circulates among the community of settlers, of white people, also includes on its backside a faith-like commitment to exclude the Indian from that community. Charismatic performance that seems to be securing authority for personal pecuniary gains is actually entangled in an ecology of authority that legitimates genocide and its afterlives.

The microcosm of charismatic authority that Melville dramatizes in *The Confidence Man* might be read as existing in an environment of uncertainty, but more precisely it exists in an environment of incalculability. It is suffused with excess and deficiency. This is the world of charisma, for charisma names a gift, seemingly from the divine, clearly from beyond the world. The confidence man plays in this economy: he elicits philanthropy, charity, and affect (and material resources) unrequired by rules, overflowing from the giver in the direction of those around them. American superabundance. The confidence man's peculiarity, the sense that he possesses the extraordinary in the ordinary, solicits a response that is over the top. Indeed, whenever the confidence man's interlocutors slip into a framework of exchange and obligation, he pulls away, with the result that they reframe their motivation in terms of excess (e.g., "I give away money, but never loan it"). This is the spirit of American democracy, a political culture satisfied not with choosing between the options on the table or calculating risks and rewards, but with relishing new ways of imagining life together—which may, Melville warns, really be a scam.

Critics of *The Confidence Man* often note the shifting economic mode that the novel depicts. It is a world where money is an abstraction, recorded in ledgers and stock certificates rather than concretized in land or material possessions. It is also, at its heart, an economy of debt. Just as the confidence man elicits charity, money that overflows, he also elicits the opposite: loans, money that pulls. Here is the meaning of BELIEF—*credo*, the root of credit. To have faith in another means to form relationships that are not based on calculation, that involve the pull of obligation, credit. Debt is born of love: in a world, or boat, full of those who love each other, debts flow freely. But then we have to remember that the confidence man is a con-man: the wisdom he disseminates deceives. Another risk of charisma: the charismatic leader seems to be obliged to you, to owe you a debt. You have opened yourself to them, deferred to the authority of charisma, and through that deference you have an investment in the charismatic leader—you and those around you who also defer. But this obligation is hollow. You will not be enlarged; you will lose your investment.

At the end of the day, however, no one is particularly upset by the confidence man. As one interlocutor describes him, he is a "man-charmer," suggesting the powers of hypnosis, but he is also "quite an original" (332). As another character puts it, "a philanthropist is necessarily an enthusiast" (57). In an environment where relationships are characterized by excess and deficiency, not reciprocity, being an original counts for a whole lot. And this is the landscape of American democracy. It is full of singular performances, giving it vitality. These performances solicit deference. Even more, they call for faith and love. Concealed in these seemingly extraordinary performances, and powered by them, are forms of systemic domination. Put another way, free of the domination of past generations and the domination of legalism and rationalism, American democratic culture confronts domination in the realm of charisma—and with the resources of charisma.

The lesson of Melville's novel is about the virtues of spectatorship. Given the context in which we live, we are tasked with witnessing performance after performance of charisma. Some of these pull toward a richer, more vibrant democratic culture; others pull in the opposite direction, sometimes frighteningly. Democratic and authoritarian charisma intermingle in the world; they can never be sorted neatly. What we can do is focus our attention on whether charisma is pulling us beyond the world or binding us to the world. The media through which charisma operates today are different from those of the nineteenth century—Twitter and Instagram charisma look different than microphone, television, or novel charisma—but the mechanism at work persists, together with its risks and rewards, its promise of grace and its counterfeit debts.

Notes

1. Max Weber, *On Charisma and Institution Building* (Chicago, IL: University of Chicago Press, 1968), chapter 6.
2. Philip Rieff, *Charisma: The Gift of Grace, and How It Has Been Taken Away from Us* (New York: Pantheon, 2007).
3. Herman Melville, *The Confidence-Man: His Masquerade* (London: Longman, Brown, 1857), 9. Hereafter cited parenthetically.
4. Kathryn Lofton, *Oprah: The Gospel of an Icon* (Berkeley, CA: University of California Press, 2011).

Further Reading

Some of Max Weber's agenda-setting writings on charisma are collected in *On Charisma and Institution Building* (Chicago, IL: University of Chicago Press, 1968); see also *Charisma and Disenchantment* (New York: New York Review of Books, 2019). For a discussion of the theological background of Weber's scholarship, see David Norman Smith, "Faith, Reason, and Charisma: Rudolf Sohm, Max Weber, and the Theology of Grace," *Sociological Inquiry* 68, no. 1 (1998): 32–60. Weber's reflections are brought into conversation with contemporary democratic theory by Jean-Claude Monod in *Qu'est-ce qu'un chef en démocratie? Politiques du charisme* (Paris: Éditions Points, 2017).

Jeremy C. Young carefully studies nineteenth- and early-twentieth-century archival material to reconstruct the culture of charisma in *The Age of Charisma: Leaders, Followers, and Emotions in American Society, 1870–1940* (New York: Cambridge University Press, 2017). Young's study is usefully contrasted with Sharon Marcus's study of celebrity during a similar period: *The Drama of Celebrity* (Princeton, NJ: Princeton University Press, 2019). Moving away from the nineteenth century, Erica Edwards offers a very smart study of how charisma is entangled with patriarchy and homophobia in Black culture, and the way Black women writers responded; see *Charisma and the Fictions of Black Leadership* (Minneapolis, MN: University of Minnesota Press, 2012). My own argument about democratic and authoritarian charisma is more fully developed, in dialogue with twentieth-century American literature, in *In Defense of Charisma* (New York: Columbia University Press, 2018).

14

Partisan

John Funchion

As part of its series of Gamemaster strategy games, toy manufacturer Milton Bradley released the 1986 board game Fortress America: The United States Under Attack. Saturated with Cold War paranoia, the game operates on the premise that the Soviet Union has shifted the global balance of power in its favor after discovering the United States has developed a secret Star Wars laser defense system. Under direction from the Kremlin, global military forces invade the United States from the east and west coasts and from the southern border. Beginning the game with a diminished national defense budget, the US player thus must wage a war on three fronts with limited conventional military resources, giving the opposing players an asymmetrical advantage at the start of gameplay. The US player's only hope is a deck of "Partisan Cards" that provide reinforcements in the form of partisans, or local citizen militias, that have constituted themselves to protect their own land. As the game progresses, more of these units appear behind enemy lines to create insurgent havoc for the invading forces. With special dice bonuses tied to defending their particular localities, partisans rather than the regular military grant the US player the best chance of securing victory with "the advantage of surprise attacks against invaders!"[1]

Clearly speaking to Reagan-era fears associated with military superiority and Soviet influence, Fortress America also taps into a long-held American infatuation with the partisan or guerrilla fighter. From the mythology surrounding the Minutemen to the spread of Stand Your Ground laws, many Americans imagine they must own firearms because they alone will be capable of defending their property against an invading force or despotic government. The idea that ordinary Americans with firearms, not the uniformed military, serve as the nation's real defenders was similarly dramatized

John Funchion, *Partisan* In: *Democracies in America: Keywords for the Nineteenth Century and Today.*
Edited by: D. Berton Emerson and Gregory Laski, Oxford University Press. © D. Berton Emerson and Gregory Laski 2023.
DOI: 10.1093/oso/9780198865698.003.0015

in John Milius's film *Red Dawn* (1984), featuring a band of high school students who become partisans to terrorize Latin American communist occupiers in Colorado. Like the Milton Bradley game, *Red Dawn* celebrates a political subject whose sovereignty resides with the bullet, not the ballot.

Today, by contrast, when someone uses the phrase *partisan politics*, it calls to mind a different but more familiar notion linked to political polarization and factionalism: "an adherent or proponent of a party, cause, person, etc." Current dictionaries still provide the military definition, "a member of a small body of light or irregular troops operating independently and engaging in surprise attacks," but sometimes flag this second meaning somewhat comfortingly as *rare* or *historical*.[2] Yet a survey of nineteenth-century dictionaries, military tracts, government treatises, and literary materials reveals that the two definitions of "partisan" share a deeply troubling common etymological lineage and language. Not everyone who takes up arms in defense of one's land, family, or freedom gets to claim the partisan mantle. Anyone can be a brigand, an outlaw, or even a guerrilla warrior. But the partisan fantasy in the United States has historically been tied to one subject: the white, propertied man and his defense of white supremacy.

Historical definitions of "partisan" all exhibit undercurrents of violence. Tracing the term back to a Middle French word with the same spelling, one late-nineteenth-century dictionary notes "partisan" emerges from the Latin *partiri*, "to divide, to part" into a "party, a faction," so that one becomes "violently attached to party or interest" or "engaged in desultory warfare."[3] Others echo these characterizations when they describe the partisan as "one who is violently and passionately devoted to a party or interest," with the military entry also identifying this individual as "a member of a party" skilled at "obtaining intelligence, intercepting convoys, or otherwise annoying an enemy."[4] Those who wrote about factionalism employ similar language. Notably, James Madison opens *Federalist* 10, one of the most well-known American meditations on the dangers posed by partisanship, by referencing the "violence of faction." As Madison feared, the "public good is disregarded in the conflicts of rival parties" precisely when interests become intractable because partisans wage war upon their adversaries.[5] The many political novels that appeared a century later, after the second founding of the Civil War and Reconstruction, returned to these concerns. In *Democracy* (1880), for instance, Henry Adams casts the character Senator Silas P. Ratcliffe's "doctrine of party allegiance" as one requiring him to "abdicate reason" to fanatically serve his party's and his own political aims.[6] Hamlin Garland renders visible factionalism's violent subtext when he introduces an Iowa politician in *A Spoil of Office* (1892) who "could wield the Democratic party like a pistol."[7] Partisan politics endangers the state by pursuing antagonism over deliberation at the expense of the public good; political victory occurs only by vanquishing the enemy and never through compromise.

Madison, Adams, and Garland, to varying degrees, all saw partisanship as a symptom of corruption. But that diagnosis does not adequately explain why some citizens elect and actively seek out uncompromising partisans. The answer to that question resides in how partisans derive their power through the production of enmity and an attachment to local communities. Here we cannot let partisanship, as it too often does, subsume all forms of political disagreement. Since the Constitution's ratification, moral minorities and African American print culture eschewed strict party allegiances to redefine American democracy by advocating for more expansive definitions of CITIZENSHIP.[8] But these movements called for legislative reforms, not the DISFRANCHISEMENT of their political rivals. Even when describing a zealous party loyalist, the term "partisan" retains its militaristic tenor. Whether belonging to the majority or the minority party, the partisan keeps politics on the battlefield and, in the United States, tightens white supremacy's grip on American democracy.[9] The partisan's military and cultural backstory teaches us that it rejects the promise of democratic disagreement among equals by instead securing power through deception and belligerence. Even when penning legislation, the partisan readies the sword.

During the first decade of the twenty-first century, the US public became acquainted with General David Petraeus and his "counterinsurgency" precepts. In both the manual Petraeus cowrote with then Lieutenant General James Mattis and in a separate report issued by the Department of Defense, they acknowledge that insurgency usually gets labeled as a form of irregular warfare because combatants typically do not don an official army uniform or report directly to a state authority. Insurgents may fight on behalf of a nation, but their nationalism typically rebels against an existing state to bring a future one into being. The Department of Defense thus rightly regards irregular warfare as a "complex, 'messy,' and ambiguous social phenomenon that does not lend itself to clean, neat, concise, or precise definition."[10]

Ambiguity often gets extolled as an aesthetic virtue, and in this case it would appear to have a similar effect: like an innovative work of art, irregular warfare defies generic expectations. It upends convention, assaulting the intellect and the senses through acts of subterfuge and deception while also challenging the laws that govern conventional war.

Treatises exclusively devoted to what we now call the subjects of insurgency and counterinsurgency first surfaced in the eighteenth century. Colonialism in North America and the Caribbean, the mass forced migration of enslaved people from Africa, and the revolutions throughout the Atlantic world meant regular armies often took heavy casualties when squaring off against the unconventional tactics employed by Indigenous and insurrectionary populations. Partisan militias appropriated these irregular tactics, carrying out sabotage, supply raids, ambushes, subterfuge, and psychological operations. French tacticians referred to this mode of fighting as *le petite guerre*, directly translated into English as "the small war" and of course eventually as guerrilla war.[11] After both the French and Indian War and the US Revolution, the term "partisan" came to describe the individual who executed these combat maneuvers in the United States. Although partisans received criticism for their unconventional tactics and poor training, their successes in these conflicts endeared them to many white Americans. In his guide to forming a partisan corps, eighteenth-century strategist Roger Stevenson maintained that while "attacks of criticism . . . are never spared to the partisan," the French and Indian War had lately made their combat practices more acceptable.[12] Military tracts such as Stevenson's, along with stories that lauded Revolutionary partisan heroes Ethan Allen and Francis Marion, inaugurated an often-celebratory conversation about the politically disruptive features of the partisan on as well as off the battlefield.

Those who wrote about military codes of conduct still struggled with the partisan's legal standing. Tacticians and legal authorities differentiated the partisan from other unconventional fighting forces. When the Confederate States of America passed the Partisan Ranger Act in 1862, confederate irregulars known as bushwhackers wreaked havoc in border communities that lacked conventional forces. Their atrocious treatment of civilians even prompted Jefferson Davis to ban most partisan units and compelled Union Major General Henry W. Halleck to commission the esteemed jurist Francis Lieber to compose a set of legal guidelines on irregular combatants. Lieber uses guerrilla warfare as a broad category referring to actions performed by "the Freebooter, the Marauder, the Brigand, the Partisan, the Free-corps, the Spy, the Rebel, the Conspirator, [and] the Robber." Only the partisan, he concludes, is "entitled to the privileges of the law of war, so long as he does not transgress it," because this warrior still answers to the organized army and assaults only military targets. Lieber nevertheless stumbles when acknowledging that Halleck himself "seems to consider 'self-constitution' a characteristic of the partisan."[13] He must concede that typically they are self-constituted rather than commissioned units. As such, they retain an insurgent character, operating extralegally until they retroactively establish their legal standing by founding a new or restoring an old state.

Lieber found partisans' legal status vexing because while they did not pillage and plunder, they defied state authority. He failed to recognize that, even on the battlefield, the partisan asserts a political identity. A century after Lieber issued his legal guidelines, the political philosopher Carl Schmitt clarified the partisan's legal status as a non-state actor. He argued that "the partisan fights at a political front, and precisely the political character of his acts restores the original meaning of the word *partisan*." A Nazi apologist best known for his meditations on totalitarian rule and states of emergency, Schmitt enumerated the partisan's political characteristics in a series of lectures published under the title *Theory of the Partisan* (1963). He attributes partisans' blurry legal status to both their questionable tactics and their fundamental allegiance to a party rather than a state. He further stresses, "the illegal resistance fighter and underground activist are made the true type of partisan." While the state may contain multitudes, the partisan engages in a "war of absolute enmity," cohering around a shared and total commitment to eliminating their party's appointed enemy.[14] Schmitt essentially affirms Madison's worst fears: the partisan not only practices a set of military tactics but also seeks to destroy the existing political and social order to impose its party's will over a population.

Schmitt regards the "telluric character" of the partisan as another of its essential features.[15] He means that the partisan has ties to a specific region. These connections to the land grant the partisan tactical advantages (i.e., they know their terrain better than the occupying force does) and an essential bond with their local community. He thus puts partisan sovereignty at odds with both the impersonality of classical republicanism and the self-interest of classical liberalism, the two dominant political philosophies that undergirded US political thinking from its start. Partisans do not consent to be governed, exercising instead their self-proclaimed right to decide whether anyone who would threaten their party or property should live or die.

Schmitt's study applies to eighteenth- and nineteenth-century views of the partisan. Ethan Allen, for example, depicts his decision "to raise the Green Mountain Boys" as an expression of his manhood and "natural-born liberties."[16] Allen's legendary militia, which originally formed to reject New York's attempt to control the territory in 1770, harassed settlers from that colony by destroying their property or flogging them. From its formation, the Green Mountain Boys embodied Schmitt's ideas by remaining locally loyal to Vermont. Accordingly, when Vermont became its own independent republic from 1777 to 1791, it made the individual right to bear arms for self-defense an unambiguous part of its constitution.

Those who opposed early Federalists often appealed to partisan sovereignty when contesting standing armies and insisting that "no law shall be passed for disarming the people."[17] Writing in 1792, the South Carolinian jurist Thomas Cooper regarded partisan militias as the martial embodiment of popular sovereignty because volunteer militiamen "feel themselves Citizens as well as Soldiers."[18] Those who join a professional army pledge allegiance to a ruler or a centralized ruling body, he averred, that is not directly accountable to or in sympathy with the people. Cooper and others validated the underlying claim behind the Whiskey Rebellion and other frontier insurrections that maintained a continuing "right of revolution."[19] Bearing arms, from this perspective, guaranteed the protection of individual natural rights in ways that voter enfranchisement did not.

These natural rights, however, fundamentally applied only to white people. These writings draw sharp distinctions between white people and people of color rather than appealing to universal rights. Black revolts such as the Haitian Revolution or Nat Turner's Insurrection never merit the partisan label. Instead, people of color, whether Indigenous warriors or enslaved revolutionaries, threaten rather than embody the partisan liberty in this body of work. Nineteenth-century novels about insurgency cemented these dividing lines by directly tying the partisan's political subjectivity to white supremacy.

The Scottish writer Jane Porter helped inaugurate the insurgent novel genre, finding a captive audience in the United States, where her romance *The Scottish Chiefs* (1810) became a runaway bestseller.[20] Although readers today may have never heard of Porter or *The Scottish Chiefs*, most people know its story well—William Wallace's fight for Scottish independence— thanks to Mel Gibson's film *Braveheart* (1995). Wallace's stratagems, which include ambushes and espionage coupled with the underlying assumption that his forces possess special territorial attachments to the lands upon which they fight, bear the hallmarks associated with the partisan. He also repeatedly utters versions of the oath, "I swore to free Scotland or die" as he ensures "every fortress is filled with a native garrison."[21] Such passages resonate with US Revolutionary battle cries and consolidate Wallace's partisan political identity. His fight to restore ancient Scottish feudalism remains consistent with his commitment to PERSONAL LIBERTY because his sword and martial prowess guarantee that freedom more than any legislative body could. US receptions of Wallace's story reveal an important but sometimes concealed feature of the partisan romance: its association with white supremacy. In 1915, the Ku Klux Klan began burning crosses to recall *crann tara*, an ancient Scottish practice used to call clans to arms, mimicking scenes found in historically embellished films and novels that lionized the Klan's initial formation after the Civil War.[22] And white patriot or militia groups, beginning in the late 1990s, claimed Wallace's legacy to promote their rejection of the federal government.[23]

The white Southern author William Gilmore Simms produced some of the most culturally significant insurgent romances during the first half of the nineteenth century. He wrote a book explicitly titled *The Partisan: A Romance of the Revolution* (1835), which tracks activities carried out by a band of fictional revolutionaries. Carrying out irregular warfare in vivid detail, Simms's rebels profess their disdain for monarchial rule because it derives its legitimacy from "immutable systems of human government [despite] humanity itself being mutable, hourly undergoing change, and hourly in advance of government." Tellingly, they deem all types of state sovereignty as mutable rather than monarchial rule alone. The notion that any state authority should be respected for any length of time falls under tremendous scrutiny. By contrast, he glorifies partisans for exercising unqualified individual freedom, triumphantly noting how they always "stood their ground" in defiance of the British. Simms also juxtaposes the white partisans' heroics with the character Goggle, who "is a half-breed Indian, or mestizo, or something" who proves morally and intellectually bankrupt.[24] Goggle may have connections to the local community, but his race explains his cowardice, disloyalty, and ineptness. He could never become a partisan. What emerges in Simms's romance, then, is a fictional depiction of the partisan's political character that closely aligns with Schmitt's philosophical account.

At the beginning of the twentieth century, Thomas Dixon's Klan trilogy mobilized the partisan mythology initially brought into being by nineteenth-century writers such as Porter and Simms to anchor it overtly to white supremacy. Dixon applies the label "partisan" disparagingly and rhetorically to newspapers and politicians that support Reconstruction in order to treat the federal government as an illegitimate and occupying force in the South. Based on this premise, the Klan forms as a paramilitary organization fanatically loyal to its party's cause: the subjugation of African Americans to save white civilization. While scenes of physical violence abound in these narratives, Dixon's hooded partisans rally around one tactic in particular: threatening every Black man "as he values his life, not to approach the polls."[25] Granting Black enfranchisement gets characterized as constitutionally dubious but "protected by the bayonet."[26] Here Dixon completely erases any distinction one might wish to draw between the political and military definitions of the partisan: white men must use whatever means necessary to defy the federal state's protection of Black rights. Following the partisan pursuit of absolute enmity, Dixon identifies Black people and their allies as enemies who must be vanquished.

As Dixon penned his white Southern partisan hagiographies, African American writers chronicled the terrors white partisanship visited upon them, whether exercised through repressive legislation or violent vigilantism. Charles Chesnutt deftly unmasks the intersections of white partisan violence in *The Marrow of Tradition* (1901), a fictionalized account of the Massacre of 1898 in which a group of white Democratic elites orchestrated the removal of an elected body of Black and white politicians from office. When a white partisan newspaper fails to oust its political opponents by publishing factually dubious propaganda, its editors lead an assault on the local Black population. Unable to prevent the excessive violence Lieber aligned only with nonpartisan irregular warriors, this white mob carries out senseless slaughter to assert white party dominance. Chesnutt affirms Schmitt's contention that partisans are anti-democratic subjects who "override the laws" to achieve their political interests "at any cost!"[27] This novel reveals that the partisan's extreme individual sovereignty rooted in party allegiance and wrapped in martial metaphors and actions will ultimately destroy democratic republics when their structures no longer serve their ends.

Partisans, Chesnutt observes, even when pursuing their party's interests electorally, are a "grave menace to the peace of the state and the liberties of the people,—by which is meant the whole people, and not any one class, sought to be built up at the expense of another."[28] He sees the embrace of the partisan's unchecked individualism for what it truly is in the United

States: a fantasy about perpetual white supremacy that persists into the twenty-first century. One need not look too closely at Fortress America's original box to notice that it portrays armies of people of color breaching the United States' borders that the game suggests only the partisans can stop.

Notes

1. Michael Gray, *Fortress America Game Play Manual* (Pawtucket, RI: Milton Bradley, 1986), 8.
2. "partisan, n.2 and adj.," *OED Online*, December 2019, Oxford University Press, www.oed.com.
3. James Stormonth, *A Dictionary of the English Language*, rev. ed. (Edinburgh: William Blackwood and Sons, 1895), 709.
4. John Oglive, *The Imperial Dictionary of the English Language*, vol. 3, rev. ed. (London: Blackie & Son, 1883), 381.
5. James Madison, *Federalist* 10, in *The Federalist*, ed. Robert Scigliano (New York: Modern Library, 2001), 53, 54.
6. Henry Adams, *Democracy: An American Novel* (New York: Henry Holt and Company, 1908), 110.
7. Hamlin Garland, *A Spoil of Office: A Story of the Modern West* (Boston, MA: Arena Publishing Company, 1892), 183.
8. See Kyle G. Volk, *Moral Minorities and the Making of American Democracy* (New York: Oxford University Press, 2014), 22–25, and Derrick R. Spires, *The Practice of Citizenship: Black Politics and Print Culture in the Early United States* (Philadelphia, PA: University of Pennsylvania Press, 2019), 6–26.
9. Outside the United States, a wide array of paramilitary movements also claim the partisan label, but their insurgent projects do not always advance white supremacy.
10. United States Department of Defense, *Irregular Warfare (IW) Joint Operating Concept (JOC)* (Washington, DC, September 11, 2007), 6. See also Department of the Army, *Insurgencies and Countering Insurgencies* by David Petraeus and James Mattis (Washington, DC, May 2014).
11. Armand-François de La Croix, *Traité de la Petite Guerre pour les Compagnies Franches* (Paris: Antoine Boudet, 1752).
12. Roger Stevenson, *Military Instructions for Officers Detached in the Field: Containing, A Scheme for Forming a Corps of a Partisan* (Philadelphia, PA: Robert Aitken, 1775), 45.
13. Francis Lieber, *Guerrilla Parties Considered with Reference to the Laws and Usages of War* (New York: D. Van Nostrand, 1862), 9, 11, 18.
14. Carl Schmitt, *Theory of the Partisan: Intermediate Commentary on the Concept of the Political* (New York: Telos Press Publishing, 2007), 15, 18, 52.
15. Ibid., 22.

16. Ethan Allen, *Ethan Allen's Narrative of the Capture of Ticonderoga and of His Captivity and Treatment by the British*, 5th ed. (Burlington, VT: C. Goodrich & S. B. Nichols, 1849), 7.

17. "The Address and Reasons of Dissent of the Minority of the Convention of Pennsylvania to Their Constitution," *The Anti-Federalist*, ed. Herbert J. Strong (Chicago, IL: University of Chicago Press, 1981), 207.

18. Thomas Cooper, *Reply to Mr. Burke's Invective against Mr. Cooper, and Mr. Watt in the House of Commons, on the 30th of April, 1792* (London: J. Johnson, 1792), 58.

19. Saul Cornell, *A Well-Regulated Militia: The Founding Fathers and the Origins of Gun Control in America* (New York: Oxford University Press, 2006), 82.

20. Frank Luther Mott lists *The Scottish Chiefs* as an overall bestseller in the United States in *Golden Multitudes: The Story of Best Sellers in the United States* (New York: Macmillan Company, 1947), 305.

21. Jane Porter, *The Scottish Chiefs: A Romance*, rev. ed. (New York: D. Appleton and Company, 1866), 431.

22. The first Klan during Reconstruction did not burn crosses, but Thomas Dixon depicted the practice in *The Clansman* (1905) explicitly because of its associations with Scottish lore. Adapting *The Clansman* for the screen, D. W. Griffith inspired the second Klan to imitate the cross burning depicted in *The Birth of a Nation* (1915).

23. Gerard Seenan, "Klansmen take their lead from Scots," *The Guardian*, January 20, 1999, https://www.theguardian.com/world/1999/jan/30/3.

24. William Gilmore Simms, *The Partisan: A Romance the Revolution*, ed. Stephen E. Meats (Fayetteville, AR: University of Arkansas Press, 2011), 116, 21, 151.

25. Dixon, *The Leopard's Spots: A Romance of the White Man's Burden—1865–1900* (New York: Doubleday, Page & Company, 1903), 162.

26. Dixon, *The Clansman: An Historical Romance of the Ku Klux Klan* (New York: A. Wessels Company, 1905), 247.

27. Charles W. Chesnutt, *The Marrow of Tradition*, ed. Eric Sundquist (New York: Penguin, 1993), 320.

28. Ibid., 92.

Further Reading

A good starting point is Carl Schmitt's *Theory of the Partisan: Intermediate Commentary on the Concept of the Political* (New York: Telos Press Publishing, 2007). For an historical account of early US factionalist politics, see Gerald Leonard and Saul Cornell, *The Partisan Republic: Democracy, Exclusion, and the Fall of the Founders' Constitution, 1780s–1830s* (Cambridge: Cambridge University Press, 2019). Matthew Christopher Hulbert charts the transformation of Confederate partisans into western outlaws in *The Ghosts of Guerrilla Memory: How Civil War Bushwhackers Became Gunslingers in the American West* (Athens, GA: University of Georgia Press, 2016).

Although partisan fantasies exclude Black people, Jennifer C. James powerfully establishes the crucial role African American war literature played in shaping conversations about Black sovereignty in *A Freedom Bought with Blood: African American War Literature from the Civil War to World War II* (Chapel Hill, NC: University of North Carolina Press, 2007). Excellent primary materials associated with the kinds of Black and Indigenous resistance disregarded by white partisan discourse include William Wells Brown, *The Negro in the American Rebellion: His Heroism and Fidelity* (Boston, MA: Lee and Shepard, 1867) and Ohíye S'a (Charles A. Eastman), *Indian Heroes and Great Chieftains* (New York: Little, Brown, and Company, 1918).

15

Disgust

Jason Frank

In a 1794 letter to Thomas Dwight, Fisher Ames expressed disgust at the proliferating "cancer" of the Democratic-Republican societies. Ames characterized the societies as the "root of an extracted cancer, which will soon eat again and destroy... Any taint of that poison left behind will infect the seemingly cured body; therefore the knife should now be used to cut off the tubercles."[1] This was not the only time that Ames employed metaphors of ulcers, cancers, and open wounds to describe popular enactment within the body politic, and he was not alone among Federalists in recurring to metaphors of bodily disfiguration to describe the radical democratizing undercurrents of the 1790s. "Our disease is democracy," Ames wrote, "it is not the skin that festers—our very bones are carious and their marrow blackens with gangrene."[2]

Edmund Burke mobilized a similar host of metaphors in his antirevolutionary writings. For Burke, the French Revolution was about more than the replacement of royal political authority with democratic republicanism. It initiated "a system which is by its essence inimical to all other governments," not just the legal institutions of the state but the manifold subordination of human conduct to "the discipline of social life."[3] This democratic disorder was felt "throughout all the relations of life... [It] inverted the natural order in all things, setting up high in the air what is required to be low on the ground."[4] Like Ames, Burke invoked natural disgust to defend the inherited social order from the incursions of the "swinish multitude." Their widely shared depiction of democracy as a monstrous violation of the order, proportion, and norms dictated by God or nature suggests an inner entailment between democracy and disgust in the conservative writing from this Revolutionary era and beyond, thereby revealing not only the

Jason Frank, *Disgust* In: *Democracies in America: Keywords for the Nineteenth Century and Today.*
Edited by: D. Berton Emerson and Gregory Laski, Oxford University Press.
© D. Berton Emerson and Gregory Laski 2023. DOI: 10.1093/oso/9780198865698.003.0016

political contours of the affect of disgust but also something distinctive about the spirit of democracy.

The conservative pairing of democracy with disgust often drew upon the canonical association of political order with health and popular politics with disease in Western political thought and its governing metaphor of the body politic, a metaphor that, as Judith Shklar writes, "assigned a proper place to each person and group so that all could perform functions in maintaining the whole."[5] According to Livy, Agrippa Menenius Lanatus invoked the fable of the body politic, and the irrationality of a revolt of one part of the body against the other, to bring the seceding plebs of Aventine back into the reigning order of Rome. Thomas Hobbes mobilized it during the English Civil War when he analogized the powers that tend to "weaken" or "dissolve" the "Common-wealth" with "diseases of a natural body," "biles and scabs," "Worms," "Wounds," and "Wens."[6] During the constitutional ratifying debates, Alexander Hamilton described "seditions and insurrections" as "unhappy maladies as inseparable from the body politic, as tumours and eruptions from the natural body."[7] Anti-democratic writers tapped into this long history of conceptualizing insurgent egalitarian politics through the grotesque figure of the disorganized and deterritorialized body.

Body metaphors, in this sense, offer a compelling historical index to the naturalization of hierarchical social and political relations democratic movements sought to contest (even when asserting their own forms of hierarchy and domination, such as the racial categorizations of American Herrenvolk Democracy). Disgust has an uncomfortably symbiotic relationship with democracy because the latter is so closely associated with defiling or contaminating powers, with those who speak when they are not to speak, who, in the words of Jacques Rancière, "part-take" in what they have no part in, who through enacting displacements refigure the authoritative "allocation of ways of doing, ways of being, and ways of saying."[8] We may learn something important about democracy itself, in other words, if we listen to the eloquent hatred of democracy's critics—figures such as Ames, Burke, and, as we will see in this essay, William Cobbett—because they suggest that democracy was rightly understood to threaten the hierarchical unity anchored in the God-given naturalness of the body, a unity in which every part had its proper place. While this symbolism is rooted in premodern political cosmologies, it persists amid the so-called "disenchantments" of the modern age. The "social naturalism" of so much eighteenth-century thought, for example, rendered the transcendental hierarchies and moral regulations of the Great Chain of Being, as well as the complex discursive inheritances of Stoicism, immanent to both nature and ultimately society itself.[9] The relationship between democracy and disgust in periods of radical democratic transition corroborates ancient as well as modern democracy's close historical association with the absence of the proper qualification for rule enacted by "subjects that do not coincide with the parties of the state or of society, floating subjects that deregulate all representation of places and portions."[10]

Few things can more reliably elicit disgust than bodies in decomposition or whose parts are not found in their proper place, and democracy invariably deals with "matter out of place."[11] As a disruption of the reigning configuration of political arrangements, democracy was greeted in the 1790s with a moralizing disgust by elites policing the institutional and affective contours of the inherited order. Like Burke, American Federalists saw democratic disorder in the political world as necessarily connected to democratic disorder in the moral, aesthetic, and economic worlds. "The people have become impatient of government restraint," Archibald Henderson wrote, "and have lost all reverence for established usages and the settled order of things."[12] "Established usages" in daily behavior animated and sustained the governing order, and conservatives sought to preserve these rules of propriety and authorization not only in formal legal institutions but also in the deportment and composure of everyday life. They fought against the multifaceted threat democracy posed to "the habit of subordination," which, as David Hackett Fischer writes, "served to cement a functional society more effectively than legislative restraints or constitutional restrictions. The dropping of a curtsy, the doffing of a cap, the raising of a deferential finger to the brow—these were the superficial symbols of a spirit which ran deep and strong in the minds and hearts of men."[13] Conservatives have always been acutely attuned to the practical nuances and affective textures of the politics of the ordinary; they have affirmed the importance of sustaining authority not only in the relationship between governors and governed, aristocrats and commoners, priests and parishioners, but also between employers and employees, husbands and wives, parents and children.

As an aversive affect, disgust is particularly well suited to combat challenges to these everyday "habits of subordination." Disgust entered the English language in the seventeenth century, but it flourished in the eighteenth with emerging discourses of moral sentimentalism and aesthetic concerns with taste. The word "disgust" (or *degout* in French) literally means "bad taste." It is sharply, viscerally evaluative, and involves immediate and unreflective judgment, which makes it such an important affect for political consideration. Disgust is a judgment backed by the body, viscerally certain, and free of ambivalence. It also moves beyond individual assessment and into the political world because it demands the assent of others, which leads William Ian Miller to emphasize disgust's "communalizing" tendency. "The avowal of disgust expects concurrence," Miller writes. "It carries with it the notion of its own indisputability... the sheer obviousness of the claim."[14] If someone is indifferent to something that disgusts me, it is unlikely that I will be able to persuade them into sharing it. To the contrary, this indifference, and the person expressing it, may also become an object of disgust. Disgust enjoins us not only to reject its object but also to demand that others join us in that rejection. Disgust mobilizes a collective affect of cohesion through shared visceral aversion.

The proliferation of disgust in the conservative political discourses of the 1790s emerged as egalitarian pressures challenged the established hierarchies of the social and political order. Disgust, like contempt, plays an important role in securing and maintaining status and class distinctions, but where contempt remains removed and detached, even coolly indifferent, disgust mingles with threat and surprise and cannot tolerate or remain in the proximity of its object. Contempt is an aversive passion that works to reinforce existing social hierarchies, but disgust is a passion elicited by social hierarchies under duress. Disgust asserts "a claim to superiority that at the same time recognizes the vulnerability of that superiority to the defiling powers of the low."[15] "We are sliding down into the mire of a democracy," Ames declared, "which pollutes the morals of the citizens before it swallows up their liberties."[16]

Few writers relied more fulsomely on the rhetorical elicitation of disgust than William Cobbett, radical social conservative, anti-Semite, defender of the "right" of slavery, and arguably the most popular writer in America during the era of the French Revolution. The radical publicist in monarchial Britain was a High Tory pamphleteer in republican America. In the nineteenth century, Cobbett would rage against the social dislocations and injustices of industrial capitalism, but in America during the 1790s, often writing under the pseudonym "Peter Porcupine," Cobbett was the most vehement critic of the French Revolution's contaminating influences. In both instances, Cobbett's criticism was philosophically conservative, defending an inherited social order threatened by the industrial revolution, on the one hand,

and democratic revolution, on the other. His nostalgic longing for a lost social organicism animated a flurry of publications in which he sought to police the boundaries of propriety against democratic incursions, especially as enacted by women, Jews, Blacks, purported homosexuals, and just about anybody else who Cobbett thought might contaminate the healthy body politic. As the great nineteenth-century critic and essayist William Hazlitt argued, Cobbett's primary "principle is repulsion, his nature contradiction; he is made up of mere antipathies, an Ishmaelite indeed without a fellow."[17]

Like Ames and Burke, Cobbett believed that democracy's "crawling demagogues and popular parasites" revolutionized the political, economic, social, moral, and aesthetic spheres of daily life. Just as democracy disrupted property relations in society, argued Cobbett, so did it undermine the Christian basis of morality essential to civilized behavior. Democracy threatened the sanctity and patriarchal authority of the family, and democrats were, therefore, typically cast by Cobbett as social miscreants. At the conclusion of one of his many diatribes against Thomas Paine, for example, Cobbett wed the disgust of Paine's situation in Revolutionary France to political or moral approbation in the most obvious of ways. Describing Paine's imprisonment under the Convention, Cobbett linked this degraded and degrading image to Paine's political positions and principles:

> Let us now return to the blasphemer at the bottom of his dungeon. There he lies! Manacled, besmeared in filth, crawling with vermin, loaded with years of infamy. This, reader, whatever you may think of him, is the author of the Rights of Man, the eulogist of French liberty... Look at him! Do you think now, in your conscience, that he has the appearance of a legislator, a civilian, a constitution maker?

In appealing to the "conscience" of his public, Cobbett is actually invoking their aesthetic response: "Look at him!" Paine's disgusting appearance— "besmeared in filth, crawling with vermin, loaded with years of infamy"— evidences his lack of moral fitness to be "a legislator, a civilian, a constitution maker."[18] As Raymond Williams perceptively notes, "it was difficult to find [in Cobbett's writing] a democrat or rebel who was not also a bad husband, father, brother, or son."[19] "Thus Paine was not only 'the prince of demagogues' but 'infamous,' an 'old ruffian,' a poor, mean-spirited miscreant' and a 'vile wretch.'"[20] The collapse of the moral and aesthetic registers in Cobbett's writing indicates his broader attempt to engender a particular mood or disposition in his reading public—repulsion and disgust—and to marshal these responses against reform and in service of the existing political order.

Cobbett argued democratic efforts to reform social institutions, economic arrangements, and daily behavior resulted in a general disorganization of the body politic, which he described as a "natural oeconomy," and which he asserted must be combated simultaneously and on all fronts.[21] In his very first American publication, "On the Emigration of Dr. Joseph Priestley," Cobbett presented a fable to exemplify democracy's relationship to a disruption of the existing distribution of orders and roles within the body politic. In this overwrought tale, a cabinet filled with china, ceramics, water pitchers, and chamber pots is thrown into disorienting insurrection. The pitchers and the ceramics—which Cobbett, referring to the specter of revolutionary slave rebellion in Haiti, refers to as the "brown brethren"— challenge the traditional authority of the ever-white china. Time and again in his writing, Cobbett connected the democratic revolutions of the eighteenth century to the specter of future insurrections among slaves. In Cobbett's allegory, at the insurrection's end, the glistening wet chamber pot shines upon the table, longing to "kiss the lip and ornament the cup-board." As the reigning order is upended by democratically self-created authorities (the ceramics in the fable make a constituent claim to transformative political power), the container for defecation becomes a vessel for drinking. The belabored moral of the story is provided by the "wise water pitcher," who echoes Agrippa Menenius Lanatus at Aventine: "We are all of the same clay, 'tis true; but he who made us, formed different functions. One is for ornament, another for use. The posts the least important are often the most necessary."[22]

Cobbett had a particular revulsion for those Democratic-Republicans who formed clubs modeled—or so Cobbett and other Federalists continually insisted—on the Jacobin clubs in France. He likened American Jacobins to a "sort of flesh flies that naturally settle on the excremental and corrupted parts of the body politic."[23] If French Jacobins were "bloodthirsty cannibals" who sat in judgment with "their shirt sleeves tucked up to their elbows; their arms and hands, and even the goblets they were drinking out of . . . besmeared with human blood,"[24] American Jacobins were similarly "Bacchanalians whose beverage is the blood of their benefactors" and whose mouths catch "anarchical belches."[25] The insolent "self-created" authority of these societies exemplified for Cobbett and other conservatives the dangerous social inversions of the Revolutionary era, which, in Burke's words, set "up high in the air what the solidity of the structure requires to be on the ground."[26]

Like Burke, Cobbett also repeatedly returned to the egalitarian violation of gender and sexual norms. Miscegenation, "French" sexual mores, emasculated men, and masculine women are central figures in Cobbett's portrayals of the democratic opposition. Cobbett converts the much-touted fraternity, camaraderie, and conviviality of republican citizens of different races and sexes into sexualized improprieties and promiscuities meant to elicit a defensive disgust in his readers. Parodying the Revolutionary French reception of insurgent slaves from Saint Domingue, for example, Cobbett writes, "the *white* man first flew into his arms, and was embraced most tenderly—the *mulatto* was hugged with still more affection—but when it came to the *negro*, had it been a *mistress*, he could not have pressed her more ardently! The next day they voted the *emancipation of the slaves*, and declared, that they would form with *all negroes and mulattoes a* 'tri-coloured coalition,' which would soon destroy the combined powers of aristocracy and tyranny."[27]

Similarly, during Citizen Genêt's notorious term as the French ambassador to the United States, Cobbett accused the Jacobin clubs of "licking" and "saluting" the Citizen's body (in all its parts) as a part of his general attack on the suspiciously erotic fraternization of their members and democrats more broadly. "If they stood ever so fair in the opinion of the ladies," Cobbett wrote, "must not their gander-frolicks, and their squeezing, and hugging, and kissing one another be expected to cause a good deal of pouting and jealousy?"[28] Just as the clubs were figured as dangerous aberrations within the constitutional political order—George Washington derided them as "self-created" societies and blamed them for instigating the Whiskey Rebellion—their behavior and manners seemed to simultaneously challenge a natural sexual order. Jacobin effeminacy and "gander-frolicks" were conversely related to the ugly masculinity of republican women. "The instant a lady turns to politics say farewell to smiles," goes one typical formulation.[29] Like many other conservatives, Cobbett assailed Mary Wollstonecraft with particular venom, emphasizing her monstrously hermaphroditic character, "masculine, feminine, and neuter all at once."[30]

These close associations of democracy and disgust should not be understood as merely reactionary aberrations, because they vividly illuminate the egalitarian challenge democracy posed to defenders of the inherited order during this period of revolutionary transition. This rhetoric recalls the radicalism of democracy's basic claims, usually buried beneath encomiums and platitudes, because democracy involves "forms of subjectification through which any order of distribution of bodies into functions corresponding to their 'nature' and places corresponding to their functions is undermined and thrown back on its contingency."[31] In contrast to normative arguments against disgust in contemporary democratic theory—most prominently by Martha Nussbaum—the historical entanglement of democracy and disgust suggests the relationship might be constitutive and irresolvable. Because democracy enacts a reconfiguration of the sensible that elicits order-preserving disgust, disgust cannot be finally overcome but must be politically confronted and tactically engaged. Disgust shapes the affective contours of our democratic life, and to aspire for a politics beyond its terms is to disavow the fundamental challenge of democratic politics. To recover a fuller appreciation of democracy's forgotten radicalism, it is productive to return to the eloquent hatred—*and* disgust—of its most trenchant critics.

Notes

1. Fisher Ames, "Letter to Thomas Dwight, September 11, 1794," in W. B. Allen, ed., *The Works of Fisher Ames: Volume II* (Indianapolis, IN: Liberty Fund, 1983), 1048–1050.
2. Fisher Ames, "Letter to Timothy Pickering, March 10, 1806," in *The Works of Fisher Ames: Volume II*, 1516–1518.
3. Edmund Burke, *Letters on a Regicide Peace* (Indianapolis, IN: Liberty Fund, 1999), 250.
4. Ibid., 325.
5. Judith N. Shklar, *Men and Citizens: A Study of Rousseau's Social Theory* (New York: Cambridge University Press, 1985), 198–199.
6. Thomas Hobbes, *Leviathan*, ed. Richard Tuck (New York: Cambridge University Press, 1996), 221–230.
7. Alexander Hamilton, *Federalist* 28, in Jacob E. Cooke, ed., *The Federalist* (Middletown, CT: Wesleyan University Press, 1961), 176.
8. Jacques Rancière, *Disagreement: Politics and Philosophy*, trans. Julie Rose (Minneapolis, MN: University of Minnesota Press, 1999), 29.
9. See Dan Edelstein, *On the Spirit of Rights* (Chicago, IL: University of Chicago Press, 2019).
10. Ibid., 100–101.
11. Mary Douglas, *Purity and Danger* (New York: Routledge, 1966).
12. Quoted in Linda K. Kerber, *Federalists in Dissent: Imagery and Ideology in Jeffersonian America* (Ithaca, NY: Cornell University Press, 1980), 213.
13. David Hackett Fischer, *The Revolution of American Conservatism: The Federalist Party in the Era of Jeffersonian Democracy* (New York: Harper & Row, 1965), xiv.
14. William Ian Miller, *Anatomy of Disgust* (Cambridge, MA: Harvard University Press, 1997), 194.
15. Ibid., 9.

16. Fisher Ames, "Political Thoughts," *Monthly Anthology and Boston Review II* (November 1805): 565–566.

17. William Hazlitt, "Character of Cobbett," in P. P. Howe, ed., *The Complete Works of William Hazlitt*, 21 vols. (London: J. M. Dent and Sons, 1931), 8: 54–55.

18. Ibid., 219–223, 296.

19. Raymond Williams, *Cobbett* (Oxford: Oxford University Press, 1983), 9.

20. William Cobbett, "Cobbett on Thomas Paine," in David A. Wilson, ed., *Peter Porcupine in America: Pamphlets on Republicanism and Revolution* (Ithaca, NY: Cornell University Press, 1994), 219–223.

21. William Cobbett, "A Bone to Gnaw, for the Democrats," in *Peter Porcupine in America*, 91.

22. William Cobbett, "Observations on the Emigration of Dr. Joseph Priestley: To Which Is Added a Comprehensive Story of a Farmer's Bull," in *Peter Porcupine in America*, 76.

23. William Cobbett, "History of the American Jacobins, Commonly Denominated Democrats," in *Peter Porcupine in America*, 185.

24. William Cobbett, "Observations on the Emigration of Dr. Joseph Priestley," 63.

25. William Cobbett, "A Bone to Gnaw," 97, 110.

26. Edmund Burke, *Reflections on the French Revolution* (New York: P. F. Collier & Son, 1909–14), 79.

27. William Cobbett, "A Picture of France in 1794, in a Letter from a Gentleman in Switzerland, to his Friend in America," *Porcupine's Gazette*, April 25, 1797; reprinted in William Cobbett, ed., *Porcupine's Works*, 12 vols. (London: Cobbett and Morgan, 1801), vol. 5, 183.

28. Cobbett, "A Bone to Gnaw," 113.

29. Ibid., 90.

30. William Cobbett, "A Kick for a Bite," in *Peter Porcupine in America*, 130.

31. Rancière, *Disagreement*, 101.

Further Reading

There has been an outpouring of interdisciplinary scholarship on the politics of disgust over the past two decades, much of it driven by path-breaking research in experimental psychology that clinically demonstrates the affinity between disgust and ideological conservatism explored historically here. Good overviews of this work can be found in Daniel Kelly's *Yuck! The Nature and Moral Significance of Disgust* (Cambridge, MA: MIT Press, 2013), Susan Miller's *Disgust: The Gatekeeper Emotion* (London: Routledge, 2004), and William Ian Miller's *The Anatomy of Disgust* (Cambridge, MA: Harvard University Press, 1997). Philosophical investigations of disgust have been published by Aurel Kolnai from the perspective of phenomenology (*On Disgust* [Chicago, IL: Open Court, 2004]) and by Colin McGinn from the perspective of analytic philosophy (*The Meaning of Disgust* [New York:

Oxford University Press, 2011]). The seminal theoretical works of Mary Douglas in *Purity and Danger: An Analysis of Concepts of Pollution and Taboo* (London: Routledge, 1966) and Julia Kristeva in *The Powers of Horror: An Essay on Abjection* (New York: Columbia University Press, 1982) remain important to the contemporary conversation. Aesthetic and literary examinations of disgust can be found in Sarah Ahmed's *The Cultural Politics of Emotion* (Edinburgh: Edinburgh University Press, 2014), Carolyn Korsmeyer's *Savoring Disgust: The Foul and the Fair in Aesthetics* (New York: Oxford University Press, 2011), Winfried Menninghaus's *Disgust: Theory and History of a Strong Emotion* (Albany, NY: SUNY Press, 2003), and Robert Rawdon Wilson's *The Hydra's Tale: Imagining Disgust* (Edmonton: University of Alberta Press, 2002). Martha Nussbaum has written several influential studies of the illiberal life of disgust in the law, with a focus on racial and sexual discrimination. See, especially, *Hiding from Humanity: Disgust, Shame, and the Law* (Princeton, NJ: Princeton University Press, 2004) and the comparative study of these issues in the edited volume *The Empire of Disgust: Prejudice, Discrimination, and Policy in India and the US* (Oxford: Oxford University Press, 2018). The political scientist Ange Marie Hancock explores the role of racialized disgust in shaping contemporary US welfare policy in *The Politics of Disgust: The Public Identity of the Welfare Queen* (New York: New York University Press, 2004).

16

Moderation

Jean Ferguson Carr

The injunction to learn to be moderate—to avoid extremes, to contain passions, appetites, and resentments, to use speech to defuse conflict—was a key discourse and practice in the long nineteenth century in the United States. "Let Moderation begin its reign," the British rhetorician Hugh Blair wrote for a sermon published in 1790. "Train your minds to moderate views of human life, and human happiness."[1] The elocutionary readers published in Britain and the United States took up Blair's call, circulating texts and developing pedagogical practices to help students (and thereby citizens) aspire to moderation. This vast array of schoolbooks, addressed to all levels and kinds of students, reprinted poetry, prose, and select sentences, approved a vocabulary and modeled forms of syntax, and developed an argument about how such texts should be read and performed. They transmitted to generations of schoolchildren a ubiquitous faith in moderation. But they also suggested some of its problems: the difficulty of identifying its shifting and relational qualities, the tension between moderation and political action, and the challenge of knowing how to perform it.

The call for moderation links personal self-culture with political behavior. Politicians and citizens were urged to practice moderation but also to recognize that the times, the situation, or a particular offense might demand stronger words and actions. Indeed, although discourses of moderation suggest a wariness about political passion (as excess or lack of control), they also propose ways to channel passions into collective action or compromise. Moderation has often been a way of containing the behavior of the people, but it is also a way of limiting the reach of rulers, guarding against TYRANNY or overweening uses of force. The nineteenth century's interest in moderation as a discipline for governing the passions and desires has become in our times

Jean Ferguson Carr, *Moderation* In: *Democracies in America: Keywords for the Nineteenth Century and Today.* Edited by: D. Berton Emerson and Gregory Laski, Oxford University Press. © D. Berton Emerson and Gregory Laski 2023. DOI: 10.1093/oso/9780198865698.003.0017 a call to act in public spaces and situations with respect for traditions of decorum and civic exchange. Moderation is evident in protocols for speaking to colleagues on the floors of Congress and in restraints about how to characterize opponents in the press or in public debate—in other words, in relationships that often seem a vestige of past congeniality and nonpartisan cooperation. Calls for moderation undergird the BELIEF in working across the aisle, in seeing both sides of an issue, or in engaging in measured debate. A critique of moderation is that it may be limited to custom or courtesy, thus masking more substantial differences or suppressing argument and opposition. And it may constrain protest or criticism under the guise of obedience to procedure. But the practices of moderation also undergird the hope of public discourse, of civic community and shared values.

Inherited as a value from the British eighteenth-century treatises, magazines, and anthologies on which such books depend, moderation was a frame for civic discussion, a hedge against aristocratic license, and a practice of interest to both temperance and abolitionist movements. Associated with issues of control, it signaled the management of the emotions, of anger and resentment, of extreme enthusiasm or despair, and thus shaped the way a person spoke and acted in public. The moderate person strove to discipline internal feelings and thoughts for personal health and public purpose. Such uses of moderation prefigure our own time's tension about activists, and about those who seem to be going too far left or right on the political scale, who might therefore upset the status quo or act unpredictably or hastily. In the nineteenth century, as in today's personal and public arenas, what counts as the middle kept shifting and what emerges as moderation is a highly gendered, raced, and classed performance. Despite its positive associations, political writers worried that moderation could be a sign not so much of self-control or discipline but of weakness, hesitation, or lack of commitment to principles. Moderation was itself often a suspect position, a falsely secure middle for those who used self-control or civic decorum as an excuse for inaction. Moderation was less of a position than an anti-position, a relationship to other points on a SCALE, to other performances or decisions. In the elocutionary readers, moderation shifts from a stated value or fixed label to a way of living, speaking, and behaving. The readers do not promise to locate moderation for students but encourage them to practice it in speech and reading in the classroom, to try to achieve it in private and public life. It becomes a hedge against uncertainty, a way to prepare for surprise or calamity.

Moderation is a long-standing value, suggested by the Greek maxim carved on the temple of Apollo at Delphi ("nothing to excess") and validated by Aristotle's discussion of the "golden mean" and St. Thomas Aquinas's praise of temperance and modesty. Early modern writers valued moderation as a personal discipline and a public curb, a quality "extremely difficult to achieve, beyond the capacity of most if not all subjects."[2] Moderation thus became an enforced civic virtue. In 1790, Edmund Burke, meditating on the French Revolution, insisted that moderation would "temper together the opposite elements of liberty and restraint." But his often-quoted saying—"Moderation will be stigmatized as the virtue of cowards; and compromise as the prudence of traitors"—imagines moderation as an act of withholding or betrayal.[3]

Early dictionaries associated moderation with politics, attitudes, and behavior. In John Walker's *Critical Pronouncing Dictionary* (1797), it is offered as a sign of political "forbearance of extremity," a "contrary temper to parry violence," a state of mind ("calmness of mind, equanimity"), and an attitude toward expenditure ("frugality in expence").[4] Samuel Johnson's *Dictionary* (1785) suggests the term's elusiveness by defining moderation in terms of what it was *not*: "Temperate; not excessive; Not hot of temper; Not luxurious, not expensive; Not extreme in opinion, not sanguine in a tenet; Placed between; holding the mean; Of the middle rate."[5] Noah Webster's *American Dictionary* (1805) defines moderate as "temperate, sober, mild, reasonable," moderation as "forbearance of extremity, care," and a moderator as one who "restrains, rules, or presides."[6] Webster's 1828 edition focuses on the political implications of moderation, claiming it as "a due mean between extremes or excess of violence." It is a condition of personal behavior and a guard against excess zeal (the need to become "less violent, severe, rigorous or intense"), and the reward for its deployment is achieving "calmness of mind; equanimity."[7] Joseph Worcester's *Comprehensive Pronouncing and Explanatory Dictionary* (1830) emphasizes moderation as an attitude of "calmness; restraint." To act moderately is to act "temperately; mildly" and to moderate is to "regulate; to restrain; to still."[8] The 1888 edition of Worcester's *Academic Dictionary* links moderation with taking the middle road and thus with "middling" behavior, hardly a positive trait. The person who observes "a due mean between extremes," who was "temperate; not excessive; mild; reasonable; deliberate," runs the risk of being labeled "mediocre."[9]

By the nineteenth century, moderation came to be associated with the temperance movement and was thus promoted as a matter of self-discipline—of desires, consumption, and excess. Texts warn against physical display of desire and encourage readers to forgo drink or excess food, to control extravagant or overindulgent purchases, to manage the imagination, and even to control excessive novel reading. Moderation is an attribute of behavior, a practice—a desired but perhaps unreachable goal. Moderation was often starred in temperance writings as a "so-called" position, listed in quotation marks to signal it as vague or merely a way of talking. An 1832 temperance pamphlet asks "what is meant by moderation," or, to be precise, what "men blindly call moderation." Signaling a shift from seeing moderation as a "vaunting and deified" value, the pamphlet insists there is "no necromancy in the word moderation that will hold us spell-bound at the portal."[10] Temperance activists moved from advocating moderation to seeing anything less than abstinence as a "baleful error" or "fatal delusion." "The veriest drunkard who trembles at the verge of delirium," a midcentury pamphlet chides, "invariably calls himself a moderate drinker."[11] Near century's end, in *Women and Temperance*, Emma Willard dramatizes what was at stake by mocking the "Moderation bridge": "rocking and rickety, standing on the outworn piles of custom, precedent, and self-indulgence." Far more "safe and solid" is the "total abstinence bridge."[12]

Moderation was also a contentious discourse on all sides of slavery and post-emancipation. Charles C. Jones's *The Religious Instruction of the Negro* (1842) urges slaves to "learn to be patient, and to moderate your expectations," but it also warns owners to moderate punishment of the slaves "neither in anger, nor out of proportion to the offense."[13] In their narratives, Frederick Douglass and Harriet Jacobs underscore this counterpoint of moderation, depicting their own positions and ways of speaking and writing as moderate—reasonable, calm, measured—but showing slave-owners, both male and female, as immoderate in their anger and cruelty: for Jacobs, the masters spring on their victims "like a tiger"; for Douglass, they "rush" with the "fierceness of a tiger" or a "savage."[14] William Lloyd Garrison, editor of the abolitionist newspaper *The Liberator*, rejects the burden of moderation, asking in a catechism about slavery, "Why is all the prudence, moderation, judiciousness, philanthropy, piety, on the side of their opponents?" An earlier address rails against criticism of his response to slavery: "On this subject, I do not wish to think, or speak, or write, with moderation. No! no! Tell a man whose house is on fire to give a moderate alarm; tell him to moderately rescue his wife from the hands of the ravisher; tell the mother to gradually extricate her babe from the fire into which it has fallen—but urge me not to use moderation in a cause like the present."[15] After the war, Lydia Maria Child includes lessons on moderation in her book for recently freed slaves, *The Freedman's Book*, praising the value of "temperate" habits in temper, behavior, and expenditure.[16]

As these cases from slavery texts suggest, moderation cannot be simply treated as an idealized or abstract quality. It depends on who is being counseled to be moderate or whose behavior is critiqued as out of control. Elocutionary readers inherited these multiple senses of moderation and turned them toward the self-discipline needed to express oneself appropriately in public. This discipline encourages ordinary people to imitate their leaders or esteemed people from the past, while also recognizing some of the new forms of identity and hierarchy. In the United States of the nineteenth century, it is no longer a given that leaders should always be revered or that father knows best.

The textbooks thus reinscribe past relationships of political power, while also testing them in new contexts and circumstances. Moderation and its associated terms appear in the readers in practice sentences, as prompts for composition, and as themes in the reading passages. Early schoolbooks, such as Lindley Murray's *English Reader* (1799), issued hundreds of times in the United States, excerpted Hugh Blair's sermons for lessons on "Moderation in one's wishes recommended," "On the government of our thoughts," "On the proper state of our temper," and "Evils which flow from unrestrained passion." Schoolbooks like Murray's were clearly invested in using pieces that "recommend a great variety of moral duties" to "make a strong and durable impression" on students' minds.[17] Murray also recycled and disseminated Blair's elaborated investment in moderation in many of the "select sentences" offered for elocutionary practice: "Has he been moderate in his life, and temperate in all his pleasures?" and "A temperate spirit, and moderate expectations, are the best safeguards of the mind, in this uncertain and changing state."[18] Such sentences, abstracted from their earlier publication, circulated widely as literacy texts in the nineteenth century, reprinted at times for their moral import but also useful as exercises in translation (from Latin to English and back), parsing, or grammatical analysis.

Moderation was a form of civic order and discipline, a cultural project that promised a new era of enlightened behavior. Coupled with other virtues like thrift or kindness, it infused midcentury readers such as the wide-selling McGuffey's *Eclectic Readers*, which sold from the 1830s throughout the century. They distributed privileged forms of moral education from the all-male academies to the common schools, girls' schools, missions, and home schooling. Moderation thus became a value not just for well-educated gentlemen on the eastern seaboard or in the south but also for farmers and workingmen, girls and women, and freed slaves.[19] Lessons urged passionate boys to learn to control their temper, for example, or warned against acting rashly or extremely, and even small children were offered temperance tales.[20] A lesson in the *Third Reader* credited the early death of Alexander the Great to his inability to "subdue" his taste for drink—a "shocking" sign in one "who had subdued so many nations."[21] Older children were offered cautionary remarks about the ways in which intemperance affected famous writers, and a scene from Shakespeare's *Othello*, retitled "The Folly of Intoxication," warned that drunkenness would make men "bestial."[22]

Nineteenth-century schoolbooks instructed students how to put such moral values to use in their compositions or speeches. In a long list of subjects for themes, Richard Green Parker listed as suitable topics: "government of the thoughts, tongue, temper, affections," "control of the passions, temper," "rashness," "avoid extremes," "intemperance the prime minister of death," and "our tempers must be governed or they will govern us."[23] In another schoolbook, he listed six statements a student should be able to incorporate into a theme on "Moderation in our wishes necessary." The list worried through the problems of restlessness and excitement, ambition and hope, the real and the ideal, to end with "What is rational and obtainable should, therefore, be the only objects of desire."[24] In the same book, Parker prints a model "valedictory" oration, in which the student waxes eloquent (for five densely packed pages) on our "national spirit of moderation."[25]

Such didactic moralizing is not surprising in nineteenth-century educational practice, but moderation also reigns over less overt lessons about how people make decisions in times of stress. Students learn to hold ideas in opposition and to strike a balance between one side or another. They practice what eighteenth-century rhetoricians such as John Walker called the "middle voice" so as to perform and express passions without being carried away by them.[26] The books advise self-conscious students to test themselves by speaking in empty rooms, trying out appropriate stances and hand gestures for particular passions. Students were preparing themselves in classrooms for highly charged encounters, ready with balanced sentences, gestures, and ways of moderating their feelings. The schoolbooks thus suggest that public behavior is not simply a given or a natural response, but can be learned. Democracy becomes a much-valued goal, requiring considerable maintenance and preparation. Ordinary citizens as well as leaders are seen as responsible for its practices—in both their private lives and their public contributions.

By midcentury, moderation was so widely accepted that it almost went without saying, merged into lists of similar virtues (modesty, chastity, virtue, fortitude, equanimity, duty, discretion, cheerfulness, contentment). Indeed, readers of the 1850s rarely named it directly. They continued to reprint passages from texts like Blair's sermons in which moderation is delineated, but they also evoked its influence with lessons on temperance, control of anger and passion, and moderation in eating. Their technical attention to voice and gesture might now suggest a simplistic understanding of politics and affect. But although elocutionary readers insisted on repeated moral adages—rewarding virtue, noting "faults to be remedied"—they also treated private and public behavior as complicated, requiring reflection, practice, and repeated effort. The "heroes" of the elocutionary readers are rarely one-dimensional role models valued solely for their success. Lessons present significant persons— George Washington, Cromwell, Napoleon, Hamlet—depicted in moments of challenge that threaten their behavior, their reason, their balance. They are admired for their resilience in the face of failure. Lessons show politicians working to negotiate a moderate path between extremes, quelling political enmity, or calming angry mobs. They depict speakers managing their impulses to act in haste or anger, but they also show them shifting to high passion when the situation demands it (at times of war, for example, in parliament, or at trial). Democracy's heroes are known for their ability to read their times and to react with consideration and a sense of their place in a broader fabric of human wills, desires, and ambitions. They are valued for being able to move others in measured ways, not by demagoguery or rage, but by rhetorical skill.

Students were expected to improve their own behavior and way of speaking by attending to heightened rhetorical scenes (for example, Henry V calling his troops to battle, Patrick Henry speaking to the Virginia Convention, or St. Paul defending his life before King Agrippa). In Parker's *Progressive Exercises in Rhetorical Reading* (1836) this exercise in comparative identification is made explicit. Parker offers a series of analogous sentences— one drawn from the grand style and content of drama, the other from the discourse of daily life. Students are asked to "imitate" the sentence—which asks them to understand comparable syntax, subject positions, and actions. "Go show your slave how choleric you are, and bid your bondman tremble," reads one "analogical sentence." "Go tell your father how naughty you have been, and ask your mother to reprove you," reads its colloquial counterpart.[27]

The sentence compares those in power and those who fear punishment; it structures the relationship of fault and punishment, of dread and outcome. At times the comparison is comical: "Why looks your Grace so heavily to-day?" morphs into "Why did you drive your hoop so fast to-day?"[28] At other times, it suggests social and political change—distrust of tyranny, emergence of ordinary people as actors, the importance of educational over military achievement. One of the effects of such analogical exercises is to help students see the ways in which their choices and behaviors imitate those of great people. Another is to help them see the ways in which times and rhetorical imperatives have changed.

Moderation was thus a complex, contested, and valued quality, inherited from classical and British eighteenth-century writers. It migrated across the Atlantic and out from traditional centers of power and rhetorical authority to be put to use by diverse populations of students. It gained and lost power across the nineteenth century, tested by its complicated affiliation with temperance and abolitionist movements. Learning to be moderate, to speak and read with moderation, was both an ideological lesson (a way of understanding one's social or political position, of assessing the consequences) and a technical lesson (a way of modulating the voice and arranging the body). It required discipline—of the passions, the desires, and the habits but also of the voice, the gestures, and the stance. If it was at times associated with tired platitudes and simplistic morality, it was also the tool for learning to perform the complex speech acts of political passion, difference of opinion, love or hate, anger or injury. It remained a quality or stance often recommended, often urged, but difficult to define, to learn, or maintain. This nineteenth-century narrative about moderation suggests the preparation and labor necessary to sustain shared civic and social values. The term's emphasis on a middle ground—on the shifting space between and among people of different positions and powers—emphasizes moderation as a strategy or attitude rather than a fixed political position.

Notes

1. Hugh Blair, "On Moderation," *Sermons* (London: W. Strahan and T. Cadell, 1790), III, 246, 248.
2. See Ethan H. Shagan, *The Rule of Moderation: Violence, Religion and the Politics of Restraint in Early Modern England* (Cambridge: Cambridge University Press, 2011), 3, 4.

3. Edmund Burke, *Reflections on the French Revolution* (London: J. Dodsley, 1790), 353.

4. John Walker, *A Critical Pronouncing Dictionary and Expositor of the English Language* (London: G. G. and J. Robinson, 1797), 167.

5. Samuel Johnson, *A Dictionary of the English Language*. 6th ed. (London: J. F. and C. Rivington, 1785), II, 143. H. J. Todd, who issued a revised edition of Johnson's *Dictionary* in 1818 adding new words and etymologies, went to surprising lengths to rescue moderation from its etymological association with the middle (Latin), instead emphasizing its association with "rule or measure" (Hebrew).

6. Noah Webster, *A Compendious Dictionary of the English Language* (Hartford, CT: Sidney's Press, 1806), 194.

7. Noah Webster, John Walker, Chauncey A. Goodrich, and Joseph E. Worcester, *An American Dictionary of the English Language*. 5th ed. (New York: S. Converse, 1828), II, 140.

8. Joseph E. Worcester, *A Comprehensive Pronouncing and Explanatory Dictionary* (Boston, MA: Hilliard, Gray, Little, and Wilkins, 1830), 205.

9. *Worcester's Academic Dictionary* (Philadelphia, PA: J. B. Lippincott, 1888), 367.

10. "The Mystery of Moderate Spirit Drinking," *The Temperance Advocate* (Belfast: Hugh Rea, 1832), 85, 109, 86.

11. "The License System," *American Temperance Magazine* (New York: R. Van Dien, 1851), 363.

12. Emma Willard, *Women and Temperance* (Hartford, CT: Park Publishing, 1883), 390.

13. Charles C. Jones, *The Religious Instruction of the Negroes* (Savannah, GA: Thomas Purse, 1842), 188, 241.

14. Frederick Douglass, *Narrative of the Life of Frederick Douglass* (Boston, MA: Anti-Slavery Office, 1845), 60; Harriet Jacobs, *Incidents in the Life of a Slave Girl* (Boston, MA: Published for the Author, 1861), 61.

15. William Lloyd Garrison, "A Short Catechism, Adapted to all Parts of the United States," in *The Liberator* (1837): 289, and "To the Public," in *The Liberator* (1831): 63.

16. Lydia Maria Child, *The Freedman's Book* (Boston, MA: Ticknor and Fields, 1865), 272, 28, 16.

17. Lindley Murray, *The English Reader* (New York: Isaac Collins, 1799), iii–iv.

18. Ibid., 85, 2.

19. Murray's *Introduction to the English Reader* (1817) prints a sentence that appears in many language textbooks: "They who are moderate in their expectations, meet with few disappointments" (27). It appears as a select sentence, but also as a parsing or grammar exercise, in the 1828 *Ladies' Miscellany* (88), and as a text for a girl's sampler.

20. McGuffey's *Second Eclectic Reader* (Cincinnati, OH: Truman and Smith, 1836), 83; *Third Eclectic Reader* (Cincinnati, OH: Truman and Smith, 1836), 11; *Second Eclectic Reader*, 154.

21. W. H. McGuffey, *Second Eclectic Reader* (1836), 33.

22. The excerpt from *Othello* appears in the *Sixth Eclectic Reader* (Cincinnati, OH: Sargent, Wilson, and Hinkle, 1857), 240. Biographies in the revised *Sixth Eclectic Reader* (Cincinnati, OH: Van Antwerp, Bragg, 1879) caution that Dickens "seemed to speak approvingly of conviviality and dissipation" (97) and that Coleridge "fell far short of what he might have attained, through...an excessive use of opium" (462).

23. Richard Green Parker, *Progressive Exercises in English Composition* (Boston, MA: Lincoln and Edmands, 1833), 86–88.

24. Richard Green Parker, *Aids to English Composition* (Boston, MA: Robert C. Davis, 1844), 215. Parker is half-quoting Blair's sermon "On Moderation," which states, "Satisfy yourselves with what is rational and obtainable" (248).

25. Ibid., 374–379.

26. John Walker, *Elements of Elocution* (London: Printed for the Author, 1781). Subsequent readers advise moderation as if it were self-evident. Walker's elaborate "system of the passions," from which this advice derives, uses Shakespeare to illustrate complex attitudes and feelings, distinguishing "moderate" performance from those "when this passion is in excess" (354).

27. Richard Green Parker, *Progressive Exercises in Rhetorical Reading* (Boston, MA: Crocker and Brewster, 1836), 86.

28. Ibid., 88.

Further Reading

On the cultural influence of elocutionary readers, see Jean Ferguson Carr, Stephen L. Carr, and Lucille Schultz, *Archives of Instruction: Nineteenth-Century Rhetorics, Readers, and Composition Books in the United States* (Carbondale, IL: Southern Illinois University Press, 2005). See also Ruth Miller Elson, *Guardians of Tradition: American Schoolbooks of the 19th Century* (Lincoln, NE: University of Nebraska Press, 1964) and Ronald J. Zboray, *A Fictive People: Antebellum Economic Development and the American Reading Public* (New York: Oxford University Press, 1993). For the complex meanings of moderation in early modern England, see Ethan H. Shagan, *The Rule of Moderation: Violence, Religion and the Politics of Restraint in Early Modern England* (Cambridge: Cambridge University Press, 2011). On temperance, see Carol Mattingly, *Well-Tempered Women: Nineteenth-Century Temperance Rhetoric* (Carbondale, IL: Southern Illinois University Press, 1998). On rhetoric and activism, see Jacqueline Jones Royster, *Traces of a Stream: Literacy and Social Change among African American Women* (Pittsburgh, PA: University of Pittsburgh Press, 2000). On the notion of "schooled commonplaces," see Susan Miller, *Assuming the Positions: Cultural Pedagogy and the Politics of Commonplace Writing* (Pittsburgh, PA: University of Pittsburgh Press, 1998).

17

Comfort

Michelle Sizemore

How does democracy *feel*? For midcentury domestic reformers, the answer was "comfortable." Exactly like their parlors. For comfort had become one of the most desirable features of the middle-class home and the parlor the most fussed-over room in the house. Discussion of comfort's domestic virtues saturated household advice manuals, house pattern books, magazines, and domestic fiction. Embraced by moral reformers as varied as Catharine Beecher, Andrew Jackson Downing, and Robert Hartley, comfort gained prominence as theories of environmental determinism newly envisioned the house as a built environment with the capacity to shape human character. Details such as the layout of rooms, choice of fabrics, and cut of drapes accrued immense importance as household activists sought the proper moral influences of comfortable surroundings. But what did living-room quality possibly have to do with democratic striving?

Comfort wasn't always a private commodity vended by home improvement channels and design vlogs. In a chapter from *Democracy in America* titled "Particular Effects of the Love of Physical Gratification in Democratic Times," Alexis de Tocqueville discusses comfort as a "moderate and tranquil" degree of "physical pleasure" whose common pursuit strengthens social order. The typical American is motivated by modest material rewards: by "comfort" as opposed to "opulence" in aristocratic societies. In "democratic nations," he claims, "[t]here is no question of building vast palaces, conquering or going against nature, or sucking the world dry, the better to satisfy one man's passions; all that is needed is to add a few yards to one's fields, to plant an orchard, to enlarge one's house ... without trouble and almost without expense."[1] For Tocqueville, the aspiration for small gratifications

Michelle Sizemore, *Comfort* In: *Democracies in America: Keywords for the Nineteenth Century and Today.*
Edited by: D. Berton Emerson and Gregory Laski, Oxford University Press. © D. Berton Emerson and Gregory Laski 2023.
DOI: 10.1093/oso/9780198865698.003.0018

promotes industry and restraint, individual virtues that increase the common good.

Over the next two decades Tocqueville would be joined by a brigade of commentators extolling the virtues of comfort. And the desirable corporeal sensibility felt in parlors above Bleeker became the guidepost of an accelerating New York City housing reform movement aimed at the Lower East Side and Five Points in the 1840s and 1850s—a full half-century before the well-documented efforts of Progressive-Era activists such as Jacob Riis. These men and women insisted suitable living conditions for everyone were fundamental to the democratic project and leveraged amenity for reform. As tents, cars, streets, and shelters increasingly serve as primary dwellings across the United States, we would do well to contemplate the democratic principle of EQUALITY informing this earlier movement, the proposition that universal and inalienable rights to "life, liberty, and the pursuit of happiness" confer access to satisfactory living conditions—not income, or employment status, or the moral standards of the privileged classes.

How do feelings like comfort influence our capacity to act on behalf of a cause? How might affective attunement with others advance democratic goals and democratic relations? Contemporary theorists of emotions remain preoccupied with such questions, turning to affect as a corrective to Western political philosophy's overestimation of the role of reason in formulating political opinions, judgments, and decisions. These practitioners presuppose that humans are corporeal creatures with subliminal affective intensities and resonances that inflect beliefs and actions. Still, all affects do not convey the same effects. Some of the leading critics on the subject have assumed that "weak" affects like comfort obstruct or suspend agency. This essay suggests, to the contrary, that comfort and its converse, discomfort, were primers for political action in nineteenth-century New York's long crusade for adequate housing. Thus, if democracy evoked DISGUST for conservative political thinkers in the 1790s, decades later the egalitarianism of sociopolitical order evoked the pleasant sensations of corporeal harmony and contentment for social progressives.

For centuries, "comfort" was primarily a moral term describing emotional and spiritual support in difficult circumstances. It referred to strength or solace in times of distress such as the death of a loved one. Beginning in the eighteenth century, Americans increasingly used the word "comfort" to indicate the enjoyment of one's physical surroundings. The explicit physical dimension of the term represented an important transition from its designation of relations between people to its designation of worldly goods thought to enhance mental and physical well-being. Redefined in this way, "comfort" came to describe an attribute of things, a change due in part to the consumer revolution. The material significance of the term originated in political economists' analysis of differences between luxury and necessity and increasingly applied to commodities occupying a middle ground between wants and needs. "Comforts" and the related terms "conveniences" and "decencies" referred to goods offering modest improvements of basic human necessities.

Thus, by the end of the eighteenth century comfort was understood as a property of the material object itself, but this conception is not identical with later definitions of physical corporeal comfort emphasizing "the self-conscious satisfaction between the human body and its immediate physical environment."[2] Not until the middle of the nineteenth century did comfort regularly denote a pleasurable physical state, thereby approaching contemporary definitions that prioritize the interaction between body and environment. Most experts maintain that comfort derives from our sensory reaction to stimuli such as heat, cold, smell, noise, light, and air supply. Yet it is not strictly a physiological phenomenon, the sole effect of sensory input transmitted to receptor cells and nerve cells along neural pathways to the brain. The pleasure of this physical state is also learned, shaped by experience and culture.

My recommendation is that we conceive of comfort as a mood engendered by humans' mingled sensory and cognitive perception of place; in this case, the domestic environment. Moods are ambient feeling-states that surround subjects. They are diffuse, nebulous, vague. Simultaneously physiological and psychological, moods are feelings that color our thoughts and perceptions, as Rene Rosfort writes, "suffus[ing] our experience as a whole with a certain affective hue or tinge, and thus qualify[ing] the way we experience the world, *other* people, and ourselves."[3] Comprehending comfort as a mood seems especially fitting given the atmospheric qualities that bring about comfort, from clean air to mild temperature.

This understanding muddles the mind–body dualism persisting in Western thought, a split almost always privileging the thinking brain. Take, for example, the notion of a "comfort zone." Comfort zones have become integrated into our everyday knowledge as "a place or situation in which a person feels secure or at ease," so much so that few question this purely psychological explanation of comfort's causes (conditions of security or familiarity).[4] Yet it is a challenge to pinpoint the precise cause of comfort. Are we comfortable because our minds are at ease with the familiarity of the setting? Because our bodies are at ease with the lighting, the plush seating? Yes and yes. Comprehending comfort as a mood requires that body and mind be taken as a continuous entity such that comfort arises non-linearly from a generalized atmosphere working on the mind–body system; and insofar as comfort "incites," it does so through a similarly generalized atmospheric shift in attitude and perception.

To foreground the mood of domestic comfort in a discussion of democracy is to take seriously the wager that bodies do politics on the neural and physiological levels. It is to insist that something subtly felt, even if not consciously registered, can modulate our tendencies and capacities, often faintly and gradually. The notion of "democratic moods" presents an alternative to models of democratic engagement that prioritize either rational deliberation or strong reactionary emotions. Change was granular in the arena of housing reform, emerging from the embodied experiences of thousands of ordinary people carrying out the prosaic work of professions and philanthropies that brought them into cross-class contact with the city's slums.

No other dwelling in the nineteenth century represented the antithesis of comfort more powerfully than tenement housing. Following an already steep population increase over the previous two decades, New York's population exploded from 324,000 to over 1 million between 1840 and 1860 as Irish, German, and British immigrants and village migrants from New England, New Jersey, and Long Island made Manhattan and Brooklyn their home. The addition of 750,000 residents created a severe housing shortage. Landlords and developers responded to this urgent demand by packing tenants into existing dwellings or by building new multifamily housing, called tenements. It was not unusual to find five- to seven-story buildings divided into 100 apartments containing 150 families. And these were the front buildings. Very often in the backyard were rear tenements half the size. Some property-owners threw up a third tenement or jerry-rigged apartments from cellars, attics, and shacks, wringing as much rent money as possible from their lots.

With six to eight people or more crowding rooms of 120 square feet, the Five Points earned the notorious distinction of the most densely populated neighborhood in the world. The slums of the Sixth Ward made regular appearances in tourist accounts such as Davy Crockett's *Tour to the North and Down East* (1834) and Charles Dickens's *American Notes* (1842), as well as city-commissioned studies. Journalists reported abominable conditions in local papers and national magazines. In a widely read 1845 report, Dr. John Griscom, City Inspector, writes: "The tenements, in order to admit a greater number of families, are divided into small apartments, as numerous as decency will admit. Regard to *comfort*, convenience, and health, is the last motive."[5] Throughout the prolific writing on the slums during this period, the extreme discomfort of living conditions attracted as much attention as or perhaps even more than the health risks. Comfort quickly became a watchword as habitat moved to the front and center of reformers' concerns.

Gaining momentum in the 1840s, New York housing reform joined advocates in arenas as wide-ranging as city and state government, medicine, sanitation, education, religion, architecture, and interior design. The population surge forced the issue of adequate housing into public awareness, and several concurrent developments contributed to housing reform, including the pragmatism of newer scientific philanthropy and advances in epidemiology and sanitation science. Guiding this campaign were changing attitudes toward the poor prompted by a more forgiving explanation of their degradation: the environment was replacing personal depravity as the cause. Robert Hartley succinctly expresses this view in an 1853 report on the laboring classes: "Physical evils produce moral evils. Degrade men to the condition of brutes, and they will have brutal propensities and passions."[6] The growing conviction of "moral environmentalism," in Stanley Schultz's coinage, was the amendment of moral behavior via improvements to the physical environment.[7]

Perhaps most instrumental of all was the abundance of writing on tenement life. Alongside these other efforts, writers helped to change living conditions for the better by steadily promoting the equality of basic human needs. The urban exposé was especially influential, spanning a variety of fictional and nonfictional genres including tabloid journalism, government reports such as Griscom's, city mystery-and-misery novels, and urban sketches. Flavoring reform with sensation, the exposé brought to light the lurid underworld of Gotham, often through the revelations of an anonymous first-person narrator who relates his "observations and investigations" to readers accompanying his trek through the metropolis.[8] Much of the fiction shared with its nonfictional counterparts a more realistic reportorial style and a commitment to documenting the urban environment. These works were sympathetic to the poor, indicting the rich and powerful who exploit the unfortunate as well as the indifferent bourgeoisie who allow the degrading conditions to persist.

The genre's runaway bestseller, Solon Robinson's *Hot Corn*, serialized in the *New York Tribune* in August 1853, focuses on the hardships of Little Katy, a hot-corn seller who dies from exposure after spending the night on the street. Expanding upon the original serialized story in 1854, Robinson published a collection of interwoven sketches, *Hot Corn: Life Scenes in New York Illustrated*, which spotlights the everyday struggles of the city's destitute and aims criticism at the manifold problems of slum life. The book sold 50,000 copies in six months. Little Katy was such a phenomenon that the serial spawned watercolors, broadsides, dozens of songs, and three theatrical versions with concurrent runs even before the book debuted.

Much of Robinson's attention turns on the squalid conditions of the city and the unnamed middle-class narrator's visceral experience of this setting. On the opening page, he invites uninitiated readers to "walk with [him]...through the streets of New York" to the cramped and polluted spaces of Cow Bay—a Five Points district that journalists agreed was the worst of the worst.[9] The narrator's immersion in these scenes produces an oppressive multisensory encounter vital to *Hot Corn*'s representation of discomfort. The Five Points are an assault on the senses, in particular the "lower" senses of touch, taste, and smell, as scholars of the day conceived of them. The nineteenth century had formalized the notion that "high" culture required the suppression of the "lower" senses. To achieve respectability, individuals and societies needed to rise above the animal life of the body. Touch was considered the most inferior, a vulgar and uncivilized mode of perception belonging to primitive cultures and the lower classes. Tactile experience dominates in Cow Bay. The narrator records bodies in contact with each other (three families in a 10 × 12 garret), bodies in contact with habitation ("low cellars," "narrow passages"), bodies in contact with "steaming filth" (110, 213, 70). Prolific descriptions of overcrowding reinforce contemporary hierarchies of sensory experience. Countless "hole-in-the-ground" dwellings, like dugouts for moles, create subhuman imagery. "Surely human beings cannot live there!" exclaims the scandalized reader (54). Because of their accommodations, the city's poor live in violation of Victorian prohibitions against physical intimacy: above all, interpersonal touch and direct full-body contact with the rudiments of the environment, such as streets and floors where residents are constantly strewn and heaped together.

Unpleasant sensations harass the narrator (and reader) apart from the physical encroachment they both witness and endure. Sweltering heat in "holes almost as hot as the hot corn" activates another form of tactile experience: the sense of thermoception, or temperature perception (44). Indeed, distinctive qualities belonging to the air—excessive heat and cold, stagnancy due to poor ventilation, foul smell—occupy much of the narrative focus. As the narrator describes his visit to Little Katy's death bed: "The fetid odor of this filthy lane had been made more fetid by the late and almost scalding hot rains, until it seemed to us that such an air was only fit for a charnel house" (110). A vague "pestilence" permeates the atmosphere and it is this "air...fit for a charnel house" to which Little Katy succumbs. By the narrator's account, she is "poisoned with the sleep-inhaled miasma of the filth-reeking gutter" (105).

Robinson fixates on air quality both to pronounce on the current miasmic theory of disease and to project an atmosphere for the negative moral influences of alcoholism, prostitution, child-beating, wife-beating, and theft attending the vicinity. To this end, the illustrations attempt to visibly render invisible effluvia, as in an image where noxious air girdles Katy much like her damp shawl. This vaguely perceptible sphere of vapors is a fitting expression for the new and imperfectly understood notion of the physical environment's influence on the moral condition and social behavior of the inhabitants. In his report, Griscom had been so convinced of the determinism of built environments he declared that the removal of "respectable" individuals from "the [correct] *moral atmosphere* in which they move" would make their "evil passions...rise."[10] This miasmic medium foregrounds the mediated nature of experience, both in the sense that surroundings imprint character and that the framing, vaporous as it may be, shapes perception and interpretation.

The slums find a stark contrast with the "snug, comfortable house" of a family lifted from poverty, a technique by which Robinson charts social progress through setting and ambiance in *Hot Corn* (72). One year later, he devoted an entire book to the middle-class ideal of comfort. *Home Comforts* is a fictional narrative on the domestic economy of a respectable carpenter's family, one that focuses minute attention on contentment between the body and its physical environment. Mrs. Savery's modest sitting room is, as her name suggests, pleasant to the taste and smell as well as to the touch, sight, and sound. By far the most outstanding feature of the room is aroma— from corn cakes on the griddle topped with quince preserves, "air fresh and sweet from the flower garden," a trunk filled with cedar shavings and sassa-fras, and so on.[11] Also, the delicate warmth of the fire from a coal stove newly distributing heat throughout the room "enables the occupants to sit quite back, with more comfort than they used to find in close proximity with the stove" (37). Comfort's subtle atmosphere is notable for its enhance-ment of rapport. Mrs. Savery, her children, and her neighbors are ensconced together—connected—through the warmth of the fire and the redolence of coal burning and cakes baking. No one is making direct or conscious contact; instead the gentle medium of warmth, scent, and flavor fosters inti-macy and accord.

Mobilizing comfort (and discomfort) in the cause of equitable housing may seem farfetched or doomed, especially as we now tend to associate comfort with complacency and moods in general with inertia. Can we imagine Mrs. Savery rushing from parlor to protest? We don't need to. Housing reform came about incrementally. While in the first half of the nineteenth century city commissions formed and tenant legislation passed, New York's first Tenement House Act did not materialize until 1867. A sec-ond Tenement House Act followed in 1879, and a third in 1901, each cor-recting the one before. A series of significant legislative amendments also occurred in between these three acts. Legislation, scientific studies, tene-ment planning and construction, and bad publicity all slowly regulated and improved living conditions. Undergirding all of these efforts was not only a belief about the right of everyone to a basic standard of comfort but also a somatic, sensible discernment of the problem. Comfort must be viewed as a crucial development in the politics of perception. Jacques Rancière's notion of the "distribution of the sensible" is instructive on this front. In *Disagreement*, he describes an aesthetic-political world variously divided into regimes of perception that govern what is and isn't sensible. According to Rancière, the essence of politics consists in reconfiguring the distribution of the sensible by including that which was previously excluded from the perceptual field, and for him this means greater visibility and audibility.[12] But as this essay has been suggesting, domestic comfort becomes perceptible as much through tactile, olfactory, and gustatory sensation as through vision and hearing—through aesthetic attunement to the air.

The mounting housing crises of the twenty-first century make comfort timely for appraisal as the topic continues to figure in local and national discussions about affordable housing for low-income Americans. Today, we must ask whether and how something as airy as comfort might be implemented in current US housing reform. Were the Department of Housing and Urban Development to marshal a theory of comfort for democratic praxis, it would need to be intentional about who owns the theory governing reform. Just as conceptions of comfort were dictated by those with economic, cultural, and racial privilege in the nineteenth century, all too often now housing initiatives are set into motion without consulting the communities involved. The enduring challenge for any plan that depends on apprehending the affective resonance of humans in relation to their built environments lies in fathoming and legislating for the particularities of bodies and their comfort within uneven structures of power.

Notes

1. Alexis de Tocqueville, *Democracy in America and Two Essays on America* (1835, 1840; repr., London: Penguin, 2003), 617, 619.

2. John E. Crowley, *The Invention of Comfort: Sensibilities and Design in Early Modern Britain and Early America* (Baltimore, MD: Johns Hopkins University Press, 2001).

3. Rene Rosfort and Giovanni Stanghellini, "In the Mood for Thought: Feeling and Thinking in Philosophy," *New Literary History* 43, no. 3 (2012): 408.

4. "comfort zone, n.," *OED Online*, June 2019, Oxford University Press, www.oed.com (accessed August 26, 2019).

5. John Griscom, *The Sanitary Condition of the Laboring Population of New York, With Suggestions for Its Improvement* (New York: Harper and Brothers, 1845), 6; emphasis mine.

6. Robert Hartley, Association for Improving the Condition of the Poor, *First Report of a Committee on the Sanitary Condition of the Laboring Classes in the City of New York, with Remedial Suggestions* (New York: John F. Trow, 1853), 26.

7. Stanley K. Schultz, *Constructing Urban Culture: American Cities and City Planning, 1800–1920* (Philadelphia, PA: Temple University Press, 1989), 112.

8. George G. Foster, *New York Naked* (1854; repr., New York: DeWitt & Davenport, 1856), 8.

9. Solon Robinson, *Hot Corn: Life Scenes in New York Illustrated* (New York: DeWitt and Davenport, 1854), 13. Hereafter cited parenthetically.

10. Griscom, *Sanitary Condition of the Laboring Population of New York*, 23; emphasis mine.

11. Solon Robinson, *Home Comforts; or, Economy Illustrated, by Familiar Scenes of Everyday Life* (New York: Bunce and Brothers, 1855), 15. Hereafter cited parenthetically.

12. Jacques Rancière, *Disagreement: Politics and Philosophy*, trans. Julie Rose (Minneapolis, MN: University of Minnesota Press, 2004).

Further Reading

For an introduction to affects and politics, see Ruth Leys, "The Turn to Affect: A Critique," *Critical Inquiry* 37, no. 3 (2011): 434–472; Gregory Seigworth and Melissa Gregg, "An Inventory of Shimmers," in Gregory Seigworth and Melissa Gregg, eds., *The Affect Theory Reader* (Durham, NC: Duke University Press, 2010); John Protevi, *Political Affect: Connecting the Social and the Somatic* (Minneapolis, MN: University of Minnesota Press, 2009); and Brian Massumi, *Politics of Affect* (Cambridge: Polity, 2015). Research on comfort spans cultural history, cultural studies, sociology, architecture, and the building sciences. See Katherine C. Grier, *Culture and Comfort: Parlor Making and Middle-Class Identity, 1850–1930* (Washington, DC: Smithsonian Institution Press, 1988); Philomena M. Bluyssen, *The Indoor Environment Handbook: How to Make Buildings Healthy and Comfortable* (London: Earthscan, 2009); Elizabeth Shove, *Comfort, Cleanliness, and Convenience: The Social Organization of Normality* (Oxford: Berg, 2003). For midcentury histories of New York tenements and slums, the following sources are both useful and accessible: James Ford, *Slums and Housing* (Cambridge, MA: Harvard University Press, 1936); Tyler Anbinder, *Five Points* (New York: Plume, 2002); Paul Boyer, *Urban Masses and Moral Order in America, 1820–1920* (Cambridge, MA: Harvard University Press, 1978); Caroll Smith Rosenberg, *Religion and the Rise of the American City: The New York City Mission Movement, 1812–1870* (New York: Cornell University Press, 1971); and Edwin G. Burrows and Mike Wallace, *Gotham: A History of New York City to 1898* (New York: Oxford University Press, 2000).

PART
IV

Ambitions and Distortions

The unsettling fact is that ruling ourselves is not a predictable or stable enterprise, but this is as much a cause for jubilation as despair. This seemingly fatal flaw is also the source of democracy's strength. Its fragmentary, unfinished nature poses a challenge to all of us who want to be both equal and free.

Astra Taylor, *Democracy May Not Exist, but We'll Miss It When It's Gone* (2019)[1]

Democracy can be a dream, but it can also be a nightmare. Resting on what the historian James Kloppenberg has called an "ethical ideal," democracy depends on a belief—a lofty and perhaps even utopian one—that people can govern themselves.[2] This ideal comes to life in a messy reality; it gets enacted in everyday, on-the-ground exchanges between people whose own beliefs about and views of others may be hardened, cruel, and exclusionary. Writing from the standpoint of one of those excluded groups, the African American scholar W. E. B. Du Bois framed the matter with an uncomfortable clarity. "The theory of democratic government is not that the will of the people is always right," he remarked in 1910, "but rather that normal human beings of average intelligence will, if given a chance, learn the right and best course by bitter experience."[3]

The essays composing the final Part of this book invite you to reflect on this inescapable paradox. As you read about THE COMMONS, TYRANNY, SHAM, DISFRANCHISEMENT, SECURITY, SETTLEMENT, DOUBT, and NEIGHBORS, ponder: How does democracy negotiate the tensions between its grand ideals and the realities of forging a common life among a diverse people? When democracy gets stuck, is it enough to try to narrow the gap between values and practices? Or do the values themselves need revision? What role do universals such as "natural" or "higher law" or "self-evident truths" play in that process? Must we have faith in such ideals? How can we commit to believing in such ideals and still commit to progress and change? Does democracy guarantee progress? What is the line between democracy and tyranny, and how do we recognize and navigate it?

The long nineteenth century reveals the ways in which the ambitions and distortions of democracy are often mirror images of one another. Take *doubt*: the deformation of trust in others can be damaging to democracy. But as Jane Addams, founder of the Chicago Hull House community, maintained, it also can be made into a virtue, even something utterly necessary if people work to turn this doubt into the inquiry and openness that living in common with others different from oneself demands. Similarly, one of the nation's formative political documents, the Declaration of Independence, situated democratic rule as the antithesis of tyrannical force. But it all too frequently fell to enslaved people, Indigenous Americans, and women's rights advocates to show how "the people" could easily slip into cruel and absolutist modes.

Ultimately, the essays in this Part show again and again that the lines between the ideal and the real, between ambition and distortion, between dream and nightmare are fine indeed, and the movement of those lines requires constant monitoring. It is for this reason that the twenty-first-century democratic activist and thinker Astra Taylor encourages us to replace the well-worn figure of the "Founding Fathers" with the less familiar "perennial midwives" as our governing metaphor of American democracy, in order to better capture the nature of collective self-rule as an endeavor.[4]

How, then, can a democratic people walk this path, aware of the historical risks and mindful of the necessary constraints, but with a spirit of generation and possibility?

Notes

1. Astra Taylor, *Democracy May Not Exist, but We'll Miss It When It's Gone* (New York: Metropolitan Books, 2019), 311–312.
2. James T. Kloppenberg, *Toward Democracy: The Struggle for Self-Rule in European and American Thought* (New York: Oxford University Press, 2016), 14.
3. W. E. Burghardt Du Bois, "Reconstruction and Its Benefits," *American Historical Review* 15, no. 4 (1910): 781–799.
4. Taylor, *Democracy May Not Exist*, 312.

18

The Commons

Dana D. Nelson

The knowledge- and resource-sharing practices that characterize our online lives may be the first thing we think of if asked to name a "commons." Wikipedia is a robust example of a user-based knowledge commons, a free, open-access encyclopedia that has proven to be as reliable as expertly produced commercial encyclopedias (sometimes even more so). Linux is another notable achievement, a non-proprietary and user-based family of free and open-source software operating systems initiated by Linus Torvalds in 1991. Wikipedia has spawned a plethora of wiki-cousins, and we've seen the rapid emergence of peer-to-peer sharing practices such as Uber, Lyft, Airbnb, Spinlister (bicycles), Zaarly (home services), Dog Vacay, Lending Club, Fon (wifi), Poshmark, and Neighborgoods (clothes), just to name a few. This resource-sharing—ride-, apartment-, room-sharing, and home loaning, peer-to-peer lending, reselling, coworking, and talent-sharing—deploys peer networks and the internet to expand the use of existing goods. These platforms sometimes (though not always) aim at some kind of profit, but they also cultivate behaviors that are about collaboration and sharing, about interdependence and sufficiency. In this, they impact and importantly redirect our culture's strong emphasis on consumerism and individual accumulation.

The other strong association we have with the commons has to do with natural resources—water, pastures, fisheries, wood for buildings and fires, flora and fauna. We've been taught, most famously by Garret Hardin's widely read and quoted essay on "The Tragedy of the Commons," that man's intrinsic selfishness inevitably imperils such resources and that the best way to "save nature" is to put it beyond the reach of ordinary, unthinkingly venal actors and let government or private business manage it for us.[1] The problem

Dana D. Nelson, *The Commons* In: *Democracies in America: Keywords for the Nineteenth Century and Today.*
Edited by: D. Berton Emerson and Gregory Laski, Oxford University Press. © D. Berton Emerson and Gregory Laski 2023.
DOI: 10.1093/oso/9780198865698.003.0019

with his story about natural resource commons, though, is that it rests on a flawed premise (one we can quickly see by thinking about my first set of examples): commons, simply put, don't preexist human input and management. Humans, acting separately or selfishly, can most certainly imperil the abundance—and even the existence—of a given natural resource. But commons schemes have emerged in history and today *precisely to redress* the threat of scarcity. Though commons schemes can fail, they can also succeed: they are by no means *inevitably* "tragic." Over the course of her impressive career, Nobel Prize-winning economist Elinor Ostrom documented many successful commons schemes in history and into today that preserve and maximize natural goods such as water, pastures or fish, and municipal, civic and human resources, too, succeeding precisely because of good human self-management.

Commons, in other words, are self-governing schemes for natural-, knowledge-, and civic-resource generation and management. And put that way, we can see why commons and the practice of commoning could be a resource for thinking about and practicing democracy today. Though we easily associate "commons" with knowledge and natural resources, we seldom stop to consider how the work of their administration produces a *civic* good—an experience of communal self-governing and resource allocation for commoners themselves. At their best, commons can produce a democratically generated political power along with a political subjectivity grounded in interdependence. Thus commoning practices might be an important tool for democratic revitalization.

Interestingly, it's possible to argue that practices of commoning were foundational to the ideas and strategies that drove the American Revolution. Historians have mostly discounted the practices of commoning in the British colonies, citing, for instance, the pilgrims' early abandonment of common-field agriculture after they realized that residents of the colony worked harder to self-provision than they did for community stores. In this familiar account, British colonists almost immediately rejected resource-sharing in favor of private accumulation. Commoning practices in the colonies have thus received very little attention. But like Hardin's conclusion about the tragedy of the commons, this one too easily assumes the abandonment of shared cropping in Plymouth meant a total rejection across the colonies of the entrenched practices settlers carried with them across the Atlantic for sharing resources—the exercise of common right in wetlands, coastal areas, forests, rivers, and oceans; the sharing of fires, beds, and folk knowledge. It further assumes that commoning couldn't exist alongside practices of private property, and also that practices of commoning were stuck in time as well as place, unable to evolve as people moved and times progressed.

More and more, as historians begin to probe the legacies of ordinary and poor settlers in the American colonies, these assumptions are turning out to be wrong. America is, in a familiar phrase, the "land of the common man." This is so for a reason: historian Allan Kulikoff details how many of the early British settlers in the colonies—commoners who came on their own as well as the many who came under indenture or criminal penalty—came to the Americas steeped in commoning traditions, traditions that concerned the sharing and management not just of natural resources such as firewood and pastures but domestic, cultural, and civic resources as well, and with a political sensibility tempered by decades of resistance to enclosure in England. Thus many British and European colonists came seeking access to a livelihood and way of life no longer accessible to them in England. They brought with them the informal practices and traditions of commoning they had been raised in and some had fought to save. To this day, holders of private land must post "do not trespass" signs if they don't want people hunting on their property—so deep and nevertheless hidden is the assumption of commoning in US law.

In her important book *Freedoms We Lost: Consent and Resistance in Revolutionary America*, historian Barbara Smith details the customs and mobilizing theories of the democratic participation among ordinary American colonists—practices and ideas that drove the Patriot cause. In her account, ordinary folk in the British colonies cultivated two signal principles—neighboring and competency—that contributed practically and ideologically to the revolutionary cause. Neighboring was an ethic that evolved organically across the colonies from a suite of compatible beliefs—for instance, Puritans came to be "knit together" in a covenantal community and Quakers came to Pennsylvania and New Jersey in particular to practice their faith as a Society of Friends. Whatever the faith of the European settlers, high mortality rates in the early years of colonization also contributed by forcing new inhabitants to innovate traditions that replaced lost kinship networks. Intriguingly, too, settlers from northern Holland may well have brought to America a set of beliefs—and a word, "naoberschap"—about the responsibility of NEIGHBORS to organize life events like weddings and funerals. These various intertwining practices of "neighboring" made local social interconnections a fabric of life, an active practice: an ethic.

At the same time, colonists developed economic ethics that similarly emphasized interdependence and community accountability. Competence has long conjured the drive toward the fabled independence of American revolution. But Smith points out that in emphasizing independence, we've forgotten an equally crucial aspect: "while possession of a competency suggested an experience of nondependence, it was not truly an experience of independence, if by that we mean self-sufficiency or a construction of one's identity as somehow 'self-made.' The goal of a competency did not suggest or even allow independence from one's neighbors or the commercial market."[2] In Smith's account, neighboring and competency guided British colonists toward their Declaration of Independence from England in ways that also made it, Smith underscores, a declaration of American *interdependence*.

It's hard not to see competence and neighboring as related to common-ing, especially if we think of them in the context of contemporary reports like J. Hector St. John de Crèvecoeur's accounts of the late colonies. *Letters from an American Farmer* (1782) and letters later collected in *Eighteenth-Century Sketches* (1925) document the broad dimensions of commoning in the run-up to Revolution in America, describing colonists' traditions of communal provisioning and mutual support. Crèvecoeur shows how colonists routinely shared natural resources (like seeds, firewood, and herbal reme-dies), as well as labor and creative resources (like traditional folk ballads, or sharing beds and fires with strangers, barn and house-raisings, local tradi-tions for peacekeeping and fairness, or serving in the militia). He indicates the extent to which logics of commoning flourished in eighteenth-century British America, and Smith shows how fully these practices provided a prac-tical basis for the colonists' revolutionary belief in their ability to self-govern. The locally based powers and enthusiasm of colonists urging for independ-ence from England propelled the political elite into supporting them and their energies drove the Revolution, as historian Woody Holton details in his book *Forced Founders*. The community-based power of ordinary people authorized and was recognized by most early state constitutions. It's plausible, then, to assert that the American Revolution was driven in crucial ways by experiences of self-governing connected to practices of interdependency—of commoning.

Importantly, though, *inter*dependence is neither what we remember nor treasure about the American Revolution. This is so for two reasons. First is the resonant claim of political independence from England enshrined in the Declaration. Second is the popular sovereignty memorably invoked by the Preamble to the American Constitution: "We the People." The popular sovereignty recognized and claimed by the US Constitution and its first ten amendments was a grant to *individual* citizens, who received from that CONSTITUTION a different kind of freedom from that on offer by interdependence, the freedom associated with liberal individualism. Political philosophers frequently characterize this freedom as *negative*: freedom *from* government scrutiny or coercion, which Isaiah Berlin neatly encapsulated as the "new idea . . . that there is a province of life—private life—within which it is thought undesirable, save in exceptional circumstances, for public authority to interfere."[3] In this way, the Constitution's protections of, for example, freedom of conscience, speech, unreasonable search and seizure, and excessive bail insulate individual citizens from unreasonable state actions. The Constitution thus enshrined citizenship as an individual good, a set of protected and importantly *private* rights. It recognized the integrity, autonomy, and power of individual citizens as a byproduct of national power, where individual freedom came as citizens acquiesced to national power. In this way, the Constitution's framing underscored the seventeenth-century individualism of Locke and presaged emerging doctrines of liberalism that would be memorably articulated by such notable nineteenth-century intellectuals as Benjamin Constant and Alexis de Tocqueville in France, Jeremy Bentham and John Stuart Mill in England, and William Lloyd Garrison and Ralph Waldo Emerson in the United States. This individualist framing soon overshadowed the model of CITIZENSHIP envisioned by the ordinary Patriots who motored the Revolution.

The political freedom sought by the Patriot movement did not reference emerging ideals of individual private freedom. Rather, the Patriots claimed the collective right of ordinary citizens to participate publicly in self-governing. Political theorists and philosophers often describe this as an "ancient" form of political freedom, in contrast to liberal individualism, since granting political power to ordinary (poor) citizens was the innovation of classical Greek democracy, signaled in the word itself: demos (common or poor people) + kratia (power). For the Patriots, acting in local committees across the colonies and into the early United States, this ideal was not ancient. It was *revolutionary*: the self-claimed right emerging among ordinary American colonists to participate in the making and execution of

government, policy, and law. For Crèvecoeur, this power to self-govern constituted what we've since come to call the "American Dream." His term for
it was "the municipal blessing"—the remarkably wide ability of ordinary
colonists to gain a freehold and competency, enabling their participation in
the work of collective self-governing.[4]

It's clear that the political elite—the storied founders and framers—were
mobilized by the Patriots' equalitarian political and economic ideals in the
1770s. But many began pulling back from those ideals in the 1780s as they
sought to put in place structures of government and fiscal policy that would
attract international investment and thus cultivate national power and even
preeminence for the new United States. Their early moves (often in the
form of tax collection) were resisted by ordinary citizens across all the states
in the form of debt protests and citizen "regulations" (actions by which
ordinary citizens exercised what they saw as their right to enforce "good
government" when their political leaders failed to do so). This is why the
political elite sought to replace the Articles of Confederation with the new
Federal Constitution, and it's also why that convention was "closed-door":
its doors were closed *specifically against* the direct input (or "advice") of ordinary
citizens into the Constitution's design (as is the Constitution). The framers
aimed to tame the movement toward popular democracy by substituting
a representative republican government for the more direct participatory
forms citizens were pushing for. They enacted this substitution carefully,
though, drawing on democratic rhetoric. As Holton notes in his study of the
Constitution's framing, the framers carefully disguised their political reser-
vations about direct participation in the Constitution itself, never approving
"an inflammatory proposal if they could accomplish the same objective using
a mechanism their fellow citizens would find easier to swallow."[5]

The Patriot movement idealized citizen association—citizens acting
freely together in public to frame and enact laws. The era of ratification
became, in Smith's analysis, an era of "dissociation." As the political elite
backed out of their revolutionary coalition with ordinary political actors,
they offered the mechanisms of political REPRESENTATION like a Trojan horse.
Structures of political representation promised the popular, democratic access
to governing they were actually designed to limit. Under the Constitution,
the people would no longer act together in public in the making or enforcing
of law but rather would be "represented" by political and legal professionals:
"once the Constitution was ratified," as Smith pithily summarizes, "the

desires of political majorities would not easily determine political pol-icy."[6] Individual citizens got an expanded right to vote for political leaders, but lost the right to lead themselves.

After ratification, ordinary citizens continued to associate, forming "Democratic-Republican societies" of correspondence across the new nation. The Whiskey Regulation—or Rebellion, as Alexander Hamilton insisted it be called—was the outcome of political association. From 1791 to 1794, ordinary people protested the first national excise tax, which they felt unfairly burdened small farmers in the west. President Washington responded to the protest by calling up more troops—some 13,000—than he had commanded during the American Revolution to march to western Pennsylvania and end the protest. But the habits of association ran deep. Even some forty years later, Tocqueville would characterize the spirit of association that he observed ongoing in America as the very backbone of its democracy. In *Democracy in America*, Tocqueville described democracy in the United States not as a set of institutions but as a *society*. From his perspective, what distinguished American democracy was its routine inte-gration in the lives of ordinary Americans. Notably in his description, the social experience of each person was shaped by collective practices of democratic power that did not aim at formal institutions of government. As he describes it,

> The inhabitant of the United States learns from birth that he must rely on himself to combat the ills and trials of life; he is restless and defiant in his out-look toward the authority of society and appeals to its power only when he cannot do without it. The beginnings of this attitude first appear in school, where the children even in their games, submit to rules settled by themselves and punish offenses which they have defined themselves. The same attitude turns up again in all the affairs of social life. If some obstacle blocks the public road halting the circulation of traffic, the neighbors at once form a deliberative body; this improvised assembly produces an executive authority which reme-dies the trouble before anyone has thought of the possibility of some previ-ously constituted authority beyond that of those concerned. Where enjoyment is concerned, people associate to make the festivities grander and more orderly. Finally, associations are formed to combat exclusively moral troubles: intem-perance is fought in common. Public security, trade and industry, and morals and religion all provide the aims for associations in the United States. There is no end which the human will despairs of attaining by the free action of the collective power of individuals.[7]

In Tocqueville's account, the vitality of democracy in the American 1830s had nothing to do with sovereignty. Rather, the spirit of democracy was fostered by citizens' ability to craft and cultivate a democratic sensibility collaboratively, by working together, by participating regularly in democratic problem-solving. In Tocqueville's powerful conclusion, "the free action of the collective power of individuals" created an extraordinary agency for regular people. What he described in the 1830s was precisely the "public happiness" that Jefferson had praised in the 1770s—and is likely what he meant, as Hannah Arendt observes, by "the pursuit of happiness" when he drafted the Declaration.[8]

These community-based cooperative practices faded over time. That makes it easy to demonize the framers, to see them as "bad guys" trying to squash democracy. But that's not a fair conclusion. The framers undeniably aimed to limit and contain popular democratic power: many routinely expressed their impatience and sometimes even contempt for the "rage for democracy." Yet it's fair to say that while framers did aim to brake the democratic energies of citizens, they did not actually intend to *break* them. They may not even have imagined this could be possible, given how robust these practices were at the time of—and remained in the years after—ratification. We can see them behind the Farmers' Alliance cooperative movement that fought against large business monopolies in the late nineteenth century. We can see them in the secret fraternal orders, like the Masons, that thrived in the nineteenth and twentieth centuries and even today still produce civic goods through the twenty-two hospitals that make up the Shriners Hospital for Children, where children in need are treated without regard to their families' ability to pay. We can see them lingering in credit unions and health-care cooperatives. It's arguable that the associational impulse that Tocqueville saw as characterizing US democratic society didn't begin to fade until the late twentieth century, when a suite of political, economic, and social factors that coalesced and accelerated in the era of the internet and social media led to the severe diminishing of social capital and civil society.

So it's hard to blame the framers many years later (more than 200!) for the diminishing of civic commoning. In fact, from a different angle, we might also want to admire the Constitution for its much-lauded innovation of distributing power at different scales, between the states and the national government. Elinor Ostrom has praised this model of federalism for its "nesting scales" of self-governing, a model for the distribution of power and oversight that importantly assists, in her careful historical and structural analysis of successful commons, the effective management of shared resources.[9] By her account, commons need checking and balancing at different scales because of human frailty. Hardin was wrong in "Tragedy of the Commons" to imagine that humans are inevitably selfish, but he's not wrong that we *often* are. Ostrom argues that commons management schemes need layers of government precisely to help guard against the kinds of misinformation, both from the bottom up and from the top down, that can lead to the collapse of a common-pool resource. And we need these varying interacting scales of government to guard against local TYRANNY, the kinds of majoritarian unfairness that can also lead to commons collapse. Ostrom's careful point here is that commons *can* be democratic but they are not necessarily so: it's exactly the kind of checking and balancing that comes with governing schemes that intermix scales of self-governing (for instance, local, towns, counties, regions and federal) that help move commons schemes toward greater fairness, effectiveness, and accountability.

In this way, we can see positive legacies both from the robust participatory practices of civic democratic commons bequeathed by ordinary Patriots and the structural cautions and institutional mechanisms bequeathed by the framers for our contemporary interest in revitalizing the commons. It's worth cultivating an appreciation for both these legacies. Commons enthusiasts today often proceed as though all commons are robust and infinitely expanding, like the knowledge and internet commons. Indeed, Wikipedia itself tells us that the commons "is the cultural and natural resources accessible to *all* members of a society."[10] With regard to limited and fragile natural and civic resources, Wikipedia's definition leads straight to Hardin's tragedy. As Ostrom and her teams of researchers are at pains to emphasize, commons emerge in the face of scarcity and they are vulnerable in many ways to collapse and failure. Every successful commons has rules both for who can participate and who *cannot*. In other words, commons may provide local solutions for local problems but they are not the ultimate solution for anything—democracy, economic justice, or water supply.

But they are an important practicing ground—as those who've contributed to Wikipedia, or who prefer Uber to taxis, or who have participated in a food co-op or a time bank know—for cultivating skills for *inter*dependency. Commoning can offer experiences fundamental to the practice and growth of democracy. They can generate collective experiences of self-governing, the free sharing of and participation in collaborative problem-solving. Successful commoning allows participants to experience the power that can be gained by pooling our resources. And, as such, they could be a powerful auxiliary to the formal institutions of US democracy, a practice in which we ourselves act as co-creators of good government and experience our inter-dependent abilities to lead together, rather than relying on leaders we vote for to solve all our problems for us.

Notes

1. Garrett Hardin, "The Tragedy of the Commons," *Science* 162 (December 1968): 1243–1248.
2. Barbara Smith, *The Freedoms We Lost: Consent and Resistance in Revolutionary America* (New York: New Press, 2010), 59.
3. Isaiah Berlin, *Liberty*, ed. Henry Hardy (New York: Oxford University Press, 2002), 283.
4. J. Hector St. John de Crèvecoeur, *Letters from an American Farmer and Sketches from the Eighteenth Century* (New York: Penguin Books, 1981), 83.
5. Woody Holton, *Unruly Americans and the Origins of the Constitution* (New York: Hill and Wang, 2008), 184.
6. Smith, *Freedoms We Lost*, 184.
7. Alexis de Tocqueville, *Democracy in America*, trans. George Lawrence, ed. J. P. Mayer (New York: Harper and Row, 1966), vol. 1, pt. 2, 189–190.
8. Hannah Arendt, *On Revolution* (New York: Penguin Books, 1965), 225–235.
9. Elinor Ostrom, "Polycentricity, Complexity and the Commons," *The Good Society: A PEGS Journal* 9, no. 2 (1999): 37–41.
10. Wikipedia, "Commons," https://en.wikipedia.org/wiki/Commons, emphasis added.

Further Reading

The topic of the commons for students in the humanities seldom begins with the important work of Elinor Ostrom but should always, especially *Governing the Commons* (Cambridge: Cambridge University Press, 1990). For thinking about the commons in American colonial history, see Allan Kulikoff, *From British Peasants to Colonial American Farmers* (Chapel Hill, NC: University of North Carolina Press, 2000), Terry Bouton, *Taming Democracy* (New York: Oxford University Press, 2009), Barbara Smith, *Freedoms We Lost* (New York: New Press, 2010), Woody Holton, *Forced Founders* (Chapel Hill, NC: University of North Carolina Press, 1999) and

Unruly Americans (New York: Hill and Wang, 2008), Elizabeth Maddock Dillon, *New World Drama* (Durham, NC: Duke University Press, 2014), and Stuart Banner, *Legal Systems in Conflict* (Norman, OK: University of Oklahoma Press, 2000). For other important historical and theoretical accounts of commoning and commons, see J. M. Neeson, *Commoners* (Cambridge: Cambridge University Press, 1996), E. P. Thompson, *Customs in Common* (New York: New Press, 1993), Leela Gandhi, *The Common Cause* (Chicago, IL: University of Chicago Press, 2014), and Anna Lowenhaupt Tsing, *The Mushroom at the End of the World* (Princeton, NJ: Princeton University Press, 2017).

19

Tyranny

Angélica María Bernal

Over the past decade there has been a resurgence in "tyranny" talk. In the aftermath of the global financial crisis of 2008, a new movement calling itself the Tea Party emerged to denounce the policies of the administration of President Barack Obama. These policies included bailouts and assistance for homeowners and banks, the passage of the Affordable Care Act, and the Deferred Action for Childhood Arrivals (DACA) policy to support immigrants brought to the United States as minors. Tea Party activists denounced these moves as the country's decline into "tyranny."[1] Discourses of tyranny continued and intensified in ensuing years with the rise of the Make America Great Again (MAGA) movement and President Donald Trump, on both sides of the ideological divide. MAGA activists and politicians situated their movement as a repudiation of tyranny brought on by progressive governments, courts, and culture. Critics of the MAGA movement and President Trump's policies—including the ban on immigration from predominantly Muslim countries, repeals of DACA and environmental protection measures, firings of critics, and claims of election fraud in the 2020 presidential race—denounced these as the actions of a tyrant. These discourses on tyranny were most vividly on view on January 6, 2021, when Trump supporters stormed the US Capitol, flanked not only by flags of the MAGA movement but also older symbols invoking the American Revolution and discourses of resistance to tyranny.

These events add urgency to the need to ask ourselves what we mean when we appeal to the term "tyranny." What is a tyranny? What universe of political critiques and ideas are we invoking in calling someone a tyrant? And what is the line between tyranny and democracy?

Angélica María Bernal, *Tyranny* In: *Democracies in America: Keywords for the Nineteenth Century and Today.*
Edited by: D. Berton Emerson and Gregory Laski, Oxford University Press. © D. Berton Emerson and Gregory Laski 2023.
DOI: 10.1093/oso/9780198865698.003.0020

To begin tackling these questions, let us return to their political origins in the historical site that ignites today's tyranny discourses: the American Revolution and founding. One of the most famous responses comes via the Declaration of Independence (1776), which presented to the world the case for revolution and independence as follows: "The history of the present King of Great Britain is a history of repeated injuries and usurpations, all having in direct object the establishment of an absolute Tyranny over these States...A Prince whose character is thus marked by every act which may define a Tyrant, is unfit to be the ruler of a free people."[2] Tyranny for the US revolutionaries represented a state of governance and a type of rule and ruler that was oppressive, unjust, arbitrary, and absolutist. King George had acted as a tyrant because he had imposed absolute rule over the colonies by taxing them without their consent, quartering soldiers in their homes, subverting their self-government and their own authorities, and inciting insurrection between the colonies themselves, to name a few of the injuries stated. To act as a tyrant and impose a tyranny was to act against the people and deprive them of freedom.

But what this freedom meant also differed according to who asserted it within the colonial context. For Jefferson and the other authors of the Declaration, this freedom was situated in their natural rights, which were above and prior to any government, "inalienable rights" to "life, liberty, and the pursuit of happiness." But moving from these abstract norms to the historical and political context, concretely this meant the right to maintain the freedom to govern themselves that the colonies had enjoyed for nearly 200 years already since the first permanent colony was established in Virginia in 1607.

For others who were not the descendants of British colonists but were descendants of or themselves forcibly brought as slaves, with the beginning of the slave trade in Virginia in 1619, tyranny referred to a state both external, coming from an imperial power, and internal, within the colonies themselves.[3] Writing in 1772, poet Phillis Wheatley evoked this difference when she related the colonist's appeals against tyrannous rule to her own experiences as a slave:

> I, young in life, by seeming cruel fate
> Was snatch'd from *Afric's* fancy'd happy seat...
> such was my case. And can I then but pray
> Others may never feel tyrannic sway?[4]

The power of the slave-owner over the slave was the epitome of tyranny. As revolution spread in the colonies, so too did appeals by enslaved Blacks for freedom, appeals that argued for the abolition of slavery as a tyrannical condition that went against natural rights to life and liberty in all of humanity. Speaking at the African Lodge in Massachusetts in 1797, Black abolitionist Prince Hall called on fellow Masons to fight against slavery as "the iron hand of tyranny and oppression" that dragged people "from their native land...from their dear friends and connections" and delivered them into a condition of "cruelty" only relieved by death.[5] Tyranny, as Hall and Wheatley defined it, thus meant not only a state of oppression that interfered with self-governance but also one of total domination.

The problem of tyranny as domination raises further questions about the *who* (its agent), *why* (its causes), and *what* (the context in which it occurs). These questions have themselves been intimately intertwined with the question of democracy, or what it means to have a government defined by the self-rule of a people.

The Constitution famously begins by declaring "We, the People" as that which is at the heart of the US form of government. We sometimes debate the differences inherent in a DEMOCRACY VERSUS REPUBLIC, but what was centrally at stake for the founders was the idea that in both republics and democracies this figure called "the people"—and the mode of REPRESENTATION—played a critical role. For classical and early modern republican thought in Rome and later in seventeenth-century England, the entity known as "the people" was closely linked to liberty: placing freedom and authority within the people would be the bulwark that could protect and maintain liberty from its usurpation by a tyrant.

One of the great debates of the founding period was whether this adage of republican thought still held true in the modern era of expansive constitutional republics: Were the people the saviors or the threats to liberty? This debate played out in its most heated form during the ratification debates of the Constitution, and the answers to this question polarized the early republic. In *The Federalist Papers*, a middle ground was proposed: that a system of free government could be best attained by providing institutional checks and balances and separations of powers against one of the most prominent causes of a tyranny: the usurpation of power by the one (a president), a few (rising oligarchs), or the many (the legislature). To prevent the rise of a tyrant or a tyranny, the powers of the president and of the legislature would be kept in check by other branches and the powers of government would be divided throughout the branches of government, with each also checking the others, so that no one would be able to absorb them all. As Publius, the pseudonym used by the authors of *The Federalist Papers*, stated in *Federalist 51*, "Ambition must be made to counteract ambition."[6] With this we can see one answer to the question of tyranny: that it refers to the usurpation of power by those in power, our elected officials.

Another dangerous source of tyranny was the usurpation of power by one segment of the population and their wielding it to dominate another. This is the problem of factionalism introduced in *Federalist 10*. Factionalism, for Publius and other founders, was an inevitable aspect of a free government. People would come together politically according to their self-interests and passions. But these passions could easily turn violent and ambitious, leading people to act less toward the common good of their fellow citizens and the country. And the problem, for Publius, was particularly pernicious when that faction was a majority. "If a faction consists of less than a majority," then a majority could defeat it through voting. But "when a majority is included in a faction, the form of popular government, on the other hand, enables it to sacrifice to its ruling passion or interest both the public good and the rights of other citizens."[7]

The "people," and with them democracy itself, harbored the possibility of slippage into tyranny. The continual domination by a singular majority over the rest would not install a free government. Why would rule by a majority be a problem? The French theorist Alexis de Tocqueville offers us answers to this question with the memorable phrase: *tyranny of the majority*. In *Democracy in America* (1835), Tocqueville writes, "Hence the majority in the United States has immense actual power and a power of opinion which is almost as great. When once its mind is made up on any question, there are, so to say, no obstacles which can retard, much less halt, its progress and give it time to hear the wails of those it crushes as it passes."[8] The line between tyranny and democracy could be erased by the power of a majority and its continual omnipotence.

If we return to the founders, one solution given to the problem was the CONSTITUTION itself as a vehicle for establishing rule of law and guarantees of protected basic rights for individuals. The arbitrary exercise of power was one of the signals of slippage into tyranny, thus the establishment of the rule of law—or in the words of John Adams, "an empire of laws, and not of not men," would be its bulwark.[9] The equal application of the law to all and basic guarantee of rights would therefore protect citizens, and particularly "unpopular minorities," from tyrannous politicians or majorities.

But what if the laws themselves supported a condition of tyranny? The issues of slavery and colonialism raised this very question. In his *Appeal to the Coloured Citizens of the World* (1829), David Walker importantly inverts prior tyranny discourses, which had used slavery as a metaphor to define modes of unfreedom. We saw these discourses throughout the Revolutionary period: cries against the tyrannical rule of the British and depictions of such tyranny as a mode of enslavement. What this obscured, Walker makes clear: tyranny is not a mode of enslavement; rather, slavery is literally tyranny.

Against apologists such as Thomas Jefferson, who in his *Notes on the State of Virginia* diminished slavery in the United States as less harsh than slavery in the ancient world, Walker decried slavery as a tyranny, and slaveholders and their supporters as tyrants.[10] "Now, Americans! I ask you candidly, was your sufferings under Great Britain, one hundredth part as cruel and tyrannical as you have rendered ours under you?" The United States—"this *Republican Land of Liberty*"—in fact rests on tyranny given the prevalence of slavery, its inhumanity, and moreover its *political* status as a system supported by the institutions and laws of the US government. "Have you not brought us among you, in chains and handcuffs, like brutes, and treated us with all the cruelties and rigour your ingenuity could invent, consistent with the laws of your country, which (for the blacks) are tyrannical enough?"[11] The laws, enacted by democratic majorities, supported a tyranny in the form of prohibitions against intermarriage, protections for slaveholders in their human property making it illegal to teach slaves to read and write, bans against Blacks holding office, and restrictions against slaves from buying their own freedom.[12] Walker ends his exhortation to all Americans by recalling the words of the Declaration and its argument that it is a right and duty to rebel against a tyrannical government and institute a new one that is truly based on the consent of *all* the governed.

Writing around the same time but in a different context—that of Indigenous land claims by the Mashpee tribe against the state of Massachusetts—the Pequot thinker and activist William Apess brings to the fore the coexistence of tyrannical oppression within a democracy based on violent SETTLEMENT. While the Mashpee had enjoyed self-government rights under British rule, by the 1780s the Massachusetts government defied these charters and Native rights and instead asserted authority to lease Mashpee land and resources through a "guardianship" system. In *Indian Nullification of the Unconstitutional Laws of Massachusetts Relative to the Mashpee Tribe* (1835), Apess, acting as an advocate for the Mashpee, outlines the problems with this system. The state of Massachusetts, Apess argues, had *no authority* to act as they had and take away the Mashpee's land and property. As the opening letter by three Mashpee representatives emphasized, whites were themselves invaders on Native land: "The red children of the soil of America address themselves to the descendants of the pale men who came across the big waters to seek among them a refuge from tyranny and oppression."[13]

Rather than compare the injustice of their actions to that of the British, Apess invokes the current situation of enslaved Americans: "In the enslavement of two millions of American people in the Southern States, the tyranny of this nation assumes a gigantic form."[14] For Apess, the situation of Indigenous peoples was another manifestation of the tyranny of the United States. For Indigenous peoples, this tyranny was experienced through illegal and violent land appropriation, which reduced them to "absolute pauperism." It also deprived them of their freedoms of self-governance and, through "paternal guardianship" systems and laws, created the conditions to "keep them in the chains of a servile dependence."[15] Tyranny, then, meant a state of oppression that encompassed not only self-government claims but also a wider constellation that included economic, territorial, cultural, psychological, and social modes of domination brought on by the onslaught of colonialism.

Earlier writers had suggested that the recourse was a duty to rebel against tyrannies and tyrants. But what if exercise of this duty was punished? Apess and the Mashpee had indeed rejected—or in Apess's language "nullified"— Massachusetts's unjust laws, declaring "that as a tribe we will rule ourselves" and that it was their right under the Constitution as free men.[16] As a consequence, Apess and others were jailed and charged as "rioters." Once again, the language of tyranny reappears, this time to bring to light the issue of legitimacy within this duty of rebellion against tyranny—or *who* has a right to rebel. "Governor Lincoln denounces it as *sedition*, the Legislature are exhorted to turn a deaf ear, and the Indians are left their choice of submission to tyrannical laws, or having a militia called out to shoot them."[17] The law and democratic majorities become here vehicles for imposing tyranny by also squashing dissent.

The presence of tyranny within democratic systems also emerges as an important argument made by early feminists. Whereas for Walker and Apess, tyranny defined a condition between racialized groups, feminists bring to the fore arguments for a different tyranny between men and women that is itself also supported by political systems, institutions, and laws. Echoing the Declaration of Independence in its style and explicit denunciation of tyranny, the Seneca Falls Declaration (1848) argued that, "The history of mankind is a history of repeated injuries and usurpations on the part of man toward woman, having in direct object the establishment of an absolute tyranny over her."[18] Authored principally by Elizabeth Cady Stanton, this Declaration describes tyranny in great detail, encompassing a host of deprivations that included: the denial of inalienable rights to the freedoms of equal CITIZENSHIP such as voting and holding public office; taking away women's right to property and legal personhood upon marriage; taking away women's wages and monopolizing "nearly all profitable employment"; and denying women an education. As Stanton describes, in the context of marriage men become women's masters, compelling them into obedience and submission with "the law giving him power to deprive her of her liberty, and to administer chastisement."[19] Patriarchy, then, established a tyranny for women that literally meant loss of freedoms in a range of spheres that included both political citizenship and economic rights but also those within the domestic sphere, the effect of which meant reducing women's capacity for exit from their condition of oppression (such as loss of children in the case of divorce, punishment by husbands, lack of economic opportunities, and lack of personhood under the law). It also impacted their capacity for action at a psychological level by affecting women's "confidence in her own powers...her self-respect."[20] Tyranny, then, as Stanton writes, represented a state of loss of rights and freedoms that resulted in a state of "degradation," of loss of dignity and deprivation of personhood.

As Stanton, Apess, and Walker all highlight, tyranny represents more than the unjust rule of a single leader or elite group, and instead represents systems of power within a society. Democratic systems themselves were by no means immune but also could give rise to and maintain tyranny, capturing a deep tension within the democratic ideal of rule by the people: "the people" represented a more enlightened mode of governance than, say, monarchial rule by proposing a government where the ruled actually also (even if indirectly) rule. This was supposed to be the antithesis of the despotic and absolutist rule of a king. And yet "the people" could act in unenlightened, unjust, cruel, and violent ways.

In the post-Reconstruction context, the Black activist and journalist Ida B. Wells suggested another approach. In "Lynch Law in All Its Phases"

(1893), Wells outlines in painful detail the rising tide of "lynch law" throughout the South. In case after case, Blacks were brought up before the law on false charges and, rather than attain due process, hordes of whites with the support of local authorities and elites enacted "lynch law," submitting them to torture, hanging, burning, and ultimately death. While slavery had been formally abolished through the Civil War, the Emancipation Proclamation, and de jure the Thirteenth Amendment in 1865, these rampant manifestations of ANTI-BLACK VIOLENCE suggested for Wells that "That same tyrant is at work under a new name and guise." The tyranny of slavery manifested itself within Jim Crow and racial violence such that, Wells argued, in "one section... of our common country, a government of the people, by the people, and for the people, means a government by the mob." A government by the will of the mob is for Wells "lawlessness." Wells situates mob rule as an aberration of popular rule and as grounded not just in a numeral majority across the whole of the United States but localized in parts and situated in a *racialized* majority. What constitutes this majority as a mob and its actions as violent mob rule expressing a tyranny is that much like a singular tyrant, "the rule of the mob is absolute." It rules because mobs operate with impunity in the South, but also because elsewhere in the United States citizens are willing to "stand by in silence and utter indifference."[21]

Absolutist rule by either one leader, an elite, or masses is thus an important thread in the definition of tyranny. As we've also seen, such rule can coexist within a democracy and be intertwined within various spheres of a society. One of these, an undercurrent seen in the pervasive metaphor used to describe tyranny as "slavery," is the economic sphere. Along with slavery, racism, colonialism, and patriarchy, by the end of the nineteenth century critiques against the tyranny of an American economic order emerged that echo particularly in the twenty-first century, with the ravages of the COVID-19 pandemic, rising unemployment, and vast income inequality.

In the nineteenth century, the rise of industrial capitalism and rapid growth appeared to give rise to a "Gilded Age" of progress, and yet for the vast majorities of Americans the opposite would be true. Unchecked "laissez-faire" capitalism resulted in immense accumulation of wealth by a new tycoon class on the backs of unjust labor practices—unsafe working conditions and hours, child labor practices, and wage-capture and indebtedness to companies—and the exploitation of workers. As workers today decry inhumane conditions that include few bathroom breaks, lack of sick leave or hazard pay as front-line workers, and minimum-wage pay that by today's standards is no longer a living wage, the critiques of activists such as Emma Goldman and Lucy Parsons ring true.[22] In an 1886 speech, Goldman denounced the tyranny of the capitalist system and its imposition of tyrannical work relations for the majority of people to the point of reducing them into a new mode of slavery: wage slavery. "I admit that you are not slaves in the sense that you are sold upon a block, but you are slaves nevertheless. The only difference is that you are hired slaves instead of block slaves. You have to dread the idea of being unemployed and of being compelled to support your masters."[23] Born enslaved, Lucy Parsons described the tyrannous relation between worker and employer as also analogous to that of enslaver and enslaved: "How many of the wage class, are there who can avoid obeying the commands of the master (employing) class, as a class? Not many are there?"[24] Tyrants, then, were not just politicians, demagogues, or kings, but could also exist in the relationships of absolute rule and subordination between bosses and employees in countless workplace settings. The antidote to tyranny that both Parsons and Goldman championed involved revolutionary acts of emancipation in the economic domain, acts that created more cooperative systems and democratized places of work—proposals that presaged contemporary discussions challenging economic inequality and wealth disparity in movements such as Occupy Wall Street.

Ultimately, the problem of tyranny is more comprehensive than a form of government or leader alone. Rather, it involves systems of power that give rise to modes of subordination and absolutist rule in politics, economics, social, cultural, symbolic, territorial, and intimate spheres. That it can take place within a democracy and be maintained and enabled by democratic institutions, laws, and the people itself is a crucial lesson from the long nineteenth century for the present, as we seek to address issues from racial injustice and colonial violence to extremism, sexism, and economic injustice and disparity.

Notes

1. Theda Skocpol and Vanessa Williamson, *The Tea Party and the Remaking of Republican Conservatism* (New York: Oxford University Press, 2016).
2. "Declaration of Independence: A Transcription," National Archives, https://www.archives.gov/founding-docs/declaration-transcript.

3. The 1619 Project, *New York Times*, https://www.nytimes.com/interactive/2019/08/14/magazine/1619-america-slavery.html.

4. Phillis Wheatley, "On Being Brought from Africa to America" (1773), in Mason Lowance, ed., *Against Slavery: An Abolitionist Reader* (New York: Penguin Classics, 2000), 25.

5. Prince Hall, "A charge delivered to the African Lodge, June 24, 1797," *Freemasons, African Lodge No. 459*, Evans Early American Imprint Collection, University of Michigan, 4, https://quod.lib.umich.edu/e/evans/N24354.0001.001/1:2?rgn=div1;view=fulltext.

6. James Madison, *Federalist 51*, in Clinton Rossiter, ed., *The Federalist Papers* (New York: Signet Classic, 1999), 319.

7. Ibid., 75.

8. Alexis de Tocqueville, *Democracy in America*, trans. George Lawrence, ed. J. P. Mayer (New York: Perennial Classics, 1969), 248.

9. John Adams, "Thoughts on Government (1776)," in Isaac Kramnick and Theodore J. Lowi, eds., *American Political Thought: A Norton Anthology* (New York: Norton, 2009), 125.

10. See Elizabeth Duquette, "Tyranny in America, or, the *Appeal to the Coloured Citizens of the World*," *American Literary History* 33, no. 1 (2021): 1–28.

11. David Walker, *Walker's Appeal, in Four Articles; Together with a Preamble, To the Coloured Citizens of the World, But in Particular, and Very Expressly, to Those of the United States of America* (Chapel Hill, NC: University of North Carolina Press, 2011), 86, 9, 48.

12. Ibid., 21, 53.

13. Quoted in Adam Dahl, "Nullifying Settler Democracy: William Apess and the Paradox of Settler Sovereignty," *Polity* 48, no. 2 (2016): 9.

14. William Apess, *Indian Nullification of the Unconstitutional Laws of Massachusetts Relative to the Marshpee Tribe, Or, The Pretended Riot Explained* (Press of Jonathan Howe, 1835), 91, https://archives.lib.state.ma.us/bitstream/handle/2452/795666/ocm1662408.pdf?sequence=1&isAllowed=y.

15. Ibid., 92.

16. Dahl, "Nullifying Settler Democracy," 7.

17. Apess, *Indian Nullification*, 97.

18. Elizabeth Cady Stanton, "Declaration of Sentiments," in Isaac Kramnick and Theodore J. Lowi, eds., *American Political Thought: A Norton Anthology* (New York: Norton, 2009), 530.

19. Ibid.

20. Ibid., 531.

21. Ida B. Wells, "Lynch Law in All Its Phases (13 February 1893)," *Voices of Democracy: The US Oratory Project*, https://voicesofdemocracy.umd.edu/wells-lynch-law-speech-text.

22. Alex Gourevitch, "Bernie Sanders was right to talk about wage slavery. We should talk about it, too," January 24, 2000, *Jacobin Magazine*, https://www.jacobinmag.com/2020/01/wage-slavery-bernie-sanders-labor.

23. Candace Falk, ed., *Emma Goldman: A Documentary History of the American Years, Volume 1: Made for America, 1890–1901* (Urbana, IL: University of Illinois Press, 2008), 283.

24. Quoted in Gourevitch, "Bernie Sanders was right."

Further Reading

The American Revolution and founding period sets the discourses on tyranny. Several good starting points are Gordon Wood, *The Creation of the American Republic: 1776–1787* (Chapel Hill, NC: University of North Carolina Press, 1998); Jacob E. Cooke, ed., *The Federalist* (Middletown, CT: Wesleyan University Press, 1983); and Herbert J. Storing, ed., *The Anti-Federalist* (Chicago, IL: University of Chicago Press, 1985). To understand tyranny in relation to US slavery and racism, abolitionist writers and Black political thinkers are critical. Two helpful anthologies are *Against Slavery: An Abolitionist Reader* (New York: Penguin Classics, 2000) and Melvin L. Rogers and Jack Turner, eds., *African American Political Thought* (Chicago, IL: University of Chicago Press, 2021). For discussions relating to colonialism and Native American political thought, two canonical resources are Roxanne Dunbar-Ortiz, *An Indigenous Peoples' History of the United States for Young People* (Boston, MA: Beacon Press, 2019) and Vine Deloria Jr., *Custer Died for Your Sins: An Indian Manifesto* (Norman, OK: University of Oklahoma Press, 1988). Discussions of the tyranny of patriarchy over women traverse multiple fields, but a classic that covers vast terrain including the tyranny discourses of the founders and Emma Goldman is Carole Pateman's *The Sexual Contract* (Stanford, CA: Stanford University Press, 1998).

20

Sham

Derrick R. Spires

"Fellow-citizens!" Frederick Douglass proclaimed on July 5, 1852, to his largely white abolitionist audience in Rochester, NY, "I will not enlarge further on your national inconsistencies. The existence of slavery in this country brands your republicanism as a sham, your humanity as a base pretense, and your Christianity as a lie."[1] Speaking in the wake of the Compromise of 1850, which reinforced the Constitution's fugitive slave provisions by requiring local governments to support fugitive capture and incentivized court findings in favor of enslavers, Douglass was attempting to thread a needle: he wanted to maintain his anti-slavery interpretation of the Constitution and his faith in republicanism even as the United States deployed democratic processes toward anti-democratic, anti-Black ends. In wielding the word "sham," Douglass indicates not simply a falsehood or incompletion; he signals ongoing acts of deception. Enslavement, white supremacy, and racially exploitive capitalism had rendered US political systems a sham because they were inconsistent with republican forms of governance. Democracy, as Douglass understood it, requires a cultural and material infrastructure that empowers people to engage in shaping their communities and mechanisms for "those said to be without rights [to] make claims and 'room for themselves.'" For, as historian Martha S. Jones posits, such pathways are "fundamental to democracy."[2] Lacking this commitment, US democracy remained a sham—a veil, a drama, a national counterfeit.

Democracy in the United States has always been aspirational rather than actual. At best, it has been a lodestar spurring action and civic faith; more often, it has functioned as a sleight of hand in which white majoritarian rule has stood in for rule "by the people," with whiteness as sovereignty's ensign and ANTI-BLACK VIOLENCE its calling card. Across the long nineteenth

Derrick R. Spires, *Sham* In: *Democracies in America: Keywords for the Nineteenth Century and Today.*
Edited by: D. Berton Emerson and Gregory Laski, Oxford University Press. © D. Berton Emerson and
Gregory Laski 2023. DOI: 10.1093/oso/9780198865698.003.0021

century, in fact, white majorities worked to make the imagined white republic a reality and to devise systems that could rationalize this reality. Black Michiganders put it well during their 1843 state convention. Despite recent history in which "*your* fathers and *ours*, fought side by side . . . for the Independence of this, our beloved, country," white citizens had "trampled our Liberties in the dust, and thus standing with the iron-heel of Oppression upon our heads, bid us rise to a level with yourselves; and because we do not rise, you . . . say, that we are an inferior race by nature."[3] Michigan lawmakers created racialized differences that they then claimed were "natural" through a self-fulfilling prophecy. This pattern bears mentioning explicitly: representative democratic institutions across the nineteenth century often supported anti-democratic, racist measures, and their practitioners often structured— that is, shammed—their mechanisms to create, mask, and perpetuate inequality. Black Michiganders joined conventioneers throughout the country in making clear that the justifications for excluding Black and other citizens from the governing polity were shamefully duplicitous, a sham that created the conditions used, retroactively, to justify them.

Nineteenth-century Black intellectuals—including Douglass, Frances Ellen Watkins Harper, and convention collectives—chronicled this shamming in real time and offer language for reading sham democracy today. They document how sham democracy uses formally democratic institutions to undermine democratic practices or to ensure that government is legitimate only when it serves white people. Whether white supremacy was the end goal or a "passport to power," as Black Pennsylvanians called it in 1848, matters less than the ongoing fact of its effectiveness.[4] In this sense, sham democracy is less a technical term, in the sense of whether the United States is a DEMOCRACY VERSUS REPUBLIC. Rather, "sham" describes a national pattern of protecting whiteness and property over equality and justice, where the "popular" in "popular sovereignty" is a code—a sham—for white.

First, some definitions. "Sham": fraud, cover, false front, deception, counterfeit, veil, made for display. The *Oxford English Dictionary* suggests "sham" emerged around 1677, potentially in relation to "shame." One early usage connects "sham" to "a Town Lady of Diversion" disguised in "Country Maid's Cloaths, who to make good her Disguise, pretends to be so *sham'd*!" The unfortunate "maimed Lover" who encountered her was said to have "met with a *Sham*." Whether or not this genealogy holds, it illuminates the sense that a sham is not accidental or simply imperfect or incomplete. Shams are "devised to impose upon or disappoint expectation," an ongoing attempt to "sell" the fraud "with deceitful purpose." Sham can refer to a deceitful action (as in "their gesture was a sham") or an object passed off as something it is not ("that document is a sham"). It can refer to a covering, whether a shirt, pillowcase, or bed skirt, designed to protect clean underclothes, to give the false impression of cleanliness, or to keep disorderly or otherwise unmentionable components out of sight. Sham suggests actions "pretended, feigned, false, counterfeit; not genuine or true" (as in a sham trial in which judgment is predetermined or substantively irrelevant). Effective shams require planning and careful attention to viewer expectations. They require ongoing maintenance and are often supported by the structures they cover, whether the body they keep clean or the institution for which they provide cover.[5]

Twenty-first-century writers tend to apply "sham democracy" to regimes that use a form of constitutional democracy to mask authoritarianism and corruption. As of this writing, Google searches for "sham democracy" point to articles about Canada, the European Union, the United Kingdom, vague references to "African countries," and India. In each case, writers question the nature of the government: Do the practices match the outward projection? None of the top results references the United States, not even in relation to ongoing voter suppression.

If we search mid-nineteenth-century newspapers, however, we find "Sham Democracy" held a distinctly US flavor attached to chattel slavery and threats of violence. Articles, speeches, and convention proceedings referring to members of the Democratic Party and those who supported enslavement, especially those in northern states, as "Sham Democracy" appeared throughout the mainstream, abolitionist, and Black presses. A resolution in the 1852 National Free Soil Convention Platform, for instance, named their new party "the Democratic League" to distinguish themselves "from the sham Democracy called the Democratic party."[6] The phrase emerged most forcefully during debates over the Kansas-Nebraska Act (1854) in which Senator Stephen A. Douglas and others appealed to "popular sovereignty" to justify allowing new states to vote on enslavement. At the same time, commentary around the presidential election of 1856 suggested that sham democracy maintained its hold—that is, held the sham in place—through violence by *making a down-right threat of dissolving the Union, unless it meets with success.* "The back-bone of the Sham Democracy," this July 24, 1856, *National Era* article concludes, "is *Disunion*, held up continually *in terrorem* over the North."[7] Such is sham democracy's nature: it incorporates critics through threats of violence (fast and slow), coercion, and fear.

In the wake of the Civil War, and despite the Confederacy's defeat, writers for the *Christian Recorder* and other Black newspapers warned that the "old alliance between the sham Democracy of the North and the slave Aristocracy of the South is to be renewed and perpetuated" to continue to give new form to the slave regime, "which has once carried this government and country through to the brink of destruction."[8] The white-edited *New York Tribune* similarly linked sham to those opposing the package of laws that would constitute Reconstruction and who sought to return former insurrectionists to property and political power. "The Right to Suffrage," a widely reprinted February 22, 1865, *Tribune* editorial, summarizes sham democracy's political strategy, a precursor to the "southern strategy" the Republican Party deployed almost 100 years later: "Let Whites who have been plotting or fighting to subvert and destroy the Union be restored at the earliest moment to all the privileges of American citizenship; and Let Blacks who have been fighting to uphold and preserve the Union be deprived and debarred forever of all the privileges and franchises of American citizenship." These uses of sham democracy echo sham's relation to "shame": these sham democrats—first members of the Democratic Party, but increasingly applied to politicians more broadly—had shamed the nation's republican principles. "Isn't this a lovely exemplification of 'State Sovereignty,' and 'local self-government?' " the *Tribune* asks.[9]

Where the political senses of "sham democracy" pointed to a partisan intention to deceive, Douglass's "What to the Slave Is the Fourth of July?" addresses a form of structural self-deception or veiling that willfully mistakes republican forms for republican practices. The nation's spirit—its pretentions to justice, Christianity, liberalism, and shared governance—were all a sham covering an insidious rot suffusing every cultural, political, economic, and religious institution. The nation-state maintained a sheen legitimacy through its ensigns: flags, parades, ceremonies around electoral politics, an outsized concern with "unity," and celebration of a sanitized past to deflect from present "sins." The combination produced "a thin veil to cover up crimes which would disgrace a nation of savages."[10] Worse, Douglass argues, the compromises undertaken to avoid division, including the Fugitive Slave

Act, betrayed the Constitution's principles and would ultimately rend the union asunder.

Rather than a call to act in the name of defending democracy or a day of mourning remembrance for democratic dreams deferred, white abolitionists had, Douglass contends, used Independence Day celebrations to mask their shame:

> your celebration is a sham; your boasted liberty, an unholy license; your national greatness, swelling vanity; your sounds of rejoicing are empty and heartless; your denunciations of tyrants, brass fronted impudence; your shouts of liberty and equality, hollow mockery; your prayers and hymns, your sermons and thanksgivings, with all your religious parade, and solemnity, are, to [enslaved African Americans], mere bombast, fraud, deception, impiety, and hypocrisy—a thin veil to cover up crimes which would disgrace a nation of savages.[11]

Douglass reminds his white abolitionist listeners that they can hardly afford to indulge in the sham of a progressive account of history—where the future always looks better. Though white Americans have a constitution that ensures a republican form of government and the legacy of the revolution to draw on, their democracy remains a hollow display-piece because it actively ignores and perpetuates injustice. Douglass reorients his listener's perspective so that they are forced to see the sham from "the gross injustice and cruelty to which [enslaved people are] the constant victim."[12] In so doing, he reveals that regardless of how closely a sham mimics the real thing, a sham is *built* for deception. The fact that one mistakes the sham for the thing itself only speaks to its effectiveness and a refusal to read it for what it covers.

Throughout the speech, Douglass draws on biblical injunctions against taking one's salvation—or, in this case, republicanism—for granted based on form or lineage. Douglass's intertexts, the gospels of Matthew and Luke and Paul's first letter to the Corinthians, offer jeremiad warnings of "wrath to come" and calls to "Bring forth therefore fruits worthy of repentance" rather than continue, knowingly, in wrongdoing behind a front of righteousness. Douglass's implication is clear for an audience attuned to biblical allusions: Revolutionary heritage is no substitute for revolutionary actions. Repent and rededicate yourselves to republicanism now, or others—perhaps Douglass's enslaved brothers and sisters—will replace you as the inheritors of the democracy to come.

Where Douglass presents sham democracy as a cultural and ethical concern at odds with the Constitution's premises, his contemporary, Frances Harper, sees the CONSTITUTION itself as part of the sham. For her, its language and the framers' prioritizing of compromise and profit over principle are one of sham democracy's principal features. In a letter published in *National Anti-Slavery Standard* in 1859, Harper notes US law has "veiled" enslavement and white supremacy "under words so specious that a stranger unacquainted with our nefarious government would not know that such a thing was meant by it."[13] Harper's letter repeats the figure of the veil Douglass invoked in 1852 and anticipates later writers—from W. E. B. Du Bois to Ta-Nehisi Coates—who invoke the veil as a metaphor for ongoing attempts to partition Black citizens out of democratic CITIZENSHIP.[14]

For Harper, legal language veils intention through obfuscation and silence, relying on shared value for white life and prosperity to smooth differences. "Oh, was it not strangely inconsistent," Harper asks, "that men fresh, so fresh, from the baptism of the Revolution should make such concession to the foul spirit of Despotism! that...they could permit the African slave trade—could let their national flag hang a sign of death on Guinee's coast and Congo's shore!"[15] Harper's letter riffs on insights concerning the Constitution that emerged with the publication of James Madison's notes on the 1787 Convention in 1836. These notes, white abolitionist Wendell Phillips observes, "prove the melancholy fact, that willingly, with deliberate purpose, our fathers bartered honesty for gain, and became partners with tyrants, that they might share in the profits of their tyranny."[16] What Benjamin Rush, a signer of the Declaration of Independence, described in 1782 as "a new spectacle to the world, of men just emerging from a war in favor of liberty...fitting out vessels to import their fellow creatures from Africa to reduce them afterwards to slavery," must have seemed to Harper a twice-told tale some seventy-seven years later.[17] The 1850 Fugitive Slave Act that provides Harper's example was not new; it reaffirmed and expanded Article IV, Section 2, of the US Constitution: "No person held to service or labor in one state, under the laws thereof, escaping into another, shall, in consequence of any law or regulation therein, be discharged from such service or labor, but shall be delivered up on claim of the party to whom such service or labor may be due."[18] This boomerang trajectory was not, from Harper's view, "strangely inconsistent" so much as it was ironically consistent in its anti-democratic trajectory.

While Douglass, Abraham Lincoln, and others would argue that the Constitution's silences suggested an anti-slavery bent, Harper joined Rush and Phillips (whose commentary inspired her letter) in noting how silences rarely worked in favor of equality in a white republic. Harper does not call the Constitution a proslavery document; instead, she emphasizes how constitution-making and compromise helped consolidate and recruit even dissenters into the project of enslavement. The silences functioned as cover for oppression even as they revealed legislators' knowledge that they ought not say what they mean before the candid observers of the world.

Though Harper and Douglass approach sham from different vectors, they reach similar conclusions. The nation as constructed could never faithfully support democracy because, Douglass reminded listeners in 1852, "the whole political power of the nation (as embodied in the two great political parties) is solemnly pledged to support and perpetuate the enslavement of three millions of your countrymen."[19] Calling US democracy a sham does not erase political differences, dissent, or flashes of expanding democratic engagement (formal and otherwise). Instead, sham suggests that even the most revolutionary moments might not have as lasting a structural effect as they appear to have. Lasting democracy must be explicit and intentional.

After the Civil War, Douglass, Harper, and others focused even more intensely on white supremacy as the "Great Problem to be Solved" if the republic were to survive. The Reconstruction Amendments (Thirteenth to Fifteenth) may have begun expanding US democracy, but the law could not withstand ongoing assaults from white supremacy and the pervasive sense that the problems of Reconstruction were the presence of African Americans and not the enslavement from which many had emerged. Black intellectuals co-opted and inverted the "problem" rhetoric forwarded most infamously in Thomas Jefferson's wondering, in *Notes on the State of Virginia*, what "is to be done" with African-descended people once emancipated.[20] Contra Jefferson, they asked, could white Americans meet the challenge democratic principles set before them and include the nation's whole body—its "constitution"—not just its white parts?

Harper invokes this question near Reconstruction's end, as white backlash transmogrified brief hopes into the dread of retrenchment:

> The great problem to be solved by the American people, if I understand it is this—whether or not there is strength enough in democracy, virtue enough in our civilization, and power enough in our religion to have mercy and deal justly with four millions of people but lately translated from the old oligarchy of slavery to the new commonwealth of freedom.[21]

"The right solution of this question," Harper prophesizes, will determine the nation's future. Harper offered this assessment in 1875, just one year removed from the "Coup of 1874," when white violence and terrorist strategies handed the unreconstructed South and (sham) Democrats massive electoral wins, despite Black majorities in several Southern states. This question went well beyond PARTISAN politics—beyond "simply what the Democratic party may do against us or the Republican party do for us"—because white-dominated political parties had demonstrated that they could not be trusted.[22] In a political world of hollow shams, Black citizens needed to continue the independent organizing that helped sustain them—free and enslaved—before emancipation.

Almost twenty years after Harper's speech and only three years before *Plessy v. Ferguson* (1896) would enshrine "separate but equal" as the law of the land, Douglass would echo Harper's sentiments: "There is no negro problem." "The problem," Douglass argued before white hecklers at the 1893 World's Columbian Exposition, "is whether the American people have loyalty enough, honor enough, patriotism enough, to live up to their own constitution." The marker for answering such a question, however, could not be white Americans' self-conception—its shams—but rather how and whether the United States empowered the "humblest citizen" to engage, meaningfully, in the republic.[23]

If we make the case that the United States is a democracy, then, this series of shams—disfranchisements, removal of rights, and clarifications about who could and could not participate across the nineteenth century—shows some serious limitations to democratic governance. If we make the case that this era was not, on the whole, democratic, then we face other questions: When did the sham end, functionally? Granting WOMEN'S SUFFRAGE via the Nineteenth Amendment works, until you remember that Jim Crow continued curtailing Black voting rights, regardless of gender. And these advances still map onto a Black–white binary that does not account, for instance, for ongoing struggles over Indigenous sovereignty or for the exclusion acts restricting Asian immigration through discriminatory quotas until 1965. The 1960s Civil Rights Acts offer a more promising start, a "third founding," as some have called it. Yet, mass incarceration has driven the DISFRANCHISEMENT of poor, Black, Indigenous, and Latinx Americans, and the affirmative programs developed to address Jim Crow's material effects benefited white women more than any other demographic, even as white Americans became increasingly hostile toward such programs. The range of new restrictive voting laws proposed in the first decades of the twenty-first century continues a pattern of meeting expanding equality with backlash and cultural, political, and social strategies that profit from reassuring significant numbers of white Americans that they are still more equal than others—a passport to power, indeed.[24] That is not democracy; it is a sham.

Our answers need not be all or none, but Douglass and Harper compel us to be clear about naming "the problem." As the United States enters a new phase of public conversations around racism and history, novelist and critic Kiese Laymon warns of one more sham: "Paradigm-shifting change will remain painfully impossible," Laymon writes, "if we insist on targeting the symbolism of the insult [e.g., flags] while neglecting and often benefiting from the ongoing violence of the injuries."[25] Nineteenth-century Black activists met these shams with vigilance and radical truth-telling, a strategy repeated across the centuries as Black activists—through conventions, civic and religious institutions, and grassroots organizing—continued working toward democracy in the face of white supremacy.

Notes

1. Frederick Douglass, "What to the Slave Is the Fourth of July?," speech delivered on July 5, 1852, *BlackPast.org*, https://www.blackpast.org/african-american-history/speeches-african-american-history/1852-frederick-douglass-what-slave-fourth-july.

2. Martha S. Jones, *Birthright Citizens: A History of Race and Rights in Antebellum America* (New York: Cambridge University Press, 2018), 11.

3. "Minutes of the State Convention, of the Colored Citizens of the State of Michigan, Held in the City of Detroit on the 26th & 27th of October, 1843," in Philip S. Foner and George E. Walker, eds., *Proceedings of the Black State Conventions, 1840–1865* (Philadelphia, PA: Temple University Press, 1970), 1:192. *ColoredConventions.org*, https://omeka.coloredconventions.org/items/show/245.

4. "Minutes of the State Convention of Colored Citizens of Pennsylvania, Convened at Harrisburg, December 13–14, 1848," *ColoredConventions.org*, https://omeka.coloredconventions.org/items/show/241.

5. "sham," *OED Online*, www.oed.com.

6. "National Free Soil Convention Platform," *The Liberator*, August 20, 1852, 134.

7. "The Disunionists," *The National Era*, July 24, 1856, Accessible Archives.

8. "What the South Intends," *The Christian Recorder*, August 12, 1865, Accessible Archives.

9. "The Right of Suffrage," *New York Daily Tribune*, February 22, 1865, ProQuest Historical Newspapers.

10. Douglass, "What to the Slave?"

11. Ibid.

12. Ibid.

13. Frances Ellen Watkins Harper, "Miss Watkins and the Constitution," *National Anti-Slavery Standard*, April 9, 1859, in Frances Smith Foster, ed., *A Brighter Coming Day: A Frances Ellen Watkins Harper Reader* (New York: The Feminist Press, 1990), 48.

14. W. E. B. Du Bois, *The Souls of Black Folk: Essays and Sketches* (Chicago, IL: A. C. McClurg & Co., 1903). *Documenting the American South*, https://docsouth. unc.edu/church/duboissouls/dubois.html.

15. Harper, "Miss Watkins," 47–48.

16. Wendell Phillips, *The Constitution a Pro-Slavery Compact; or, Selections from the Madison Papers*, 2nd ed. (New York: American Anti-Slavery Society, 1845), 8.

17. Benjamin Rush to Nathaniel Greene, September 16, 1782, in *Letters of Benjamin Rush*, ed. L. H. Butterfield (Princeton, NJ: Princeton University Press, 1951), 1: 286.

18. US Constitution, https://www.law.cornell.edu/constitution/index.html.

19. Douglass, "What to the Slave?"

20. Thomas Jefferson, *Notes on the State of Virginia* (Philadelphia, PA: Prichard and Hall, 1788), 154. *Documenting the American South*, https://docsouth.unc.edu/ southlit/jefferson/jefferson.html.

21. Harper, "The Great Problem to Be Solved," speech delivered on April 14, 1875, in Foster, *A Brighter Coming Day*, 219–222. BlackPast.org, https://www.blackpast. org/african-american-history/1875-frances-ellen-watkins-harper-great-problem- be-solved.

22. Ibid.

23. Quoted in David W. Blight, *Frederick Douglass: Prophet of Freedom* (New York: Simon & Schuster), 736.

24. Koritha Mitchell, *From Slave Cabins to the White House: Homemade Citizenship in African American Culture* (Urbana, IL: University of Illinois Press, 2020), 2–6.

25. Kiese Laymon, *How to Slowly Kill Yourself and Others in America: Essays* (New York: Scribner, 2020), 53.

Further Reading

A common perception is that nineteenth-century Black activists focused their attention solely on abolition, but there's a robust tradition of African American thought on democracy and politics. Jane H. Pease and William H. Pease, *They Who Would Be Free: Blacks' Search for Freedom, 1830–1861* (New York: Athenaeum, 1974) provides a classic intellectual history. Recent scholarship includes Christopher Bonner, *Remaking the Republic: Black Politics and the Creation of American Citizenship*

(Philadelphia, PA: University of Pennsylvania Press, 2020); Martha S. Jones, *Vanguard: How Black Women Broke Barriers, Won the Vote, and Insisted on Equality for All* (New York: Basic Books, 2020); and Derrick R. Spires, *The Practice of Citizenship: Black Politics and Print Culture in the Early United States* (Philadelphia, PA: University of Pennsylvania Press, 2019). For accounts of the relation between racism, white supremacy, and US democracy, see Carol Anderson, *White Rage: The Unspoken Truth of Our Racial Divide* (New York: Bloomsbury, 2016); Karen E. Fields and Barbara Jeanne Fields, *Racecraft: The Soul of Inequality in American Life* (New York: Verso, 2012); and Cheryl Harris, "Whiteness as Property," *Harvard Law Review* 106, no. 8 (1993): 1707–1791. On the Constitution, see David Waldstreicher, *Slavery's Constitution: From Revolution to Ratification* (New York: Hill and Wang, 2009); and James Oakes, *The Crooked Path to Abolition: Abraham Lincoln and the Antislavery Constitution* (New York: Norton, 2021).

The Colored Conventions Movement: Black Organizing in the Nineteenth Century, ed. P. Gabrielle Foreman, Jim Casey, and Sarah Lynn Patterson (Chapel Hill, NC: University of North Carolina Press, 2021), offers the first scholarly collection to address the Colored Conventions Movement, which spanned the nineteenth century and provides a sustained theorizing on US democracy. For convention minutes, see the Colored Conventions Project at https://coloredconventions.org. For a sampling of Harper's writing, see *A Brighter Coming Day: A Frances Ellen Watkins Harper Reader*, ed. Frances Smith Foster (New York: The Feminist Press, 1990). For a sampling of Douglass's writing, see *Frederick Douglass: Selected Speeches and Writings*, ed. Philip S. Foner and Yuval Taylor (Chicago, IL: Lawrence Hill Books, 1999).

21

Disfranchisement

Tess Chakkalakal

From one angle, voting and democracy are nearly synonymous. And yet, when we talk about voting as a characteristic of democracy, we must first recognize how difficult the concept of universal suffrage has been to achieve. Indeed, the value of the right to vote in the United States may best be measured by the eagerness of some groups and individuals to impose restrictions on who can and cannot vote. Perhaps no group felt the power of those restrictions, and hence the importance of exercising their right to vote, more than American citizens of African descent. Restrictions imposed on African American voting rights both before and well after the Civil War have been essential to shaping a distinct African American political identity that remains salient to understanding American democracy today. The intersection of race and voting rights continues to challenge the ideals of democracy in the United States, namely the commitment to political EQUALITY enabled by the franchise.

Formed in 2016, "BlackPac" is an organization that embodies the dilemmas surrounding this ideal in the twenty-first century. Committed to "galvanizing Black voters to the polls to elect Governors, Lt. Governors, Attorneys General, US Senators, and State Legislators," BlackPac holds that African Americans comprise a singular voting constituency, regardless of state or regional differences.[1] The formation of this constituency stretches back to the period after 1865, when racial slavery was abolished, and the movement known as "Universal Negro Suffrage" sought to enfranchise African Americans, a goal that was ultimately realized (for men) with the ratification of the Fifteenth Amendment to the Constitution in 1870.

"Universal" suffrage meant unrestricted manhood suffrage except for age and residence requirements. Denying African American men the right to

Tess Chakkalakal, *Disfranchisement* In: *Democracies in America: Keywords for the Nineteenth Century and Today.* Edited by: D. Berton Emerson and Gregory Laski, Oxford University Press. © D. Berton Emerson and Gregory Laski 2023. DOI: 10.1093/oso/9780198865698.003.0022 vote had long been a feature of American democracy. Enslaved people, of course, were prohibited from voting. Before the Civil War, however, free Blacks in some Southern and Northern states exercised the right to vote. Free African Americans in North Carolina, for instance, exercised suffrage rights until 1835, when the state constitution was amended to restrict this privilege to white men. This was a trend for many states in the 1820s and 1830s. When the federal Constitution was adopted in 1788, voting was generally limited to property-owners, meaning that non-property-owners—Black and white—were disfranchised. Over the coming decades, property qualifications were dropped in many states, granting working-class and poor Americans the right to vote for the first time while explicitly limiting the franchise for Black men who had previously possessed voting rights. New York, for instance, removed property requirements in 1822 but left a requirement in place for Blacks. In 1840, 300 of the nearly 30,000 Black men in New York were eligible to vote. Within the United States, five states in New England, with the exception of Connecticut, allowed free Black men to vote on the eve of the Civil War.

Following this widespread disfranchisement, renewed political debate on Black suffrage began right around the time that Black men were permitted to enlist in the Union Army in 1862. African American leaders such as Frederick Douglass encouraged Black men to become soldiers on the grounds that doing so would lead eventually to full CITIZENSHIP. Implicit in such a promise was the idea that if a man was willing to die for his nation, he could not be denied the right to vote in its elections.

Black suffrage was central to Northern war aims. Republican control of Congress might be imperiled if the Southern states were readmitted without being required to enfranchise African Americans, especially since by counting all former slaves for apportionment roughly fifteen Southern seats had been added to the House of Representatives. As Senator Charles Sumner of Massachusetts believed, the former slave's freedom would be rendered meaningless unless he had the ballot for both protection and representation. In the words of Sumner: "The old champions reappear under other names and from other States, crying out, that, under the National Constitution, notwithstanding its supplementary amendments, a state may deny political rights on account of race or color and thus establish that violent institution . . . an Oligarchy of the skin."[2] Put in such terms, the Civil War became viewed not just as a battle between the North and South over slavery but a war of republicanism against oligarchy that could only be won by granting Black men full and equal political REPRESENTATION.

The passage of the Fifteenth Amendment on February 3, 1870, was supposed to have been the final nail in the coffin burying slavery. The last of the Reconstruction Amendments (generally understood as the Thirteenth through the Fifteenth), its primary objective was to end racial discrimination in voting practices. Considered to be "the climax of the crusade," the idea of institutionalizing national Black suffrage was viewed as necessary to securing not only the slave's newfound freedom but also the rights of all African Americans.[3] Essentially, the Fifteenth Amendment prevents the federal government and each state from denying a citizen the right to vote based on "race, color, or previous condition of servitude."[4] At the time of its passage, opposition to the Amendment was fierce, as was to be expected from the former slaveholding South, but had also come from surprising sources, namely the anti-slavery North. One northerner and the self-described poet of American democracy, Walt Whitman, was a strong advocate of emancipation during the Civil War. And yet he also believed Black suffrage would threaten "a well-contested national election," what he considers in *Democratic Vistas* (1871) to be the "sublimest part of human history" and essential to his vision of American democracy.[5]

For Whitman, a major problem with Black suffrage was that African Americans, given their collective experience of slavery, would vote only in a bloc and would not think as individuals about issues and candidates. Twenty years later, he was still concerned about this tendency, noting that he agreed with the Southern journalist Henry Watterson's view "that the Negro franchise would never be truly granted till the Negro vote was a divided, not a class one."[6] The idea that African Americans would always vote together (and for Republicans, who stood at the time for granting African Americans political rights) was something of a racial fiction created to diminish their power in the political sphere. Despite considerable opposition to the movement on both sides of the Mason–Dixon line and among both Republicans and Democrats, the Fifteenth Amendment became law. In general, the Amendment was considered to mean what it said. Though the primary power to determine the right and exercise of suffrage remained with the states, that power was not unlimited, since it was restricted by the express restraint contained in the prohibition of racial tests for suffrage under the first section of the Fifteenth Amendment: "The right of citizens of the United States to vote shall not be denied or abridged by the United States or by any State on account of race, color, or previous condition of servitude."[7] In other words, the color bar was outlawed, but state jurisdiction over elections and qualifications remained. Poll taxes and literacy tests were not outlawed by the Amendment. That reality opened up the long and steady road to disfranchisement.

Beginning in 1890, roughly two decades after the Fifteenth Amendment had asserted the right of Black men to vote, Mississippi acted on an initiative that was made possible by the steady federal retreat from Reconstruction and the abandonment of military force in the state. At the Mississippi Constitutional Convention, delegates amended the state constitution to grant the franchise only to those who met the state residence requirement of two years, who were free from criminal records, who had paid the poll tax of two years, and who could read or understand any section of the state constitution. While the residency requirement and the poll tax stipulation could be evaluated precisely, without discrimination, the third, involving literacy and known as the "understanding clause," was left to the discretion and judgment of the registering (state) officer. As other states followed Mississippi's lead, the restrictions became even more pointed. Alabama and Virginia enacted a hereditary qualification, known as the "grandfather clause," whereby any son or descendant of a solider and the descendant of any person who had the right to vote on January 1, 1867, inherited that same right. Given that January 1, 1867, fell three years before Black men had been given the right to vote by the Fifteenth Amendment, the clear, though unstated, purpose of these amendments to state constitutions was to evade the force of the Fifteenth Amendment, rendering its antidiscrimination stipulations on the matter of voting rights virtually null and void.

Whereas debates on the Fifteenth Amendment took place on Capitol Hill, with the House of Representatives and the Senate struggling to attain "impartial suffrage," as Frederick Douglass put it, the response to the Southern states' later efforts to disfranchise Black voters by holding constitutional conventions came largely from those Black voters who had been disfranchised in the Southern states.[8] That this group lacked the authority and political clout of those who had participated in the debate over the Fifteenth Amendment two decades earlier is too obvious to mention. But who were these men, speaking out against their disfranchisement, and how did they attempt to persuade those occupying positions of political power to take up their cause? The little-known case of a slave-turned-government official named Jackson V. Giles gives us one portrait.

Like Mississippi, Alabama ratified its new constitution in 1901, putting in place a set of processes that would allow state legislators to disfranchise almost all Black voters while ostensibly complying with the terms of the Fifteenth Amendment. The commitment to ensuring the enforcement of the Amendment formed the baseline of Black political discourse during the early twentieth century. But Alabama's Black citizens would launch a number of legal challenges to its constitution. The most notable of these was *Giles v. Harris*, which was argued before the Supreme Court in April 1903 and became known as "The Second *Dred Scott* Case," a reference to the historic antebellum Supreme Court decision of 1856. In that most famous of cases, the court returned Dred Scott to slavery, even though he and his wife had been living in a free state; the effect was to deny citizenship to women and men born into slavery, thus repealing Article IV, Section 2, of the CONSTITUTION so far as it applied to them: "The citizens of each State shall be entitled to all privileges and immunities of citizens of the several states."[9] Though less well known, *Giles v. Harris* was the first of the anti-disfranchisement cases argued on Fifteenth Amendment grounds before the US Supreme Court and was the subject of much discussion among prominent African American writers at the time, who used their fictional output to disprove assumptions about Black inferiority. The case proved to be a landmark decision, altering the landscape of American politics by creating divisions that remained in place until the Voting Rights Act of 1965 was signed into law by President Lyndon B. Johnson more than a half-century later.

The man at the center of the case, Jackson W. Giles, who was born enslaved in 1859, worked as a cotton sampler in his twenties; by his early forties, he had won a coveted job as a US Postal Service office clerk and served as president of the Colored Men's Suffrage Association of Alabama. Like Dred Scott, Giles had filed a suit in federal court to have his rights as a free man protected. Unlike Scott, Giles had already been declared legally free when slavery was abolished by the Thirteenth Amendment and so had, for over twenty years, enjoyed his rights as a free citizen of the United States until Alabama's 1901 constitutional convention, which brought disfranchisement to the state in which he lived.

Giles fought back. With the financial support of one of the most famous African Americans of the time, Booker T. Washington, he filed a petition to force the Montgomery County Board of Registrars to register him and 5,000 other African American men in the county as voters. Just as in

Dred Scott, decided almost fifty years before *Giles*, the court ruled against Giles and the 5,000 African American men he represented. But in this case the court simply instructed Giles to take his argument elsewhere, to Congress or the Alabama legislature. Given the language of the Fifteenth Amendment, the courts could not rule on the restrictions to voting that were not directly opposed by the Constitution. If the states wanted to employ literacy tests and poll taxes on voting, which ostensibly had nothing to do with race, color, or previous conditions of servitude, they had the power to do so. If African Americans wanted to vote, they would have to launch a political battle, persuading those who could vote of the importance of protecting their right to vote. But, restricted from voting in the Southern states and now without the support of the courts, African Americans would have to make their case against disfranchisement outside of the institutional structures of power in the United States.

In contrast to Whitman's fear of bloc-voting among African Americans, the post-Reconstruction period showed African Americans divided along ideological and strategic lines, debating not just how to achieve political representation but also its value in ensuring the economic prosperity of the newly freed. Ironically, one of the most vocal advocates for limiting and even discouraging African Americans from voting for the sake of economic progress was Booker T. Washington. This public pronouncement, however, needs to be read with Washington's more private financial support to the *Giles* case. On September 18, 1895, as the most visible spokesperson for Black Americans on the national stage, Washington had addressed the nation at the Atlanta Cotton States and International Exposition, delivering what became known by his critics as the "Atlanta Compromise Address," in which he signaled that Blacks would be willing to accept a limited franchise in exchange for a segregated role in rebuilding the South's agricultural and manufacturing infrastructure as thrifty manual laborers and domestic workers. In one of the most memorable lines from that speech Washington had declared, "In all things that are purely social we can be as separate as the fingers, yet one as the hand in all things essential to mutual progress."[10]

Washington's attempted compromise with Southern whites who had successfully instituted restrictions on Black suffrage through constitutional conventions had what many considered to be a devastating effect on African American political progress. In response to Washington's compromise, Charles W. Chesnutt, a long-time friend, lawyer, and well-known novelist of the late nineteenth century, offered some of the most persuasive arguments for protecting the right of African Americans to vote as promised by the Fifteenth Amendment. Chesnutt's arguments, written in the era of disfranchisement, are worth recalling today, as current legal and political battles over the right to vote are being fought on numerous fronts such as efforts to enfranchise former convicted felons in Florida and elsewhere.

Alongside W. E. B. Du Bois, Chesnutt and Washington both contributed original essays to the landmark 1903 volume *The Negro Problem*. Published just months after the *Giles* decision was announced, Chesnutt's essay marked his most public statement against Washington's "policy of conciliation," which, he believed, had led to "the Disfranchisment of the Negro." This, Chesnutt wrote, was the most urgent problem of the twentieth century and required an immediate solution. The solution could be found, he asserted, not in the courts or Congress, as many at the time believed, but by changing PUBLIC OPINION:

> There are three tribunals to which the colored people may justly appeal for the protection of their rights: the United States Courts, Congress and public opinion. At present all three seem mainly indifferent to any question of human rights under the Constitution. Indeed, Congress and the Courts merely follow public opinion, seldom lead it. Congress never enacts a measure which is believed to oppose public opinion;—your Congressmen keeps his ear to the ground. The high, serene atmosphere of the Courts is not impervious to its voice, they rarely enforce a law contrary to public opinion, even the Supreme Court being able, as Charles Sumner put it, to find a reason for every decision it may wish to render; or, as experience has shown, a method to evade any question which it cannot decently decide in accordance with public opinion.[11]

Following the publication of his classic novel *The Marrow of Tradition* (1901), an account of the 1898 Wilmington, North Carolina, massacre of Black Americans by white supremacists, Chesnutt turned much of his literary labor to convincing doubters like Washington of "the value of the franchise." Washington's bitter dispute with Du Bois over Black education is by now familiar history. Less well known is the fact that Washington and Chesnutt shared an intimate friendship for more than a decade. While they would continue to be friends until Washington's death in 1915, their disagreement over the question of the franchise took a toll on their friendship. Chesnutt took issue with Washington's claim that "there is something deeper in human progress than the mere act of voting." Chesnutt presented his opposition to Washington's support of a restricted suffrage with both respect and frankness in their personal correspondence:

I appreciate all you say and have written about education and property, but they are not everything. There is no good reason why we should not acquire them all the more readily because of our equality of rights. I have no confidence in that friendship of the whites which is to take the place of rights, and no expectation of justice at their hands unless it is founded on law.[12]

Chesnutt also made his opposition public, declaring that Washington had advised Black people to go slow in seeking to enforce their civil and political rights, which, in effect, means silent submission to injustice. Departing from Washington and the "fashionable" view of the time that the Fifteenth Amendment was a mistake, Chesnutt "believed it to have been an act of the highest statesmanship, based upon the fundamental idea of the Republic, entirely justified by conditions."[13]

Despite the passage of the Fifteenth Amendment in 1870 and the Voting Rights Act in 1965, attempts to restrict the franchise in the United States continue today by a commitment to racial categories. This is something Chesnutt foresaw. As he succinctly put it in one of his longest personal letters to Washington, "It is the *differences* which make the trouble."[14] These abiding efforts to curtail voting rights evince the power of voting to separate the powerful from the powerless in a nation governed by the people for the people. They also reveal the degree to which questions of voting are also always questions about how individuals represent themselves as members of "the people." Indeed, the assertion of individual authority through voting rights is why authors such as Whitman, Douglass, and Chesnutt made voting a central feature of their visions of American democracy. The abiding question is: What happens to people when they are denied the right to vote? The people inevitably diminish and all that is left is a government that rules for its own sake.

Notes

1. "Our Mission," *Black Pac*, https://blackpac.com.
2. Quoted in Carl M. Frasure, "Charles Sumner and the Rights of the Negro," *The Journal of Negro History* 13, no. 2 (1928): 143–144.
3. James M. McPherson, *The Struggle for Equality: Abolitionists and the Negro in the Civil War and Reconstruction* (Princeton, NJ: Princeton University Press, 1992), 417–432.
4. US Constitution, https://www.law.cornell.edu/constitution/index.html.

5. Walt Whitman, *Democratic Vistas*, ed. Ed Folsom (Iowa City, IA: University of Iowa Press, 2010), 31.
6. Ed Folsom, "The Vistas of *Democratic Vistas*," in *Democratic Vistas* (Iowa City, IA: University of Iowa Press, 2010), xxx.
7. US Constitution.
8. Frederick Douglass, "Appeal to Congress for Impartial Suffrage," speech delivered in January 1867, https://www.blackpast.org/african-american-history/1867-frederick-douglass-appeal-congress-impartial-suffrage.
9. US Constitution.
10. Booker T. Washington, "Atlanta Exposition Address," September 18, 1895, in Louis R. Harlan, ed., *The Booker T. Washington Papers* (Urbana, IL: University of Illinois Press, 1977), 4: 583–587.
11. Charles W. Chesnutt, "The Disfranchisement of the Negro," in *The Negro Problem: A Series of Articles by Representative American Negroes of To-Day* (New York: James Pott & Company, 1903), 114.
12. Charles W. Chesnutt, *"To Be an Author": Letters of Charles W. Chesnutt, 1889–1905*, ed. Joseph R. McElrath Jr. and Robert C. Leitz III (Princeton, NJ: Princeton University Press), 182.
13. Chesnutt, "Disfranchisement," 111.
14. Ibid., 188.

Further Reading

Alexander Keyssar, *The Right to Vote: The Contested History of Democracy in the United States* (New York: Basic Books, 2000) effectively explores the debates over the limitations on the right to vote from the revolution to the late twentieth century, showing how those debates and contests contributed to the meaning of democracy in American political life and culture. Keyssar's book also provides detailed tables with lists of voting restrictions broken down by state and year beginning in 1790 up to the late nineteenth century. William Gillette, *The Right to Vote: Politics and the Passage of the Fifteenth Amendment* (Baltimore, MD: Johns Hopkins University Press, 1965) offers a thorough historical account of the politics of the Fifteenth Amendment and its aftermath. Eric Foner also explores this history in *The Second Founding: How the Civil War and Reconstruction Remade the Constitution* (New York: Norton, 2019).

Scenes of African American men voting were a mainstay of the literary fiction of the period and provide valuable texture to historical investigations. Aside from Anna E. Dickinson's *What Answer?* (1868) and Frances E. W. Harper's *Iola Leroy; Or, Shadows Uplifted* (1892), which depict the violence and misinformation related to African American men exercising their vote, Albion W. Tourgée's *Bricks without Straw* (1880) devotes considerable space to scenes of African American men voting.

Anti-disfranchisement literature expanded during the turn to the twentieth century with the publication of novels by African American writers such as Sutton E. Griggs and James McHenry Jones, among others. For a good scholarly treatment of this literature, see Tess Chakkalakal and Kenneth Warren, eds., *Literature, Jim Crow, and the Legacy of Sutton E. Griggs* (Athens, GA: University of Georgia Press, 2013).

22

Security

Russ Castronovo

The military forces of fascist Germany had overrun the democracies of Europe months before Franklin Delano Roosevelt delivered the 1941 State of the Union address, a speech now better known as the Four Freedoms. "The democratic way of life is at this moment being directly assailed in every part of the world.... Let us say to the democracies...which dare to resist their [dictators'] aggression," the president urged, that the United States will help defend the freedom that is under attack from bombs and bullets. He went a step further by arguing that at no time in history had "American security" been so profoundly threatened. Yet even as Roosevelt warned that American democracy could not flourish without security, he also expressed a fundamental concern that any bargain made to ensure safety would jeopardize the substance of liberty. He underscored the point by invoking Benjamin Franklin's famous saying, "Those, who would give up essential liberty to purchase a little temporary safety, deserve neither liberty nor safety."[1] Franklin was not the first to articulate what we might call the liberty/security tradeoff, but his ability to condense this conflict into a handy aphorism provides an opportunity to examine an inherent tension that underlies a set of complex and perhaps irresolvable questions about the relationship of security to democracy.

Do liberty and security oppose one another? Does security threaten civil liberties, or does a robust sense of political freedom require security as a safeguard? Franklin's characterization of liberty as "essential," in contrast to the "temporary" aspect of security, would seem to tip the scales in favor of liberty, but what precepts should the citizens of a democracy use in finding a proper balance between the two? At what point does a lack of border security, economic security, environmental security, and other forms of

Russ Castronovo, *Security* In: *Democracies in America: Keywords for the Nineteenth Century and Today.*
Edited by: D. Berton Emerson and Gregory Laski, Oxford University Press. © D. Berton Emerson and Gregory Laski 2023.
DOI: 10.1093/oso/9780198865698.003.0023

vulnerability endanger political freedom? Contrastingly, at what point do surveillance, policing, border control, and other measures hollow out people's liberty? Such questions reveal that the story of the social contract, as told by political theorists, has long been unsettled by the persistent tensions of the liberty/security tradeoff. While John Locke, whose *Second Treatise of Government* (1689) served as a touchstone for eighteenth-century proponents of American democracy, depicted the state of nature "as very unsafe, very insecure," the security guaranteed by the social contract has been a source of citizens' consternation for just as long.[2] Such unease and the justifiable paranoia it can lead to has intensified since the Information Age, when governments and corporations possess the capability to search and store "zettabytes and yottabytes of information—enough space to store years' worth of data and voice communications generated by everyone in the United States."[3] Yet the problem of security with respect to the Constitution's "We, the People" predates an era of unimaginable technological sophistication. Long before champions of civil liberties began to worry that security measures associated with what Cathy O'Neil calls "weapons of math destruction" can "undermine democracy," Revolutionary figures as diverse as Franklin, Tom Paine, and Alexander Hamilton discerned how efforts to secure democracy render freedom uncertain and fragile.[4]

Ever since Franklin outlined the liberty/security tradeoff in 1757, it has been reanimated many times by those seeking to defend democratic freedoms from government overreach, as well as by those arguing that civil liberties necessarily require some limitations in the interests of security. Making significant adjustments to the original, one elected official declared in 2015, "Ben Franklin essentially said at one point, those who would trade privacy for a bit of security deserve neither privacy nor security."[5] It was probably Franklin himself who was the first to recycle his formulation when tensions in the British colonies of North America were boiling over. This tension shows up in debates about terrorism, immigration, cellular technology, and dataveillance, but its sources extend back to prototypical understandings of the social contract under which people supposedly agree to sacrifice some amount of freedom in exchange for the protections guaranteed by the monarch, the state, or the commonwealth—or, most importantly for this volume, the democracy that they themselves constitute.

The balancing of liberty and security has oscillated wildly during this span. While Franklin presented security as a threat to political freedom, today's advocates for security frequently argue that civil liberties have to be scaled back and that emergency police and military powers have to be expanded. "Most liberal democratic governments presume that they cannot be effective against the threat [of terrorism] unless they sacrifice some of their democratic substance," concludes one researcher after an extensive study of parliamentary debates in Europe after the attacks of September 11, 2001.[6] Where Franklin once placed security and liberty in opposition, today the two have been collapsed into one another so that liberty itself becomes something that must be secured. In the George W. Bush era, US Attorney General John Ashcroft and Assistant Attorney General Viet D. Dinh could thus reject the notion of balance altogether by stating that "security, then, is not a counterweight to freedom.... Searching for a 'balance' between liberty and security is counterproductive because such an approach is based on a false dichotomy."[7] By this logic, security and liberty have become one and the same. "Freedom must be secured," advise Ashcroft and Dinh, radically eroding the conceptual distance between liberty and security that Franklin sought to maintain.[8]

As definitions of security have grown increasingly mobile and made it possible to speak of financial security, border security, nuclear security, food security, network security, and so on, it might be best to go back to the beginning.

Benjamin Franklin first pitted "essential liberty" against "temporary safety" during a crisis in border security along the Pennsylvania frontier in 1755. For eighteenth-century Philadelphians, rumors of an imminent attack by French troops and their Native allies upon the city had created "Circumstances of Alarm and Terror."[9] Franklin charged, however, that the crisis was artificial, a false panic orchestrated by the colonial governor in a brazen attempt to make the Pennsylvania General Assembly appear weak and unsuited to managing frontier defenses essential to public safety. Irate settlers responded to this fearmongering by dumping the scalped bodies of their murdered neighbors on the steps of the statehouse—which would later be renamed Independence Hall. By dragging its feet and not authorizing money to purchase arms and troops to protect settlers, the Assembly members "were to be considered *public Enemies*," if one believed Governor Robert H. Morris's scripting of the crisis.[10]

Whatever the governor's (mis)characterization, Morris rightly discerned the conflict over security as a struggle between democratic and authoritarian power, with the category "the people" pinioned between the two. He thus cast Franklin's remarks as "a very extraordinary measure, as the people will be thereby taught to depend on an Assembly for what they should only receive from the Government."[11] Should "the people" seek security from their elected representatives? Or was an appointed—not elected—government better able to safeguard the public welfare? The governor had his answer, but Franklin persisted in viewing Morris's position as dangerous both to security and liberty. Security, because it inevitably raises questions about who is best able to ensure safety and for how long, is always beset by ambivalence, perceived at once as protection for and a threat to the people's liberty. For his part, Morris was untroubled by any uncertainty, writing of Franklin's scheming to entrust the people's security to the Assembly, "if it is not criminal I am sure it ought to be so."[12]

Franklin saw through this argument as well as the governor's alarmist theatrics. "A provincial Dictator he wanted to be constituted," as Franklin characterized the governor's true motivation.[13] In portraying the democratically elected assembly (though, of course, this was a democracy severely limited by racial status, property qualifications, and sex) as ineffective, the governor was asserting that a singular authority could better ensure the security of the colony's inhabitants. In reality, however, it was the governor, acting in collusion with absentee landowners, who had consistently vetoed Assembly measures to make allocations for the defense of frontier settlements. In a letter sent to Governor Morris, the Assembly asserted that it took seriously the need for "*further Security*" along an "extended Frontier, settled by *scattered single* Families at two or three Miles Distance" and would have done much "to secure them from the insidious Attacks of small Parties of *skulking Murderers*" had not the governor himself blocked the security provisions.[14] The vociferous response of the Assembly framed the disagreement as part of a larger crisis over the issue of whether white colonists, by freely exercising "the just Rights of Freeman," had the liberty to "defend themselves" or whether they should temporarily relinquish this responsibility to others.[15] When Franklin later wrote a history of the Pennsylvania colony, he celebrated the Assembly's letter (which, of course, he had written himself) as a perfect expression of the people's sovereignty: "There is not in any Volume . . . a Passage to be found better worth the Veneration of Freemen, than this, 'Those who would give up *essential Liberty*, to purchase a little *temporary Safety*, DESERVE neither *Liberty* nor *Safety*.'"[16]

A closer look at the context of Franklin's stirring motto reveals that fear and violence are always part of the original bargain between liberty and security. His reference to "*skulking Murderers*" injects a lethal racial component into the equation, demonizing the Delaware and Shawnee tribes for attacks on the SETTLEMENT efforts of whites. As the Pennsylvania Assembly was squaring off with Governor Morris, Franklin was also dispensing advice to settlers about using dogs to track, corner, and maul Native Americans. Best to have the dogs tied up before turning them loose on their human quarry, since it will make them "fresher and fiercer."[17] These graphic details illustrate how security for some people entails the production of insecurity for other people, particularly those viewed as outsiders. " 'Our' security always rests on the insecurity and suffering of an-other," contends Anthony Burke.[18]

At the same time, however, the quest for security also creates feelings of insecurity at home. For the individual subject of democracy, civil liberties are always at risk from security forces—the police, the military, a government agency such as the National Security Agency (NSA). For Judith Shklar, the ever-present fear "that the governments of this world with their overwhelming power to kill, maim, indoctrinate, and make war" can at any moment disregard personal freedoms in the name of security keeps citizens unhinged and on edge.[19] The tensions generated by the liberty/security tradeoff are as palpable as they are irresolvable: on the one hand, liberal democracy aims "to secure the political conditions that are necessary for the exercise of personal freedom"; on the other, the bid for security can endanger the very freedoms that are to be secured.[20]

The quick passage of surveillance measures such as the USA Patriot Act after 9/11 offers a reminder of how the perceived need for security, often stoked by fear, has set the stage for the exercise of emergency powers to suspend democratic liberties. Examples prior to the twenty-first century are not hard to find: the Alien and Sedition Acts of John Adams's administration, the suspension of habeas corpus during Abraham Lincoln's, the detention of Japanese Americans in internment camps during the Second World War by Roosevelt's. The turnabout can be swift: the Four Freedoms speech ends on a note of national self-congratulation by recalling that the United States has pursued "a perpetual peaceful revolution ... without the concentration camp or the quick-lime in the ditch," yet the creation of Heart Mountain, Topaz, Manzanar and other internment camps would soon contradict that optimism.[21] Little more than a year after Roosevelt's speech, the president issued Executive Order 9066 for supposed security reasons to provide "every possible protection against espionage and against sabotage," resulting in the incarceration of 120,000 people of Japanese ancestry.[22] Emergency measures are often implemented in the name of "a little temporary safety," to recall Franklin's phrase, but such arrangements made in the name of necessity, even if they do not become permanent, distort the balance between liberty and security by shifting "essential" notions of what is acceptable.

By 1775, the notion of what constitutes an acceptable compromise to historic English liberties had shifted alarmingly for Franklin. In commenting on a plan for reconciliation between the colonies and Britain, Franklin stipulated that rather than suffer any abrogation of the charters and laws governing the colonies, Americans would be better off risking "the Hazards and Mischiefs of War."[23] He then underscored the point by deploying the language he had used twenty years earlier: "They who can give up essential Liberty to obtain a little temporary Safety, deserve neither Liberty nor Safety."[24] While the changes to the original wording and emphasis are minor, the historical context had altered in subtle but meaningful ways. In 1755, the complaint had targeted a colonial governor's attempts to trade the people's self-rule for the promise of security; now, twenty years later, the liberty/ security formula received a fresh application that seemed directed not at an aggrandizing governor, but at timorous compatriots who might be tempted to exchange reduced autonomy for the opportunity to patch things up with their mother country.

The following year, 1776, Tom Paine issued a stirring salvo that undercut the position of anyone seeking "a little temporary safety." Although *Common Sense* is regularly viewed as more a rhetorical feat than a theoretical one, Paine's retelling of the story behind the social contract involves a critical reevaluation of security. He begins with a dutiful overview of Locke's argument, describing how the political subject "finds it necessary to surrender up a part of his property to furnish means for the protection of the rest."[25] The innovation of the American revolutionaries would be to replace Locke's property with liberty. Paine's conclusion seems unambiguous: "security being the true design and end of government," people have the right to unite around their common interests and form a government that best fulfills this promise—and to reject one that does not.[26] But a note of uncertainty precedes this statement, as Paine instead wonders if government itself exposes people to greater insecurities than they might experience in the fabled state of nature. "We suffer... the same miseries *by a government* which we might expect in a country *without government*," and "our calamity is heightened" when the people stop to consider that they themselves seemingly have agreed to a social contract that exchanges liberty and property for protection.[27] The blessing of security, for Paine, can just as easily be a curse, forcing him to ask if by comparison lawlessness might be preferable to safety.

When Paine later circles back to the proposition that "security" is "the true design and end of government," he makes a small but significant addition by defining "the design and end of government, viz., freedom and security."[28] Security alone is not enough. What remains unclear at this juncture, however, is the balance between the two. The remainder of *Common Sense* is something of a seesaw battle between security cast in negative terms and the positive blessings of liberty. That is, security is expressed as security "from invaders," concretized in the "locks and bolts to our doors or windows" to protect against piracy, and associated with what Paine views as the dangerous quietism of the Quakers who pray for "the king, and the safety of our nation."[29] In contrast, the "free will" to make decisions, the "liberty of choosing" representatives, and the "liberty to act as [one] pleases" more than outweigh the necessities of safety and security.[30]

Perhaps most remarkable is Paine's use of security against his political enemies. Addressing the Tories remaining loyal to the Crown, Paine counsels that it would be wise to support measures that "protected them from popular rage." If their desire is "continuing [a stable form of government] securely to them," then Tories should jump at the prospect of independence.[31] The alternative is exposure to ongoing discord and unrest. Equal parts advice and threat, Paine's marshaling of the "popular rage" is nothing less than an attempt to promote *in*security among Loyalists to the king. Those outside of what Paine delimits as the secure zone of political belief literally become outsiders, left insecure and vulnerable to mob rule. Paine reworks the liberty/security tradeoff so that those most opposed to American independence also have the least security. Fears of anarchy and factional strife, he suggests, should have Loyalists clamoring for American liberty as the source of security. With its exuberant republicanism, *Common Sense* shifts the balance so that the pursuit of liberty becomes the best guarantor of the Tories' personal safety and private property. In contrast to Ashcroft and Dinh, who will later subsume liberty under security, Paine taps into the democratic spirit of the revolutionary Atlantic world to present the "liberties of the continent" as coextensive with protection, stability, and security.

Any argument made in favor of the proposed federal CONSTITUTION would have to reckon with the terms first articulated in Franklin's tradeoff, as Alexander Hamilton recognized in *Federalist* 8. Even though memory was fresh of what it was like to have standing armies in one's midst, the example of European nations suggested that a large security force would increase a country's stability. Yet Hamilton also quickly recognized how a continual military and police presence exert "a malignant aspect to liberty and economy."[32] Like Paine, Hamilton sensed how political animosities could destabilize the American republic, but he lacked Paine's buoyant faith that freedom on its own could ensure continued peace and tranquility. Wouldn't the new American states attack and plunder one another in the absence of a federal union? Particularly alarming was the threat of internal dissension—faction—that needed to be quelled if this new political union was to have any hope of longevity. At some point, nations are forced to make a decision: "To be more safe, they, at length, become willing to run the risk of being less free."[33] In the end, however, the people may well regret their choice after they have given "security to institutions which have a tendency to destroy their civil and political rights."[34]

Hamilton does more than rehash the opposition that Franklin had laid out, however. He significantly adds to the debate by discerning the affective components that accompany the liberty/security tradeoff. No people can thrive in a state of vulnerability and unceasing worry. Hamilton's repetitions become crucial here, as he paints a picture of a citizenry made fragile by its own fears. "Constant apprehension" begets "constant preparation" for the worst. Living in "a state of continual danger" requires "continual effort and alarm." Exhausted by these political anxieties, people become incautious—they "run the risk"—and are guided by emotions.[35] The result is that people become trapped in a paradox of their own making, opting to protect their liberties by adopting security measures that imperil the existence of those very liberties. Their choice is not a rational one but is instead impelled by an affective overinvestment in security and safety. Writing as "Publius," Hamilton is now ready to drive home the argument for the Constitution. Only this ambitious plan to form a national union can allay feelings of vulnerability: the Constitution, in effect, will make the people safe from their own yearning for security.

The Constitution's Preamble thus promises to "secure the Blessings of Liberty to ourselves and Posterity." The genius of the founders, in the eyes of many commentators, lies in fixing the conundrum of liberty and security. "Liberty" is the thing to be achieved, named here as the substantive goal whose job it is this Constitution to "secure." Liberty remains the endpoint;

security is simply the means of getting there. Others, however, are not so sure and have warned that security always has the capacity to overtake democracy. Neither Hamilton nor the Constitution he helped ratify resolved the paradox that security creates for democracy. The nineteenth-century author and intellectual Ralph Waldo Emerson, for instance, worried that the desire for safety could become its own raison d'être: "Society is a joint-stock company, in which the members agree, for the better securing of his bread to each shareholder, to surrender the liberty and culture of the eater."[36] The search for a bit of basic political sustenance obscures the loftier and more fulfilling goal of liberty and, in fact, becomes a source of insecurity. If "we, the people" place too much stock in security, ironically, we expose our most highly safeguarded democratic values to insecurity. And although Emerson suggests that the social contract might be better construed as a "surrender," the liberty/security tradeoff very much remains an active contest, a battleground upon which citizens continue to wrestle with the tensions laid out in Ben Franklin's historic maxim.

Notes

1. Franklin D. Roosevelt, "1941 State of the Union Address 'The Four Freedoms' (6 January 1941)," https://voicesofdemocracy.umd.edu/fdr-the-four-freedoms-speech-text.
2. John Locke, *Second Treatise of Government*, https://www.earlymoderntexts.com/assets/pdfs/locke1689a.pdf.
3. David Gray, *The Fourth Amendment in the Age of Surveillance* (New York: Cambridge University Press, 2017), 4.
4. Cathy O'Neil, *Weapons of Math Destruction: How Big Data Increases Inequality and Threatens Democracy* (New York: Crown, 2016), 199.
5. "Ben Franklin's famous 'liberty, safety' quote lost its context in 21st century," *All Things Considered*, March 2, 2015, https://www.npr.org/2015/03/02/390245038/ben-franklins-famous-liberty-safety-quote-lost-its-context-in-21st-century.
6. Anastassia Tsoukala, "Democracy in the Light of Security: British and French Political Discourses on Domestic Counter-Terrorism Policies," *Political Studies* 54 (2006): 608.
7. John D. Ashcroft and Viet D. Dinh, "Liberty, Security, and the USA Patriot Act," in Dean Reuter and John Yoo, eds., *Confronting Terror: 9/11 and the Future of American National Security* (New York: Encounter Books, 2011), 188–189.
8. Ibid., 188.
9. Benjamin Franklin, *An Historical Review of the Constitution and Government of Pennsylvania* (New York: Arno Press, 1972), 277.

10. Ibid., 278.
11. Morris's letter is quoted in J. A. Leo Lemay, *The Life of Benjamin Franklin, Volume 3. Soldier, Scientist, and Politician, 1748–1757* (Philadelphia, PA: University of Pennsylvania Press, 2009), 475–476.
12. Ibid., 476.
13. Franklin, *Historical Review*, 278.
14. Ibid., 290.
15. Ibid., 289.
16. Ibid.
17. Benjamin Franklin to James Read, November 2, 1755, in *The Papers of Benjamin Franklin* (New Haven, CT: Yale University Press, 1963), 6: 235.
18. Anthony Burke, "Aporias of Security," *Alternatives* 27 (2002): 2.
19. Judith N. Shklar, "The Liberalism of Fear," in Nancy Rosenblum, ed., *Liberalism and the Moral Life* (Cambridge, MA: Harvard University Press, 1989), 23, 30.
20. Ibid., 21.
21. Roosevelt, "Four Freedoms."
22. Franklin Delano Roosevelt, Executive Order 9066, http://historymatters.gmu.edu/d/5154.
23. Benjamin Franklin, "Objections to Barclay's Draft Articles of February 16," in *Papers of Benjamin Franklin*, 21: 498.
24. Ibid.
25. Thomas Paine, *Common Sense*, in *The Thomas Paine Reader* (New York: Penguin, 1987), 67.
26. Ibid.
27. Ibid., 66.
28. Ibid., 68.
29. Ibid., 83, 97, 113.
30. Ibid., 77, 79, 107.
31. Ibid., 109.
32. Alexander Hamilton, *Federalist 8*, in *The Federalist Papers* (New York: Mentor, 1961), 66.
33. Ibid., 67.
34. Ibid.
35. Ibid., 67–68.
36. Ralph Waldo Emerson, "Self-Reliance," in *Essays and Lectures* (New York: Library of America, 1983), 261.

Further Reading

The topic of security crosses multiple fields and is often closely aligned with studies of surveillance. The work of Michel Foucault is an important starting place, especially *Security, Territory, Population: Lectures at the Collège de France*

1977–1978 (New York: Picador, 2009) and *"Society Must Be Defended": Lectures at the Collège de France 1975–1976* (New York: Picador, 2003). Simone Brown's *Dark Matters: On the Surveillance of Blackness* (Durham, NC: Duke University Press, 2015), John T. Hamilton's *Security: Politics, Humanity, and the Philology of Care* (Princeton, NJ: Princeton University Press, 2013), Matthew Potolsky's *The National Security Sublime: On the Aesthetics of Government Secrecy* (New York: Routledge, 2019), and Johannes Voelz's *The Poetics of Insecurity: American Fiction and the Uses of Threat* (New York: Cambridge University Press, 2018) all provide literary and philosophical approaches to the topic. Much of the work in what has become known as critical security studies is the subject of geography, criminology, and international relations. Examples include Mark Necleous's *Critique of Security* (Edinburgh: Edinburgh University Press, 2008) and Ian Loader and Neil Walker's *Civilizing Security* (New York: Cambridge University Press, 2007).

23

Settlement

Alaina E. Roberts

The Declaration of Independence mentions Indigenous peoples only once. In enumerating the king of England's alleged "injuries and usurpations," Thomas Jefferson and the framers describe how George III "has excited domestic insurrections amongst us, and has endeavored to bring on the inhabitants of our frontiers, the merciless Indian Savages, whose known rule of warfare, is an undistinguished destruction of all ages, sexes, and conditions."[1] This brief reference offers an important glimpse of two of the "Founding Fathers'" central beliefs about Native peoples, which would scarcely change over the next decades and forever shape interactions between Native and non-Native peoples on this continent. First, even at this early stage in the evolution of the United States, white Euro-Americans believed that they had a certain claim to space in the Americas. While in this document the framers acknowledge a "frontier," which bifurcated land claimed by the United States and land claimed by Native tribes, eventually this demarcation would narrow and then disappear entirely. Second, most Euro-Americans saw Native Americans as substantially different from themselves. By portraying Native peoples as racial others, Euro-Americans could justify treating them in a manner they would not employ toward other whites, such as stealing their land, engaging in one-sided military massacres, and rejecting their treaty rights. It is apt, then, that the Declaration of Independence, a document considered so foundational to American democracy, establishes ideas about race and land that would go on to shape relations between white Americans and Native Americans. Approached in this way, the Declaration discloses a self-evident truth that remains largely unrecognized: from the very birth of the country, democracy was predicated

Alaina E. Roberts, *Settlement* In: *Democracies in America: Keywords for the Nineteenth Century and Today.*
Edited by: D. Berton Emerson and Gregory Laski, Oxford University Press. © D. Berton Emerson and Gregory Laski 2023.
DOI: 10.1093/oso/9780198865698.003.0024

on settler colonialism, which allowed for Indigenous land theft and the delegitimization of Indigenous culture, law, and ownership.

The experiences of the Chickasaw, Choctaw, Cherokee, Creek, and Seminole Nations (collectively known as the Five Tribes) demonstrate how these issues of land and race came to a head in the Reconstruction era, defined here as the period from 1863 to 1907. Throughout the nineteenth century, the removal, resettlement, and process of land absorption and buy-out that the United States perpetrated against the Five Tribes is proof that the United States voided its own treaties and sanctioned mass white settle-ment on land promised indefinitely to Native Americans. After the Civil War, the reconciliation of former Confederates and Unionists exemplified the part that coercive acquisition of western Indian land played in allowing both white and Black Americans to reimagine the United States as a democratic nation in the wake of racial slavery, while ignoring ongoing injustices against Native peoples. A studied consideration of these historical events must factor into any attempt to account for America as a nation founded on the principles of liberty and EQUALITY for all. Rather, the belief that Indigenous peoples were unequal to whites is what accorded Americans the land and economic capital to forge the United States as we know it today.

Settler colonialism, the forcible resettlement of Native people and their replacement by white settlers who then moved onto their lands, was a proc-ess that occurred from the time of contact through the twentieth century. While the colonial period saw Native peoples and Europeans negotiating settlement through treaty, violence, and bargaining on a relatively even ground (with Native people holding more military and economic power in certain instances), after the Revolutionary War coercive white encroach-ment on Native American lands steadily increased as settlers sought resources and homesteads.[2] As plantation-style slavery spread through the nineteenth century, the Five Tribes found their lush, agriculturally rich southeastern lands under attack. White settlers began illegally squatting on tribal lands, and state governments followed their lead by sanctioning this trespassing and extending their state laws to Native Americans and their lands. Mississippi began talks about such an effort in 1820 and took legislative action in 1829.[3] Around this time, Alabama and Georgia did the same.[4] These changes placed Native nations under the jurisdiction of American county courts and outlawed their tribal governments, destroying their right to legally protect themselves and their lands from encroaching whites and undermining the principal of tribal sovereignty.[5] Tribal sovereignty is the idea that Indigenous nations have the right to create their own legislation, police themselves, retain ownership and access to their homelands, forge alliances with other sovereign nations, and, generally, oversee their own affairs and tribal members.

If these Southern states succeeded in bringing Native people and their nations under their authority, Indigenous Americans would either have to remain in the South under the limited rights of free people of color or move west. This was only the latest effort to move Native Americans west of the Mississippi River. After the Louisiana Purchase in 1803, Thomas Jefferson had contemplated creating a region that would only be populated by Native Americans and had encouraged south and southeastern Native peoples to move voluntarily.[6] As slavery became increasingly profitable, this long-held concept became a concrete reality as a way to not only separate the races but also transfer ownership of valuable plantation lands from Native hands into white American possession.

Land transfer was previously largely beholden to a set of social rules that acknowledged Native peoples' rights to particular spaces. Though they thought of Indigenous people as uncivilized, Euro-American colonists created treaties with various Native American tribes and leaders to keep the peace. These treaties outlined agreements between Native Americans and colonists about land claims, trade, war (or peace), and any other significant matter. By their very existence, they also recognized the legitimacy of Native nations as independent political, social, and economic entities. For, if Euro-Americans did not believe that Native nations possessed a legitimate claim to land (and represented a potent military threat), they surely would not have bothered treating with them. Mississippi, Alabama, and Georgia's actions represented a break from this legal acknowledgment of qualified tribal sovereignty, and the reverberations manifest themselves in the interactions between Americans and Indian nations from this moment forward.

In 1831, the Cherokee Nation filed suit against the state of Georgia in the US Supreme Court when Georgia arrested a Cherokee citizen, George Tassel, for murdering another Cherokee citizen in the Cherokee Nation. The United States' Congressional and executive branches had signaled their support for white Southern planters and settlers with the Indian Removal Act of 1830, which authorized President Andrew Jackson to grant lands west of the Mississippi River to Native people living east of the Mississippi (encompassing southeastern and midwestern Indian tribes) in exchange for their homelands. The Cherokee Nation commenced a legal battle in response. In the suit, *Cherokee Nation v. Georgia*, the Indian nation alleged that only Cherokee courts had the right to try the case because Georgia laws had no validity within the Cherokee Nation, and thus could not be enforced.[7] In the midst of the trial, the state of Georgia executed the accused murderer. The Supreme Court declined to rule on the case, as it determined that as a "foreign nation" the Cherokee Nation had no standing before the court. However, in his written opinion, Chief Justice John Marshall coined a term that continues to define the idea of tribal sovereignty within the United States.

Marshall wrote that Indian nations could not perfectly be called "foreign." Rather, they could "perhaps, be denominated domestic dependent nations [because] they look to our Government for protection, rely upon its kindness and its power, appeal to it for relief to their wants, and address the President as their Great Father."[8] This important delineation designated Native nations as entities that had a right to create their own laws and regulate their own citizens; it also circumscribed the United States' role in its relationships with Native nations: the United States had a duty to honor contracts and treaties made with Indian nations. Marshall's specification that Indian nations were not foreign governments provided a loophole for an American citizen who *did* have standing before the court to file suit on the Cherokees' behalf, and the Cherokees quickly seized this opportunity. The next year, in 1832, a Christian missionary named Samuel Worcester served as the plaintiff for just such a case in *Worcester v. Georgia*. This case was successful, with the Supreme Court ruling that Georgia law was not valid within the Cherokee Nation, and it would go on to serve as the legal groundwork for the twentieth-century movement to strengthen tribal sovereignty. But in the nineteenth century, it did not stop Indian removal.

Worcester v. Georgia should have forced the state of Georgia to stop white settlers from encroaching on Cherokee land. Instead, the federal government showed its support for Georgia. President Jackson put his support behind the Southern states and pushed the American military to forcibly remove Native people instead of using voluntary treaty agreements per the Indian Removal Act. About 100,000 Native Americans were rounded up and put in camps to await their journeys and many would die on their trips, traveling hundreds of miles to Indian Territory (modern-day Oklahoma) during the agonizing heat of summer and freezing cold of winter, without sufficient food, clothing, or resources. White Americans had adjusted their willingness to honor treaties and even their own judicial system, two of the most vital markers of their democratic society, when it came to the acquisition of Indian land. But the "frontier" mentioned in the Declaration was not yet gone. Even though their movements were coerced, the Five Tribes still signed treaties wherein the American government promised to pay them for the lands they were leaving behind and provide for them in other ways, and they still had a new place set aside from whites to call their own, at least for the time being.

In their removal treaties, the United States promised, in varying language, that the Five Tribes would have claim to their lands in Indian Territory forever. For example, the Choctaw Nation's treaty assured the Choctaws that they and their descendants would live on their land "while they shall exist as a nation and live on it."[9] Similarly, the United States promised the Cherokees that their land would "in no future time without their consent, be included within the territorial limits or jurisdiction of any State or Territory."[10] But this was not to be. For when the rules of engagement as defined by white Americans changed once more after the Civil War, and Native Americans' status as racial others allowed for unfair mistreatment in order to obtain land, these promises would prove meaningless.

Once in Indian Territory, the Five Tribes rebuilt throughout the 1830s and 1840s. Some members of these Indian nations owned Black slaves and they, along with their owners, built the literal and metaphorical foundations of new nations once in their western home. These enslavers grew wealthy, and as some of the most powerful men in these nations, their opinions dictated tribal governance. It is no surprise, then, that when the Civil War erupted, large portions of all the Five Tribes allied with the Confederacy. Confederate representatives promised these nations Congressional representation, which the Cherokees had long lobbied for, as well as protection and annuities from the sale of their southeastern lands, which had been slow in coming from the US federal government.[11]

Although some of the tribal elites who dominated the governments officially sided with the Confederacy, opinions were divided, and some portions of each nation supported the Union or tried to avoid the war entirely. But in the aftermath of the war, in a bid to use their supposed disloyalty as an excuse to advance the white American goal of moving white settlement west, into Indian Territory, the United States generalized the Five Tribes' actions and treated them as if all of their tribal members had entered into a treaty with the Confederacy.[12] The US federal government argued that the Five Tribes had broken their existing treaties through their involvement in the war on the side of the South, and that they would have to agree to new treaty provisions in order to reinstate their relationships with the United States. The United States was willing to withhold provisions promised in the Five Tribes' removal treaties in order to get them to the negotiating table and, unsurprisingly, the new treaty provisions the United States was interested in were in line with white settlers' and businessmen's goals, rather than those of Native people.

The United States compelled the Five Tribes, through treaty negotiations, and then through legislation in the 1880s, to free and enfranchise their slaves, allow railroad construction within their borders, and allot their communally held land into individual parcels, among other stipulations.[13] These postwar treaties, collectively referred to as the Treaties of 1866, essentially prepped Indian Territory to be taken over by the United States in violation of the United States' own promises a mere twenty-odd years before. The railroad provision set the stage for American corporations' entrance into the region. Black emancipation and enfranchisement had to be realized in order to align with the Republicans' hopes for African Americans' social and political rights in the United States. Breaking up the Five Tribes' communally owned land into individual parcels would force Native people into the capitalist mode of American individualism. The Black former slaves of members of the Five Tribes and Native citizens themselves would each receive an allotment through their heads of household, and after these allotments were assigned, the "leftover" land could be settled by Americans. American settlement would introduce American values to the region and provide a foundation for Indian Territory to eventually be made into an American state.

The historical importance of the racial distinction white Americans made between themselves and Native Americans is demonstrably clear when we examine the parallel example of Southern Confederates. The "Lost Cause," the idea of a ransacked, oppressed South, dominated the narrative of the Reconstruction era from the late nineteenth century to the mid-twentieth century, and many today still accept it as truth. But, in reality, Confederates suffered little comeuppance in the Reconstruction era; their situation was settled quite differently than the Five Tribes'. President Andrew Johnson offered general amnesty to southerners except a group of prominent Confederates, whom he required to submit individual petitions for amnesty. Though Johnson required rebellious southerners to pledge oaths to "support, protect, and defend the Constitution of the United States, and...pledge to support all laws and proclamations concerning the emancipation of slaves," his amnesty plan restored plantations to former Confederates who took this oath, denying formerly enslaved people in the United States the opportunity to procure and reside on this land.[14] Like his predecessor Abraham Lincoln, Johnson placed a greater emphasis on reuniting the nation than on advocating for Black rights.

For his fellow white Americans, Johnson placed property rights, a basic American value, above all, even when it came to those who were undeniably traitors to their country. And while Southern Democrats may have complained about the Reconstruction Amendments, it was still their own countrymen legislating the restoration of their country. In a supposedly democratic society that claimed all men had equal rights, Americans' racialized othering of Native people gave them license to ignore their right to own and control their own property and decide their own laws. In Indian Territory, a foreign government (the United States) put together a Reconstruction plan that discarded any pretense of acknowledgment of Indian sovereignty.

Cherokee Nation v. Georgia (1831), *Worcester v. Georgia* (1832), and the Five Tribes' treaties promising them land and autonomy should have protected Indian Territory from American intervention. And yet, in the Reconstruction era, white legislators and politicians were the ones making decisions about the Five Tribes' land—not tribal leaders and their sovereign governments. Indians were not voters and could not vote out the men who made these decisions. Nor would there be a moment where they would reestablish power and undo the actions taken by these decision-makers, as there was for former Confederates.

US imperialism in Indian Territory allowed for American democracy to grow through the land settlement, economic development, and national ideology it implemented. After the Civil War, thousands of white and Black Americans streamed into Indian Territory and other western regions seeking new starts and land to call their own. Even before the land allotment agreed upon in the Treaties of 1866 took place, settlers began building homes and businesses, squatting on Indian land, and marrying Native people and former slaves who were to receive land. The Homestead Act of 1862, which allowed white settlers to claim 160 acres of free land after living on and improving it for five years, initially only applied to unoccupied land. But in 1889, Congress authorized the opening of certain regions within Indian Territory, and both whites and Blacks raced to move and occupy this land. Between 1890 and 1907, the Black population of Indian Territory increased from 19,000 to over 80,000 and the white population increased from 109,400 to 538,500, while the Indian population remained stable at roughly 61,000.[15] Along with these settlers came the capitalistic arm of American society. Railroads brought accompanying businesses, with white settlers opening taverns, stores, and newspapers, which took profit away from Native-owned businesses. Oil and gas were discovered throughout the territory and clever crooks often deceived illiterate Native and Black land-owners into signing away their valuable land and mineral rights.[16]

As more Americans invaded the West, the region grew in fame, taking on a fanciful sheen in which it represented individualism and industry, though it was very much created through federal intervention. Both former Confederates and Unionists began to envision the West as a space that might be shaped by a new, unified nation. Former Confederates, who had been firmly invested in a weak federal government, found that they could accept federal intervention if it created space for their settlement and economic interests in the West. And northerners formed the backbone of the indus-trial involvement that economically shaped the West. As in the South, the reconciliation between Unionists and Confederates was only possible through the rejection of rights for people of color. In the West, as white political and economic power increased through the 1890s, culminating in Oklahoma statehood in 1907, white Americans agreed that Native Americans (and African Americans) were fundamentally different from them and therefore did not have the same rights to property or prosperity.

Though settler colonialism in (what would become) the United States did not begin with an all-powerful nation-state dictating to Native nations where they would live and what rights they would have, the policies put in place during the removal era and the post-Civil War consolidation of federal power dismantled Native sovereignty and denied Native humanity. The reconstruction of the Five Tribes is just one example of how Native nations and peoples were forced to remake themselves in order to embody the American values of capitalism and individualism. While they were long told about the democratic ideals of this nation, they never experienced the realization of these ideas for themselves. Instead, imperialism characterized their lives for decades.

In the twenty-first century, the colonization of Indian nations still sus-tains American democracy. The Keystone Pipeline, part of an oil transport system known for failure and environmental disaster, penetrated several Indian nations despite the mass protests of Native populations, whose voices were ignored because they are seen as less human and as an insignificant voting population. Yet, the pipeline makes it possible for Americans around the country to receive oil and gas; it makes it possible for the federal government, state governments, and private companies to make money. Designers use Native motifs to ornament clothing without paying tribes for the rights to their designs. Americans sprinkle in Native terms (let's "pow wow"; this dog is my "spirit animal"; I've found my "tribe" here) without any reference to the cultures from which they are taken.

Native people remain a constant point of reference for American society: their culture, land, and image remain a site of settlement even as they, now as American citizens, remain unable to access the privileges and rights one would expect in a democracy. Their situation should make us question our idea of "democracy" and the sacrifices Indigenous women and men made historically, and continue to make today, to maintain it.

Notes

1. "Declaration of Independence: A Transcription," National Archives, https://www.archives.gov/founding-docs/declaration-transcript.
2. Frederic Gleach, *Powhatans World and Colonial Virginia: A Conflict of Cultures* (Lincoln, NE: University of Nebraska Press, 1997).
3. Amanda L. Paige, Fuller L. Bumpers, and Daniel F. Littlefield, Jr., *Chickasaw Removal* (Ada, OK: Chickasaw Press, 2010), 17.
4. Theda Perdue and Michael D. Green, *The Cherokee Removal: A Brief History with Documents* (Boston, MA: Bedford/St. Martin's, 2005), 18–21.
5. Paige et al., *Chickasaw Removal*, 17.
6. "Memorandum for Henry Dearborn on Indian Policy," *The Papers of Thomas Jefferson, Volume 39: 13 November 1802 to 3 March 1803* (Princeton, NJ: Princeton University Press, 2012), 231–234.
7. Perdue and Green, *Cherokee Removal*, 79–80.
8. *Cherokee Nation v. Georgia*, 30 US 1 (1831), https://supreme.justia.com/cases/federal/us/30/1.
9. "Treaty with the Choctaw, 1839," *Indian Affairs: Laws and Treaties, Vol. 2* (treaties), ed. Charles Kappler, accessed via Oklahoma State University Digital Collections, 311.
10. "Treaty with the Cherokee, 1835," *Indian Affairs, Vol. 2* (treaties), 442.
11. Annie Heloise Abel, *The American Indian as Slaveholder and Secessionist*, 2nd ed. (Lincoln, NE: University of Nebraska Press, 1992), 161–162; Grant Foreman, *The Five Civilized Tribes* (Norman, OK: University of Oklahoma Press, 1934), 130, 158–161; "Southern superintendency," Annual report of the commissioner

of Indian affairs, for the year 1859, United States Office of Indian Affairs, University of Wisconsin-Madison Libraries Digital Collections, http://digital. library.wisc.edu/1711.dl/History.AnnRep59, 188.

12. "Southern superintendency," Annual report of the commissioner of Indian affairs, for the year 1862, United States Office of Indian Affairs, University of Wisconsin-Madison Libraries Digital Collections, http://digital.library.wisc. edu/1711.dl/History.AnnRep62, 167.

13. "Treaty with the Choctaw and Chickasaw, 1866," *Indian Affairs, Vol. 2* (treaties); "Treaty with the Creek, 1866," *Indian Affairs, Vol. 2* (treaties); "Treaty with the Cherokees, 1866," *Indian Affairs, Vol. 2* (treaties); "Treaty with the Seminole, 1866," *Indian Affairs, Vol. 2* (treaties).

14. "Prest. Johnson's amnesty proclamation," Library of Congress, http://hdl.loc. gov/loc.rbc/rbpe.23502500.

15. US Bureau of the Census, *Extra Census Bulletin: The Five Civilized Tribes of the Indian Territory* (Washington, DC: Government Printing Office, 1894), 7–8; US Bureau of the Census, *Statistics for Oklahoma,* Thirteenth Census of the United States, 1910 (Washington, DC: Government Printing Office, 1913), 695.

16. Gabe James, January 14, 1899, Letters Sent and Received and Other Documents, Chickasaw, Undated and January 15, 1899 to April 28, 1899, Oklahoma Historical Society Microfilm Publications, DC Roll 051.

Further Reading

Indian removal and the related change in Euro-American thinking about the malleability of Indians' racial characteristics has a large historiography as one of the most well-known events, or processes, in Native American history. See Theda Perdue and Mike D. Green's *The Cherokee Nation and the Trail of Tears* (New York: Viking, 2007) for further reading on the Cherokees. For a newer take on removal, see Christopher D. Haveman's *Rivers of Sand: Creek Indian Emigration, Relocation, and Ethnic Cleansing in the American South* (Lincoln, NE: University of Nebraska Press, 2016). Readers interested in learning more about land allotment in Indian Territory should consult Angie Debo's classic study, *And Still the Waters Run: The Betrayal of the Five Civilized Tribes* (Princeton, NJ: Princeton University Press, 1940). David Chang's more recent *The Color of the Land: Race, Nation, and the Politics of Land Ownership in Oklahoma, 1832–1929* (Chapel Hill, NC: University of North Carolina Press, 2010) is also educational, as he follows the different claims of Native Americans, African Americans, and whites to the land in Indian Territory. On the role of the West as a ground of American reconciliation, see Heather Cox Richardson's *West from Appomattox: The Reconstruction of America after the Civil War* (New Haven, CT: Yale University Press, 2007), which argues that Western expansion was key to postwar reconciliation and the creation of a new national identity based around an idealized West.

24

Doubt

John Pell and William Duffy

A merica's "Founding Fathers" were a learned group. Many of them had
classical educations steeped in Greek and Latin. But while the nation's
founders sought to borrow from old ideas to invent a new kind of modern
government, a democratic republic freed from the strictures of European
monarchy, it took a bit longer for there to emerge a uniquely American
philosophical tradition, which came to be known as pragmatism. Writing
more than a century after its emergence in 2001, Louis Menand summarizes
the significance of this philosophy: when stripped down to its primary
value, American pragmatism is all about tolerance. Not tolerance in some
abstract, sentimental sense, but rather "the tolerance, say, of a piece of steel";
that is, the founders of American pragmatism "wanted to create more social
room for error because they thought this would give good outcomes a better
chance to emerge."[1] What we see in the nineteenth-century origins of
American pragmatism is a roadmap for embracing fallibility and doubt as
democratic virtues that rely on and in turn promote curiosity and
open-mindedness.

Accordingly, an ethical imperative at work in American pragmatism
insists on the importance of maintaining avenues for continued interaction and exchange among those with competing political commitments,
religious beliefs, and social values. Although the term "pragmatic" is often
conflated in contemporary politics and business contexts with a style of
leadership that values taking action to reach a sensible end or goal, whatever the outcomes, philosophical pragmatism refers to a method of thinking that puts emphasis on the agency we have to test and learn from the
consequences of our beliefs. This method manifests in the insistence on
observing and learning from the consequences of our commitments. In short,

John Pell and William Duffy, *Doubt* In: *Democracies in America*. Edited by: D. Berton Emerson and Gregory Laski,
Oxford University Press. © D. Berton Emerson and Gregory Laski 2023. DOI: 10.1093/oso/9780198865698.003.0025

pragmatism requires that we recognize that certainty is anathema to the interaction and exchange that keeps a democracy alive.[2]

But even the idea of democracy is not an abstract, sentimental construct for pragmatist thinkers, nor is their concern for its health. The founders of American pragmatism were keenly aware of what happens when we forgo conversation to take up arms: violence begets more violence. This realization marks the beginning of American pragmatist philosophy, a way of thinking about thinking that found its genesis in the turmoil of Reconstruction. Consider, for example, how Oliver Wendell Holmes Jr., another of pragmatism's founders, preserved his bloodied uniforms from the Union Army—along with two musket balls removed from his body—as an ostensible reminder of his experience with war. Pragmatism demands us to understand that not only do our beliefs have consequences but that we can and should be willing to study these consequences as a method for testing the usefulness of our beliefs. Put simply, as democratic citizens we can learn to change our minds, and we must.

It was the aim of American pragmatism to develop a method for dealing with this kind of doubt, that thing with which all beliefs must wrestle, an understanding that is especially crucial for the workings of democracy. The early pragmatists confronted the uncertainties facing the American experiment following the Civil War by supplying intellectual and discursive resources for citizens antagonized by competing ideologies as they reconsidered their civic commitments in order to imagine a collective future. Pragmatist rhetorical practice encourages citizens to adopt a productive relationship to disagreement by refiguring doubt as a catalyst for civic engagement. Engaging with doubt pragmatically first requires intersubjectivity—deliberate action with others (especially others who think differently) to continually cultivate the common ground that supports our interaction and exchange. To be clear, doubt in a democratic collective can be highly problematic; repeated questioning of expertise and reliable governance can lead to fatal consequences. The founders of American pragmatism worked out their ideas in just this sort of unstable time. Their commitment to common interaction, however, for pragmatists *is* democracy: the practice of being with others in order to assuage doubts about a common world.

American pragmatist philosophy has auspicious beginnings in the philosophical writings of Charles Sanders Peirce in the 1870s. He was an unapologetic intellectual who would have recoiled at later definitions of pragmatism as an "anti-intellectualistic revolt, an embrace of the 'will to believe' pathetic in its methodological feebleness."³ Peirce articulated what became pragmatism's central maxim: "consider what effects, that might conceivably have practical bearings, we conceive the object of our conception to have. Then, our conception of these effects is the whole of our conception of the object." This maxim offers an elegant "logical rule" for how beliefs emerge from experiences in the world.⁴ Peirce was dubious about Cartesian metaphysics, which he considered audacious and naive. Pragmatism, as Peirce asserts, offers a definition of belief that is consistent with human fallibility. The beliefs we hold, he argues, are not based on the congruence between our internal mental states and the external material world; rather, a belief is "a rule for action" intended to help us navigate the myriad decisions we make on a daily basis. Like other animals, humans seek habituation—we like routines—and because of this our most important beliefs have little to do with satisfying the "hair-splitting philosopher's" metaphysical questions about the nature of things and everything to do with establishing the "habits" that allow us to obtain equilibrium with our surroundings. Habits are, in short, the "essence of belief."⁵

But how do our habits of belief develop? These rules of action are responses to what Peirce calls "irritations of doubt," which he defines as "some indecision" requiring the mental activity of determining the course of action that will "cessate the doubt."⁶ Sometimes our doubts are profound—*are government health agencies adequately responding to global pandemics?*—but most of the time mundanity defines our doubts—*should I pay the toll with the last two-dollar bills in my wallet or with the pile of coins in the cup holder?* In either case, none of our prior beliefs—that is, none of the habitual patterns of action we currently employ—will always be sufficient to confront all of the various problems we must negotiate when doubt emerges. But as it turns out, Peirce says, this irritation of doubt "is the motive for thinking." Habits are those previously established rules for action that achieve desired results in a particular situation. It is no surprise, then, that we are cognitively predisposed to remain wedded to our beliefs. Habitual action, Peirce reminds us, requires less mental energy, for when we operate from habit we are not engaging in the "action of thinking" but rather working from the "stopping point" of thought.⁷

Yet new doubts arise as a result of our relations with others in the world. When our ideas, values, and beliefs encounter those of others and thereby create moments of doubt, we are hesitant to change our minds. A person may go through life "systematically keeping out of view all that might cause a change in his opinions" in order to hide from uncertainty. It is inevitable that we will encounter others who do not share our beliefs, and in rare moments of self-awareness, Peirce suggests, we come to the realization "that another man's thoughts or sentiment may be equivalent to one's own."[8] Recognizing that other's beliefs, established through the same inferential and experiential processes by which we establish our own, are valid is an important step in determining the veracity of our own beliefs. If we accept that others establish their beliefs through inferential processes similar to our own, then the doubts that emerge from our interactions with others are not the product of someone's wrong thinking, but rather the result of lacking shared experiences. Peirce's pragmatism thus animates doubt, making it a central feature of the democratic process.

Doubt as a catalyst for deliberation was also a central tenet of William James's pragmatism, yet with key differences. Whereas for Peirce doubt is a condition we cannot help but want to neutralize, James understands it more conditionally as a tool with which we can cultivate BELIEF. James transformed Peirce's pragmatic understanding of doubt into a line of inquiry for exploring the therapeutic dimensions of belief, the way we cultivate and hold onto beliefs not because we have to but because we choose to. Not surprisingly, James took a keen interest in the psychology of religion. *The Varieties of Religious Experience* (1902) compares the ways religious commitments manifest in the private practices of individual believers. Peirce had thought the scientific method the best avenue for testing beliefs, but James recognized that abstract phenomena couldn't be grappled with in such an objective manner, even though such phenomena were just as "real" to our experience as material reality. "This absolute determinability of our mind by abstraction is one of the cardinal facts of our human constitution," James writes. "Polarizing and magnetizing us as [beliefs] do, we turn towards them and from them, we seek them, hold them, hate them, bless them, just as if they were so many concrete beings."[9] James cautions that inventing a belief that we come to hold as true doesn't mean such belief is infallible; it only means that the belief is useful for understanding some aspect of our lived experience. James had no patience with an absolutist attitude, even though he recognized people construct creeds as a consequence of what is an otherwise natural human drive. What we know and what we believe we know will always be partial, so we shouldn't hide from doubt or treat it as a harbinger of unbelief. Instead we should welcome doubt and embrace what ultimately is its call to inquiry, for this is what doubt is for pragmatism: a catalyst for inquiry, an invaluable resource for any democracy.

Doubt as the beginning of inquiry gains further development in the work of the educator and philosopher John Dewey, who is perhaps American pragmatism's most prolific thinker and whose ideas developed and underwent noticeable shifts over the course of his career. In one of his earliest essays about democracy, Dewey argues that the ideals of classical liberalism—that way of thinking about freedom as collections of rights to which individuals are inherently entitled—misrepresent the reality that such rights are *social* goods, which is to say the liberal ideals that inform modern democracy depend on positive, productive relations among the members of the collective. "To define democracy simply as the rule of the many, as sovereignty chopped up into mince meat," Dewey says in one representative passage, "is to define it as abrogation of society, as society dissolved, annihilated."[10] A democracy is worthless, in other words, if we don't acknowledge our social obligations to one another. If Dewey had been around during the COVID-19 pandemic in 2020, he would have said that protesters assembling outside city halls and state capital buildings because they thought quarantine orders violated their civil rights were missing what makes democracy viable. Early in his career, for Dewey, democracy is not the inscription of a constitution or set of abstract rights so much as it is a collective social sentiment rooted in the value of cooperation.

In time, Dewey's political philosophy developed into an understanding of democracy as not just a social organism but a continuous process of inquiry, one wherein its ideal ends are not nearly as important as its much messier means. In other words, Dewey came to underscore the importance of the processes through which we act together as a collective. His thinking about democracy developed alongside his own pragmatic theory of knowledge, one that emphasized knowledge not as a kind of possession that we wield but instead as an activity we engage in. Specifically, Dewey came to understand knowledge as problem-solving, the working out of questions as they present themselves through experience.

Dewey's earlier interest in the ideal ends of a social democracy thus shifted toward an emphasis on the ways people work through the immediate problems of the present. In *The Quest for Certainty* (1929), Dewey puts it this way: we can attempt to change the world through introspection, through attempting to carve out a better idea of what the world should be, or we can pursue "the method of changing the world through action." While this might sound like a commonsense idea today, it wasn't at the time. Not only was Dewey critiquing a large swath of the philosophical tradition reaching all the way back to Plato and the search for ideal knowledge, he was also suggesting that ideal knowledge was itself a false idol. How we develop knowledge, Dewey argues, is through the trial and error that comes with everyday experience and the efficacy of our communication. Our daily lives are constantly bombarded with problems, many of them small and inconsequential, but as we learn to work through them, we develop practical wisdom, what the Greeks called *phronesis*. Most of the problems we face don't have clear-cut solutions, so we must make informed guesses as to whether this or that course of action will lead to the most satisfying outcome. And this means we have to grow comfortable with doubt. As Dewey says, "the most distinctive characteristic of practical activity, one which is so inherent that it cannot be eliminated, is the uncertainty that attends it."[11] As he came to emphasize the need to acknowledge uncertainty as a critical component in the development of knowledge, he did so while also emphasizing that just as our experience is always partial, so too is the knowledge that results from it; the more wide and varied our experiences, the more tested and thus more functional—or practically wise—is our knowledge.

Whereas Dewey produced the most published work of all the early American pragmatists, Jane Addams most embodied this pragmatic commitment to seek wide and varied experiences.[12] As co-founder of Chicago's famed Hull House, a community and civic outreach center where social workers lived so as to be in constant "interconnection" with the neighborhood, she earned international acclaim as a social philosopher and peace activist, becoming the first American woman to receive the Nobel Peace Prize. Addams's pragmatism was grounded in a commitment to social amelioration: the improvement of social conditions through cooperative labor. That is, she believed social problems had to be remedied through social action, and this in turn required articulating a social ethics that she developed across her many works of public philosophy. "We are learning that a standard of social ethics is not attained by travelling a sequestered byway, but by mixing on the thronged and common road where all must turn out for one another, and to at least see the size of one another's burdens," Addams writes.[13] But to mix "on the thronged and common road" means that we must be willing to share a common road to begin with, which means we must be willing to embrace "social intercourse."[14] Addams recognized that, pragmatically speaking, tackling society's most pressing problems required building a social infrastructure that would allow for more and better interaction and exchange among America's diverse citizenry.

Here we can begin to see the role of doubt in Addams's social philosophy. Specifically, Addams was invested in promoting a view of society that didn't parse people into conflicting categories who competed against one another, but instead as a diverse collective of fellow humans who must work together to remedy problems like poverty and child labor. However, before these social problems could be solved, it "requires at the very outset a definite abandonment of the eighteenth-century philosophy upon which so much of our present democratic and philanthropic activity depends."[15] Addams shared Dewey's doubts about the philosophical focus on individually centered, rights-based ethics. The collective ethos Addams and Dewey seek requires the cultivation of mutual respect and support. But this ethos can only be built with patience, by allowing our own ideas and beliefs to be influenced by those of others.

More than anything, Addams shows us what a commitment to doubt looks like as a critical component to a social philosophy rooted in the power of grassroots action. We can "never settle our perplexities by mere good fighting," she writes in an 1895 essay.[16] By "good fighting" she meant competition, the parsing of winners and losers. The resolution of our social problems instead lies in understanding these "perplexities" themselves, in learning to identify shared problems and making these perplexities sources for generative conversation.

When Oliver Wendell Holmes Jr. preserved his bloodstained uniforms from the Civil War, he created a material reminder of what can happen when we decide to put arbitrary limits on democracy. In the case of that conflict, half the nation decided that some people were better suited as human chattel, and Holmes understood that volunteering to fight for the Union was his moral duty. After fighting for the preservation of the United States in war, he carried his practice of moral duty into the field of law, eventually winning appointment to the Supreme Court.

Bringing pragmatist thought to the legal world, Holmes is most known for his 1881 book *The Common Law*, which begins, "The life of the law has not been logic, it has been experience."[17] Once again the connection between the necessity of experience and the conditionality of thought appears. When it comes to the law, Holmes believed that just as our lives are guided by how we change and adapt to new experiences, so too should our legal system be able to change and adapt. Judicial reasoning based on a view of the law as a preexisting, static set of standards—the philosophical term is "natural law"—perverts what Holmes understood as the way laws are actually developed and deployed, namely through the give and take of adjudicating specific questions at specific times with specific circumstances at play. The law is at best an imperfect guide, one that we can and should use to guide our judicial system but that also needs continuous revision. First principles, those ideas we believe without doubt, will always require reevaluation, even if such reevaluation only serves to affirm them.

He explores this idea in a 1915 essay that tackles the idea of doubt. Holmes begins by stating that even though he holds beliefs that he himself cannot help but hold—beliefs he *cannot* doubt—this doesn't mean he treats these beliefs as inerrant. After all, he says, "as there are many things that I cannot help doing that the universe can, I do not venture that my inabilities in the way of thought are inabilities of the universe." Just as we saw with Dewey's understanding that practical problems require a kind of practical wisdom to resolve, or *phronesis*, Holmes reiterates how we negotiate the complicated calculus that results from mingling legal claims with moral claims: "To get a little nearer to the practical, our current ethics and our current satisfaction with conventional legal rules... can be purged to a certain extent without reference to what our final ideal may be. To rest upon a formula is a slumber that, prolonged, means death."[18] Here Holmes provides a concise summary of the pragmatic method. To get nearer to the practical—to figure out what practical difference a belief makes and whether that belief is worthwhile—we need to observe cause and effect and adjust our behavior accordingly.

So all of us who claim our place in a democracy must be willing and able, according to pragmatist philosophers, to engage in deliberate discourse, the back and forth between parties, in order to locate solutions that can account for the greatest range of experience. Of course, as Peirce and James remind us, there will always be others we encounter with whom our interactions will likely cause doubt to again emerge. In short, our knowledge and beliefs are contingent and, hopefully, mutable. In order to avoid what Holmes saw as the violence that comes from certainty, the pragmatist encouraged democratic processes rooted in human fallibility and attuned to doubt.

In a democracy, to doubt is not a weakness but a virtue. It is the mental capacity to hold our beliefs at a distance, to turn them over and see how and why they work, how and why they might need adjustment, and how and why they will always need to be tested with further experience.

Notes

1. Louis Menand, *The Metaphysical Club: A Story of Ideas in America* (New York: Farrar, Straus, and Giroux, 2001), 439, 440.
2. Charles S. Peirce, "The Fixation of Belief," in Philip P. Wiener, ed., *Selected Writings* (New York: Dover Publications, 1958), 102.
3. Justus Buchler, "Introduction," in *Philosophical Writings of Peirce* (New York: Dover Publications, 1958), xi.
4. Charles S. Peirce, "How to Make Our Ideas Clear," in Justus Buchler, ed., *Philosophical Writings of Peirce* (New York: Dover Publications, 1955), 31.
5. Ibid., 121.
6. Peirce, "The Fixation of Belief," 10.
7. Peirce, "How to Make Our Ideas Clear," 121.
8. Peirce, "The Fixation of Belief," 12.
9. William James, *The Varieties of Religious Experience: A Study in Human Nature* (1907; New York: The Modern Library, 2002), 65.
10. John Dewey, "The Ethics of Democracy," in Louis Menand, ed., *Pragmatism: A Reader* (New York: Vintage Books, 1997), 186.
11. John Dewey, *The Quest for Certainty: A Study of the Relation of Knowledge and Action* (New York: Minton, Balch & Company, 1929), 3, 6.
12. It's no coincidence that the history of American pragmatism has focused on the work of men, especially given the subjugation of women across virtually every segment of society at the time. In addition to Jane Addams, other American women who arguably contributed to the development of pragmatist philosophy during this period include Ida B. Wells, Charlotte Perkins Gillman, Florence Kelley, Alice Hamilton, and Mary Parker Follett, just to name a few.
13. Jane Addams, *Democracy and Social Ethics* (New York: Macmillan, 1902), 6.
14. Jane Addams, "The Subjective Necessity of Social Settlements" (1893), in Jean Bethke Elshtain, ed., *The Jane Addams Reader* (New York: Basic Books, 2002), 14.
15. Jane Addams, *Newer Ideals of Peace* (New York: Macmillan, 1906), 28.
16. Jane Addams, "The Settle as a Factor in the Labor Movement" (1895), in *The Jane Addams Reader*, 57.
17. Oliver Wendell Holmes Jr., *The Common Law* (Boston, MA: Little, Brown, and Co., 1881), 1.
18. Oliver Wendell Holmes Jr. "Ideals and Doubts" (1915), in *Pragmatism: A Reader*, 170–171.

Further Reading

While white male voices dominate American pragmatism's early canon, African American thinkers and scholars have both revised and vitalized the pragmatic method. The essays in *Race Contacts and Interracial Relations: Lectures on the Theory and*

Practice of Race (Washington, DC: Howard University Press, 1992) highlight Alain Locke's nuanced thinking on the value of pluralism, while W. E. B. Du Bois's *The Souls of Black Folk* (New York: Longman, 2002) brings the pragmatic method to bear on issues of race, ethnicity, and the plight of African Americans at the turn of the twentieth century. Cornel West offers both a critique and revision of pragmatism in *The Evasion of American Philosophy* (Madison, WI: University of Wisconsin Press, 1989). A contemporary of Jane Addams and John Dewey, the sociologist George Herbert Mead used pragmatism to invigorate metaphysics and the social sciences. *The Philosophy of the Present* (New York: Prometheus, 2002) serves as a concise introduction to Mead's expansive thinking and pragmatism's methodological potential. Those interested in connections between rhetoric, pragmatism, and democracy should consider Nathaniel Crick's *Democracy and Rhetoric* (Columbia, SC: University of South Carolina Press, 2010), Robert Danisch's *Pragmatism, Democracy and the Necessity of Rhetoric* (Columbia, SC: University of South Carolina Press, 2007), Keith Gilyard's *Composition and Cornel West* (Carbondale, IL: Southern Illinois University Press, 2008), and Hephzibah Roskelly and Kate Ronald's *Reason to Believe* (Albany, NY: SUNY Press, 1998).

25

Neighbors

Nancy Rosenblum

Take the "good neighbor" literally: people who live nearby and contribute to—or do not derange—the quality of life at home. Neighbors exhibit solicitude and hospitality but also unleash their demons on us, or in our view. Snobbery, betrayal, hypocrisy, and cruelty wreck our sleep, our nerves. Relentlessly barking dogs, blaring televisions, incessant quarrels, an excess of domestic odors. Sounds that startle us at night and disturb our sleep. Bedraggled yards. Snooping and interfering. Killing time. Wounding reputation. We are, too, the beneficiaries of ordinary kindnesses. Anything is possible, from a nod of recognition to a spark of mutual sympathy and the rare unlooked-for favor that alters the day.

Proximity creates occasion for arguments, slights, acts of aggression, and assistance. Family aside, we have no more constant or intimate stage for exhibiting graciousness or foul temper, or worse, than where we live. Neighbors are not just people living nearby, friendly or unfriendly, trustworthy or treacherous, intrusive or withdrawn. Neighbors are our environment. They are the background to our private lives at home. The unique power they hold over our lives is explained in that one word: they affect us where we live, at *home*.

We shouldn't underestimate the significance of mundane trespasses and kindnesses. The quotidian is precisely their interest. The local and personal matter immensely. "To affect the quality of the day is the highest of arts," wrote the great mid-nineteenth-century theorist of neighborliness, Henry David Thoreau, in *Walden* (1854), and neighbors brighten or degrade the day, every day.[1] The phenomenology of everyday encounters is my standpoint: ordinary good turns and ordinary vices, the give and take of greetings, favors, and offenses in this place whose meaning for us is different from any

Nancy Rosenblum, *Neighbors* In: *Democracies in America*. Edited by: D. Berton Emerson and Gregory Laski,
Oxford University Press. © D. Berton Emerson and Gregory Laski 2023. DOI: 10.1093/oso/9780198865698.003.0026

other. Extreme conditions and frightful degradation of everyday life at home are common enough, however, and then neighbors' responses can be life-altering: often enough, neighbors hold our lives in their hands.

It is hard to think of another sustained interaction except friendship that floats so free of the institutional securities, rules and processes, shared purposes, and agreed-on outcomes that define roles and shape relations in other settings. We could try to posit general norms of neighborliness: sociability, say, or helpfulness, but these apply in every social domain. And in the United States amorphous general "neighborliness" is overlaid by something more. Being a good neighbor is shaped by what I call "the democracy of everyday life."

The democratic ethos of being a good neighbor is a component of how we think about ourselves, an element of Americans' moral identity. With its historical roots in settler and immigrant experiences, its grounding in reciprocity, and its incarnations in popular culture, the norm of the good neighbor is deeply engrained. For most of us (not all) much of the time (not always), it has regulative force. We are seldom prepared to cast ourselves out of the company of good neighbors; indeed, we may see ourselves as enforcers. We are inclined to blame and shame and speak out against bad neighbors who stand accused not just of selfishness, carelessness, or malice but also of a deeper failing: falling off from this aspirational but real enough regulative ideal.

At the same time that the good neighbor is an element of personal identity, it is a proverbial representation of national character, as familiar as the self-portrait of America as a nation of volunteers performing good works and rivaling the representation of America as a nation of public-spirited citizens. Indeed, the national self-image of the good neighbor is arguably more deeply rooted than these, and has surprising continuity. In the face of historic changes in economy and demography, regional and social differences, enormous variation in neighbors' dependency on one another to meet basic needs (contrast nineteenth-century settlers with twentieth-century suburbanites), ever-changing residential patterns, domestic lifestyles, and local etiquettes, the good neighbor is a steady, symbolic American. Collective self-representation of America as a "good neighbor nation" is a point of pride. We should recognize the democracy of everyday life as a deep substrate of democracy in America.

What defines it? One signature element of the democracy of everyday life is reciprocity. There is enormous latitude in the business neighbors have with one another, and reciprocity is direct, face to face, and open-ended. Our history of encounters with neighbors and the expectation that these will continue into the future incline us to return good turns, which often consist of nothing more than a wave or the standard, solicitous, but not insignificant "How are you feeling today?" The utility of reciprocity is certainly not lost on us. We assess the rewards and the costs of offers and rebuffs all the time.

But a purely transactional understanding of neighborliness leads us astray. Reciprocity, which provides a foothold on the difficult terrain of neighborliness, is mischaracterized as strategic cooperation or a network of negotiated support. Instrumentalism is not the whole of neighbor interactions. As Thoreau observed, "It is difficult to begin without borrowing, but perhaps it is the most generous course thus to permit your fellow-men to have an interest in your enterprise" (31). For, in fact, the dynamic works as often in reverse. Good turns are the occasion for encounters, not the reason for them. Give and take may have little purpose except as a way of initiating and sustaining relations day to day, as Thoreau acknowledged in his account of building his hut at Walden Pond: "At length, in the beginning of May, with the help of some of my acquaintances, rather to improve so good an occasion for neighborliness than from any necessity, I set up the frame of my house" (34).

The specifically "democratic" in relations shaped by the democracy of everyday life is in part a matter of rough parity in the terms of reciprocity. It is also a matter of who counts as my neighbor in the dance of give and take. A common term of reference for neighbors in the settler, immigrant, and suburban narratives that are our canonical sources is "decent folk." "Decent folk" gathers in the qualities—practical and moral—we weigh when we size up the couple next door to decide whether we will open ourselves to or close ourselves off from willing encounters. It reflects a modest, sensible assessment that these neighbors are trustworthy for the purposes of ordinary give and take, however minimal. The criterion is not character overall, and our judgment does not turn on any special action or exhibition of virtue. Its democratic ethos lies in the fact that the judgment is personal and individual and that we decline to approach neighbors as representatives or symbols. In some societies neighbor encounters and the terms of reciprocity are governed by the rules of entrenched social hierarchy, rank, class, kinship, or sectarianism; give and take is regulated by tribe or tradition or clientelism. "Decent folk" designates our equality in just this one respect: as neighbors. Reciprocity is *comparatively* detached from the considerations that govern interactions in spheres outside home. Reciprocity cast in terms of rough equality among neighbors as "decent folk" is a defining characteristic of the democracy of everyday life.

Of course, individually we fall off from the democratizing import of reciprocity among neighbors; collectively, too, the democracy of everyday life is imperfectly realized, and our momentous national failings are not safely in the past. Under some conditions, then, neighbors as "decent folk" is a fighting creed. And yet popular culture is rife with stories of neighbors engaged in easy give and take, first finding people living nearby alien and threatening, and then acknowledging them as "decent folk." The democratic ethos is delivered to us in popular fiction (*To Kill a Mockingbird*), on television (*The Honeymooners*), and in educational programs directed at children (*Sesame Street*). We might be tempted to view this as sentimentality and wishful thinking. We might think it an achievement beyond imagination if we had not experienced and witnessed the rough egalitarianism of reciprocity among neighbors ourselves.

The injunction "live and let live" and its close cousin, "minding our own business," is the second element of the democracy of everyday life. The phrase "minding our own business" is commonly taken as a rebuke when we trespass, snoop, interfere, admonish, advise, correct, and enforce. It is a demand to back off. By their existence, neighbors contract the sphere of privacy and we often learn about one another's lives unwillingly, just by our presence. So, minding our own business is often strictly impossible—wanted or not, we have epistemic opportunity to learn things about the people living nearby. Then, "live and let live" is a matter of what we do with what we know. Do we exploit the accident of proximity? Do we comment, admonish, report, agitate? "Live and let live" demands stern self-discipline. It commends reticence, keeping what we know or think we know to ourselves; call it "unacknowledgment."

"Live and let live" is not at all a matter of the shrug of indifference the colloquial phrase implies. It enjoins us to protect neighbors' control over their environment at home. We acknowledge that we are not well insulated from our neighbors' situation, nor they from ours. We require a certain distance that is more than physical. As Thoreau insisted, "Individuals, like nations, must have suitable broad and natural boundaries, even a considerable neutral ground, between them" (98). "Minding our own business" makes us hesitant to publicize, pronounce, and tell others about our neighbors' misdeeds or to report the undocumented family next door to authorities.

Under repressive political conditions, we are liable to become agents in a system of surveillance, and then whether or not we follow the injunction to "live and let live" can be life-saving.

For the same reasons and to the same purpose, "live and let live" prescribes a particular sort of positive action—a signal and an offer. In mistrust-creating situations, with a gesture or word we acknowledge that we are regular presences, not hostile strangers. We signal that we are safe with one another and will not disturb, injure, or exploit our neighbor. We decline to erect walls or to refuse to deal. We understand that our encounters are ongoing, our vulnerability mutual. "Live and let live" does not register indifference, then, or the disposition to wash our hands of these neighbors. We are paying attention. We are extending ourselves.

The injunction to "live and let live" can become a casualty of hostile condition. When officials encourage mistrust or condone violence, when everyday life is deranged by atrocity, even the most modest gesture has enormous significance. Writing about the horror inflicted on civilians in war, Vasily Grossman observed: "No-one during this terrible time was moved by blood suffering and death; what surprised and shook people was kindness and love... [T]he old teacher was... the only person left... who still asked, 'How are you feeling today?'"[2] Where we proffer this iota of acknowledgment, "live and let live" is a residual of normalcy and a powerful reassurance. The quintessential American case of intimate violence at the hands of neighbors we thought we knew is lynching; even then, some neighbors warn, protect, comfort, rescue, and offer hope for ordinary reciprocity among decent folk.

The democracy of everyday life has its own place, then. Its domain is quotidian life around the home. After we take account of organized politics, work, membership groups, social circles, friends, and family, there is this remainder. This domain is key to understanding the democracy of everyday life. The good neighbor is not a redescription of good citizen, and the democracy of everyday life is not democratic public life writ small or preparation for it. There is no "logic of congruence" among different social spheres, only some of which are inflected with a democratic ethos of some kind. The point is: the good neighbor should not be conflated with public principles of justice, formal democratic practices and institutions, legal rights, or civic virtue.

True, the spheres are not walled off from one another: neighbors organize voluntary associations; civic activists recruit members from among their neighbors. But there is no imperative dynamic from reciprocity as neighbors to collective political action. And declining to participate in local organizations is not derogation from the norm of good neighbor. Indeed, to represent the democracy of everyday life as if it were a matter of translating public democratic principles to apply to direct personal relations among neighbors at home is a distortion. We simply do not experience neighbor relations in these terms. We don't ask whether give and take with the people next door contributes to distributive justice. We don't comprehend the rough EQUALITY of reciprocity as a local application of principles of fairness or nondiscrimination. We don't invoke civil or political rights when we grapple with neighbors who give ordinary offense.

Nor should neighborliness be cast as a model of good citizenship. Both conflations fail to appreciate the moral uses of pluralism. If neighbors are seen as a waystation to civic engagement or neighbor relations are infused with a sort of romantic glow and seen as exemplary citizenship, we suffer a truncated view of democracy in America. We eclipse democracy's pluralism.

We learn from settler, immigrant, and suburban narratives and from our own experience that neighbors can provide aid and company, signal that we are safe with one another, offer small gestures of recognition that enhance the quality of life, especially under exigent conditions, help repair newcomers' ignorance, and show us how to practice in the world. But as neighbors we are not civic activists, agents of social justice, guardians of equal rights, or citizens committed to reform.

The good neighbor is a true democratic ideal but a false ideal for democratic CITIZENSHIP. For reciprocity among neighbors as decent folk turns on the real possibility of disregarding precisely the social inequalities, ethnic and sectarian differences, conflicting interests and ideological commitments that citizens bring to public life. The good neighbor ideal, practiced often enough, disregards these differences, which cannot and should not be disregarded in public affairs. They just *are* the circumstances of politics. They provide both the perspectives and the substantive matters for political decision-making, which is partial and PARTISAN. The collapse of citizen into neighbor or neighbor into citizen obscures the purposes, motives, interests, and justifications that shape democratic public life.

We understand democracy in America more accurately and deeply by keeping the phenomenology of good neighbors and the independence of the democracy of everyday life in view—if for no other reason than to give the quotidian its due, but also in order to accurately grasp the significance the democracy of everyday life holds for democratic politics in America.

So, what is the significance for democratic political practices and institutions of the good neighbor as an independent moral identity at home in its own sphere? The American story was from the start a history of neighbors and only later of the development of political institutions and articulation of democratic principles and processes.[3] Neighbor relations with its democratic ethos came first. Self-governing neighbors preceded and underwrote the formation of democratic institutions, conforming fairly enough to Alexis de Tocqueville's story. The democracy of everyday life emerges as the enduring deep structure of democracy in America. And the good neighbor emerges in Thoreau's work as the vital "saving remnant" of democracy in America when democratic politics and the relation of citizens to government is degraded and morally unabideable.

In *Walden* Thoreau reflects on neighbors in America; on the quality of life rooted at home, in this place, alongside these people who live nearby. Neighbors are everywhere in *Walden*, a persistent theme. We see that Thoreau heightens the democracy of everyday life. True, the quotidian can by definition be identified with the ordinary, but rightly encountered, life among neighbors is extraordinary and neighbors figure as one of the necessaries of life.

Thoreau begins his reflections with antipathy toward neighbors and deliberate self-distancing. Life in the woods, which as he reminds us more than once began on Independence Day 1845, is an experiment in the art of living. "I lived alone, in the woods, a mile from any neighbor, in a house which I had built myself, on the shore of Walden Pond, in Concord, Massachusetts, and earned my living by the labor of my hands only" (92). The first pose he assumes toward neighbors is aversive: he retreats to the woods, to his "withdrawing room." He tells us why: he is averse to the oppressive press of proximity, the surfeit of distracting news and gossip. "To be in company, even with the best, is soon wearisome and dissipating" (94). With neighbors we are mostly killing time. "We meet at very short intervals, not having had time to acquire any new value for each other . . . and give each other a new taste of that old musty cheese that we are" (95). In the same spirit, Robert Frost cautioned: "We're too unseparated. And going home/From company means coming to our senses."[4]

"Let every one mind his own business, and endeavor to be what he was made," Thoreau declares (219). That business is care of the self, and Thoreau details the techniques of care. It entails attentiveness to the natural world—to the particular individual trees and creatures and ponds that are our neighbors.

And from our vantage point as witnesses to the lives of our human neighbors, we gain insight into our own. They shed light on our vulnerabilities, moral resources, and the terms of our happiness. Surprisingly often, then, the path to care of the self runs through them. In Thoreau's encounters with neighbors, as in the company of natural things, as in every transcendental experience, they appear transfigured. We experience not the old musty cheese of familiars but "the flower and fruit of a man" that improves the quality of the day. "I want the flower and fruit of a man; that some fragrance be wafted over from him to me, and some ripeness of flavor our intercourse" (56). We experience our neighbor in the round as absolutely unique and interesting to us. That is neighbors' true value. That is real philanthropy: not doing good but giving neighbors a strong dose of ourselves.

There is more: we can know neighbors, see them with fresh eyes, and see in these familiars the infinite scope of what it is possible to become. In his lecture defending the violent actions of the white abolitionist John Brown at Harpers Ferry in 1859, Thoreau opined, "We dream of foreign countries, of other times and races of men placing them at a distance in history or space [but] we discover often, this distance and strangeness in our midst, between us and our nearest neighbors. *They* are our Austrias and Chinas, and South Sea Islands."[5] If we recognized our neighbors' sheer individuality, their foreignness, he learned, "we should live in all the ages of the world in an hour" (10).

Thoreau did not remain at Walden Pond; he never intended to. "I left the woods for as good a reason as I went there.... It is remarkable how easily and insensibly we fall into a particular route, and make a beaten track for ourselves." He went on: "Perhaps it seemed to me that I had several more lives to live" (21). Thoreau, and we, are made to shift back and forth among spheres of life over the course of our lives, and over the course of the day. Both as a condition for the deliberate endeavor of care of the self and as practical necessity, we must inhabit several worlds. We flourish when we open ourselves to the moral uses of pluralism. There is no better formulation than Thoreau's: "thank heaven, here is not all the world" (214). We have several lives to live. One is the democracy of everyday life among neighbors; another is the public life of citizens of a democracy.

Thoreau enters that life, too, of course. He is chanticleer, waking his neighbors up to the calamity of American democracy and to their own ongoing part in America's greatest national crime, slavery. Thoreau pronounces the neighbor as the singular relation in which we demonstrate respect for one another, as we cannot live as citizens in relation to one another or in relation to government in a slaveholding, war-mongering democracy. In "Civil Disobedience," Thoreau challenges authorities to treat us as the status of neighbor demands: "How shall he ever know well what he is and does as an officer of the government, or as a man, until he is obliged to consider whether he shall treat me, his neighbor, for whom he has respect, as a neighbor and well-disposed man."[6] A government that makes its citizens agents of injustice injures us—treats us with the most profound disrespect. Under these conditions it is intolerable to continue to speak practically and as a citizen, and Thoreau casts reciprocity, equality as a neighbor, and live and let live as our recourse when the CONSTITUTION and formal democratic processes fail.

The democracy of everyday life is both a resource and an index of political catastrophe. When officials create mistrust, incite betrayal, set neighbors against one another, or condone violence so that everyday life is horribly deranged, we recognize that democracy is diminished in a deeper way than exclusively political standards allow us to see. Again in "Civil Disobedience," Thoreau writes, "I please myself imagining a State at last which can afford to be just to all men, and to treat the individual with respect as a neighbor; which even would not think it inconsistent with its own repose, if a few were to live aloof from it, not meddling with it, nor embraced by it, who fulfill all the duties of neighbors and fellow-men."[7]

Thoreau's reflections on neighborliness are one source of my phenomenology of the democracy of everyday life. All the elements are there, transposed in his gorgeous language and "extra-vagrant" terms. What is Thoreau's distance and neutral ground, his "let every one mind his own business, and endeavor to be what he was made," but a rich form of "live and let live" (219)? "Giving a strong dose of ourselves" is reciprocity among neighbors who give and take their unique individual flower and fragrance. Both reciprocity and a detachment are internal to the good neighbor, and he showed why. Our status as "decent folk" and rough equals is transfigured by Thoreau, making the familiar foreign, exciting interest and possibilities. Recognize Thoreau's shifts of perspective on the democratic ethos of neighbors for what they are: good neighbors refracted through a great intelligence and with perfect confidence in the possibility of self- and political transformation.

The democracy of everyday life is no substitute for political democracy. The good neighbor is neither a preparation nor a model for democratic citizenship. That is a sentimental romance. But when "decivilization" threatens, the good neighbor can be seen as democracy's "saving remnant." That was Thoreau's provocative conclusion; treating one another with respect as neighbors is available to us when our government and we as citizens have fallen into evil or just fallen off the rails. *Walden* and "Civil Disobedience" work together as scripts for the democracy of everyday life and a scripture for American democracy.

Notes

1. Henry D. Thoreau, *Walden, Civil Disobedience and Other Writings* (New York: Norton, 2008), 65. Further quotations are from this volume and cited parenthetically in text.
2. Vasily Grossman, "The Old Teacher," in *The Road*, trans. Robert and Elizabeth Chandler (London: MacLehose, 2010), 4.
3. Whether the democracy of everyday life is a cause or precondition for democratic political development overall is an empirical question, as is whether the democracy of everyday life can exist under anti-democratic government.
4. Robert Frost, "Build Soil, a Political Pastoral," in *Collected Poems, Prose, and Plays* (New York: Library of America, 1995), 297.
5. Henry David Thoreau, "A Plea for Captain John Brown" (1859), in Nancy L. Rosenblum, ed., *Political Writings* (Cambridge: Cambridge University Press, 1996), 51.
6. Henry David Thoreau, "Civil Disobedience," in *Political Writings*, 10.
7. Ibid., 21.

Further Reading

This essay is adapted from different moments in Nancy L. Rosenblum's *Good Neighbors: The Democracy of Everyday Life in America* (Princeton, NJ: Princeton University Press, 2016). For more on Thoreau, read any of the texts cited herein, and see Robert Richardson, *Henry Thoreau: A Life of the Mind* (Berkeley, CA: University of California Press, 1988) and Laura Dassow Walls's *Henry David Thoreau: A Life* (Chicago, IL: University of Chicago Press, 2017). For another case against conflating democratic neighborliness and democratic citizenship, see Robert B. Talisse, *Overdoing Democracy: Why We Must Put Politics in Its Place* (New York: Oxford University Press, 2019). For a classic argument contrary to Rosenblum's, see Mary Parker Follett, *The New State: Group Organization the Solution of Popular Government* (Mansfield Centre, CT: Martino Publishing, 2016), which argues that the good neighbor is the foundation of democratic citizenship.

Further Reading and
Additional Resources

Each entry in this volume concludes with suggestions for continued study particular to the term. Here, as both an ending to this project and a potential new beginning for future projects, we offer selected works and resources that can serve as useful general overviews and case studies of the key elements and conflicts of American democracy from a variety of angles.

On the early history of democratic thought from 1600 to 1900, with a focus on "principles" and "underlying premises," see James T. Kloppenberg, *Toward Democracy: The Struggle for Self-Rule in European and American Thought* (New York: Oxford University Press, 2016). Especially in its introduction, Jill Lepore's *These Truths: A History of the United States* (New York: Norton, 2018) underscores the role of inquiry, evidence, and deliberation in democracy. Gregory P. Downs's *The Second American Revolution: The Civil War-Era Struggle Over Cuba and the Rebirth of the American Republic* (Chapel Hill, NC: University of North Carolina Press, 2019) offers a challenging account of how the crises of the mid-nineteenth century tested fundamental assumptions about democratic principles.

Ranging widely in historical focus but anchoring each chapter to an enduring contradiction is Astra Taylor's illuminating *Democracy May Not Exist, but We'll Miss It When It's Gone* (New York: Henry Holt, 2019). The political scientist Robert Dahl, in *On Democracy* (New Haven, CT: Yale University Press, 1998), presents a helpful primer that tackles conceptual and empirical questions; the book was reissued by Yale in 2015 with a preface and new material by Ian Shapiro. Similarly useful is Bernard Crick's *Democracy: A Very Short Introduction* (Oxford: Oxford University Press, 2002).

For precursors and potential companions to *Democracies in America*, see Russ Castronovo and Dana D. Nelson, *Materializing Democracy: Toward a Revitalized Cultural Politics* (Durham, NC: Duke University Press, 2002), which convenes literary and cultural critics to reflect on the material properties of democracy; Seyla Benhabib's *Democracy and Difference: Contesting the Boundaries of the Political* (Princeton, NJ: Princeton University Press, 1996), which constitutes a collection of leading political theorists assessing the politics of identity; and, more recently, *Democracy in What State?* (New York: Columbia University Press, 2011), which assembles essays by critical theorists to deliberate about "democracy" and its range of meanings.

On the implications of the need for shared vocabulary in American political life, see in particular the work of Danielle Allen: "Here's one more question parents should think about during back-to-school season," *Washington Post*, September 5, 2019, https://www.washingtonpost.com/opinions/we-need-civics-education-in-schools-to-build-effective-democratic-citizens/2019/09/05/3280dea4-cfe6-11e9-b29b-a528dc82154a_story.html and *Education and Equality* (Chicago, IL: University of Chicago Press, 2016), which installs "verbal empowerment" as a key feature of civic education. On the difficulties of achieving a common frame of reference, see Morgan Marietta and David C. Barker, *One Nation, Two Realities: Dueling Facts in American Democracy* (New York: Oxford University Press, 2019).

With debates about shared language in mind, *Democracies in America* may helpfully be read or assigned alongside many of the keyword volumes that focus on American studies, such as Bruce Burgett and Glenn Hendler, *Keywords for American Cultural Studies*, 3rd ed. (New York: New York University Press, 2020). These projects take as their cue Raymond Williams's original vocabulary, whose contents have been updated in *Keywords for Today: A 21st Century Vocabulary*, ed. Colin McCabe and Holly Yanacek (New York: Oxford University Press, 2018).

For those interested in the educational and public policy implications of democratic contestations, *The Drama of Diversity and Democracy: Higher Education and American Commitments*, an Association of American Colleges and Universities study first published in 1995 and reissued in a second edition in 2011, explores concrete ways that college campuses can conjoin conversations about democracy and diversity, which often go unlinked. Two more recent reports are also of great value in reinvigorating discussions of democracy and can be studied in a variety of formal and informal educational settings: *Our Common Purpose: Reinventing Democracy for the 21st Century* (https://www.amacad.org/ourcommonpurpose/report), the result of the bipartisan Commission on the Practice of Democratic Citizenship, sponsored by the American Academy of Arts and Sciences and released in 2020, and *Educating for American Democracy: Excellence in History and Civics for All Learners* (www.educatingforamericandemocracy.org), a 2021 report and accompanying curricular roadmap, issued by iCivics and funded by the National Endowment for the Humanities and the US Department of Education, among other organizations.

Finally, a number of online resources can support deliberations about democracy. The Ezra Klein Show features two useful podcasts: "An inspiring conversation about democracy" (a conversation with Danielle Allen) and "Astra Taylor will change how you think about democracy" (https://www.vox.com/ezra-klein-show-podcast). Democracy Works, produced by the McCourtney Institute for Democracy at Penn State University, features a wide range of conversations from the perspective of political science (https://www.democracyworkspodcast.com/episodes). The Colored Conventions project (http://coloredconventions.org)

archives an array of primary documents that give access to the history of African American political organizing in the long nineteenth century. A print companion to this digital effort is *The Colored Conventions Movement: Black Organizing in the Nineteenth Century*, ed. P. Gabrielle Foreman, Jim Casey, and Sarah Lynn Patterson (Chapel Hill, NC: University of North Carolina Press, 2021).

Index